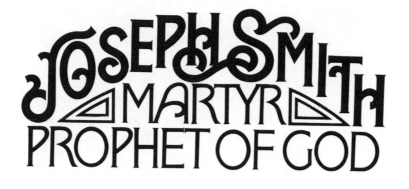

Joseph Smith
Martyr
Prophet of God

Francis M. Gibbons

Deseret Book Company
Salt Lake City, Utah
1977

Library of Congress Cataloging in Publication Data

Gibbons, Francis M   1921-
    Joseph Smith, martyr, prophet of God.

    Bibliography: p.
    Includes index.
        1.   Smith, Joseph, 1805-1844.   2.   Mormons and
Mormonism in the United States—Biography.
3.   Mormons and Mormonism—History.   I.   Title.
BX8695.S6G52   289.3′092′4 [B]   77-2019
ISBN 0-87747-637-3

Contents

Preface

It is the distinction between Joseph Smith the Prophet and Joseph the fallible, imperfect man that creates so much confusion and controversy among those who study his life. He endeavored once to draw this distinction for a couple who held the erroneous belief that "a prophet is always a prophet." He corrected them by saying that "a prophet was a prophet only when he was acting as such." (HC 5:265.) A failure to keep this distinction in mind often causes one either to reject Joseph Smith because he sees imperfection in him, or to accept without question all that he said or did.

Joseph himself never lost sight of this distinction. He was the first to recognize imperfections in himself. An autobiographical sketch he wrote frankly acknowledges that the second major spiritual experience he enjoyed occurred as he supplicated God for forgiveness of his follies and imperfections. On the other hand, he was never reluctant to acknowledge his own worth and the surpassing value and importance of the work he produced. Without hesitancy, he pronounced the Book of Mormon the most nearly perfect book that had ever been written. And one of the revelations he received he designated as the Olive Leaf "which we have plucked from the Tree of Paradise." In a letter with which a copy of this revelation was transmitted to an associate, he unabashedly said, "We have the satisfaction of knowing that the Lord approves of us, and has accepted us." (HC 1:316.)

It is a paradox that a man of such candor and openness could have produced the kind of violent controversy that surrounded him from his boyhood. Few people who knew him could maintain an attitude of neutrality toward him. He was capable of inspiring the greatest loyalty in some, while arousing the most bitter enmity in others. The explanation of this paradox lies partially in the character and personality of the man. But it lies mostly in the nature of his work and in the startling import of the message he bore to the world. In an age of religious questioning and disbelief, this man declared with boldness and finality that, like the prophets of old, he had been in direct communication with the Creator of the world and had seen and conversed with Him. He also declared bluntly that all religious sects and teachers of the day were false because they taught man-made commandments as though they were doctrine, whereas they had only the form and not the power of godliness. Predictably, this attack upon organized religion and religious teachers evoked a vigorous, and often violent, response. It is not surprising, therefore, that throughout a life of persecution, mobbings, and drivings, many professors and teachers of religion were found in the vanguard of those who harassed the Prophet.

Both the detractors and the supporters of Joseph Smith have been zealous in trying to convince others of the correctness of their respective opinions of his character and motives. As a result, a formidable body of literature has sprung up that analyzes, dissects, criticizes, lauds, or chronicles his life and works. There also exists a vast amount of relevant historical material that must be taken into account. It is from these rich and seemingly inexhaustible sources that the writer must select the materials to be incorporated in a biography of Joseph Smith. Inevitably, the process of selection will reflect the bias of the writer and his preconceived ideas about the character of the man of whom he writes. This life sketch is no exception. The reader will not have progressed far before discovering that the author is one who accepts Joseph Smith for what he represents himself to be—a prophet of God. This accounts for the interchangeable use of the terms "Joseph" and "the Prophet" to identify the subject of this biography.

It is hoped, however, that the author's convictions about Joseph Smith have not blinded him to reality, and that the portrayal will be an honest one, taking into account both the strengths and the weaknesses of this unusual man.

While some may question Joseph Smith and his work, depending upon whose testimony one is willing to accept, there can be no dispute about the character and the accomplishments of the religious organization he brought into being, The Church of Jesus Christ of Latter-day Saints, commonly called the Mormon Church. At this writing, more than 145 years after its organization, it comprises over three million members, distributed worldwide. Members of the Church, which is recognized as one of the fastest-growing churches today, are distinguished by their sobriety, thrift, and prosperity, by their high level of educational achievements, their robust health, their penchant for hard work, and their endurance and patience in the face of adversity. While many other churches are waning in size and in their influence and authority, this church, by contrast, has an ever-stronger effect upon its rapidly increasing membership.

It has been said that any organization is but the lengthened shadow of one man. To the extent that this maxim has any validity, one must search for an explanation of the phenomenal growth and vitality of the Mormon Church in the life of its founder, Joseph Smith. It is toward this end that this volume is directed.

In turning to the task, one thought keeps recurring that was aptly expressed by the noted author and hero-worshiper, Thomas Carlyle: "A false man found a religion? Why, a false man cannot build a brick house! If he [does] not know and follow truly the properties of mortar, burned clay, and what else he works in, it is no house that he makes, but a rubbish heap. It will not stand. . . . It will fall straightway."

KEY TO ABBREVIATIONS IN SOURCES

HC: *History of the Church* (sometimes referred to as *Documentary History of the Church*), by Joseph Smith.

CHC: *Comprehensive History of the Church,* by B. H. Roberts.

JD: *Journal of Discourses.*

D&C: Doctrine and Covenants, one of the four standard scriptural works of The Church of Jesus Christ of Latter-day Saints.

(A more detailed bibliography appears under the title "Sources Cited" at the end of the book.)

Chapter One

Prayer
The Foundation of
Joseph Smith's Power

A salient characteristic of Joseph Smith's life, both as a youth and as an adult, was his persistent reliance on the power of prayer. He used it as a tool in solving problems, as a means of worshiping and expressing gratitude to the Lord, and as a device for obtaining comfort and peace of mind.

The epochal event of his life came about in the spring of 1820 as he offered his first vocal prayer, and the Father and the Son revealed themselves to him. He also told how the Angel Moroni appeared to him for the first time as a result of a fervent prayer offered to ascertain his standing before the Lord. Every important revelation of truth that he received occurred in response to earnest supplication. John the Baptist appeared to him and Oliver Cowdery because of an anxious prayer they offered to inquire about baptism. (See Chapter 4.)

All these, of course, represent major incidents in the history of the Church and have been exhaustively treated by friend and foe alike; they are, therefore, well known to all who have read a biography of the Prophet. Little known, however, are the numerous incidents when Joseph offered prayers for commonplace things and felt so keenly about them that he left a record of them in his journal.

Thus, in November 1834, we find him and Oliver Cowdery imploring the Lord for "the continuance of blessings" and expressing thanks for "opening the hearts of the brethren from the east, to loan us $430. . . ." (HC 2:174-75.)

Several months later, we see him join with Oliver and several other brethren, praying "That the Lord would give us means sufficient to deliver us from all our afflictions and difficulties wherein we are placed by reason of our debts; that He would open the way and deliver Zion in the appointed time, and that without the shedding of blood; that He would hold our lives precious, and grant that we may live to the common age of man, and never fall into the hands nor power of the mob in Missouri, nor in any other place; . . . and finally, that in the end He would save us in His celestial kingdom." (HC 2:291.) During a critical time in Kirtland, Ohio, when Joseph and the Church were in a state of poverty and distress, he and five other brethren joined in urgent prayer in which they asked for six specific things. These included: "That the Lord would grant that Brother Joseph might prevail over his enemy . . . who has threatened his life, whom Joseph has caused to be taken with a precept; that the Lord would fill the heart of the court with a spirit to do justice, and cause that the law of the land may be magnified in bringing Hurlburt to justice" and "That the Lord would protect our printing press from the hands of evil men, and give us means to send forth His record, even His Gospel, that the ears of all may hear it. . . ." (HC 2:3.)

At this time, the problems of debt and the agitation created by apostates were foremost in the Prophet's mind. Consequently, these subjects were frequently mentioned in his recorded prayers. Under date of April 7, 1834, he recorded this "special prayer": "Bishop Whitney, Elder Frederick G. Williams, Oliver Cowdery, Heber C. Kimball, and myself, met in the council room, and bowed down before the Lord, and prayed that He would furnish the means to deliver the Firm from debt, that they might be set at liberty; also, that I might prevail against that wicked man Hurlburt, and that he might be put to shame." (HC 2:47-48.)

At that day, disease and injury were constant threats. Accordingly, prayers for relief from these dangers frequently found their way into Joseph's journal. Under date of October 11, 1835, appears this revealing entry pertaining to a serious illness of his father: "Waited on my father again, who was very sick. In secret prayer in the morning, the Lord said, 'My servant, thy father shall live.' I waited on him all this day with my heart raised to God in the name of Jesus Christ, that He would restore him to health, that I might be blessed with his company and advice. . . . At evening Brother David Whitmer came in. We called on the Lord in mighty prayer in the name of Jesus Christ, and laid our hands on him, and rebuked the disease. And God heard and answered our prayers—to the great joy and satisfaction of our souls. Our aged father arose and dressed himself, shouted, and praised the Lord. Called Brother William Smith, who had retired to rest, that he might praise the Lord with us, by joining in songs of praise to the Most High." (HC 2:289.)

Only a few days after this crisis, Joseph's sister-in-law, the wife of Samuel, lay critically ill. Of this incident, the Prophet recorded: "I went out into the field and bowed before the Lord and called upon Him in mighty prayer in her behalf. And the word of the Lord came unto me, saying, 'My servant Frederick shall come, and shall have wisdom given him to deal prudently, and my handmaid shall be delivered of a living child, and be spared.' The doctor came in about one hour afterwards, and in the course of two hours she was delivered, and thus what God had manifested to me was fulfilled every whit." (HC 2:292-93.)

So it was that all of Joseph's difficulties, regardless of size, were taken to the Lord in prayer. In this practice was reflected the teaching and example of his parents, Joseph and Lucy Mack Smith, Sr.; his paternal grandparents, Asael and Mary Duty Smith; and his maternal grandparents, Solomon and Lydia Gates Mack. His parents and grandparents, like Joseph, were accustomed to solving their problems on their knees. As an infant and as a child, Joseph was subjected to the strong influence of these relatives, and it is only natural that he grew up reflecting their qualities in his conduct and attitudes. It is an interesting exercise, therefore, to trace into the lives of his progenitors some of the Prophet's outstanding characteristics, including his ingrained habit of seeking answers to his questions through prayer.

Chapter Two

The Prophet's Ancestry

The Prophet's ancestral roots on his mother's side extend into Scotland. His great-great-grandfather, John Mack, came from Inverness, Scotland, and arrived in Boston Harbor in about 1669, when he was sixteen years old. At age thirty-eight, John Mack married Sarah Bagley. They lived successively in Salisbury, Massachusetts; Concord, Massachusetts; and Lyme, Connecticut. The eighth of their twelve children was Ebenezer Mack, who became the pastor of the Second Congregational Church in Lyme. Ebenezer married Hannah Huntley, a daughter of Aaron and Deborah de Wolf Huntley, and to them were born five children, including Solomon Mack.

In a remarkable autobiographical sketch, or narrative, written in his old age, Solomon gives a brief glimpse of his parents. Of his mother, he said: ". . . she experienced the power of God from an early age, with all the good morals of life, and instructing the youth for about thirty years." (Richard Lloyd Anderson, *Joseph Smith's New England Heritage* [Salt Lake City: Deseret Book Co., 1971], p. 34.)

The Macks are reported to have had "a large property" and to have "lived in good style" for a time. Through various misfortunes, however, they lost their property, and so, at the age of four, Solomon was "bound out" to a farmer in the neighborhood with whom he remained as an indentured servant for seventeen years. This period of indenture was an exceedingly trying one. In his old age, Solomon recalled these years: "I was treated by my master as his property and not as his fellow mortal. He taught me to work and was very careful that I should have little or no rest. . . . he never taught me to read or spoke to me at all on the subject of religion." (Anderson, p. 34.)

Upon fulfilling the term of his indenture, Solomon enlisted in the army and saw extensive service during the French and Indian War. Following his release from military service, he endeavored to become established in an occupation that would provide him with independence. He invested his military savings in a large tract of land in Granville, New York, which he apparently intended to subdivide and develop. This enterprise failed as did most of the others he undertook. He was in turn a farmer, a sutler, a real estate developer, a privateer (during the war of independence), and a coastal shipper.

Throughout his life Solomon was afflicted with what would appear to be an almost endless series of accidents or illnesses. In 1810, during the seventy-sixth year of his life, he was confined to his bed during most of the winter with a severe case of rheumatism. During this period he commenced for the first time to study the scriptures and to pray with real intent. In this he was helped by his faithful wife, who, he says, was "my only instructor." His interest in the scriptures was triggered by a recollection of the content of Matthew 11:28-29. When his wife assured him that these words were from the Bible, he began to search the scriptures and, for the first time, to pray with fervency.

According to his narrative, Solomon "called upon the Lord the greatest part of the winter." (Anderson, p. 55.) In the process, he experienced a series of remarkable spiritual manifestations. The first occurred one night as he lay in bed reflecting upon the scriptures and his own failure to live in accordance with their teachings. "About midnight," he said, "I saw a light about a foot from my face as bright as fire; the doors were all shut and no one stirring in the house. I thought by this that I had but a few moments to live, and oh what distress I was in. I prayed that the Lord would have mercy on my soul and deliver me from this horrible pit of sin." This remarkable experience was repeated another night soon after when Solomon saw "another light as bright as the first, at a small distance from [his] face." Again, as was true on the first occasion, Solomon interpreted this manifestation to presage the end of his life, and he felt that he had "but a few moments to live." On still another occasion that winter he experienced a vivid dream in which he thought he heard the Lord call him by his Christian name and that he had "but a moment to live." (Anderson, pp. 54-55.)

These manifestations were accompanied by repeated, fervent prayer on the part of Solomon that the Lord would "have mercy" on his soul, for he considered himself to be a "vile wretch" because of his misdeeds and his failure to heed the "calls" from the Lord and "the invitations and warnings" from his wife. It was then that he had a religious experience that radically altered his life and set him on the path of evangelism that he pursued until his death. He related the experience thus: "All the winter I was laid up with the rheumatism, so that my wife was obliged to help me to bed and up again, but in the spring the Lord appeared to be with me. But for my own satisfaction, I thought like this, as I was sitting one evening by the fire. I prayed to the Lord, if he was with me, that I might know it by this token—that my pains might all be eased for that night. And blessed be the Lord, I was entirely free from pain that night." This dramatic witness inspired Solomon to utter this rhapsody of praise and thanksgiving: "And I rejoiced in the God of my salvation—and found Christ's promises verified that what things soever ye ask in prayer, believing, ye shall receive—and found that Christ would fulfil all his promises, and not one jot or tittle could fail. And the Lord so shined light into my soul that everything appeared new and beautiful. Oh how I loved my neighbors. How I loved my enemies—I could pray for them. Everything appeared delightful. The love of Christ is beautiful. There is more satisfaction to be taken in the enjoyment of Christ one day, than in half a century serving our master, the devil." (Anderson, pp. 55-56.) This pivotal experience in Solomon Mack's life occurred in 1810, when his grandson, Joseph Smith, was an impressionable five years of age. The Prophet was actually born on a farm owned by Solomon that had been leased to Joseph Smith, Sr. All through the Prophet's earliest years until he was about eleven, Grandfather Solomon Mack lived nearby. In fact, during part of this time Solomon's wife lived in the Prophet's home, and it is possible, therefore, that Solomon lived there with her. If not, it is a certainty that he was a frequent visitor there and that he shared with the Prophet and the other members of his family his convictions about God and the way in which those convictions came to him through prayer.

Since Lydia Gates Mack was not literary as was Solomon, we must depend for an understanding of her characteristics and qualities upon the occasional references to her in the writings of family members, particularly her husband and her daughter Lucy, and upon the scanty historical records that bear directly upon her life.

Her father, Daniel Gates, was a tanner by trade and was

reputed to be a man of some means. That he had a religious bent is evidenced by the fact that he served as a deacon of his church and had his children baptized shortly after their births. This characteristic found apt expression in his will: "I would . . . commit my soul into the hands of God, who gave it, hoping and believing that I shall obtain remission of all my sins through the alone merits of Jesus Christ, my only Savior, and that for his sake I shall be admitted into life eternal." (Anderson, p. 26.)

This same quality was evident in Lydia's life. When Lucy was eight, Lydia suffered a "severe fit of sickness." So grave was her condition that her family feared for her life. She summoned the children to her bedside and exhorted them "always to remember the instructions which she had given them—to fear God and walk uprightly before him." (Anderson, p. 27.) Solomon observed that Lydia was accustomed to calling the children about her "both morning and evening and teaching them to pray, meanwhile urging upon them the necessity of love towards each other as well as devotional feelings towards him who made them." (Ibid.) Significantly, Solomon did not lead in these prayers, since at that time, according to his own admission, he was almost completely indifferent toward religion.

Asael Smith and Mary Duty Smith

The Prophet's paternal grandfather, Asael Smith, was the great-grandson of Robert Smith, who arrived in Boston in 1638 as a twelve-year-old immigrant from London, England. Robert, a tailor by trade, eventually purchased a good-sized farm located partly in Boxford and Topsfield townships, Massachusetts. His descendants' occupancy of this farm commenced a tenure by the Smith line through several generations, which resulted in their being called "the Topsfield Smiths." (John Henry Evans, *Joseph Smith: An American Prophet* [Salt Lake City: Deseret Book Co., 1966], p. 24.) Here Asael was born on March 7, 1744, a son of Samuel Smith II.

Samuel, Asael's father, fought in the American Revolution and was a prominent citizen of Topsfield. He was also a deeply religious man. Of him it was written that "he subscribed to the Christian conviction that by 'the mighty power of God' he would stand again at 'the general resurrection.' A highly religious man who took his Congregational covenant seriously, he was active in public worship. His five children were all baptized in the Topsfield church, including youngest Asael four days after birth." (Anderson, p. 89.)

Asael appears to have emulated the example of his father in almost every particular, combining the business of farming with public service. Like his father, Asael was also interested in religion and appears to have accepted the basic beliefs of the Universalists. According to his grandson, George Albert Smith, Asael "wrote many quires of paper on the doctrines of universal restoration" not long before his death. (Anderson, p. 105.)

For a reason not readily discernible from the known facts of his life, Asael Smith is pictured by some writers as being irreligious, if not agnostic. Perhaps this can be explained by his independent cast of mind and his unorthodoxy. One cannot read his known writings or biographical sketches by those who knew him best without detecting a deeply spiritual nature. Being a Universalist, he adhered to the basic tenets of that sect expressed by a Universalist convention: "We believe there is one God, whose nature is love, revealed in one Lord Jesus Christ, by one Holy Spirit of grace, who will finally restore the whole family of mankind to holiness and happiness." (Ibid.)

The most convincing evidence of Asael's spiritual nature is the remarkable "Address" written to his family on April 10, 1799, at a time when he did not expect to live long. At the outset, he invoked the blessings of God upon his family, counseling them to "put [their] whole trust solely" in God, who never did "nor never will forsake any that trusted in him." Then he launched into a detailed and revealing exposition of his deepest convictions: "And now my dear children, let me pour out my heart to you and speak first to you of immortality in your souls. Trifle not in this point: the soul is immortal. You have to deal with an infinite majesty; you go upon life and death. Therefore, in this point be serious. Do all to God in a serious manner. When you think of him, speak of him, pray to him, or in any way make your addresses to his great majesty, be in good earnest. Trifle not with his name nor with his attributes, nor call him to witness to anything but is absolute truth; nor then, but when sound reason or serious consideration requires it. And as to religion, I would not wish to point out any particular form to you; but first I would wish you to search the scriptures and consult sound [rea]son, and see if they (which I take to [be] two witnesses that stand by the God of the whole earth) are not sufficient to evince to you that religion is a necessary theme. Then I would wish you to study the nature of religion, and see whether it consists in outward formalities, or in the hidden man of the heart; whether you can by outward forms, rites and ordinances save yourselves, or whether there is a necessity of your having help from any other hand than your own. . . . But mind that you admit no others as evidences but the two that God hath appointed, viz., scripture and sound reason." (Anderson, pp. 124-25.)

The beginning and the end of Asael's address to his family resemble the invocation and the benediction of a sermon. Both emphasize the Savior's perfection and the undeviating quality of His love and concern for mankind. At the outset Asael reminded his family to put their whole trust in Him, while at the end he declared, "Sure I am my Savior, Christ, is perfect, and never will fail in one circumstance. To him I commit your souls, bodies, estates, names, characters, lives, deaths and all—and myself, waiting when he shall change my vile body and make it like his own most glorious body." (Anderson, p. 129.)

In Asael's old age, his son Joseph Smith, Sr., brought him a copy of the Book of Mormon along with an account of the many revelations and spiritual manifestations the Prophet had received. Although he was in his eighty-eighth year, Asael read the book nearly through without the aid of glasses. Without doubt or hesitancy, he pronounced it authentic; and before his death, which followed in a few months, he declared that a new religious age was upon the world. He also confided to members of his family that "he always knew that God was going to raise up some branch of his family to be a great benefit to mankind."

The maiden name of the Prophet's paternal grandmother, Mary Duty Smith, seems to symbolize her chief personal characteristic. Fragmentary references to her disclose that she was a dutiful wife, mother, and grandmother, and the qualities she exhibited in later life imply that she was also a dutiful daughter and sister. Little is known of her ancestry. Even John Smith, the most active biographer of all her children, was forced to concede, "Of her parentage I have but a little knowledge." (Anderson, p. 147.) The salient known fact about her life is that she bore eleven children and raised them all to maturity. This seems to be a little short of miraculous when one considers the remote character of the area and the rudimentary state of medical knowledge at the time. We are given an insight into the physical attributes and the character of Mary and her family by Eliza R. Snow, who wrote about Mary's visit to the Prophet's family in Kirtland, Ohio, in her old age:

"The next day after her arrival at the house of the Prophet, where she was welcomed with every manifestation of kindness and affection, her children, grandchildren, and great-grandchildren—all who were residents of Kirtland, and two of her sons, who arrived with her—came together to enjoy with her a social family meeting. And a happy one it was—a season of pure reciprocal conviviality, in which her buoyancy of spirit greatly augmented the general joy. Let the reader imagine for a moment this aged matron, surrounded by her four sons, Joseph, Asael, Silas and John, all of them, as well as several of her grandsons, upwards of six feet in height, with a score of great-grandchildren of various sizes intermixed." (Anderson, p. 115.)

Like her husband, Asael, Mary Duty Smith accepted the testimony of her grandson. In making the pilgrimage to Kirtland in her old age, she told her daughter-in-law, Lucy Mack Smith, "I am going to have your Joseph [Jr.] baptize me, and my Joseph [Sr.] bless me." (Ibid.) Four of her sons—Joseph, Asael Jr., Silas, and John—also accepted the testimony of the Prophet and were baptized into the Church. All four became high priests and died in full fellowship in the Church after having rendered significant service. Joseph, the father of the Prophet, was the first Patriarch to the Church. Asael, Jr., served on two high councils and later was called as a patriarch. Silas, who had been a captain in the Vermont militia, became a high priest. And John, the youngest brother, served as the first Salt Lake Stake president after having filled positions of high leadership in Ohio, Missouri, and Illinois.

The chief holdout from Mormonism among the children of Asael and Mary Duty Smith was their eldest son, Jesse, who adamantly refused to place any credence in the claim of the Prophet or his followers. The intensity of his opposition is revealed in a letter written to Hyrum, the Prophet's brother. Among his fulminations is this offering: "your good, pious, and Methodistical Uncle Asael induced his father to give credit to your tale of nonsense." He later characterized the story of the restoration as the "blasphemous stuff." (Anderson, p. 112.)

The "nonsense" and "blasphemy" to which Jesse alludes is a

charge that could be laid at the door of anyone who accepts the reality of God's existence and the fact that He ministers to men in the flesh, either personally or through intermediaries. Whether the charge has any substance must be ascertained either through personal revelation or an objective weighing of the facts. It cannot be decided, as some are inclined to do, merely because Jesse made it, especially since he stood alone among his family in open dissent. Both of his parents and his four living brothers accepted the Prophet's testimony, a most singular fact considering the Prophet's youth and lack of schooling and the propensity of the Smith family toward independent thought.

Joseph Smith, Sr., and Lucy Mack Smith

The paths of Joseph Smith, Sr., and Lucy Mack, the Prophet's parents, crossed in Tunbridge, Vermont. Joseph lived there with his parents; Lucy had gone there to stay with an elder brother, Stephen Mack.

They were married in Tunbridge on January 24, 1796, when Joseph was 24 and Lucy, 19. Gauged by the standards of the day, they commenced married life in very comfortable circumstances. Joseph operated one of Asael's farms on a sharing basis. In a letter written to Jacob Towne ten days before the marriage, Asael noted: "I have set me up a new house since Mr. Wildes was here, and expect to remove into it next spring and to begin again on an entire new farm. And my son Joseph will live on the old farm (if this that has been but four years occupied can be called old) and carry it on at the halves, which half I hope will nearly furnish my family with food, whilst I with my four youngest sons shall endeavor to bring to another farm, etc." (Anderson, p. 118.) Thus, the newlyweds not only had a comfortable home and an established farm, but Lucy apparently brought means to the marriage, perhaps a dowry, with which to purchase furnishings for the home. In addition, Lucy's brother Stephen and his partner, John Mudget, had given Lucy a thousand dollars cash as a wedding gift.

Joseph and Lucy lived in these comfortable, secure circumstances for about six years. It was there in Tunbridge that their eldest son, Alvin, was born in 1798, and their second son, Hyrum, was born in 1800. In 1802, Joseph was attracted to the little town of Randolph, where he engaged in a mercantile business. Monetarily, it proved to be a disastrous move. He invested all his means in an enterprise to export crystallized ginseng root to China. A combination of his lack of business acumen and the dishonesty of an agent with whom he entrusted a large shipment of the commodity resulted in a complete business failure. Not only did he lose all he had invested in the enterprise, but he also had to liquidate his interest in the farm and to use Lucy's dowry to satisfy his debtors.

Thus, at age 31, Joseph found himself penniless with a wife and two young sons. It was this state of affairs that precipitated the family's move to Sharon, Windsor County, Vermont, where they leased the Solomon Mack farm. There their third son, Joseph, Jr., was born on December 23, 1805.

By farming in the summer and teaching school in the winter, Joseph, Sr., was eventually able to reestablish his financial stability. Since he was a tenant farmer, however, it was not possible for him to remain long in one place. Therefore, between 1805 and 1816 the family lived successively at Tunbridge, Vermont; Royalton, Vermont; Lebanon, New Hampshire; and Norwich, Vermont.

Meanwhile, the family continued to grow. Samuel Harrison was born in Tunbridge in 1808; Ephraim and William, in Royalton in 1810 and 1811 respectively; Catherine, in Lebanon in 1812; and Don Carlos, in Norwich in 1816.

After three successive crop failures at Norwich because of untimely frosts, Joseph, Sr., decided to seek a more moderate climate. While Lucy remained at Norwich with the children, he went to Palmyra, New York, in the summer of 1816 and made preparations for them to join him there. Within two years the hard-working family had saved enough for a down payment on the farm where, in the spring of 1820, Joseph, Jr., was to experience the first of an amazing series of spiritual manifestations that preceded the restoration of the gospel of Jesus Christ and the subsequent organization of The Church of Jesus Christ of Latter-day Saints.

From outward appearances, there was little to distinguish the Smith family from hundreds of others of that day. They lived a tenuous, nomadic life as they endeavored to extract a living from the soil. The vagaries of the weather created special hazards and introduced into their lives an element of uncertainty that seemed to pervade everything they did. But along with this uncertainty in their outward lives, there existed within them faith in a Supreme Being, which manifested itself in the form of prayer, Bible reading, and regular attendance at religious gatherings, including vigorous and ofttimes loud camp meetings.

While Joseph and Lucy exhibited most of the qualities that characterized so many of their contemporaries, theirs had a special dimension and significance. This likely resulted in large part from the influence and example of their parents, whose unusual spiritual qualities have already been indicated. Yet family influence alone cannot explain the depth and scope of the religious sense found in these parents of the young man who was soon to become the Prophet of the restoration.

The first significant stirrings in Lucy's spiritual life occurred when she was a teenager, when her beloved sister Lovina died. As so often happens, this personal contact with the reality of death led to an introspective appraisal of life's meaning and purpose. Her own words clearly reveal the violence of the inner struggle that ensued: "The grief occasioned by the death of Lovina was preying upon my health and threatened my constitution with serious injury, and they hoped that to accompany my brother home might serve to divert my mind and thus prove a benefit to me. For I was pensive and melancholy and often in my reflections I thought that life was not worth possessing. In the midst of this anxiety of mind, I determined to obtain that which I had heard spoken so much from the pulpit—a change of heart. To accomplish this I spent much of my time reading the Bible and praying." (Lucy Mack Smith, *History of Joseph Smith, by His Mother* [Salt Lake City: Bookcraft, 1958], p. 32. All of the quotations by Lucy Mack Smith that follow are from this source.)

Notwithstanding her fervent and determined effort toward that end, Lucy did not experience a spiritual conversion or, as she put it, "a change of heart," during this critical period. She appears to have been deterred in it by conflicting sectarian beliefs and ultimately by a gradual easing of the grief and tension that had produced the crisis. Within less than two years she married the eligible young bachelor, Joseph Smith, Sr., five years older than she, and the combination of his maturity and the comfortable circumstances in which they commenced married life seem to have relieved her of the great anxieties that had precipitated her first earnest search for spiritual enlightenment.

Lucy did not again face an emotional and spiritual crisis until she and Joseph had been married for about six years and had three children. In 1802, just after they had left the comfortable security of their Tunbridge farm and had moved to Randolph, Lucy was confined to bed with fever and a heavy cold. A doctor diagnosed her illness as "confirmed consumption." Her mother was called in to act as a combination nurse, baby-sitter, and housekeeper during her illness.

Worried about the neglect of her duties as a wife and mother, and faced with thoughts of a premature death, Lucy commenced a valiant inner struggle. This resulted in what proved to be a turning point in her life and left its strong imprint on the lives of her children. These words from her pen convey only in part the magnitude of the inner battle she waged at that time: "I then looked to the Lord and begged and pleaded with him to spare my life in order that I might bring up my children and be a comfort to my husband. My mind was much agitated during the whole night. Sometimes I contemplated heaven and heavenly things, then my thoughts would turn upon those of earth—my babes and my companion." Not content merely to implore the Lord for his blessings, Lucy bargained for her life. "During this night I made a solemn covenant with God that if He would let me live I would endeavor to serve him according to the best of my abilities," she wrote. Then followed the pivotal moment in her life when for the first time she personally experienced the influence and power of God.

Until that moment, God had existed only as an idea in Lucy's mind, based upon hearsay. Thereafter he became a living reality, an actual being, who loved and was interested in her and who was ready at all times to provide guidance and aid. Lucy recorded this momentous experience in these simple words: "Shortly after this I heard a voice say to me, 'Seek, and ye shall find; knock, and it shall be opened unto you. Let your heart be comforted; ye believe in God, believe also in me.'" Following this, Lucy's mother entered the room and observed that she looked better, to which Lucy replied: "Yes, mother, the Lord will let me live, if I am faithful to the promise which I made to him, to be a comfort to my mother, my husband, and my children."

Although from this experience Lucy became convinced of God's reality and goodness, there existed in her mind some uncertainty about the manner in which she should fulfill the covenant she had made with the Lord. In an attempt to resolve this uncertainty, she "went from place to place for the purpose of getting information." Unable to find anyone who would enlighten her, or any church whose doctrines coincided with her own understanding, she resolved to be guided only by the Bible. She pursued this course for many years until she began to feel she must be baptized. She was ultimately baptized by a minister who left her "free in regard to joining any religious denomination." Thereafter, she "continued to read the Bible as formerly."

Thus Lucy experienced what the Christians of that day were prone to call "a change of heart." The conviction she thereby acquired of the Lord's existence and of his willingness to answer the sincere prayers of his children seems to have colored and influenced all her later actions. The inference is clear that this conviction was transmitted to the Prophet in his infancy and that it became the wellspring from which flowed the amazing series of spiritual manifestations that accompanied the establishment and building up of the Church.

While we are left to conjecture about the way in which Lucy conveyed to her children the assurance she had about the existence of God and the manner in which he communicates to his earthly children, there is no doubt concerning the key role she played in the conversion of her husband. Lucy records that during the time they resided at Tunbridge, Joseph, Sr., accompanied her to Methodist meetings "in order to oblige me." When Jesse Smith, her husband's oldest brother (who was always "bitterly opposed to every form of religion"), learned about this, he raised such strong objections that Joseph "thought it best to desist." Significantly, Lucy did not respond openly to this challenge. Instead, she followed a procedure that later became a way of life for her prophet-son. "I retired to a grove not far distant," she wrote, "where I prayed to the Lord in behalf of my husband—that the true gospel might be presented to him and that his heart might be softened so as to receive it, or, that he might become more religiously inclined."

That night Lucy had a vivid dream in which she saw two beautiful trees standing by a stream in an open meadow. One was encircled by a bright belt with the appearance of gold, and moved and swayed gently in the breeze, conveying "the idea of joy and gratitude." The other "stood erect and fixed as a pillar of marble," and regardless of how strong the wind blew, "not a leaf was stirred, not a bough was bent; but obstinately stiff it stood." According to the interpretation of this dream given to Lucy, these two trees represented her husband Joseph and his brother Jesse; "that the stubborn and unyielding tree was like Jesse; that the other, more pliant and flexible, was like Joseph, my husband; that the breath of heaven, which passed over them, was the pure and undefiled gospel of the Son of God, which gospel Jesse would always resist, but which Joseph, when he was more advanced in life, would hear and receive with his whole heart, and rejoice therein; and unto him would be added intelligence, happiness, glory, and everlasting life."

How accurately the substance of this dream was fulfilled is made clear from the subsequent lives of these brothers. Jesse obdurately set his mind against all religion and to the end derided the Prophet and his message. On the other hand, Joseph, Sr., became convinced of the reality and power of God, and when the message of the restoration was delivered to him by his son, he readily accepted it and affiliated with the Church, becoming its first patriarch.

For this purpose, however, the most significant thing about Lucy's dream and its fulfillment is that she appears to have been the catalyst in her husband's conversion. The depth and sincerity of that conversion are manifested by his later life, during which he showed an undeviating adherence to the religious principles he had accepted. In no instance, however, are they more dramatically portrayed than in the singular series of dreams and visions that he himself experienced. These commenced in about 1811, several years after Lucy's remarkable dream and at a time when the young prophet was only six years of age. The first of these dreams also occurred near the time when Lucy's father, Solomon Mack, experienced his near-miraculous conversion, and was preceded by a marked change in Joseph's attitude toward religion. Of this change, Lucy observed: "About this time my husband's mind became much excited upon the subject of religion; yet he would not subscribe to any particular system of faith, but contended for the ancient order, as established by our Lord and Savior Jesus Christ and His Apostles."

It was in this state of high mental excitement that Joseph had his first dream or night vision, which he related in detail to Lucy the next morning. In it he saw himself as a traveler in a land of utter barrenness accompanied only by an oracular "attendant spirit" who declared that the desolation he saw was likened to the world devoid of true religion. The spirit also told him that further along in the journey he would see a box, the contents of which would make him wise. Finding the box, he opened it and was beginning to eat its contents when a horde of beasts, horned cattle, and roaring animals "rose up on every side in the most threatening manner possible, tearing the earth, tossing their horns, and bellowing most terrifically." So endangered was he in the dream that Joseph was compelled to drop the box and flee. "Yet," he said, "in the midst of all this I was perfectly happy, though I awoke trembling." Although Joseph's second dream varied from the first in significant detail, the substance of it was essentially the same. Again he saw himself as a traveler, first in a place of desolation and then in a pleasant valley where he sampled the delicious fruit from a beautiful tree. He summoned his family to share the fruit, when they were intimidated and derided by a host of "finely dressed" people who occupied a spacious building across the valley. In the third dream, Joseph, lame from traveling a long distance on foot, found himself in a beautiful garden in which were twelve wooden images seated in two rows of six facing each other. As he walked down the separating aisle, each in turn arose and, bowing, paid obeisance to him, after which he was "entirely healed" of his lameness.

There then followed two dreams of which we have no record. Of them Lucy merely said, "I cannot remember them distinctly enough to rehearse them in full." In the sixth dream (but only the fourth that was recorded), Joseph was debarred from entering a large meetinghouse because, a porter informed him, he had arrived too late. Anguished by this rebuff and finding that "his flesh was perishing," he implored, "Oh, Lord God, I beseech thee, in the name of Jesus Christ, to forgive my sins." He then commenced to mend and was admitted to the building.

The seventh and final dream occurred in 1819, only a short while before the Prophet was visited by the Father and the Son. It culminated an eight-year period of spiritual preparation and enlightenment for the man who not only stands at the head of the Prophet's own family, but who was honored as the first patriarch of the restored church. Its symbolic significance seems to justify repeating it in full: "I dreamed, said he, that a man with a peddler's budget on his back, came in and thus addressed me: 'Sir, will you trade with me today? I have now called upon you seven times, I have traded with you each time, and have always found you strictly honest in all your dealings. Your measures are always heaped and your weights over-balance; and I have now come to tell you that this is the last time I shall ever call on you, and that there is but one thing which you lack in order to secure your salvation.' As I earnestly desired to know what it was I still lacked, I requested him to write the same upon paper. He said he would do so. I then sprang to get some paper, but in my excitement, I awoke."

Chapter Three

Joseph's Boyhood and Family Life

During the twenty-three years from 1798 to 1821, Lucy Mack Smith gave birth to ten children, only one of whom—Ephraim, who was born in 1810—died in infancy. The burdens of carrying the children during pregnancy and of washing, diapering, feeding, nursing, teaching, and comforting them would, alone, have been overwhelming. When are added to these burdens the frequent, almost nomadic, moves of the family, the lack of modern household appliances, and Lucy's activities in producing and selling oilcloth paintings (done to alleviate the family's pinched financial condition), we do not wonder that Lucy failed to keep a detailed record of her children during their formative years. Had she known in advance the dramatic life role her son Joseph was to play, she doubtless would have kept a more detailed record. As it is, we have only the most sketchy account of these early years, gleaned from Lucy's recollections and recorded years later, from oblique references made by the Prophet and others, and from inferences to be drawn from the facts known about the Smith family and the circumstances in which they lived.

The Prophet's birth on December 23, 1805, almost coincided with the official dawn of winter on Vermont's wooded, rolling hills. Nestled in a protected hollow on the partially developed farm of Solomon Mack was a plain but comfortable cabin occupied by Joseph and Lucy Mack Smith and their young brood, now grown to four with the arrival of baby Joseph. The appearance of the winter solstice two days before had marked the beginning of lengthened days, presaging both the season of heavy snow that lay immediately ahead and the verdant spring that loomed beyond. The onset of winter had suspended all of the father's farming activities except for the ever-present chores of feeding and milking the cows and caring for the other barnyard animals. Seven-year-old Alvin and five-year-old Hyrum were scarcely old enough to shoulder much of this load, although they were pressed into service to help feed the animals and chickens and do other light chores.

Lucy's days were fully occupied with the myriad household duties facing any farmer's wife, augmented by the special tasks incident to the care of a newborn infant and a two-year-old toddler, Sophronia. Although exceedingly busy because of the never-ending tasks that piled upon her daily, Lucy lived with an inner peace and serenity derived from the dramatic episode three years before in Randolph, when the Lord had spoken to her in the anguish of her soul and had promised she would be permitted to live and to be a comfort to her husband and children.

During the winter season, Joseph, Sr., was occupied teaching school for children from surrounding farms. This activity is vital to an understanding of the influences that shaped the character of the growing prophet. From his earliest days, he was exposed to an atmosphere of study, inquiry, and discussion. A favorite book in the small Smith family library was the Holy Bible, which was read and discussed regularly. The religious bent of the Prophet's parents, added to the dramatic spiritual manifestations they had experienced, make certain the fact that their study of the Bible was accompanied by a practical application of its precepts, by prayer, and by manifestations of love, humility, and reverence.

The basic attitudes then implanted in the mind of young Joseph were influenced also by frequent contact with his grandparents, who lived nearby and who lost no opportunity to share with their beloved grandchildren the one overriding interest and concern in their lives—their conviction of the reality and power of God and of the need to implore him for guidance and to keep his commandments.

Although Joseph, Sr., and Lucy moved frequently during those early years, their basic environment remained unchanged. Always present were the essential elements of frontier farm life, the endless chores and toils, the comparative isolation, the long, uninterrupted evenings, which fostered conversation and family solidarity, and the reassuring marvel of nature's cycle from seed to plant to fruit.

One of the few recorded instances of Joseph's early years occurred when he was nine years of age and the family was residing at Lebanon, New Hampshire. It was there that Catherine was born, bringing to seven the number of living Smith children, who ranged in age from fifteen to one. There occurred at this time an epidemic of typhus fever. In turn, each of the Smith children took ill, and over a period of several months they infected and reinfected each other. Sophronia, then ten years old, was the most seriously afflicted; she was attended by a physician for eighty-nine days and kept under constant medication. On the ninetieth day, the doctor despaired of her life and informed the distraught parents there was nothing else he could do for her. Pushed to the extremity of their own resources, the couple turned to the only other source of help about which they knew. "In this moment of distraction," Lucy recorded, "my husband and myself clasped our hands, fell upon our knees by the bedside, and poured out our grief to God in prayer and supplication, beseeching him to spare our child yet a little longer." An improbable, almost wild, scene ensued when the anguished mother took the ten-year-old into her arms as if she were an infant and commenced to pace the floor. Someone present remonstrated with Lucy for what appeared to be wholly irrational conduct, saying, "You are certainly crazy. Your child is dead." Undeterred, the mother continued to walk the floor until at length the child sobbed, looked up into the mother's face, and commenced to breathe quietly and freely. With a combined sense of relief and self-vindication, Lucy observed, "From this time forward Sophronia continued mending, until she entirely recovered." (Lucy Mack Smith, pp. 52-53.)

Young Joseph, who was then an observant nine-year-old, would have been witness to this dramatic episode involving his older sister and playmate. We are left to conjecture at the impact this experience had upon his attitude toward prayer and faith in God.

Joseph's siege of typhus fever appeared to be quite mild and lasted only about two weeks. The aftermath, however, produced one of the most traumatic and terrifying experiences of a life filled with woe and adversity. It started with a severe pain in his shoulder of such intensity as to cause him to scream involuntarily. The doctor diagnosed the ailment as a sprain and treated it accordingly with a remedy called "bone linament." After two weeks of excruciating pain, accompanied by the youth's protestations that he had not suffered an injury, the doctor conducted a more searching examination, which disclosed the presence of a "fever sore." When this was lanced by the doctor, a full quart of matter was discharged. No sooner had the pain subsided in Joseph's shoulder than it "shot like lightning" into his leg. Almost immediately the leg began to swell and became exceedingly painful. For two weeks he received almost constant nursing care from his mother and other members of the family, especially twelve-year-old Hyrum. During a good part of this time, Hyrum sat beside Joseph, who had been placed on a low bed to facilitate his care, and pressed the afflicted leg between his hands to help alleviate the pain. Nothing, however, gave the boy any relief. When, after three weeks, there was no improvement in his condition, the doctor was again summoned. The only remedy he could prescribe was to lance the boy's leg. Accordingly, a six-inch incision was opened up between the knee and the ankle, which seemed to afford some welcome but only temporary relief. When, within a short time, the pain returned with even greater intensity, the doctor was called again. The wound was reopened and deepened to the bone, providing some respite. Soon, however, the leg commenced to swell again and the pain became almost unbearable. At this juncture, several doctors were called in for consultation. They recommended that the boy's leg be amputated. However, so persistent and anguished were the protests of the family, especially Lucy, that the doctors were persuaded to follow an intermediate course. They would instead remove the infected portion of the bone.

One can imagine the fears and anxieties that possessed young Joseph and his family as they faced the prospect of such an operation without the benefit of hospital facilities or anesthetics. The doctors offered the only antidote they had for the excruciating pain that was sure to follow—a cord to bind his arms to prevent him from thrashing about during the ordeal, and a drink of wine to deaden his senses. Joseph declined both. Instead, he asked that his father hold him in his arms during the operation. He also insisted that his mother leave the room. These scanty preparations having been made, the surgeons commenced their work. Holes were bored into the bone on either side of the infected part; then, using pincers or forceps, the doctors tore away the diseased bone piece by piece. So intense was the pain when the first piece of bone was torn away that Joseph screamed. This brought his mother running into the room. She was promptly ushered out but was soon drawn into the room again by another terrifying scream from Joseph. Lucy penned this vivid picture of the scene: ". . . oh, my God! what a spectacle for a mother's eye! The wound torn open, the blood still gushing from it, and the bed literally covered with blood. Joseph was pale as a corpse, and large drops of sweat were rolling down his

face, whilst upon every feature was depicted the utmost agony."
(Lucy Mack Smith, p. 58.) After this intrusion, Lucy was taken
from the room and restrained from reentering until the operation
had been completed and the room tidied up.

This terrible ordeal marked the turning point in Joseph's
recovery. His body commenced to mend and with it came a release
from the tensions and anxieties that had accompanied his illness.
To help speed his recovery, he was sent to visit Uncle Jesse at
Salem where, it was hoped, the sea air and change of scene would
provide a needed tonic. Lucy reported that "in this he was not
disappointed."

It is interesting to picture this frail young convalescent, whose
prophetic character had not yet commenced to emerge, in the
home of his opinionated, agnostic uncle. Jesse's subsequent rejection of Joseph's revelations was doubtless influenced in part by his
recollection of Joseph as a dependent, almost helpless, boy.

Joseph carried the physical and emotional scars of this traumatic experience for the remainder of his life. However, he suffered
no serious impairment as a result. In fact, the experience taught
him several valuable lessons. From the intense pain came an
increased appreciation of the daily blessing of health. Faced with
death, he learned that the duration of life is tenuous and uncertain.
He learned that man's knowledge and skill are severely limited, and
that beyond the scope of man's competence lies the infinite field of
God's knowledge and power. Finally, he became conscious as never
before of the great love and concern of his family for him, especially that of his parents and his brother Hyrum. A few years later
these three were to accept without doubt or qualification the amazing disclosures of their son and younger brother, who, at this
point, seemed so vulnerable.

From Lebanon, the family moved to Norwich, Vermont,
where the harried father suffered three successive crop failures, and
where his family was enlarged to eight children with the birth of
Don Carlos. The combination of a growing family and his
unproductive farming efforts precipitated the father's decision to
move to Palmyra, New York. He went ahead to make advance arrangements while Lucy was left to wind up affairs and to move the
family and their effects. Before leaving Norwich, Joseph, Sr., had
attempted to settle accounts with all his debtors and creditors.
However, several creditors neglected to bring their accounts to the

settlement. Their claims were satisfied either by payment of cash or by the transfer of claims Joseph had against his debtors. Apparently no receipts were issued, and in view of the failure of these creditors to submit their accounts and to mark them paid, Joseph had no evidence these debts had been satisfied other than the testimony of those who attended the settlement. Lucy and the children had just completed preparations for the trip to Palmyra, with their belongings stowed on the wagon, when some of the creditors presented their uncancelled accounts for payment. Faced with the alternative of gathering the scattered witnesses together and defending a threatened lawsuit, Lucy decided to liquidate some assets to satisfy these fraudulent claims, which totaled the monumental amount of $150. Some of the parties who had attended the original settlement were incensed at this and urged Lucy to contest the matter. When she declined because of the complications created by the impending move to Palmyra, they proposed to raise the amount by donation. Manifesting admirable spunk and independence, Lucy rejected their kind offer. "The idea of receiving assistance in such a way as this was indeed very repulsive to my feelings," she declared. (Lucy Mack Smith, p. 61.)

Driven by a hired teamster named Howard, the Smith wagon, laden with the residue of their belongings after the forced liquidation, and with Lucy, her eight children, and her mother aboard, departed for Palmyra. En route, a stop was made at Royalton, where Lucy's aged mother was left to live with her son, Daniel Mack. The tearful farewell that occurred there was one that ever after would produce feelings of great sorrow in Lucy. Convinced that they would never see each other again during life, the two women each vented their tenderest feelings. Through her tears, Mother Mack admonished Lucy for the last time "to continue faithful in the service of God to the end of your days." (Lucy Mack Smith, p. 62.)

As it turned out, this sad parting was not the most trying aspect of the trip for Lucy. Not long after leaving Royalton, she encountered heavy difficulties with the teamster, Mr. Howard. With each passing day, he became more surly and uncooperative. Irritated by the children, he progressively became more snappish and rude with them. For some unexplained reason, he took a particular disliking to Joseph and frequently compelled him to walk long distances, despite the fact that the boy was still lame. The tensions and resentments generated by Mr. Howard's conduct finally erupted near Utica, New York. Enraged by some unknown incident, he unloaded the Smiths' belongings from the wagon and was preparing to leave with the team. Lucy confronted him in the presence of other travelers in an inn where the family was staying and accused him of attempting to steal the team and abandon her and her eight children. Turning to him she declared, "Sir, I now forbid you touching the team, or driving it one step further. You can go about your own business; I have no use for you. I shall take charge of the team myself, and hereafter attend to my own affairs." (Lucy Mack Smith, p. 63.) This scathing denunciation appears to have subdued the man completely, for we find no further reference to him in Lucy's narrative.

The last leg of the arduous trip, from Utica to Palmyra, was negotiated without incident. Joseph, Sr., was there to greet them and to assume again the burden of family leadership, which Lucy gladly relinquished. She noted with obvious relief, "I was quite happy in once more having the society of my husband, and in throwing myself and children upon the care and affection of a tender companion and father." (Ibid.)

The Smith family's physical resources were never again as depleted as they were when Lucy and the children arrived in Palmyra. She had just two cents in cash, and only part of the family's personal belongings, the remainder having been disposed of to satisfy the creditors' claims. Neither did Joseph, Sr., have any means. He had, however, made arrangements for temporary housing in Palmyra, where the family resided for about two years. They then moved to Manchester, where he contracted to purchase one hundred acres of virgin wooded land as a farm site.

During the first year after they moved to Manchester, the father and his sons cleared thirty acres and constructed a log house. They were able to make the first of two installment payments on the land, chiefly from the proceeds of Lucy's sale of painted oilcloth coverings. By this means, they were also able to complete the furnishing of their home. As the due date of the second installment approached, it became necessary for Alvin to hire out in order to obtain the necessary cash. Thus, through hard work and cooperative effort, the family was able to reestablish its financial stability within a few short years.

During this period young Joseph advanced into his teens. His leg now fully healed, he was able to run errands and perform light manual labor in assisting his father and two older brothers in clearing the land and building the log house. Nothing appeared yet in his character or outward demeanor that marked him as being destined for any unusual role or achievement in life. He was an obedient, cheerful boy, inclined to be gregarious, yet thoughtful and introspective. His mother reported that he was less inclined to read and study than any of the other children but was given to deep thought and meditation. Yet there was something about him that evoked deep and sometimes malignant feelings in others. We have already noted the teamster's antagonistic feelings toward him. It is also reported that near the end of the family's trip from Vermont, the son of another family that was traveling with them struck Joseph, who was on crutches at the time, and left him alongside the road; he was picked up and brought into Palmyra by another traveler. Three years after the Smiths arrived in Palmyra, an incident occurred that demonstrated that someone else had a bitter, if not murderous, attitude toward Joseph, or, at least, toward his family. One evening as he returned from an errand, someone fired a gun at him as he neared the cabin. Terrified and badly shaken, he sprang through the door to safety. His family attempted to find the would-be assassin but were unable to do so in the gathering dusk. The next morning, however, they found his tracks and the place where he had lain beneath a wagon. They also found one of their animals dead from gunshot wounds. Nothing ever came to light about the identity of the assailant or his motives.

However traumatic these incidents may have been in Joseph's early life, they were but mild precursors of the storm of abuse and vilification soon to break over his head. Unknown to Joseph, events had combined to prepare for one of the most dramatic and unusual spiritual experiences of the nineteenth century, or, in fact, of almost any preceding century.

Chapter Four

"This Is My Beloved Son. Hear Him!"

The dramatic events that were about to unfold in the life of young Joseph Smith, and that would eventually have an untold impact upon the religious destiny of the world, had, as we have seen, actually commenced in the Prophet's infancy and early youth when he was exposed to the spiritual qualities and experiences of his parents and grandparents. His mother's testimony of how the Lord had heard her prayer and spared her life; his father's recounting of the unusual dreams and visions he had experienced over a period of several years; his grandfather Mack's almost miraculous conversion in his old age and the evangelical spirit which that conversion produced; his grandfather Smith's solemn injunction to his progeny to be earnest in all matters pertaining to God; and his grandmothers' sincere, abiding faith in Deity—all these, combined, had produced in young Joseph an attitude of absolute faith in the existence and power of God. The catalyst that acted upon this attitude and produced the experience that so dramatically altered Joseph's life was an almost frenetic religious revival in and around Palmyra a few years after the Smiths arrived there.

This revival was typical of many that regularly broke like waves upon parts of the new nation. Especially susceptible to this phenomenon was the area west of the Catskill and Adirondack mountains within which Palmyra was located. So frequently had the area been caught up in the fervor of religious excitement and so searing had been the effect upon the inhabitants and their institutions that this "ecclesiastical storm center" has been labeled by historians as the "Burned-over District."

Revivals had as their main object the awakening or reinforcement of religious sentiment and commitment. Had this been the only object, it is doubtful that the revival of 1819-20 around Palmyra would have had any significant effect on Joseph other than to confirm his faith in God. However, the existence of a variety of religious sects in the neighborhood introduced into the revival a divisive, controversial element. These sects were interested not only in turning people toward God, but also in turning them toward their particular concept of the nature and attributes of God and of the purpose and ultimate goal of earth life. Differences in concept and aggressive efforts to attract converts to one sect or another transformed the revival into a turbulent, sometimes bitter, contest.

Within a radius of eight miles of the Smith farm were thirteen different religious congregations, including Quakers, Baptists, Presbyterians, and Methodists. Several members of the Smith family, including Lucy, were proselyted to the Presbyterian faith. According to his own account, Joseph "became somewhat partial to the Methodist sect." (HC 1:3.) This interest in Methodism was inspired in large part by a local Methodist minister, the Reverend Lane, who, according to Oliver Cowdery, "was a talented man possessing a good share of literary endowments and apparent humility. [His] manner of communication was peculiarly calculated to awaken the intellect of the hearer, and arouse the sinner to look about him for safety. Much good instruction was always drawn from his discourses on the scripture, and in common with others, our brother's [Joseph Smith's] mind became awakened." (CHC 1:52-53.)

In the early part of 1820, the Reverend Lane preached the most effective sermon of his career, the results of which are abundantly evident even today. On that occasion he addressed himself to the subject "What church shall I join?" taking as his text the familiar injunction found in James: "If any of you lack wisdom, let him ask of God, that giveth to all men liberally, and upbraideth not; and it shall be given him." (James 1:5.) In his audience that day was young Joseph Smith, who had been caught up in the spirit of the revival that swirled around him and who, to say the least, was perplexed by the conflicting doctrines expounded as the ministers vied for converts. The Prophet later recorded his deep feelings of confusion at the time: "So great were the confusion and strife among the different denominations, that it was impossible for a person young as I was, and so unacquainted with men and things, to come to any certain conclusion who was right and who was wrong. My mind at times was greatly excited, the cry and tumult were so great and incessant." (HC 1:3-4.)[1]

---

[1] The writings of the Prophet concerning the events that followed, including the visitation of the Father and the Son to him in a grove near his home, form the basis for the remainder of this chapter. This material can be found in Joseph Smith, *History of the Church*, 1:1-15; in the Writings of Joseph Smith, Pearl of Great Price, chapter 2.

In the midst of such turmoil, the simple injunction of James quoted was as a beacon in the mind of Joseph, showing the way out of the darkness that engulfed him. Surely God, in whom he had implicit faith, was able to shed light on the perplexing question the Reverend Lane had posed. The Prophet later explained the powerful impact this scripture had upon him at the time. "Never did any passage of Scripture come with more power to the heart of man than this did at this time to mine. It seemed to enter with great force into every feeling of my heart." (HC 1:4.)

Joseph had never before faced a crisis of this magnitude, for never before had he attempted to pray vocally and alone. On this occasion, however, so intense were his feelings and so desirous was he of obtaining an answer to the perplexing problem he faced that he determined to find a place of seclusion where, following the injunction of James, he could implore God. Near the Smith farm was a beautiful grove of trees that afforded the privacy and isolation so necessary for the purpose he had in mind. Joseph later confided that as he entered the grove, there lingered no doubt that God would hear and answer his prayer. The striking examples of his parents and grandparents in receiving answers to their prayers had convinced him that God was a reality, a benign, loving Father. The injunction found in James had also convinced him that God would give him enlightenment.

In the grove, Joseph knelt and commenced to offer his first vocal prayer. No sooner had he done so than he was seized by an evil power of such force and intensity that he felt for a time he was surely doomed to destruction. But mustering his strength, he continued to call upon God with all the fervency of his soul. At length, he was released from the evil power that had bound him and that, he declared, was not imaginary, but was the real and terrifying influence of a being from the unseen world. Simultaneously, he saw a shaft of light extending down into the grove from the heavens, in the midst of which were two personages who stood above him in the air. The Prophet made no attempt to describe these personages other than to say that their brightness and glory defied all description. Neither did he attempt to describe the feelings this extraordinary happening evoked.

As he gazed at them, one of the heavenly beings pointed to the other and, speaking to Joseph, said, *"This is My Beloved Son. Hear Him!"* As soon as Joseph was able to regain his composure, he asked the Savior which church he should join. He was directed to join none of them because all their creeds were an "abomination" in the sight of God. The Lord also excoriated the professors of those creeds as being "corrupt," as teaching for doctrine "the commandments of men," and as having "a form of godliness" but denying "the power thereof." Joseph was also told "many other things" that he was instructed not to divulge.

We are left to speculate about the time this interview occupied, about the nature and scope of the other instructions given to the Prophet, and about the transformation that occurred in Joseph that enabled him to converse with heavenly beings. We do know, however, that the instructions given by the Savior in the presence of the Holy Eternal Father, in the only known recorded instance when they appeared together to a living man, were not of a trivial nature. Subsequent events imply that they dealt in some detail with the establishment and development of The Church of Jesus Christ of Latter-day Saints, the kingdom of God on earth.

The young man who left the grove that day was hardly the same young man who entered it. His life thereafter was radically altered. He had a knowledge about the reality and attributes of God not possessed by any other mortal being. He also had keen insights into the design and purposes of God in respect to the reestablishment of the true church and the leading role he was to play in that great drama.

This experience understandably had an observable effect upon Joseph's appearance and demeanor. Shortly after it occurred, he returned to the family home. His mother immediately detected that her son did not look or act as he normally did, and she inquired about the reason. The response was hardly expected. Instead of divulging some physical ailment or emotional upset, he declared that he had found out for himself that Presbyterianism was not true—an allusion to the fact that his mother and two or more of the Smith children had affiliated with that sect. Although there are no direct statements to support it, one may assume that Joseph then confided in his mother the marvelous experience he had just had. It is a testimonial to the maturity and deep faith of Lucy and her husband that they believed the almost unbelievable story of their teenage son.

The belief and acceptance with which Joseph's family received the account of his vision hardly prepared him for the rude reception it was given outside the family circle. Especially shocking to him was the manner in which his experience was rejected and maligned by the man who had urged him to seek God for an answer to the question "Which church shall I join?" It was only natural that young Joseph would seek out the Reverend Lane to confide in him the miraculous results that occurred when Joseph had followed the direction given in the minister's sermon. Instead of commending the young man for his faith and rejoicing with him in the amazing results of his prayer, the minister scoffed at his story. "He treated my communication not only lightly, but with great contempt, saying, it was all of the devil, that there were no such things as visions or revelations in these days; that all such things had ceased with the Apostles, and that there would never be any more of them."

Under normal circumstances, one would expect that the boy's story might have been ignored or an effort might have been made to change his thinking had the Reverend Lane and others believed that he was either deluded or was deliberately telling a lie. Certainly this would not have been the first instance in which they encountered a child, or an adult, for that matter, who told a fanciful or a hard-to-believe story. But for some reason, they seemed to feel impelled to go out of their way to attack and deride the young man. As he reflected on this, he was perplexed and troubled: "It caused me serious reflection then, and often has since, how very strange it was that an obscure boy, of a little over fourteen years of age, and one, too, who was doomed to the necessity of obtaining a scanty maintenance by his daily labor, should be thought a character of sufficient importance to attract the attention of the great ones of the most popular sects of the day, and in a manner to create in them a spirit of the most bitter persecution and reviling." Joseph has left us his own interpretation of these events: "It seems as though the adversary was aware, at a very early period of my life, that I was destined to prove a disturber and an annoyer of his kingdom; else why should the powers of darkness combine against me? Why the opposition and persecution that arose against me, almost in my infancy?"

While it is true that the boy who left the grove that spring morning was never quite the same after, it is equally true that he was still a mere fourteen years of age and had much seasoning and maturing ahead of him. One should not expect that a single spiritual experience would have suddenly transformed him into a state of perfection. Certainly this was not the case with the Savior himself during his mortal probation. Though Jesus was the Only Begotten Son, we are told he learned obedience and qualified for his great mission "by the things which he suffered." So it was that after the transcendent effect of Joseph's experience in the grove had dissipated, he reverted to his accustomed role in the family of Joseph and Lucy Mack Smith. He still performed the menial but necessary tasks of a farm boy, sometimes in the employ of neighboring farmers. He was still subject to the physical infirmities of that day, and to the emotional and mental pressures to which all young men are subject. In short, he was still an imperfect, vulnerable young man who had many things to learn before he would be qualified to fill the special mission to which he had been called.

This was one of the most difficult periods of Joseph's life. He had been specially favored of the Lord with an experience the like of which had not been known for centuries, one that had marked him as a person destined for a special and significant work. Yet he had neither the means nor ability to lift himself out of the obscure and somewhat mean circumstances in which he then lived. What was worse, he found that relating his experience outside the family circle inspired bitter criticism and even persecution against him. Many years later when he recorded the events of that trying period, he gave voice to the feelings of bafflement, resentment, and isolation that they produced. He complained that he was "persecuted by those who ought to have been my friends, and to have treated me kindly, and if they supposed me to be deluded to have endeavored in a proper and affectionate manner to have reclaimed me."

Thus abandoned and rejected, and lacking the experience and maturity that would have enabled him to ignore these rebuffs or to turn them to his advantage, Joseph committed many indiscretions that caused him great remorse and that ultimately led him again to seek guidance from the Lord. He wrote: "I was left to all kinds of temptations; and mingling with all kinds of society, I frequently fell into many foolish errors, and displayed the weakness of youth, and the foibles of human nature; which, I am sorry to say, led me into divers temptations, offensive in the sight of God." To negate any implication that he had committed any especially gross or vile sins, he hastened to add: "In making this confession, no one need suppose me guilty of any great or malignant sins. A disposition to commit such was never in my nature." He then went on to define his transgression as a spirit of "levity," which caused him, on occasion, to be associated with "jovial company, etc., not consistent with that character which ought to be maintained by one who was called of God as I had been." In his own mind, then, Joseph had been convicted of hypocrisy because of differences between his conduct and the transcendent nature and implication of the heavenly vision he had beheld. In an attempt to rid himself of these feelings of unworthiness, and also to learn his status before God, Joseph therefore made a second attempt to directly invoke God's special blessing.

On September 21, 1823, some three and a half years after Joseph's dramatic experience in the grove, Joseph retired to his bedroom on the second floor of the Smiths' new home. As he was in the act of supplicating God for forgiveness of his "sins and follies" and to learn his "state and standing before Him," he saw a light appear in his room, which continued to increase until it was "lighter than at noonday." Then a personage appeared at his bedside "standing in the air, for his feet did not touch the floor." Unlike the earlier occasion when the Father and the Son appeared to him and Joseph had made no attempt to describe their appearance, he now took some pains to paint a word picture of this new visitor. "He had on a loose robe of most exquisite whiteness. It was a whiteness beyond anything earthly I had ever seen; nor do I believe that any earthly thing would be made to appear so exceedingly white and brilliant. His hands were naked and his arms also, a little above the wrist, so, also were his feet naked, as were his legs, a little above the ankles. His head and neck were also bare. I could discover that he had no other clothing on but this robe, as it was open, so that I could see into his bosom. Not only was his robe exceedingly white, but his whole person was glorious beyond description, and his countenance truly like lightning. The room was exceedingly light, but not so very bright as immediately around his person."

It comes as no surprise that Joseph was afraid when he first beheld this personage. Who among us would have reacted differently? The Savior's disciples had a similar experience when the Savior appeared to them in the upper room following his resurrection, for it is reported that they were "terrified and affrighted."

After the first shock, Joseph regained his composure and all fear left him, especially when the visitor called him by name. The visitor told him that his name was Moroni, "that he was a messenger sent from the presence of God," that God had a work for Joseph to do, and that Joseph's name "should be had for good and evil among all nations, kindreds, and tongues, or that it should be both good and evil spoken of among all people." Moroni then told him about a book written upon gold plates that contained "the fulness of the everlasting Gospel." Deposited with the book was a Urim and Thummim—two stones in silver bows fastened to a breastplate. Joseph learned that the possession and use of these were what constituted "seers" in ancient times, and that they had been prepared for the purpose of translating the inscriptions on the gold plates.

Moroni then quoted a series of scriptures from the Old and New Testaments, including the third and fourth chapters of Malachi, the eleventh chapter of Isaiah, the third chapter of Acts, and the second chapter of Joel. He quoted the first, fifth, and sixth verses of the fourth chapter of Malachi differently than they appear in the King James translation. These scriptures taken together, and as reworded and explained by the heavenly visitor, conveyed to Joseph the knowledge that the winding-up scenes of the earth drama were near at hand, that they would be accompanied by cataclysmic events and preceded by a restoration of the priesthood and the true church, and that this restoration would produce a marvelous change in the attitudes and conduct of men. Specifically, Joseph learned that men's hearts would be turned toward their departed kindred and that there would be exhibited among the living a marvelous outpouring of the Spirit, with dreams and visions and other spiritual manifestations being a commonplace among both the old and the young. The Prophet's account of this amazing experience then included this cryptic sentence, "He quoted many other passages of Scripture, and offered many explanations which cannot be mentioned here." There followed instructions concerning the care of the plates when they would ultimately be delivered into Joseph's possession, and there was opened to his understanding a vision of the precise place where the plates were then deposited. He was directed that when he obtained the plates he was to show them to no one except those to whom he would be commanded to show them. This ended the interview. The light in the room then commenced to gather around the visitor and a "conduit" opened up into heaven through which he ascended until he disappeared from view.

As Joseph lay musing upon the singularity of his experience, his room again was filled with light and the heavenly personage reappeared, repeating exactly what he had said during the first visit, except that he expounded on the fearsome judgments that were soon to be executed upon the earth and its inhabitants, accompanied by "famine, sword and pestilence." Following his ascension after the second visit, the messenger appeared still a third time and rehearsed the entire matter again without variation, except that he cautioned Joseph against any selfish motive or intention when he obtained the plates.

Since these miraculous interviews occupied most of the entire night, it is no wonder that Joseph became faint while working in the field the next day. Seeing that his son did not feel well, his father directed Joseph back to the house to rest. On the way he fell to the ground, unconscious, as he attempted to cross a fence. Reviving, he saw the same messenger again, bathed in light as before and standing above him in the air. Once again Moroni repeated all the information and instructions he had imparted the previous night. Then he commanded Joseph to tell his father what had happened. Obedient to that command, Joseph returned to the field and told his father everything. Without hesitation, Joseph, Sr., declared that "it was of God" and told Joseph to do as the messenger had instructed him.

The absolute confidence manifested in his eighteen-year-old son traced to the father's own spiritual experiences extending over a period of several years, his prior acceptance of the account of the visit of the Father and the Son, and his knowledge of young Joseph's penchant for honesty and truth. It is also likely that he recalled the oft-repeated prediction of his own father, Asael Smith, to the effect that a great prophet would be born in his line. Whatever the reason, Joseph Smith, Sr., did not then or later question the veracity of his son, whose leadership and direction he accepted in many things as if the son were his elder. This tendency to defer to young Joseph was evidenced also by the mother and by the older brothers and sister. It was a deference void of any hint of inferiority or jealousy, but was founded on a recognition that their son and brother was an agent through whom the Almighty had seen fit to manifest his will. Thus, their deferential attitude was not so much a recognition of any special qualities in young Joseph as it was a recognition of the Deity who had deigned to reveal himself through one of their own.

With his father's approbation, Joseph went to the hill that had been shown to him in vision where the gold plates were buried. So distinct had been the vision that he recognized the place immediately. After removing a stone that covered a box in which the plates and the Urim and Thummim were located, he was prevented from removing the plates by an angel who stood nearby. He told Joseph that "the time for bringing them forth had not yet arrived, neither would it, until four years from that time." He also told Joseph to come to the same place in precisely one year and for each year thereafter until the time should come for obtaining the plates.

Thus, within a period of less than one day, Joseph had had five separate interviews with a heavenly being who had given him explicit instructions about the young prophet's future work. In four of these interviews, the same subject matter had been presented with little variation. Consequently, Joseph had no doubt or uncertainty about what he was to do. The only question was whether he would be capable of fulfilling the task in light of the almost unbelievable oppositon he would face, the scope and bitterness of which had been revealed to him in part. Later events proved that while he ultimately succeeded, he was not always certain of doing so.

Chapter Five

The Emerging "Prophet, Seer, Revelator"

Following his first vision in 1820, Joseph confided in some persons outside his family circle, which brought a storm of opposition and abuse upon him. Therefore, he did not divulge the fact of Moroni's visits to anyone outside his immediate family, and he laid a strict charge upon them that they also were not to tell others. He was concerned that a premature disclosure of what had happened and what was in the offing would seriously impede, if not thwart, his mission.

But such was his confidence in his family that Joseph felt free to tell them in detail what had happened. In the evening of the day when he was visited by Moroni in the field, he related to them the marvelous events of the preceding twenty-four hours. His mother, Lucy, left this account of the family council where Joseph related these sacred events to them:

". . . by sunset the next day, we were all seated, and Joseph commenced telling us the great and glorious things which God had manifested to him; but, before proceeding, he charged us not to mention out of the family that which he was about to say to us, as the world was so wicked that when they came to a knowledge of these things they would try to take our lives; and that when we should obtain the plates, our names would be cast out as evil by all people. Hence the necessity of suppressing these things as much as possible, until the time should come for them to go forth to the world.

"After giving us this charge, he proceeded to relate further particulars concerning the work which he was appointed to do, and we received them joyfully, never mentioning them except among ourselves, agreeable to the instructions which we had received from him." (Lucy Mack Smith, p. 82.)

Later, as further instructions were given, the young prophet shared them with his family insofar as he was permitted to do so. Lucy wrote, "I presume our family presented an aspect as singular as any that ever lived upon the face of the earth—all seated in a circle, father, mother, sons and daughters, and giving the most profound attention to a boy, eighteen years of age, who had never read the Bible through in his life. . . .

"During our evening conversations, Joseph would occasionally give us some of the most amusing recitals that could be imagined. He would describe the ancient inhabitants of this continent, their dress, mode of traveling, and the animals upon which they rode; their cities, their buildings, with every particular; their mode of warfare; and also their religious worship. This he would do with as much ease, seemingly, as if he had spent his whole life among them." (Lucy Mack Smith, pp. 82-83.)

The extent to which the Prophet was instructed by heavenly visitors is not commonly known. A hint of the scope of this phenomenon is found in a letter the Prophet wrote to a newspaper editor, John Wentworth of the Chicago *Democrat,* which included this illuminating sentence: "After having received many visits from the angels of God unfolding the majesty and glory of the events that should transpire in the last days, on the morning of the 22nd of September A.D. 1827, the angel of the Lord delivered the records into my hands." (HC 4:537.) In this letter, the Prophet did not attempt to elaborate on the identity of these angels. He did so, however, in private conversation with some of his disciples.

John Taylor, third president of the Church, reported, "When Joseph Smith was raised up as a Prophet of God, Mormon, Moroni, Nephi and others of the ancient Prophets who formerly lived on this Continent, and Peter and John and others who lived on the Asiatic Continent, came to him and communicated to him certain principles pertaining to the Gospel of the Son of God." (JD 17:374.) At a later time, President Taylor elaborated upon this subject: "The principles which he had, placed him in communication with the Lord, and not only with the Lord, but with the ancient apostles and prophets; such men, for instance, as Abraham, Isaac, Jacob, Noah, Adam, Seth, Enoch, and Jesus and the Father, and the apostles that lived on this continent as well as those who lived on the Asiatic continent." (JD 21:94.)

Other writings record the appearance to the Prophet of John the Baptist, Peter, James, and John, Moses, Elias, Elijah, and others. So intimate was Joseph's knowledge of these personages that he related not only what they said but also how they looked and acted. John Taylor said that "he seemed to be as familiar with these people as we are with one another." (JD 21:94.) And again, "If you were to ask Joseph what sort of a looking man Adam was, he would tell you at once; he would tell you his size and appearance and all about him. You might have asked him what sort of men Peter, James and John were, and he could have told you." (JD 18:326.) The Prophet once compared his brother Alvin with Adam and Seth, saying that Alvin "was a very handsome man, surpassed by none but Adam and Seth, and of great strength." (HC 5:247.)

Either through neglect or because of restrictions imposed by his heavenly visitors, the Prophet failed to keep a record of the dates of their appearances or of the nature of their instructions. There were notable exceptions, as in the cases of Moroni and the personages who appeared in connection with the pentecostal outpourings at the Kirtland Temple. It would hardly have been possible not to remember the dates of Moroni's appearances because of the consecutive, repetitious visits that occurred in September 1823 and the four annual visits that followed. At Kirtland, there were others present at the visits who recorded the date. However, because the dates of the other appearances were not recorded, it is unknown which of these heavenly beings appeared to Joseph in the four-year period before he received the plates or the order of their appearances.

Joseph's vast knowledge of past and future events and the unseen world was also attributable to his sensitive, spiritual nature. At the time of Moroni's first visits, such a clear vision of the Hill Cumorah was opened in the Prophet's mind that he instantly recognized the place when he later walked to it. Subsequent events proved that this visionary gift applied to things past, present, and future. During construction of the Nauvoo Temple, the architect, William Weeks, protested the Prophet's insistence that round windows be provided in the broad sides of the building, arguing that this violated "all the known rules of architecture" and that semicircular windows should be used instead. However, the Prophet insisted that if necessary, the temple would be constructed ten feet higher in order to accommodate the circular windows. The reason for the Prophet's insistence was typical. "I have seen in vision the splendid appearance of that building illuminated, and will have it built according to the pattern shown me." (HC 6:197.)

Many of the revelations received by Joseph Smith were based

upon visions of future events or of the other world. A personal friend, Philo Dibble, left this interesting description of the Prophet and Sidney Rigdon whom he and several others saw in the process of receiving section 76 of the Doctrine and Covenants: "Joseph would, at intervals, say: 'What do I see?' as one might say while looking out of the window and beholding what all in the room could not see. Then he would relate what he had seen or what he was looking at. Then Sidney replied, 'I see the same.' Presently Sidney would say, 'What do I see' and would repeat what he had seen or was seeing, and Joseph would reply, 'I see the same.'

"This manner of conversation was repeated at short intervals to the end of the vision, and during the whole time not a word was spoken by any other person. Not a sound nor motion made by anyone but Joseph and Sidney, and it seemed to me that they never moved a joint or limb during the time I was there, which I think was over an hour, and to the end of the vision.

"Joseph sat firmly and calmly all the time in the midst of a magnificent glory, but Sidney sat limp and pale, apparently as limber as a rag, observing which, Joseph remarked, smilingly, 'Sidney is not used to it as I am.' " (Hyrum Andrus, *Joseph Smith: The Man and the Seer* [Salt Lake City: Deseret Book Co., 1960], p. 111.)

Shortly before his martyrdom, Joseph saw in vision the mountainous valleys in the west to which his people would be driven. Anson Call, who was present at the time, recorded the event. "I had before seen him in a vision, and now saw while he was talking his countenance change to white; not the deadly white of a bloodless face, but a living brilliant white. He seemed absorbed in gazing at something at a great distance, and said: 'I am gazing upon the valleys of those mountains.' This was followed by a vivid description of the scenery of these mountains, as I have since become acquainted with it. . . .

"It is impossible to represent in words this scene which is still vivid in my mind, of the grandeur of Joseph's appearance, his beautiful descriptions of this land, and his wonderful prophetic utterances as they emanated from the glorious inspiration that overshadowed him. There was a force and power in his exclamations of which the following is but a faint echo. 'Oh, the beauty of those snow-capped mountains! The cool refreshing streams that are running down through those mountain gorges!' Then gazing in another direction, as if there was a change of locality: 'Oh, the scenes that this people will pass through! The dead that will lay between here and there.' Then turning in another direction as if the scene had again changed: 'Oh the apostasy that will take place before my brethren reach that land!' " (Andrus, p. 114.)

It was Joseph's visionary qualities and his ability to communicate with beings from the unseen world that distinguished him from all others. By this means, he acquired the knowledge that enabled him to fulfill his prophetic role. Especially during the years 1823 to 1827 was he instructed in this way and prepared for the day when the sacred record would be delivered to him.

But these unusual gifts did not relieve him from the burden of laboring nor did they provide immunity from daily cares. Thus, while he was often elevated to heavenly heights, he was afterward confronted with the hard realities of life.

About a year after the Angel Moroni's first appearance, Alvin Smith, Joseph's oldest brother, died. He became ill on November 15, 1823, with what was diagnosed as "bilious colic" and died a few days later. When death seemed imminent, he asked that each of his brothers and sisters be brought to his bedside. Since he was then a mature man of 25, he seemed to them to be more of a second father than an elder brother. And he acted toward them like a father, giving each paternalistic instruction. He charged Hyrum to finish the house he, Alvin, had started. Sophronia, the eldest daughter, was admonished to care for her parents. Joseph was urged to live so as to entitle him to receive and translate the sacred record. The other children were also given specific instructions except for the baby, Lucy, for whom was reserved an especially touching scene. She clung to Alvin, calling out, "Amby, Amby," her infant version of her brother's name. After having kissed her, Alvin requested that she be taken away, for he feared that his breath offended her. This final scene having been acted out, Alvin declared, "I can now breathe out my life as calmly as a clock" and, according to his mother, "immediately closed his eyes in death." (Lucy Mack Smith, pp. 86-88.)

Judging from their frequent references to Alvin after his death, he had a powerful influence on all of his family, and his death represented the greatest tragedy that had come into their lives. His mother characterized him as "a youth of singular goodness of disposition." (Ibid.) The Prophet frequently referred to him in later years. In giving an account of the pentecostal outpourings at the time of the dedication of the Kirtland Temple, Joseph reported that he saw Alvin in the celestial kingdom. At the time, the Prophet "marvelled how it was that he had obtained an inheritance in that kingdom, seeing that he had departed this life before the Lord had set His hand to gather Israel the second time, and had not been baptized for the remission of sins." In response, the Lord gave the following revelation to the Prophet: "All who have died without a knowledge of this Gospel, who would have received it if they had been permitted to tarry, shall be heirs of the celestial kingdom of God; also all that shall die henceforth without a knowledge of it, who would have received it with all their hearts, shall be heirs of that kingdom, for I, the Lord, will judge all men according to their works, according to the desire of their hearts." (HC 2:380. See also Pearl of Great Price, Joseph Smith—Vision of the Celestial Kingdom.)

The great burden of sorrow created by Alvin's death was magnified by a malicious rumor circulated after his burial that his body had been exhumed and dissected. For the peace of mind of his family, especially Lucy, who was beside herself with grief, Joseph, Sr., had Alvin's body unearthed to show that the rumor was false. In an attempt to lay the matter at rest, he then published the following notice in the *Wayne Sentinel* on September 29, 1824, and during the succeeding week: *"TO THE PUBLIC:* Whereas reports have been industriously put in circulation that my son, Alvin, has been removed from the place of his interment and dissected; which reports every person possessed of human sensibility must know are peculiarly calculated to harrow up the mind of a parent and deeply wound the feelings of relations, I, with some of my neighbors this morning repaired to the grave, and removing the earth, found the body, which had not been disturbed. This method is taken for the purpose of satisfying the minds of those who have put it in circulation, that it is earnestly requested that they would desist therefrom; and that it is believed by some that they have been stimulated more by desire to injure the reputation of certain persons than by a philanthropy for the peace and welfare of myself and friends."

One of the most imaginative and malicious of the Prophet's biographers sees in this episode an attempt by the originators of the tale to dramatize a widely circulated gossip that the Smiths were habitual "diggers" and necromancers. Instead, the incident demonstrates, as hardly anything else could, the extreme attempts that have been made to blacken the reputation of the Smith family.

The tale that Joseph and his family were professional diggers traces back to an innocent employment of the Prophet while he prepared to receive the plates. It actually originated years after, when a malignant apostate named "Doctor" Philastus Hurlburt was excommunicated from the Church for immorality. Swearing revenge, he industriously gathered and published a series of scurrilous affidavits intended to destroy the Prophet's reputation. There is evidence that these affidavits were pure fabrication. At best, they were based upon the flimsiest kind of gossip and hearsay, were devoid of any specific factual charges, and were filled with supposition, false innuendo, and base implications. They also bear evidence of common authorship, probably Hurlburt's. A recurrent theme in most of them is that the Prophet and his family were professional diggers who made their living by preying upon the gullible and superstitious through the use of magical arts. The following excerpts demonstrate the incredible nature of these so-called affidavits: "The general employment of the family, was digging for money. I had frequent invitations to join the company, but always declined. . . . the said Joseph, Sen. told me that the best time for digging money, was, in the heat of summer, when the heat of the sun caused the chests of money to rise near the top of the ground. . . ." Another typical statement reads: "Old Joseph and one of the boys came to me one day, and said that Joseph Jr. had discovered some very remarkable and valuable treasures, which could be procured only in one way. That way, was as follows:— That a black sheep should be taken on to the ground where the treasures were concealed—that after cutting its throat, it should be led around a circle while bleeding. This being done, the wrath of the evil spirit would be appeased: the treasures could then be obtained, and my share of them was to be four fold. To gratify my curiosity, I let them have a large fat sheep. They afterwards informed me, that the sheep was killed pursuant to commandment; but as there was some mistake in the process, it did not have the desired effect. This, I believe, is the only time they ever made money-digging a profitable business." (As quoted in Fawn M. Brodie, *No Man Knows My History* [New York: Alfred A. Knopf, 1971], pp. 432, 434.)

The writings and recorded sermons of the Prophet, his family, and his ancestors will be searched in vain for anything that even remotely resembles this fanciful nonsense. Furthermore, the life and accomplishments of the Prophet, the sound and enduring character of the religious system he established, and the intelligence and industry of the men and women who were attracted to his leadership all stamp these charges as fabrications.

The germ of truth that exists in these charges is that in October 1825, Joseph was employed as a day laborer by Josiah Stowel (or Stoal) of Chenango County, New York, who had been attempting to uncover a fabled Spaniard silver mine. The Prophet gives this account of the episode: "He [Stowel] had heard something of a silver mine having been opened by the Spaniards in Harmony, Susquehanna county, state of Pennsylvania; and had, previous to my hiring to him, been digging, in order, if possible, to discover the mine. After I went to live with him, he took me, with the rest of his hands, to dig for the silver mine, at which I continued to work for nearly a month, without success in our undertaking, and finally I prevailed with the old gentleman to cease digging after it." (HC 1:17.)

During the short time Mr. Stowel remained in Susquehanna County, his hired hands, including Joseph, were boarded in the homes of local residents. Joseph stayed in the home of Isaac Hale, a farmer and noted hunter. It was there that he first met Isaac's daughter Emma, whose dark hair, luminous hazel eyes, and quiet demeanor greatly attracted him.

A personality clash appeared to exist between Isaac and young Joseph from the very beginning. Its origins are lost in obscurity and can only be inferred from a few scanty documents, the principal one being an affidavit supposedly executed by Isaac in 1834 that obviously was prepared by Philastus Hurlburt. Therefore, it predictably dwells on the digger theme. It acknowledges that Joseph was employed by those who were looking for the mine and that Isaac boarded several of these men, including Joseph, for about a month in the latter part of 1825. The statement characterized Joseph as a "careless young man—not very well educated" and reveals the chief source of Isaac's animosity toward Joseph with this unfounded charge: "Not long after this, he returned, and while I was absent from home, carried off my daughter, into the state of New York, where they were married without my approbation or consent." (Brodie, p. 439.) However, at the time this event occurred, Emma was 22 and well beyond the age of consent. In fact, judged by the comparatively early age at which most young ladies were married at that time, she could almost have been classed as a spinster. Isaac was so enraged at Emma's and Joseph's refusal to heed his advice that he never quite forgave them.

Another element in the misunderstanding between Joseph and his future father-in-law was Joseph's insistence that he had received spiritual visions and manifestations. Joseph's journal contains this revealing entry: "Owing to my continuing to assert that I had seen a vision, persecution still followed me, and my wife's father's family were very much opposed to our being married." (HC 1:17.) Isaac Hale, uneducated and lacking in spiritual perfection, could not conceive of the existence of a living God or of the possibility that if God lived he would communicate with men. So when he heard accounts of the Prophet's spiritual experiences, he arbitrarily dismissed them and concluded that Joseph was an imposter.

It was during his employment by Josiah Stowel that Joseph was first exposed to the vagaries of the American court system. Retelling his spiritual experiences had aroused bitter opposition against him on the part of some of the residents of Bainbridge, New York, where Stowel lived. So angry were they at Joseph's assertion that he had talked with God that they charged him before the local justice of the peace with being a disorderly person and an imposter. Joseph was acquitted of the charge in this, the first of a long series of litigations he faced during his short and turbulent life.

Over fifty years after this trial occurred, a Protestant minister published what he said was an official record of it, according to which Joseph was found guilty. Several facets of this record demonstrate its falsity. First, the original record has never been found. Second, a justice of the peace court is not a court of record, since the report of a justice of the peace proceeding ordinarily consists of only a minute entry containing the names of the parties, the nature of the charge, and the action taken. Third, despite the constitutional provision against self-incrimination, this spurious record has the Prophet testifying against himself and, despite the fact he was the accused, has him testifying first. Fourth, the following excerpt from the Prophet's supposed testimony shows the incredible nature of the record: ". . . that he had a certain stone, which he had occasionally looked at to determine where hidden treasures in the bowels of the earth were; that he professed to tell in this manner where gold-mines were a distance under ground, and had looked for Mr. Stowel several times, and informed him where he could find those treasures, and Mr. Stowel had been engaged in digging for them; that at Palmyra he pretended to tell, by looking at this stone, where coined money was buried in Pennsylvania, and while at Palmyra he had frequently ascertained in that way where lost property was, of various kinds; that he has occasionally been in the habit of looking through this stone to find lost property for three years, but of late had pretty much given it up on account its injuring his health, especially his eyes—made them sore. . . ." (Brodie, p. 427.)

An analysis of this statement shows how the falsifier, years after the events actually occurred, clumsily intermixed fact with fiction. For example, he took the facts that Joseph asserted the Nephite record was written on "gold plates," that he translated them with the Urim and Thummim, which had stones in it, and that he worked for Stowel, who was trying to find a "silver mine." Then he produced the falsehood that by the use of a stone Joseph could tell "where gold mines were a distance underground."

Although Joseph was acquitted, it was a source of embarrassment even to be charged and tried. Nevertheless, he continued on in Bainbridge for another ten months after the trial, dividing his time between working for Mr. Stowel and attending school. Because of the close proximity of Bainbridge to Harmony, Pennsylvania, where Isaac Hale lived, Joseph made frequent visits to Harmony to court Emma. Because of Isaac's bitter antagonism, much of their courting was of a furtive nature. Very much in love and unable to obtain the consent of her father, Emma and Joseph eloped and were married in Bainbridge by Squire Tarbill on January 18, 1827.

Lacking the means to acquire his own farm, and not wishing to inconvenience the kindly Stowels by bringing a wife to room and board with them, Joseph immediately took Emma to his father's place near Palmyra, where he farmed the next season. In doing this, he also had in mind the fact that the time for receiving the plates from the Angel Moroni was fast approaching and he wanted to be near the Hill Cumorah when that time came.

Despite the unpleasantness of the trial the year before, the Prophet left many loyal friends and supporters in the Bainbridge area when he departed for Palmyra. Chief among these were Josiah Stowel and Joseph Knight, both of whom were prosperous and highly respected farmers. These men and their families and many of their neighbors later were among the first members of the Church when it was organized four years later. Especially noted in Church history is the Colesville Branch, comprised of members from the nearby town of Colesville, New York, which later moved as a body into Ohio and then into Missouri, always retaining the identifying title to indicate their origin. The loyalty of these friends and neighbors, when compared with the bitter enmity of others in the community, shows the accuracy of the prediction made by the angel that Joseph's name would be had for both good and evil.

His relationship with Stowel and Knight also revealed a pattern that was repeated again and again during his short, turbulent life. Not counting the Prophet's father, they were the first of a long series of older, well-established, and highly respected men who accepted his story and provided support and assistance at critical times in Joseph's career. Among those included in this group were Martin Harris, Peter Whitmer, Sidney Rigdon, W.W. Phelps, Edward Partridge, Frederick G. Williams, and several of the Prophet's uncles, notably John Smith.

As he toiled through the summer of 1827 on his father's farm, Joseph's mind turned repeatedly to the momentous experience he would face in September. At that time, if he proved worthy, the plates were to be delivered to him by the Angel Moroni. While this prospect was a source of great anticipation, it also caused some concern, for he knew that once the plates were delivered to him, he would be solely responsible for their safekeeping. News of the impending delivery had been widely circulated since Joseph first divulged the fact of Moroni's visit four years before. Thus rumors were floating about of elaborate plans to get the plates once they had been delivered to him.

Some idea of the extent and intensity of the opposition the young Prophet faced at that time may be gained from this comment he later made: "The excitement, however, still continued, and rumor with her thousand tongues was all the time employed in circulating falsehoods about my father's family, and about myself. If I were to relate a thousandth part of them, it would fill up volumes." (HC 1:19.)

On the twentieth day of September, the Smiths were visited by Josiah Stowel and Joseph Knight, who ostensibly came to discuss a business matter involving the Smith farm. Later events suggest they were privy to the fact that the time was near for the delivery of the plates to Joseph. Early in the morning of September 22, Joseph borrowed Mr. Knight's horse and wagon, and some time during the day he obtained the plates, the Urim and Thummim, and the breastplate from the Angel Moroni. At that time he was informed that he would be solely responsible for them, and that if he exercised due care, they would be protected. (HC 1:18.)

Chapter Six

Translation of the Book of Mormon Begins

The two or three months after he obtained the plates tested Joseph's ingenuity almost to the breaking point. A group of men led by Willard Chase, a Methodist class leader, had learned of the expected delivery date of the plates and had organized to obtain them from Joseph. They even employed a "conjurer" to assist them in their repeated attempts to find the place where the plates were concealed.

The constant harassment to which Joseph was subjected made it impossible for him to commence the translation. He decided, therefore, to go elsewhere to find the peace and seclusion necessary to do the demanding work of translation.

By this time, the bitter antagonism of his father-in-law had abated somewhat, so in December 1827 Joseph and Emma moved to Harmony, Pennsylvania, where they took up temporary residence with Emma's family. They were assisted in this move by a voluntary gift of fifty dollars from Martin Harris, a prosperous farmer in Palmyra who, with his wife, played a key role in the unfolding drama of the translation and publication of the Book of Mormon.

Among the effects Joseph and Emma moved to Harmony was a chest that contained the plates, the breastplate, and the Urim and Thummim. Isaac Hale, who always questioned the Prophet's veracity, confirmed the existence of this chest. In an affidavit executed in 1834, he said, ". . . I was informed they had brought a wonderful box of Plates down with them. I was shown a box in which it is said they were contained, which had to all appearances been used as a glass box of the common window glass. I was allowed to feel the weight of the box, and they gave me to understand, that the book of plates was then in the box—into which, however, I was not allowed to look." (Brodie, p. 439.)

The chest was one the Prophet had obtained from his brother Hyrum. Lucy Mack Smith left this account of the circumstances under which Hyrum took the chest to Joseph when Hyrum was informed by his brother Don Carlos that the Prophet needed it: ". . . when Carlos arrived at Hyrum's, he found him at tea with two of his wife's sisters. Just as Hyrum was raising a cup to his mouth, Carlos touched his shoulder. Without waiting to hear one word from the child, he dropped the cup, sprang from the table, caught the chest, turned it upside down, and emptying its contents on the floor, left the house instantly with the chest on his shoulder." (Lucy Mack Smith, p. 109.)

In the two months between December 1827 and February 1828, Joseph did little more than acquaint himself with the plates and the Urim and Thummim, although he did some translating. He was assisted by Emma, who served as his first scribe. Since he had been forbidden to show the plates to anyone, Emma sat on one side of a room, partitioned by a blanket or curtain, while Joseph sat on the other side with the plates and interpreters. As he dictated a phrase or sentence, she would read it back for confirmation. This laborious process continued intermittently for several months, with several different scribes assisting the Prophet.

As he acquired more proficiency in using the Urim and Thummim and as he gained a greater familiarity with the ancient language in which the original record was written, the speed of translation accelerated. In the beginning, however, he moved very haltingly. Not only was he handicapped by the strangeness of this new discipline, but the domestic and other duties of Emma made it possible for her to give only occasional assistance. And the incredulous, harassing attitude of his father-in-law made it necessary for Joseph to work at uncertain, odd hours. When Isaac Hale's persistent demands to see the plates were ignored, he told Joseph "that if there was anything in my house of that description, which I could not be allowed to see, he must take it away; if he did not, I was determined to see it. After that, the Plates were said to be hid in the woods. . . ." (Brodie, p. 439.) Later, Joseph purchased from his father-in-law a small nearby farm, which included an unpretentious frame house. This offered more privacy and enabled the Prophet to work without interruption. Still, he was handicapped by lack of a full-time scribe.

By February 1828 Joseph had been able to copy a number of the characters from the plates and, with sporadic help from Emma, to translate them. This was done by prearrangement with Martin Harris, who, having provided money for the trip to Harmony, now appeared ready to make a substantial investment in time and money to help the Prophet with his work. But while Martin basically believed Joseph's story, he had some nagging doubts. These were constantly fed by his wife, Preserved Harris, who was convinced the Prophet was a fraud and was taking advantage of her husband. Through Martin, Preserved exerted pressure on the Prophet to provide some objective evidence to support his story. Joseph had been forbidden to show the plates to anyone, but he was also in sore need of the help Martin seemed willing to give, so he copied and translated some of the characters from the plates to enable Martin to corroborate his story. In February 1828, Martin went to Harmony to obtain the reproduction of the characters and the translation. In the meantime, he had learned that one of the most eminent American authorities on ancient hieroglyphic writings was Professor Charles Anthon of Columbia University in New York City. Armed with the reproduction and translation, Martin traveled to New York for an audience with Professor Anthon. Martin showed him the characters and the Prophet's translation. According to Martin, Professor Anthon identified the characters as being Egyptian, Chaldaic, Assyriac, and Arabic in origin, pronounced the translation correct, and gave him a certificate to that effect. However, when the professor learned that Joseph Smith claimed to have received the plates from an angel and to have translated them by the gift and power of God, he took back the certificate and tore it up, saying "that there was no such thing now as ministering angels, and that if [Martin] would bring the plates to him he would translate them." Martin responded "that part of the plates were sealed, and that [he] was forbidden to bring them," to which the Professor replied, "I cannot read a sealed book." (CHC 1:101-2.)

Six years after this event, Professor Anthon wrote a letter to E. D. Howe, who was compiling a vicious anti-Mormon book, acknowledging Martin's visit but denying that he had given him a statement. In 1841 he also wrote to Dr. T. W. Coit about Martin's visit, this time admitting he had given him a written statement "without hesitation." In explanation he added, "The import of what I wrote was, as far as I can now recollect, simply this, that the marks in the paper appeared to be merely an imitation of various alphabetical characters, and had, in my opinion, no meaning at all connected with them." (CHC 1:106.)

Whatever the statement or certificate said, it convinced Martin of the truthfulness of what Joseph had told him, for soon afterwards, Martin went to Harmony to act as Joseph's scribe.

Martin's wife, Preserved, still questioned the fact that Joseph Smith had the plates, so she insisted on accompanying her husband to Harmony. The account of that trip and the concern Preserved caused to her husband and the Prophet are graphically described by Lucy Mack Smith:

"Mr. Harris, having no particular objections, informed her that she . . . might go and stay one or two weeks, and then he would bring her home again, after which he would return, and resume his writing for Joseph. To this she cheerfully agreed. But Mr. Harris little suspected what he had to encounter by this move. The first time he exhibited the characters before named, she took out of her pocket an exact copy of the same; and told those present, that 'Joe Smith' was not the only one who was in possession of this great curiosity, that she had the same characters, and, they were quite as genuine as those shown by Mr. Harris. This course she continued to pursue, until they arrived at Joseph's.

"As soon as she arrived there, she informed [Joseph] that her object in coming, was to see the plates, and that she would never leave until she had accomplished it. Accordingly, without delay, she commenced ransacking every nook and corner about the house—chests, trunks, cupboards, etc; consequently, Joseph was under the necessity of removing both the breast-plate and the Record from the house, and secreting them elsewhere. Not finding them in the house, she concluded that Joseph had buried them, and the next day she commenced searching out of doors, which she continued to do. . . .

"The woman was so perplexed and disappointed in all her undertakings, that she left the house and took lodgings during her stay in Pennsylvania with a near neighbor. . . .

"While this woman remained in the neighborhood, she did all that lay in her power to injure Joseph in the estimation of his neighbors—telling them that he was a grand imposter, and, that by his specious pretentions, he had seduced her husband into the belief that he [Joseph Smith] was some great one, merely through a design upon her husband's property.

"When she returned home, . . . she endeavored to dissuade her husband from taking any further part in the publication of the

Record; however, Mr. Harris paid no attention to her, but returned and continued writing." (Lucy Mack Smith, pp. 120-22.)

The upset caused by Preserved during this two-week visit was almost negligible compared to the traumatic upheaval she brought about a few months later. In the interim, her husband moved to Harmony to work full time as the Prophet's scribe, intermittently returning to Palmyra to oversee his farming and business interests and to attempt to calm his wife. His failure at this effort is attested by the storm of adversity she was soon to bring upon the Prophet and by the fact that Martin divorced her a few years later.

Joseph Smith and his scribe presented an interesting study in contrasts as they proceeded with the translation. Seated on one side of a curtain dividing a small room was the young, handsome, intense prophet, with the interpreters at hand and the sacred plates spread before him. On the other side of the curtain, the middle-aged, plain-looking farmer sat at a solid wooden table on which were arranged pen and ink and a supply of white foolscap paper. Using the interpreters and all his powers of concentration, the Prophet grasped the sense of the inscriptions on the plates and then dictated them in English to Martin, who wrote them in long hand. Martin would then read back what he had written, and when the Prophet was satisfied that the transcription was correct, he would move on.

No attempt was made to punctuate the transcript, and the Prophet did not edit it once he had received confirmation that it was correct. At the beginning of a new day of translating, the Prophet would merely begin where he had left off the night before and, with the help of his scribe, would repeat the process.

From April to June 1828, Martin filled up 116 pages of manuscript. His constant attention to the work and his daily exposure to the spiritual influences surrounding the Prophet increased his confidence in what he was doing. During his visits home, however, Preserved would raise additional questions and plant new seeds of doubt. She continued to press Martin for more convincing, objective evidence that Joseph had the plates and that his claims of divine assistance were true. Anxious to satisfy his nagging wife and wanting something tangible to point to as evidence of the truthfulness of the Prophet's claim, Martin, in turn, importuned Joseph for the privilege of taking the manuscript home. He assured the Prophet that it would be safe in his possession and that it would be a great help in relieving the constant pressure being exerted by his wife and others.

The Prophet had grave misgivings about granting this request, especially since he had been told twice through the Urim and Thummim that he should not turn over the manuscript to Martin. However, he looked to Martin for continued assistance in translating the record and for financial backing in publishing it. Thus he felt justified in asking again for permission to let Martin borrow the manuscript. This time the answer was affirmative on condition that Martin agreed to show it only to Preserved and a few other close members of the Harris family. Upon receiving Martin's solemn promise to observe this condition and to return the manuscript promptly, the Prophet gave it to him.

The delivery of the manuscript to Martin Harris opened one of the most trying chapters in the Prophet's turbulent life. Instead of following the counsel he had been given, Martin showed the manuscript to many unauthorized people and carelessly let it out of his possession. Lucy Mack Smith records the anguish with which the Prophet received word that the work of several months had been lost. The scene was set in the home of the Prophet's parents in Palmyra, where he had gone when Martin's return was delayed. Early in the morning after his arrival, Joseph sent for Martin. Lucy tells the story: "At eight o'clock we set the victuals on the table, as we were expecting him [Martin] every moment. We waited until nine, and he came not—till ten, and he was not there—till eleven, still he did not make his appearance. But at half past twelve we saw him walking with a slow and measured tread towards the house. . . . On coming to the gate, he stopped, . . . got upon the fence, and sat there some time with his hat drawn over his eyes. At length he entered the house. Soon after which we sat down to the table, Mr. Harris with the rest. He took up his knife and fork as if he were going to use them, but immediately dropped them. Hyrum, observing this, said 'Martin, why do you not eat; are you sick?' Upon which Mr. Harris pressed his hands upon his temples, and cried out in a tone of deep anguish, 'Oh, I have lost my soul! I have lost my soul!'

"Joseph who had not expressed his fears till now, sprang from the table, exclaiming, 'Martin, have you lost that manuscript? Have you broken your oath, and brought down condemnation upon my head as well as your own?'

" 'Yes; it is gone,' replied Martin, 'and I know not where.'

" 'Oh, my God!' said Joseph, clinching his hands. 'All is lost! all is lost! What shall I do? I have sinned—it is I who tempted the wrath of God. I should have been satisfied with the first answer which I received from the Lord; for he told me that it was not safe to let the writing go out of my possession.' . . .

"At length he told Martin to go back and search again.

" 'No;' said Martin, 'it is all in vain, for I have ripped open beds and pillows; and I know it is not there.'

" 'Then must I,' said Joseph, 'return with such a tale as this? I dare not do it. And how shall I appear before the Lord? Of what rebuke am I not worthy from the angel of the Most High?'

"I besought him not to mourn so, for perhaps the Lord would forgive him, after a short session of humiliation and repentance. But what could I do to comfort him, when he saw all the family in the same situation of mind as himself; for sobs and groans, and the most bitter lamentations filled the house. However, Joseph was more distressed than the rest, as he better understood the consequences of disobedience. . . .

"The next morning, he set out for home. We parted with heavy hearts, for it now appeared that all which we had so fondly anticipated, and which had been the source of so much secret gratification, had in a moment fled, and fled forever." (Lucy Mack Smith, pp. 128-29.)

The Prophet's anguish over this tragic occurrence was heightened by the fact that his oldest son died about this time. Furthermore, the Urim and Thummim had been taken away from him because he had "wearied the Lord in asking for the privilege of letting Martin Harris take the writings." (HC 1:21.) Shattered by this series of devastating blows, it was a sad and dispirited Joseph who returned to Harmony to try to pick up the tattered threads of his life.

After a season of repentant soul searching, Joseph again found favor with the Lord. The Urim and Thummim was returned to him, and in July 1828 he received his first recorded revelation through this amazing instrument. Now identified as the third section of the Doctrine and Covenants, this revelation reproved Joseph for his neglect, warned him against future transgressions, and declared that the publication of the Book of Mormon could not be frustrated by men. The Urim and Thummim was then taken away from him again. A few days later it was returned when Joseph received his second recorded revelation, now identified as the tenth section of the Doctrine and Covenants. In it, Joseph was instructed not to translate again the portion of the abridged record contained in the lost manuscript. Instead, he was instructed to translate the same material directly from the plates of Nephi. He was told this would frustrate any attempts by his enemies to alter the lost manuscript so they could point to discrepancies between it and the second translation as evidence that Joseph was an imposter. It was also revealed that the records had been preserved by the faith and prayers of ancient prophets who lived upon the American continent and who desired that the gospel message, engraven upon the plates, reach their latter-day descendants. Finally, Joseph was told that the Lord would reestablish his church among the people if they would "harden not their hearts." (D&C 10:65.)

The ten months following the time when Joseph first received the plates from the angel had been filled with frustration and failure. He had nothing tangible to show for his arduous labors. From the standpoint of his future work, however, this period was vitally productive. It taught the Prophet humility. It taught him the need for constant diligence. It gave him essential training in gauging the character and designs of men. And, perhaps above all, it dramatically brought the realization that he was directly responsible for the work and was accountable to God for his failure to perform.

Ordinarily, this last factor would have produced an urgent sense of anxiety and concern and of the need to hurry to make up for lost time. However, such a feeling, which could have produced more error and great confusion, was effectively allayed by this significant statement in the revelation: "Do not run faster or labor more than you have strength and means provided to enable you to translate; but be diligent unto the end." (D&C 10:4.) With this admonition in mind, Joseph settled into a quiet routine. During the following nine months he fulfilled his domestic role as husband and head of a household, working in the fields and caring for his animals as he was able, and giving comfort to Emma, who still grieved over the loss of her first child. The farm on which they lived was small, and it is likely, therefore, that they received some subsidy from Emma's parents or from their many friends at Colesville or Bainbridge who were interested in the Prophet's work.

During this period, as Joseph found time, he translated from the plates of Nephi, using Emma as his scribe. He worked slowly and deliberately in full confidence that the Lord, in his own due time, would raise up those necessary to help him finish his work.

During this long and agonizing lull, two events of special significance occurred. In February of 1829 Joseph was visited by his father, who had come to inquire about the Prophet's health and the progress of the work. It was a constant source of strength to Joseph that those who knew him best trusted him most. His father had never doubted his story and had always stood ready to give assistance where needed. During this visit the Prophet divulged the details of his past labors and his plans for the future, insofar as the restrictions placed upon him by the angel would permit. As father and son conferred and prayed together, young Joseph, moved upon by the spirit of prophecy, received a special revelation for his father. Now identified as the fourth section of the Doctrine and Covenants, this short, seven-verse revelation commenced with a startling prediction that foreshadowed the completion of the work of translating the ancient record and of establishing a formal church. Father Smith was told: "Now behold, a marvelous work is about to come forth among the children of men. Therefore, O ye that embark in the service of God, see that ye serve him with all your heart, might, mind and strength, that ye may stand blameless before God at the last day." Then, following brief instructions about the credentials of those to be called to service, the revelation ended with this injunction, which seems to have been a key to all the Prophet did: "Ask, and ye shall receive; knock, and it shall be opened unto you." (D&C 4:1-2, 7.)

About a month later, Martin Harris came to see the Prophet at Harmony. This meeting evoked many unpleasant memories, for it was the disbelief and persistence of Martin Harris that had resulted in the loss of most of the Prophet's early work, in the estrangement of the Prophet from his heavenly sources of information, and in the subsequent nine months of almost total unproductivity insofar as his divine calling was concerned. Yet, here again was this faithless man, asking the Prophet to approach the Lord once more in his behalf. Perhaps because of an insight into the role Martin was yet to play in the publication of the Book of Mormon or out of sympathy for the harassment Martin had suffered at the hands of his wife, Joseph acceded to his request and sought and received his fourth formal revelation, now known as the fifth section of the Doctrine and Covenants. The first verse betrays how little Martin had learned or profited from his close association with Joseph and from his recent traumatic experience in losing the manuscript. "Behold, I say unto you, that as my servant Martin Harris has desired a witness at my hand, that you, my servant Joseph Smith, Jun., have got the plates of which you have testified and borne record that you have received of me." Despite the persistent disbelief which that verse clearly revealed, Martin was told that at an appropriate time, three special witnesses would be shown the plates and that he would be one of them if he would "humble himself in mighty prayer and faith, in the sincerity of his heart. . . ." (D&C 5:1, 24.) This revelation also contained hints about the establishment of the Church sometime in the near future. But Joseph was told, ". . . you must wait yet a little while, for ye are not yet ordained." (D&C 5:17.)

Of special significance to Joseph as he looked forward to a full resumption of the work of translation and the equally important work that lay beyond was the following: "Stop, and stand still until I command thee, and I will provide means whereby thou mayest accomplish the thing which I have commanded thee." (D&C 5:34.)

These words brought comforting assurance that at the proper time the Lord would raise up those whom the Prophet would need to help complete his important work. In fact, events were even then maturing that would bring to the Prophet's aid the man who was to be the chief scribe of the Book of Mormon and the second elder of the Church.

Several months before, Oliver Cowdery had contracted to teach school at Palmyra. He had not been in the vicinity long before he began to hear rumors about the controversial local boy, Joseph Smith, who claimed to have an ancient record that had been given to him by an angel and that he was then in the process of translating. Another young man with whom Oliver had discussed these reports was David Whitmer, who lived with his family in the nearby community of Fayette, Seneca County.

Since some of the younger Smith children were among Oliver's pupils, in due course he went to board with Joseph and Lucy Smith in partial satisfaction of the tuition for the children. There he learned more about the Prophet's spiritual experiences and about the progress, or lack of it, in translating the sacred plates. Almost instinctively, Oliver was drawn to the Prophet, although he had not met him; and, as if he were destined to do so, he sought to make his acquaintance and, if possible, to assist him.

One explanation of Oliver's powerful feelings is found in Lucy Smith's account of a conversation she and Joseph, Sr., had with the Prophet a few months after Martin lost the manuscript: " 'After the angel left me,' said he, 'I continued my supplication to God, without cessation, and on the twenty-second of September, I had the joy and satisfaction of again receiving the Urim and Thummim, with which I have again commenced translating, and Emma writes for me, but the angel said that the Lord would send me a scribe, and I trust his promise will be verified.' " (Lucy Mack Smith, p. 135.)

Knowing the Prophet's penchant for solving his problems by prayer, we can be assured that henceforth and until Oliver arrived to assist him, he regularly and diligently supplicated the Lord to send him a scribe. Lucy has left us this insight: "On account of these embarrassments [Joseph's preoccupation with secular affairs and the lack of a scribe], Joseph called upon the Lord, three days prior to the arrival of Samuel and Oliver, to send him a scribe, according to the promise of the angel; and he was informed that the same should be forthcoming in a few days." (Ibid., p. 141.)

In the meantime, "Oliver was so completely absorbed in the subject of the Record, that it seemed impossible for him to think or converse about anything else." (Ibid., p. 139.) At length he could wait no longer and decided to go to Harmony to talk to the Prophet in person in order to satisfy his own mind about the things he had heard. In company with the Prophet's brother Samuel, Oliver traveled to Harmony in the first week of April 1829 over roads that were "almost impassable," particularly in the middle of the day, because of alternate "raining, freezing, and thawing." (Ibid., p. 141.) En route, Oliver stopped in Fayette to see his friend David Whitmer, to whom he promised that he would "report his findings . . . concerning Joseph having the plates." (CHC 1:120.) Little did these two young men realize that they would soon be caught up in a drama that would be the focal point of their entire lives. Not only would they learn for themselves that the Prophet had the plates, but they would also learn that fact from an angel of the Lord.

Within a few days after Oliver's arrival in Harmony, he and the Prophet were busy at the task of translating, which was to keep them heavily occupied for the next several months. The same procedure was followed as when Martin Harris served as scribe. Joseph, seated on one side of a curtain dividing the room, gave the translation to Oliver, who recorded and then proofread the words line by line. Any editing in the substance of the text occurred at the time of this proofreading. Referring to this period, Oliver wrote, "These were days never to be forgotten—to sit under the sound of a voice dictated by the inspiration of heaven, awakened the utmost gratitude of this bosom. Day after day I continued, uninterrupted to write from his mouth, as he translated with the Urim and Thummim, or, as the Nephites would have said, 'Interpreters', the history or record called the *Book of Mormon.*" (CHC 1:122.)

Soon after Oliver commenced his work as scribe, the Prophet received through the Urim and Thummim another revelation, which confirmed Oliver's conviction of the inspired nature of his call to assist the Prophet. In it, Oliver was told: ". . . blessed art thou for what thou hast done; for thou hast inquired of me, and behold, as often as thou hast inquired thou hast received instruction of my Spirit. If it had not been so, thou wouldst not have come to the place where thou art at this time. Behold, thou knowest that thou hast inquired of me and I did enlighten thy mind; and now I tell thee these things that thou mayest know that thou hast been enlightened by the Spirit of truth; Yea, I tell thee, that thou mayest know that there is none else save God that knowest thy thoughts and the intents of thy heart." Oliver was also told that if he desired a further witness of the divinity of Joseph's work and of his call to assist, ". . . cast your mind upon the night that you cried unto me in your heart, that you might know. . . . Did I not speak peace to your mind concerning the matter? What greater witness can you have than from God." (D&C 6:14-16, 22-23.)

The revelation touched on two other matters that had a powerful bearing on Oliver's future attitudes toward Joseph and the work. First, he was told to "admonish [Joseph] in his faults, and also receive admonition of him," and second, he was told, "I grant unto you a gift, if you desire of me, to translate, even as my servant Joseph." (D&C 6:19, 25.) From these statements as well as events that were soon to occur, Oliver developed a false notion of his role in the work. Not only did he conclude that he was Joseph's equal, but later events suggest that he also thought himself to be Joseph's superior. Herein lay the seeds of Oliver's future disaffection from the Prophet and from the Church. As will be seen, however, the disaffection was based upon personal conflict and misunderstanding and not upon any question of the divinity of the work.

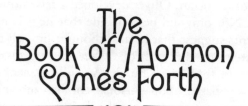

Chapter Seven

The Book of Mormon Comes Forth

By the time Oliver Cowdery came to write for him, the Prophet had had the plates and the Urim and Thummim for over eighteen months. Now, with a willing, alert scribe who, by the standards of the day and the locale, was fairly well educated, he was prepared to move rapidly. During April and May they worked steadily, without interruption. Often they discussed questions or points of interest raised by the translation. Whenever they were unable to reach agreement or understanding, they turned to the divine source of knowledge. The Prophet recorded one such occasion when a difference of opinion arose between them as to whether the apostle John "died or continued to live." At length they "agreed to settle it by the Urim and Thummim." In response Joseph received what is now section 7 of the Doctrine and Covenants, which told him that John was to continue in mortality in order that he might "minister for those who shall be heirs of salvation who dwell on the earth." (D&C 7:6.)

From almost the very beginning Oliver wanted to translate the records as well as to act as scribe. In fact, in section 7 he was told that if he desired it, he would be given the gift of translation. Thereafter, he frequently asked the Prophet if he could be permitted to translate. In response to these inquiries, the Prophet received two additional revelations. The first reaffirmed the previous revelation and told Oliver that the desired gift would be given to him if he would "ask in faith." Then followed a lucid description of the revelatory process, so essential to the work of translation: "Yea, behold, I will tell you in your mind and in your heart, by the Holy Ghost, which shall come upon you and which shall dwell in your heart. Now, behold, this is the spirit of revelation; behold, this is the spirit by which Moses brought the children of Israel through the Red Sea on dry ground." (D&C 8:2-3.)

The second of the two revelations disclosed that Oliver had somehow failed to grasp the vital interrelationship between the mind and the heart in the process of translation. Apparently he was shown some of the inscriptions from the plates and was permitted to use the Urim and Thummim in attempting to translate them. (It is doubtful that he was shown the plates themselves because of the strict charge of secrecy laid upon the Prophet. His privilege of seeing the plates was to be reserved until later.) But to his great disappointment, he failed. By way of explanation and solace, he was told: "Behold, you have not understood; you have supposed that I would give it unto you, when you took no thought save it was to ask me. But, behold, I say unto you, that you must study it out in your mind; then you must ask me if it be right, and if it is right I will cause that your bosom shall burn within you; therefore, you shall feel that it is right." (D&C 9:7-8.)

The account of Oliver's abortive attempt to translate not only demonstrates why he failed, but also throws light on why the Prophet succeeded. Translation was not merely a mechanical process. Success in it required a delicate balancing of the mental and the spiritual. Oliver seems to have failed because he did not apply himself mentally to the task; however, no amount of mental exertion would have brought success without the proper spiritual attunement. David Whitmer, who was very close to the Prophet during the latter phase of the translation, has left us insight into the spiritual discipline the work demanded:

"At times when brother Joseph would attempt to translate he would look into the hat in which the stone was placed, (to exclude the light), he found he was spiritually blind and could not translate. He told us that his mind dwelt too much on earthly things, and various causes would make him incapable of proceeding with the translation. When in this condition he would go out and pray, and when he became sufficiently humble before God, he could then proceed with the translation. Now we see how very strict the Lord is, and how he requires the heart of man to be just right in his sight before he can receive revelation from him." (CHC 1:130-31.)

In the same vein, David Whitmer wrote on another occasion: "He was a religious and straightforward man. He had to be; for he was illiterate and he could do nothing himself. He had to trust in God. He could not translate unless he was humble and possessed the right feelings towards everyone. To illustrate so you can see: One morning when he was getting ready to continue the translation, something went wrong about the house and he was put out about it. Something that Emma, his wife, had done. Oliver and I went upstairs and Joseph came up soon after to continue the translation but he could not do anything. He could not translate a single syllable. He went downstairs, out into the orchard, and made supplication to the Lord; was gone about an hour—came back to the house, and asked Emma's forgiveness and then came upstairs where we were and then the translation went on all right. He could do nothing save he was humble and faithful." (CHC 1:131.)

As the translation went forward, Joseph and Oliver continued to discuss things learned from the translation that they did not fully understand. On one such occasion in mid-May they were discussing the subject of baptism for the remission of sins, which had just come into the translation. Unable to resolve their apparent differences of opinion, they decided to pray to God for enlightenment. They sought out a place of seclusion on the banks of the nearby Susquehanna River, where they knelt in humble prayer. In response, there appeared to them a heavenly, resurrected being who identified himself as John the Baptist and who proceeded to confer the Aaronic Priesthood upon them, including the authority to baptize. Acting upon instructions from the messenger, Joseph baptized Oliver and then Oliver, in turn, baptized Joseph. Also pursuant to instructions, the two young men then ordained each other to the priesthood in the same sequence that the baptisms were performed. The messenger informed them that he was acting under the direction of Peter, James, and John, the three chief apostles of the Lord during his earthly ministry, who held the keys of the priesthood of Melchizedek. They were also told that that priesthood would be conferred upon them in due course.

Intermittently over a period of nine years, Joseph had been visited by heavenly beings. While the experience had not occurred with sufficient frequency to have become commonplace, neither had it had the shocking, even terrifying effect upon him it initially had had. Thus, his account of the incident is couched in dispassionate, almost clinical language: "While we were thus employed, praying and calling upon the Lord, a messenger from heaven descended in a cloud of light, and having laid his hands upon us, he ordained us. . . ." (HC 1:39.) Contrast this with the exuberant account left by Oliver, who had never before seen a divine being:

"I shall not attempt to paint to you the feelings of this heart, nor the majestic beauty and glory which surrounded us on this occasion; but you will believe me when I say, that earth, nor men, with the eloquence of time, cannot begin to clothe language in as interesting and sublime a manner as this holy personage. No; nor has this earth power to give the joy, to bestow the peace, or comprehend the wisdom which was contained in each sentence as it was delivered by the power of the Holy Spirit! Man may deceive his fellow man; deception may follow deception, and the children of the wicked one may have power to seduce the foolish and untaught, till naught but fiction feeds the many, and the fruit of falsehood carries in its current the giddy to the grave, but one touch with the finger of his love, yes, one ray of glory from the upper world, or one word from the mouth of the Savior, from the bosom of eternity, strikes it all into insignificance, and blots it forever from the mind! The assurance that we were in the presence of an angel; the certainty that we heard the voice of Jesus, and the truth unsullied as it flowed from a pure personage, dictated by the will of God, is to me, past description, and I shall ever look upon this expression of the Savior's goodness with wonder and thanksgiving while I am permitted to tarry, and in those mansions where perfection dwells and sin never comes, I hope to adore in that day which shall never cease." (HC 1:43.)

In accordance with the promise of John the Baptist, Joseph and Oliver were later visited by Peter, James, and John, who conferred upon them the Melchizedek Priesthood, which held the keys of presidency and the authority to administer in spiritual things. It was not until both of these priesthoods were restored to earth that Joseph was authorized to organize a church and to speak and act in the name of God. Some idea of the vast importance and potential of these priesthoods is gained from a subsequent revelation in which we learn that one who receives and magnifies them is entitled to share with God the Father in all that he has. (D&C 84.)

Knowledge of the task in which Joseph and Oliver were engaged had become generally known around Harmony within a short while after they commenced to work together. This precipitated the same feelings of enmity and opposition that had been manifested at Palmyra after Joseph first received the plates. Because of this, they were at first reluctant to tell others they had received these priesthoods at the hands of divine messengers. Soon, however, a sense of duty outweighed their concern and they "commenced to reason out of the Scriptures with [their] acquaintances and friends, as [they] happened to meet with them." (HC 1:44.) This effort brought about the first formal conversion in the person of Samuel Smith, the Prophet's younger brother, who was visiting from Palmyra at the time. Samuel's relationship to the Prophet and his acceptance of the account of the early visions did not automatically guarantee his acceptance of the need for baptism. The Smith family qualities of independent thought and prayerfulness are clearly revealed in the Prophet's account:

"He [Samuel] was not, however, very easily persuaded of these things, but after much inquiry and explanation he retired to the woods, in order that by secret and fervent prayer he might obtain of a merciful God, wisdom to enable him to judge for himself. The result was that he obtained revelation for himself sufficient to convince him of the truth of our assertions to him; and on the twenty-fifth day of that same month in which we had been baptized and ordained, Oliver Cowdery baptized him; and he returned to his father's house, greatly glorifying and praising God, being filled with the Holy Spirit." (HC 1:44.)

Shortly after Samuel's baptism, Joseph's older brother, Hyrum, came inquiring about the work and his role in it. In answer, Joseph received a revelation through the Urim and Thummim for the guidance of Hyrum, who was admonished to keep the commandments of God and to prepare for his ministry by study and prayer. (D&C 11.) For the first time in a revelation to the Prophet, specific reference was also made to the organization of a church. Hyrum was admonished: "Wait a little longer, until you shall have my word, my rock, my church, and my gospel, that you may know of a surety my doctrine." (D&C 11:16.)

By this time opposition had become so open and intense that Joseph and Oliver were being impeded in their work. It was at this juncture that David Whitmer and his family entered the picture. As the result of a letter to him from Joseph, and possibly from Oliver also, Whitmer left his family's farm at Fayette, New York, and traveled to Harmony. There he picked up Joseph and Oliver and returned them to Fayette, where they were provided board and room by his father, Peter Whitmer, until the work of translation had been completed. The Whitmer farm was later to be the place where many of the early revelations of the Church were received, where the three witnesses were shown the plates by the Angel Moroni, and where The Church of Jesus Christ of Latter-day Saints was organized on April 6, 1830.

Not only did the Whitmer family provide Joseph and Oliver with room and board, but the Whitmer sons, especially John, also aided the Prophet in the translation by alternating with Oliver as scribe.

The projected time for publication of the book was fast approaching, and the Prophet did not intend to turn over to the printer the only copy of the manuscript. Thus, while John or one of the other Whitmer boys was engaged as scribe to the Prophet, Oliver was preparing a second copy of the manuscript.

So excited were Joseph and Oliver about their work and the profound nature of the teachings in the record that they spent their spare time in expounding these teachings to the people in the neighborhood. They did not find in Fayette the bitterness and enmity so evident in Palmyra and Harmony. On the contrary, they found the neighbors "friendly, and disposed to enquire into the truth of these strange matters which now began to be noised abroad." In fact, the Prophet wrote, many "opened their houses to us, in order that we might have an opportunity of meeting with our friends for the purpose of instruction and explanation." (HC 1:51.)

As a result, several persons were converted and baptized in the summer of 1829, approximately nine months before the Church was organized. The Prophet recorded that his brother Hyrum, David Whitmer, and Peter Whitmer, Jr., were baptized in Seneca Lake in June of that year.

In the meantime, the work of translation and preparing the second copy of the manuscript went forward at an accelerated pace. Toward the end of the record, Joseph read what had been hinted at earlier in the translation and what had been explicitly said in a revelation to Martin Harris several months before: that there were to be three witnesses to whom the records would be shown. These three were to see the plates "by the power of God" as a means of establishing the truth of the Prophet's declarations and "as a testimony against the world at the last day." (Ether 5:3-4.)

Oliver Cowdery, David Whitmer, and Martin Harris (who had come from Palmyra to see about the work) asked Joseph to inquire of the Lord if they might be permitted to serve as the witnesses. At first Joseph put them off. However, they were so persistent that he finally gave in and made the inquiry. The answer came by revelation through the Urim and Thummim. In it the three were told that if they would rely upon God "with full purpose of heart," and if they would exercise that faith "which was had by the prophets of old," they would be shown not only the plates, but also the breastplate, the sword of Laban, the Urim and Thummim, and the Liahona, a set of "miraculous directors" referred to in the record that aided those whose story was told in charting a correct course in the wilderness. They were also told that once they had been shown these things, they would be expected to testify of them "by the power of God" to the end that the Lord might bring about his "righteous purposes unto the children of men in this work." (D&C 17.)

Fortified by this promise, they waited expectantly for the time of its fulfillment. Because of his previous experiences with heavenly beings, Oliver Cowdery approached the occasion with a greater sense of calm and assurance than the other two. David Whitmer had not as yet had the awesome experience of being in the presence of a personage from the eternal world, but he had enjoyed several miraculous experiences in his relationship with Joseph and Oliver; he was also a man of faith and therefore had implicit confidence in Joseph as a prophet. But while Martin Harris looked forward to the event with excitement and anticipation, he was still beset by the doubts and uncertainties that had clouded his relationship with the Prophet from the very beginning.

Shortly after the revelation identifying the three witnesses was received, Joseph's parents arrived at the Whitmer farm. They knew from a report sent to them by the Prophet that the work of translation had been completed. They had also learned from Hyrum and Samuel about the restoration of the priesthood and about the baptisms that had been performed. Manifesting that same interest in their son and his work that they had shown from the time of his first glorious manifestation nine years earlier, these faithful parents came to give encouragement and support and to share in the feelings of exultation and joy they knew would accompany the completion of so great a task.

The viewing of the plates by the three witnesses occurred the day after Joseph's parents arrived. Some of the thrilling events of that day are related by the Prophet's mother: "The next morning, after attending to the usual services, namely, reading, singing and praying, Joseph arose from his knees, and approaching Martin Harris with a solemnity that thrills through my veins to this day, when it occurs to my recollection, said, 'Martin Harris, you have got to humble yourself before God this day, that you may obtain a forgiveness of your sins. If you do, it is the will of God that you should look upon the plates, in company with Oliver Cowdery and David Whitmer.' " (Lucy Mack Smith, pp. 151-52.)

The Prophet and the three witnesses then went into some nearby woods. There they knelt and, with the Prophet commencing, each in rotation offered "fervent and humble" prayer that the Lord would grant to them a view of the plates. Nothing happened. The same procedure was followed a second time, again with a negative result. Feeling that his presence was an impediment to the success that the four men sought, Martin Harris left the circle and went alone further into the woods. After his departure, Joseph, Oliver, and David continued their fervent supplications. An account of what happened then is described in these words of the Prophet:

". . . we . . . had not been many minutes engaged in prayer, when presently we beheld a light above us in the air, of exceeding brightness; and behold, an angel stood before us. In his hands he held the plates which we had been praying for these to have a view of. He turned over the leaves one by one, so that we could see them, and discern the engravings theron distinctly. He then addressed himself to David Whitmer, and said, 'David, blessed is the Lord, and he that keeps His commandments;' when, immediately afterwards, we heard a voice from out of the bright light above us, saying, 'These plates have been revealed by the power of God, and they have been translated by the power of God. The translation of them which you have seen is correct, and I command you to bear record of what you now see and hear.' " (HC 1:54-55.)

As soon as Oliver and David had experienced this divine manifestation, Joseph went in search of Martin, whom he found nearby, engaged in fervent prayer. At Martin's request, Joseph joined him, and soon the same vision was opened to his view. In an ecstatic outburst, the Prophet's doubting friend declared: " 'Tis enough; 'tis enough; mine eyes have beheld; mine eyes have beheld." Then jumping to his feet, Martin shouted, "Hosanna," and, according to the Prophet, "otherwise rejoiced exceedingly." (HC 1:55.)

The weight of anxiety that the events of this day lifted from Joseph's shoulders is beyond calculation. Until then, the burden of testifying to the divinity of the work in which he was engaged rested upon him alone. For almost two years he had been precluded by angelic instruction from showing the plates to anyone, and so the most elaborate precautions had been taken to conceal them from the view of others. To the minds of those who questioned the Prophet's veracity, these precautions were a subterfuge, invented to mask a fradulent deception. Unable to retaliate, Joseph had borne these insults in silence. To one so imbued with the importance of honor and integrity as was he, this was a heavy and awful burden to bear, and now he had witnesses to help carry that burden, witnesses who could corroborate his story.

We gain some idea of the combined sense of exhilaration and relief Joseph experienced from this account left by Lucy Mack Smith: "When they returned to the house it was between three and four o'clock p.m. . . . On coming in, Joseph threw himself down beside me, and exclaimed, 'Father, mother, you do not know how happy I am: The Lord has now caused the plates to be shown to three more besides myself. They have seen an angel, who has testified to them, and they will have to bear witness to the truth of what I have said, for now they know for themselves, that I do not go about to deceive the people, and I feel as if I was relieved of a burden which was almost too heavy for me to bear, and it rejoices my soul, that I am not any longer to be entirely alone in the world.' " Lucy also recorded the reactions and comments of the three witnesses. She wrote that Martin Harris "seemed almost overcome with joy, and testified boldly to what he had both seen and heard." Oliver and David are reported to have said "that no tongue could express the joy of their hearts, and the greatness of the things which they had both seen and heard." (Lucy Mack Smith, pp. 152-53.)

The events of that day radically altered the lives of the three witnesses and bound them together with bonds that neither time nor adverse circumstances could sever. In years to come all of them became disaffected from the Prophet because of personal differences. But to the death, each of them retained a vivid recollection of the events of that day and bore solemn witness that an angel had shown them the plates and that they had heard the voice of the Lord declaring that the plates had been revealed and translated by the power of God.

Early critics of the Book of Mormon attributed the testimony of the three witnesses to a conspiracy between them and the Prophet. That theory lost all credibility when the witnesses continued to bear fervent testimony even after their falling out with the Prophet. At a loss to explain away the positive affirmation of these witnesses, some critics fell back to the only logical ground still available to them: the Prophet, they said, had hypnotized the witnesses and had conjured up a vision for them. One such critic wrote: "At an early age he had what only the most gifted revivalist preachers could boast of—the talent for making men see visions." (Brodie, p. 74.) This same critic also declared that the Prophet was unconscious of this gift until his experience with the three witnesses. She would have us believe, therefore, that Joseph accompanied the three into the woods with the expectation that they would have an experience similar to the several he had had, and that when it occurred he was "surprised" and discovered for the first time that he had conjurer's powers. We are also asked to accept the preposterous notion that this accidental happening, involving mature, intelligent men, stayed with them throughout their lives and directly affected their conduct to the very end.

Some idea of the persistent, almost overpowering, effect the visitation had on the three witnesses may be gained from a statement David Whitmer published fifty-two years later, made to refute a charge that he had denied his testimony. Among other things he wrote:

"It [was] represented by one John Murphy, of Polo, Caldwell County, Mo., that I, in a conversation with him last summer, denied my testimony as one of the three witnesses to the 'Book of Mormon.'

"To the end, therefore, that he may understand me now, if he did not then; and that the world may know the truth, I wish now, standing as it were, in the very sunset of life, and in the fear of God, once for all to make this public statement:

"That I have never at any time denied that testimony or any part thereof, which has so long since been published with that Book, as one of the three witnesses. Those who know me best, well know that I have always adhered to that testimony. And that no man may be misled or doubt my present views in regard to the same, I do again affirm the truth of all my statements, as then made and published.

" 'He that hath an ear to hear, let him hear;' it was no delusion! What is written is written, and he that readeth let him understand." (David Whitmer, *An Address to All Believers in Christ* [Richmond, Mo., 1887], pp. 8-9.)

The other witnesses also found it necessary from time to time to reaffirm their testimony, either to rebut false statements made by the enemies of the Church or to confirm the faith of believers who inquired about the reality of the events related in their formal testimony, which appears in the frontispiece of each published copy of the Book of Mormon.

The Prophet's account of the translation of the ancient record received additional corroboration when he was permitted to show the plates to eight other witnesses, including four other Whitmer sons; Joseph Smith, Sr., and two of his sons; and Hiram Page. Each of these men saw the record, handled it with his own hands, and was allowed to turn the leaves, or pages. They declared that the plates had "the appearance of gold" and that the inscriptions were "of curious workmanship" and "ancient" in character. Later these witnesses and others close to them "emphasized the size, weight, and metallic texture of the plates." (William Smith, as quoted in Brodie, p. 80.) Never did any of them deny the reality of what they saw and felt. On the contrary, they bore willing and fervent testimony during the remainder of their lives.

The testimony of this second set of witnesses poses an insuperable problem for critics of the Book of Mormon. They are forced to abandon the theory of conspiracy as in the case of the three witnesses. The conjuring theory has no application, because they testified that they both saw and felt the plates. Faced with this reality, most critics respond merely by turning in another direction, as did this one: "Exactly how Joseph Smith persuaded so many of the reality of the golden plates is neither so important nor so baffling as the effect of this success on Joseph himself." She then observes that Joseph showed "no evidence of cynicism even in [his] most intimate diary entries" and that "he was rapidly acquiring the language and even the accent of sincere faith." (Brodie, p. 80.) From there it is but a short step to the final conclusion now in vogue among the Prophet's critics: that the Prophet was neither a conspirator nor a deceiver, but was himself deceived and genuinely believed the stories about spiritual manifestations that he circulated.

Now that eleven other men could corroborate his story, and the work of translation had been completed, the Prophet turned his mind toward the problems of publication. Two principal concerns troubled him: money and the security of the manuscript. The first was solved when Martin Harris agreed to assume the printer's bill. Now that he had received divine confirmation of the Prophet's work, his doubts and uncertainties were less pronounced, and he came forward with his pledge to finance publication of the book. This led to a legal separation from his wife, who adamantly maintained to the end that the Prophet was a charlatan and her husband a fool. Their farm was later partitioned as part of the separation agreement, and Martin's share was sold to a Mr. Larkey for $3,000. The proceeds of this sale were used to pay the printer's bill. (CHC 1:158.)

The Prophet's traumatic experience in losing the part of the manuscript that had been entrusted to Martin had taught him a valuable lesson. Never again would he relinquish control of the original transcript. Accordingly, it was decided that the printer, Egbert B. Grandin, would be provided with an exact copy, and that he would be furnished with only enough of the manuscript at a time to keep the typesetter busy. The Prophet also saw to it that the original transcript, which was concealed at his parents' home, was kept under constant surveillance.

Later events proved that these precautions were necessary. At the same time the Book of Mormon was being printed, a Mr. Cole began publishing a weekly periodical called *Dogberry Paper On Winter Hill*. His prospectus promised his readers that he would "publish one form of 'Joe Smith's Gold Bible' each week, and thus furnish them with the principal part of the book without their being obliged to purchase it from the Smiths." (CHC 1:158.) Cole used the Grandin press in the evenings and on Sundays, which enabled him to obtain galley proofs of portions of the Book of Mormon then being printed. Using these, he is reported to have printed in several issues of his paper garbled accounts of the Nephite record. He was forced to discontinue his publication when Joseph, relying on the copyright he had obtained to the Book of Mormon, threatened legal action.

The Prophet's ownership of the copyright gave rise to a significant event during publication. Although Martin Harris's resolve was greatly strengthened by the visitation of the angel, his inherent attitude of doubt and the pressure exerted by his wife caused him to procrastinate in raising the money to pay the printer. This in turn exerted strong pressure on the Prophet to find another source of financing. He felt impressed to send someone to Canada to raise money by the sale of the Canadian copyright. According to an account of David Whitmer, published fifty-seven years after the event and at a time when he was in apostasy, Joseph "received a revelation that some of the brethren should go to Toronto, Canada, and they would sell the copyright." (CHC 1:162-63.) Pursuant to that direction, Hiram Page, one of the eight witnesses, and Oliver Cowdery traveled to Toronto but failed to find the promised purchaser. David Whitmer points to this failure as evidence that Joseph was then a false prophet. He also expressed concern about the answer given by the Prophet to explain why his prediction was not fulfilled. According to David, the Prophet inquired of the Lord and was told: "Some revelations are of God: some revelations are of man: and some revelations are of the devil." (CHC 1:163.) The implication was that in directing the brethren to Canada, the Prophet was either self-deluded or was directed by the influence of the devil. And the fact that the Prophet was less than perfect seemed to shake David's faith—in the Prophet, at least. Yet, if he had reflected more deeply and had had wider understanding in the ways of the Lord, he would have found in this experience confirmation of his faith in Joseph. Reflection would have convinced him that Joseph acted prophetically in the translation of the Book of Mormon, for an angel of God had shown David the plates and the voice declared that the plates had been translated by the gift and power of God. The Canadian incident merely demonstrated that Joseph was human and therefore subject to error. It should have also inspired greater confidence in the Prophet because of the qualities of candor, lack of dissimulation, and reliance upon God it revealed in him.

Had David had greater maturity and been better acquainted with the ways of the Lord as later revealed through the Prophet, he would have recognized that no man is infallible and that imperfection or ignorance in men sometimes distorts or clouds the meaning of messages God transmits to them. He would also have recognized that man, being a free agent, is subject to evil as well as to good influences, and is capable of independent thought and action, thus increasing the likelihood that he may err in any given situation. This concept is difficult for some to grasp, especially those who deal in absolutes. It does place a premium on one's spiritual perception and requires that he be constantly on guard against evil influences. It may be that the Prophet was misled in this instance and, if so, David would have been justified in criticizing him. But as suggested, he overshoots the mark if he takes an isolated instance of error and from that premise leaps to the unwarranted conclusion that Joseph was not a prophet—or was a fallen prophet.

All this, however, is based on the assumption that fifty-seven years after the event, David accurately reported what Joseph said to him. Memory plays strange tricks. So does bias. It is entirely conceivable that what Joseph said had become grossly distorted in David's mind as he brooded over past failures and as real or imagined slights at the hand of the Prophet were magnified all out of proportion.

The principal theme found woven throughout the Book of Mormon is that God works through men according to their faith and diligence. The scripture in James that took the Prophet into the grove also emphasizes that he who wavers "is like a wave of the sea driven with the wind and tossed" (James 1:6), and that such a man cannot expect to receive anything from the Lord. The difficulty with the Toronto incident may not have come so much from the inaccuracy of what was said as from the faithless and weak character of those who were sent. If the Prophet had sent men of the character and the spirituality of Brigham Young and Heber C. Kimball, the outcome may well have been far different. They likely would not have returned until they had found the man. But the lives of Oliver Cowdery and Hiram Page do not show them to have been men of such faith and resolution. On the contrary, they were weak and vacillating. Only a short time after the Toronto incident, Hiram Page purported to receive a series of "revelations," through the medium of a stone, pertaining to the upbuilding of Zion and the order of the Church. These he soon renounced when the Prophet convinced him he was in error. (HC 1:109-15.)

About the same time, Oliver commenced to hold himself out

as a spokesman for the Church and to presume to give direction to the Prophet. As a result, he was chastized in a revelation received in September 1830. He was told that Joseph was the only one appointed to receive revelation for the guidance of the Church and that it was improper for him to presume to "command him who is at thy head, and at the head of the church." (D&C 6.) Oliver also fell into many other errors in the years that followed and was led into apostasy. At the time of the Toronto episode, Oliver apparently entertained the same casual attitude he had had while the Book of Mormon was being translated. (See Chapter 6.) He felt that all he had to do was to travel to Toronto and there, without any effort on his part, he would find someone anxiously waiting to purchase the Canadian copyright. When that person failed to appear immediately, he and his companion returned home empty-handed. Those familiar with the Book of Mormon cannot help but be reminded of the experience of Nephi and his brothers who were sent back to Jerusalem by their father to obtain certain records. When they were first rebuffed, the older brothers were prepared to give up. It was the determination of the younger brother Nephi to try again and again that brought success.

Publication of the Book of Mormon in March 1830 marked a significant plateau in the life of the Prophet. Until then, his claims of contact with the unseen world had been circulated only by word of mouth. Now those who inquired about him, whether skeptic or believer, had some objective evidence by which to judge the validity of his story. They also had the testimony of eleven mature, reliable men found in the frontispiece of the Book of Mormon, which corroborated the Prophet's story. The accounts in the book were of a nature to stretch the imagination and credulity of the skeptic and to inspire and motivate the believer. They told of three groups of people who migrated from the Middle East to the American continent from about 2000 B.C. to 600 B.C. These groups, who came by ship, were led by inspired prophets of Israelite descent. They brought with them the sacred records and genealogy of their ancestors, who, for the most part, were descendants of Joseph who was sold into Egypt. These records included the writings and teachings of the biblical prophets up to and including the writings of Isaiah and Jeremiah. Eventually, these emigrants divided into two distinct groups, one that kept the biblical commandments and one that did not.

According to the Book of Mormon, the inhabitants of this continent were blessed by a visitation from the resurrected Lord. Ultimately, the unfaithful group annihilated the faithful group, whose records had been written on metallic plates by a long series of faithful scribes. It was these plates, buried centuries before by an ancient American prophet named Moroni, that were delivered to Joseph Smith by an angel in 1827 and that, as the record states, he translated by the gift and power of God.

Chapter Eight

The Organization of the Church

Joseph Smith was always careful to draw a distinction between knowledge of God and the authority to act in his name. During the 1820s his knowledge of God had been extended beyond that of any living man. Through personal visitations from divine beings, through the inspired translation of ancient, sacred writings, and through the gift of prophecy and revelation, he had acquired a vast and intimate understanding of the nature and the purposes and designs of the Lord. Despite this, he never presumed to speak or act in His name until the spring of 1829, when the priesthood, the authority to act for God, was conferred upon him and Oliver Cowdery. This investiture of authority occurred at a time when the translation of the Book of Mormon was drawing to a close and plans for its publication were being laid.

While there were many details to attend to during these months, the Prophet did not have the burden of care that possession of the sacred plates and interpreters had entailed. It was possible, therefore, for him to commence to give prayerful consideration to the formation of a church, which the priesthood empowered him to do. During this period he received a series of revelations that was ultimately compiled into a single document now identified as section 20 of the Doctrine and Covenants. This wide-ranging document, since referred to as the constitution of the church, covers such diverse subjects as the existence of God, the creation and fall of man, the role and mission of the Savior, the Holy Ghost and the Trinity, justification and sanctification, falling from grace, baptism, manner of baptism and confirmation, duties of members, the sacrament, duties of parents toward children, officers of the church and their duties, and church conferences. In addition, this section identified April 6 as the anniversary of the Savior's birth and designated that day as the day on which the church should be organized. Accordingly, on April 6, 1830, Joseph and a few of his followers met at the home of Peter Whitmer to effect the organization of the Church of Christ (later officially named The Church of Jesus Christ of Latter-day Saints—D&C 115:4) pursuant to the revelations Joseph had received. Of those present, six were designated as the official organizers necessary to comply with legal requirements: Joseph Smith, Jr., Oliver Cowdery, Hyrum Smith, Peter Whitmer, Jr., Samuel H. Smith, and David Whitmer. All of these persons, along with an unspecified number of others, had been baptized between May 1829 and April 6, 1830.

Despite the fact that Joseph had been commanded to organize the church and had received the priesthood through the administration of angels, he was very particular to obtain the sustaining approval of those who were to comprise the membership of the church. According to his account of the meeting, after commencing with "solemn prayer" they "proceeded, according to previous commandment, to call on our brethren to know whether they accepted us as their teachers in the things of the Kingdom of God, and whether they were satisfied that we should proceed and be organized as a Church according to said commandment which we had received. To these several propositions they consented by a unanimous vote." (HC 1:77.) Thus from the beginning, he applied the principle of common consent in his dealings with the Saints, reflecting one of the basic teachings he expounded: that the spirits of mankind are eternal and are free agents.

This concept found frequent expression in the Prophet's dealings with his brethren. While wrongfully imprisoned in a Missouri jail, he wrote a lengthy epistle that included this eloquent restatement of that principle: "No power or influence can or ought to be maintained by virtue of the priesthood, only by persuasion, by long-suffering, by gentleness and meekness, and by love unfeigned; By kindness, and pure knowledge, which shall greatly enlarge the soul without hypocrisy, and without guile." (D&C 121:41-42.) Earlier in the same letter, he deplored the tendency of men to attempt to impose their will upon others: "We have learned by sad experience that it is the nature and disposition of almost all men, as soon as they get a little authority, as they suppose, they will immediately begin to exercise unrighteous dominion." (D&C 121:39.) On another occasion when he was asked how he was able to maintain such effective control over his followers, he answered, "I teach them correct principles, and they govern themselves."

Other significant matters of business transacted at that first meeting of the Church included the following: The Prophet and Oliver Cowdery were ordained as the first and second elders of the Church; the sacrament of the Lord's supper was celebrated, using bread and wine as the emblems; and each person present who had been baptized was confirmed a member of the Church and, according to the ancient pattern, received the gift of the Holy Ghost by the laying on of hands. There then followed an outpouring of the Spirit of God and "some prophesied, whilst [they] all praised the Lord, and rejoiced exceedingly." (HC 1:78.)

One should not assume from this that the meeting was characterized by the kind of frenzied activity often associated with so-called pentacostal meetings. On the contrary, everything was done with that degree of solemnity and decorum which the importance of the occasion demanded. This is most convincingly demonstrated by the fact that during the meeting, the Prophet received and dictated a revelation now identified as section 21 of the Doctrine and Covenants. This revelation directed the Church to keep a record, designated Joseph as "a seer, a translator, a prophet, an apostle of Jesus Christ," and commanded the members to "give heed unto all his words and commandments . . . as if from mine own mouth, in all patience and faith."

This was only one of a number of revelations the Prophet received in the presence of others. Accounts by those who witnessed such incidents state that they were accompanied by a marked change in the Prophet's countenance and demeanor. We are told, for example, that his face acquired a pale, almost luminous, quality, that his eyes were either closed or half-closed, and that his whole attitude and posture conveyed an impression of the most intense concentration. He spoke slowly and distinctly so that his words could be recorded in longhand. Once dictated, a revelation was never revised except for minor changes in grammar or punctuation.

On the Sunday following the organization of the Church, the first worship service was held at the home of Peter Whitmer. The Prophet's faithful scribe, Oliver Cowdery, was the speaker on that occasion. This fact revealed a facet of Joseph's leadership that undoubtedly contributed to the rapid growth of the Church in the years that followed. He never felt impelled to do everything himself; on the contrary, he called on others to the maximum possible extent. One might have expected that at this first meeting the Prophet would have been the principal speaker. Surely he was the best qualified because of his insights into spiritual things. Yet he was content to provide Oliver with an opportunity for growth in leadership ability, something the fledgling church sorely needed at that time.

Soon after, Joseph traveled to Colesville, New York, to visit friends and family, staying with the Joseph Knight family. Aside from the social aspects of the visit, he also wanted to proselyte his friends and former neighbors. Meetings were arranged in homes in the area, at which Joseph expounded the principles of the restored gospel, discussed the scriptures, including the Book of Mormon (which was then off the press), and recounted some of the spiritual experiences he had enjoyed over the years. The impact of these meetings was electrifying. Many were converted and baptized and were later organized into the Colesville Branch. Members of this group preserved their identity as the Colesville Branch even after they migrated from the small community from which they took their name. Almost two years later, after they had migrated to far-off Missouri, the Prophet made this entry in his journal while visiting the Colesville Saints in Kaw township, a few miles west of Independence: "I visited the brethren . . . and received a welcome only known by brethren and sisters united as one in the same faith, and by the same baptism, and supported by the same Lord. The Colesville branch, in particular, rejoiced as the ancient Saints did with Paul." (HC 1:269.) The allusion to Paul, of course, related to the joy the ancient apostle had in mingling with those whom he had been instrumental in converting. But unlike Paul, Joseph spent most of his ministry in the main centers of the Saints, giving administrative direction to the burgeoning affairs of the Church. So while he was instrumental in converting many people during his short career and while he stood second to none in the influence he exerted on the Church and its membership, Colesville appears to have been the single instance in which he was responsible for the conversion of a substantial group of people.

It is not difficult to understand why the Prophet's appearance in Colesville created such a stir. Several years before, when he first came there as a laborer for Josiah Stowel (Stoal), there had been talk about his having received an unusual spiritual manifestation. Later, the curiosity and interest increased when word spread that he had returned with the plates and was in the process of translating them. At last, when word filtered out that he and one of his scribes had been visited by resurrected beings, the neighborhood erupted into uncontrolled opposition and abuse, resulting in Joseph's removal to Fayette, where he could complete the work of translation in peace. Now, almost a year later, he had returned, but not in failure as his critics had predicted. He had brought with him concrete evidence of success in the form of bound copies of the Book of Mormon, which not only contained the witness of eleven mature men attesting to the divine nature of the book, but which also contained the startling promise that anyone who read the book with an open mind and a prayerful heart could learn of its truthfulness by heavenly means.

Numerous cottage meetings were held in and near Colesville. One of the regular attenders at these meetings was Newel Knight, a son of the Prophet's long-time friend and supporter, Joseph Knight. In private conversations with Newel, Joseph emphasized the role of prayer in gaining a personal conviction of the reality and power of God. Half-convinced of the truthfulness of these assertions, Newel agreed to attempt to offer a public, vocal prayer at one of the cottage meetings. When the time came, however, he became frightened and embarrassed and, despite the urgings of the Prophet and others, declined to participate. Later he retired to some nearby woods to attempt by solitary prayer to gain the conviction he desired. As he knelt to pray, however, the recollection of his refusal to pray in public produced such guilty, remorseful feelings that he was unable to continue. Finally he abandoned all attempts to pray and returned home. By that time his inner anguish had produced in his outward appearance an ugly, frightening aspect, and he seemed to be unable to control his movements. At length, his body commenced to gyrate and to be tossed around his apartment. The noise and commotion attracted the attention of some neighbors, who came running to learn the cause. They were amazed and frightened by what they saw and found themselves powerless either to control the erratic, violent movements of Newel's body or to calm the anguished terror of his mind. In the midst of all this, Newel pleaded for his wife to summon Joseph Smith. This is the Prophet's account of what happened after he arrived:

"I succeeded in getting hold of him by the hand, when almost immediately he spoke to me, and with great earnestness requested me to cast the devil out of him, saying that he knew he was in him, and that he also knew that I could cast him out.

"I replied, 'If you know that I can, it shall be done;' and then almost unconsciously I rebuked the devil, and commanded him in the name of Jesus Christ to depart from him; when immediately Newel spoke out and said that he saw the devil leave him and vanish from his sight. This was the first miracle which was done in the Church, or by any member of it; and it was done not by man, nor by the power of man, but it was done by God, and by the power of godliness; therefore, let the honor and the praise, the dominion and the glory, be ascribed to the Father, Son, and the Holy Spirit, for ever and ever. Amen."

The Prophet then continued with his narration:

"This scene was now entirely changed, for as soon as the devil had departed from our friend, his countenance became natural, his distortions of body ceased, and almost immediately the Spirit of the Lord descended upon him, and the visions of eternity were opened to his view. So soon as consciousness returned, his bodily weakness was such that we were obliged to lay him upon his bed, and wait upon him for some time." (HC 1:82-83.)

This episode was witnessed by a number of neighbors, and the greater part of them joined the Church. Because of what they had seen for themselves, they were convinced beyond doubt of the reality and power of both God and Satan and of the authority of Joseph to speak and act in the name of God. Though this represented the first miracle performed in the newly organized church, to Joseph it was but another in the seemingly endless chain of supernatural experiences he had enjoyed during the previous decade.

News of this remarkable incident spread rapidly throughout the area. Its effect upon the hearer depended to a large extent upon his mental preconditioning. Those who truly believed in a supreme being and in the reality of the unseen world were anxious to see and hear the Prophet. The independent testimony of those who had witnessed the event caused the believer to investigate Joseph's claims in a candid and sincere way, and it was from this group that converts came. However, among Joseph's enemies and detractors and among disbelievers in the community, word of the incident was greeted with scorn and derision. Some of them were content merely to criticize and defame the Prophet; others were more malignant and seemed determined to do him bodily harm. In the forefront of this group were several prominent ministers, who lost no opportunity to agitate against the Prophet, whether in their pulpits or in private conversation.

When Joseph returned to Fayette, he found that the publication of the Book of Mormon had created great excitement and interest. Many were converted and became affiliated with the Church. There was opposition, as usual, but it lacked the overtones of violence and malignancy that had been evident at Colesville.

By June 1830 Joseph's followers had increased to the point that it was thought necessary to hold a conference to give them motivation and direction. Thus was commenced a practice that has become one of the distinguishing characteristics of the Church. About thirty members were in attendance, in addition to some friends and investigators. They were barely able to crowd into Peter Whitmer's home, the place where the Church had been organized a scant two months before. As was true with the meetings at Colesville, this conference was charged with an almost electric atmosphere, heightened by the presence of Newel Knight. The business of the conference, which included the confirmation of those who had been baptized and the conferring of the priesthood upon a number of the brethren, was followed by a period of "exhortation and instruction." What then occurred is best described by the Prophet:

". . . the Holy Ghost was poured out upon us in a miraculous manner—many of our number prophesied, whilst others had the heavens opened to their view, and were so overcome that we had to lay them on beds or other convenient places; among the rest was Brother Newel Knight. . . . By his own account of the transaction, he could not understand why we should lay him on the bed, as he felt no sense of weakness. He felt his heart was filled with love, with glory, and pleasure unspeakable, and could discern all that was going on in the room; when all of a sudden a vision of the future burst upon him. He saw there represented the great work which through my instrumentality was yet to be accomplished. He saw heaven opened, and beheld the Lord Jesus Christ, seated at the right hand of the majesty on high, and had it made plain to his understanding that the time would come when he would be admitted into His presence to enjoy His society for ever and ever. When their bodily strength was restored to these brethren, they shouted hosannas to God and the Lamb, and rehearsed the glorious things which they had seen and felt, whilst they were yet in the spirit." (HC 1:85.)

This jubilant occasion filled Joseph's followers with an almost unbounded zeal and enthusiasm. No longer was it necessary for them to rely on the borrowed light of Joseph's testimony or on that of the witnesses to the Book of Mormon. Now they had experienced the power of God themselves and ever after would be personal witnesses of it and of the divine nature of the work Joseph had founded.

Soon after this first conference, Joseph returned to Colesville to continue his proselyting activities and to set his personal affairs in order. The reception he received was one he had not fully anticipated. His followers, of course, were happy at his return. Their fervor and personal conviction had also attended many others who were anxious for baptism or to learn more about the doctrines he expounded.

Coincident with the increase of interest and devotion on the part of the Prophet's followers, however, had been the growth of a venomous spirit of opposition by his enemies. Not content to expose the Church on theological grounds, they resorted to physical violence. Learning of Joseph's plans to baptize a number of new converts in a nearby stream, mobbers tore out a dam that had impounded the water necessary for baptizing. Early the following morning Joseph's followers repaired the dam and thirteen converts were baptized. Word of the baptisms spread quickly and the mob commenced to reassemble even before the ordinances were completed. They followed the Prophet and his flock, first to the home of Joseph Knight and later to the apartment of Newel Knight. Joseph wrote: ". . . it was only by the exercise of great prudence on our part, and reliance in our heavenly Father, that they were kept from laying violent hands upon us; and so long as they chose to stay, we were obliged to answer them various unprofitable questions, and bear with insults and threatenings without number." (HC 1:88.)

Unable to deter the Saints by intimidating threats, the mobbers resorted to criminal suits. As he prepared to conduct a cottage meeting one evening, Joseph was arrested and charged with being a disorderly person. He was brought to trial in South Bainbridge, Chenango County, the next day following a terrifying night in the upper room of a tavern where, with a loaded musket, the arresting constable protected him against the threats of a mob. At the trial the charges were proven to be spurious and Joseph was discharged from custody—only to find himself served at the courthouse door with another warrant obtained from nearby Broome County. There he was tried on essentially the same charges and with the same result: acquittal. Finally his enemies organized a tar-and-feather party. However, the Prophet was able to elude them with the assistance of the constable who had arrested him and who had by then become his self-appointed protector.

Years later, the lawyer who defended the Prophet at these trials, a Mr. Reid, visited Nauvoo, Illinois, and spoke about the trials and about his acquaintance with Joseph. The fact that he never joined the Church lends special weight to his comments.

"The first acquaintance I had with Gen. Smith was about the year 1823. . . . I early discovered that his mind was constantly in search of truth, expressing an anxious desire to know the will of God concerning his children here below, often speaking of those things which professed Christians believe in. . . . After living in the neighborhood about three years, enjoying the good feelings of his acquaintances, . . . he told his particular friends that he had had a revelation from God [that] he would find hid in the earth an old history written on golden plates, which would give great light and knowledge concerning the will of God towards His people in this generation; unfolding the destiny of all nations, kindreds and tongues; he said that he distinctly heard the voice of Him that spake."

Following a reference to the circumstances under which the plates were obtained and translated, Mr. Reid continued with his narrative: "After the book was published, he came to live in the neighborhood of Father Knight's, about four miles from me, and began to preach the Gospel, and many were pricked in their hearts, believed and were baptized in the name of the Lord Jesus. He soon formed a church at Colesville, his meetings were numerously attended; the eyes of all people were upon him with astonishment. O, Mr. Chairman, the world was turned up side down at once, and the devil, . . . personified in some of the religionists, began to prick up his ears and jump and kick and run about like Jim Crow. . . . Those bigots soon made up a false accusation against him and had him arraigned before Joseph Chamberlain, a justice of the peace, a man that was always ready to deal justice to all. . . . I was called upon to defend the prisoner. The prosecutors employed the best counsel they could get, and ransacked the town of Bainbridge and county of Chenango for witnesses that would swear hard enough to convict the prisoner; but they entirely failed. *Yes, sir, let me say to you that not one blemish nor spot was found against his character, he came from that trial, notwithstanding the mighty efforts that were made to convict him of crime by his vigilant persecutors, with his character unstained by even the appearance of guilt.* . . . After a few moments' deliberation, the court pronounced the words 'not guilty,' and the prisoner was discharged. But alas! the devil, not satisfied with his defeat, stirred up a man not unlike himself, . . . to go to Colesville and get another writ. . . . I was again called upon by his friends to defend him against his malignant persecutors. . . . I made every reasonable excuse I could, as I was nearly worn down through fatigue and want of sleep . . . [but] a peculiar impression or thought struck my mind, that I must go and defend him, for he was the Lord's anointed. . . . The next morning about 10 o'clock the court was organized. . . . They employed the ablest lawyer in that county, and introduced twenty or thirty witnesses before dark, but . . . nothing was proven against him whatever. . . . The court arraigned the prisoner and said: 'Mr. Smith, we have had your case under consideration, examined the testimony and find nothing to condemn you, and therefore you are discharged.' . . . We got him away that night from the midst of three hundred people without his receiving any injury; but I am well aware that we were assisted by some higher power than man; for to look back on the scene, I cannot tell how we succeeded in getting him away. I take no glory to myself; it was the Lord's work and marvelous in our eyes." (HC 1:94-96.)

Unsatisfied by their two abortive attempts to convict him of a crime, the Colesville mobbers renewed their harassment of Joseph when he returned there a few days after the last trial. Learning of his presence at the Knight home where, with Oliver Cowdery, he had gone to confirm several new members of the Church, the mobbers gathered to express their mindless rage and frustration in the only way left to them. Milling and pushing, they shouted threats against the Prophet, sometimes in vulgar and profane language. Seeing that the mob was beyond reason or compassion, he and Oliver left immediately for Harmony.

Chapter Nine

Doctrinal Developments in the Church

A striking facet of the Prophet's character and leadership ability came to light during the hectic summer of 1830. Although heavily preoccupied in avoiding the mobs and in providing sustenance for himself and Emma, he received several significant revelations during this period. In June, he received what is now known as the book of Moses in the Pearl of Great Price, which is the transcript of a revelation given to Moses at a time when he saw God face to face in "an exceedingly high mountain." This announced that God had created "worlds without number" and that the chief work and glory of God was "to bring to pass the immortality and eternal life of man." It also contained an allusion to the Prophet: "And in a day when the children of men shall esteem my words as naught and take many of them from the book which thou shalt write, behold, I will raise up another like unto thee; and they shall be had again among the children of men—among as many as shall believe." (Moses 1:41.)

These concepts—the multiplicity of the works of God and the central role man plays in these works—form the foundation of one of the most profound and motivational doctrines expounded by the Prophet. In subsequent explanations, it was made clear that all who have lived or who will live on the earth will gain immortality through the atoning sacrifice of the Savior; however, only a select few will gain eternal life because of the discipline required to "live by every word" that proceeds from the mouth of God. Eternal life was defined as embodying all of the blessings and powers of godhood, including the ability to propagate spiritual offspring and to create and people worlds.

The distinction between immortality and eternal life reconciled the bitter arguments that had raged in the theological world over salvation by faith or works. While resurrection from the dead and reconciliation with God comes about through the grace of Christ's atoning sacrifice, the goal of eternal life or exaltation is attainable only by the constant, disciplined application of the principles that

Christ taught. Out of these concepts revealed in June 1830 also sprang the doctrine of gradations in the hereafter, which was greatly elaborated upon two years later in what is known as section 76 of the Doctrine and Covenants.

With the announcement and elaboration of these vital concepts, every facet of the lives of the Saints took on new meaning and purpose. The joys and satisfactions of life were to be savored and appreciated as mere precursors of the greater happiness yet to come—eternal life in the presence of God. Difficulties and trials were looked upon as the means of testing their faith and of honing their character in an eternal quest for excellence and perfection.

These doctrines produced in the Prophet and his followers a buoyant optimism in the face of the most trying circumstances. From the stench and squalor of a Missouri jail, he gave eloquent utterance to that optimism in these memorable words: "And if thou shouldst be cast into the pit, or into the hands of murderers, and the sentence of death passed upon thee; if thou be cast into the deep; if the billowing surge conspire against thee; if fierce winds become thine enemy; if the heavens gather blackness, and all the elements combine to hedge up the way; and above all, if the very jaws of hell shall gape open the mouth wide after thee, know thou, my son, that all these things shall give thee experience, and shall be for thy good." (D&C 122:7.) From the bleak plains beyond Illinois, where Joseph's followers buried thousands of their dead along the trail of the westward exodus, William Clayton gave voice to this irrepressible optimism: "Come, come ye saints, no toil nor labor fear,/But with joy, wend your way. . . ./And should we die before our journey's through,/Happy day, all is well." (*Hymns,* no. 13.)

In addition to the revelation containing this far-reaching doctrinal concept, the Prophet received several others that summer that were more prosaic in character. One such (section 25) was directed to his wife, Emma. In the light of subsequent events, it takes on added significance because of the insight into Emma's character that it provides. Emma was told to "murmur not because of the things which thou hast not seen, for they are withheld from thee and from the world, which is wisdom in me in a time to come." She was also warned to "beware of pride" and assured that she need not "fear" about how Joseph would support her. Finally, she was admonished to serve as a "comfort" and a "scribe" to the

Prophet and was directed to make a selection of sacred hymns for use by the Church. The inference from this revelation is that Emma was a proud, fearful, murmuring woman, and later events corroborated this analysis to a large extent. Such a harsh judgment must be tempered by the recognition, however, that the same revelation referred to Emma as an "elect lady" whom the Lord had called.

During the summer of 1830 the Prophet received several other revelations covering a wide range of subjects. Section 26 of the Doctrine and Covenants contains words of caution to Joseph Smith and Oliver Cowdery to let their time "be devoted to the studying of the scriptures, and to preaching," as well as reaffirmation of the law of common consent as a governing principle of the Church. In section 27, instructions were given authorizing the use of water instead of wine in administering the sacrament, and there was a reaffirmation of the priesthoods conferred on Joseph and Oliver by John the Baptist and by Peter, James, and John.

Amidst all this, Joseph was busy tending to his small farm in Harmony. In July, however, he was instructed: ". . . after thou hast sowed thy fields and secured them, go speedily unto the church which is in Colesville, Fayette, and Manchester. . . ." (D&C 26:3.) Soon after this revelation was received, Oliver went on to Fayette and the Prophet remained to complete his preparations.

Not long after Oliver's departure, Joseph was confronted with the first of what turned out to be a lengthy series of dissensions within the Church. After arriving at the home of the Whitmers in Fayette, Oliver became convinced he had found an error in an isolated sentence of one of the revelations the Prophet had received. Discussion with the Whitmers brought them around to Oliver's way of thinking, which emboldened him to write an impudent letter to the Prophet in which he commanded Joseph "in the name of God to erase those words." Joseph immediately answered Oliver by mail, inquiring about the authority by which he purported to command Joseph "to alter or erase, to add to or diminish from, a revelation or commandment from Almighty God." (HC 1:105.) Sensing that this incipient rebellion among some of his closest and most trusted associates could, unless checked, greatly impede the work, Joseph immediately went to Fayette to confront them. There he was able to convince them that the sentence in question was reasonable and proper, but not without extensive debate and discussion. The turning point came when he convinced Christian Whitmer, who, in turn, brought the others around to his way of thinking.

This comparatively insignificant event reveals a vital aspect of the Prophet's leadership and of the relationship between him and his followers. He obtained the concurrence of his followers not by the exercise of authority or coercion, but rather by reasoning and discussion. Also, his followers showed no reluctance to express contrary views. In fact, Oliver even felt free to challenge the Prophet openly and to arbitrarily direct him to alter one of the revelations.

The summer of 1830 brought about a final rift between the Prophet and his father-in-law, Isaac Hale. Except for short interludes, Joseph and Emma had made their home in Harmony since December 1827, either under the same roof with the Hales or on a small adjoining farm. It was here, or in the near vicinity, that most of the translation of the Book of Mormon was accomplished; that Joseph suffered the anguish of losing the 116-page manuscript that was dictated to Martin Harris; that John the Baptist and later Peter, James, and John appeared to restore the Aaronic and Melchizedek priesthoods; that many of the early significant revelations were received; and that the first branch of the Church was organized and the first miracle of the Church performed. Isaac Hale had observed or had been involved in all of these events. From the beginning he had entertained a low opinion of Joseph, which sank to the depths when the Prophet eloped with his favorite child, Emma.

From time to time, Isaac had appeared to be reconciled to the Prophet and had given him necessary sustenance and protection. In fact, during the early part of the summer of 1830 he even appeared to be genuinely interested in Joseph's work, occasioned, perhaps, by the publication of the Book of Mormon and the organization of the Church. Later that summer, however, Isaac's mind was again poisoned against the Prophet.

"About this time," the Prophet said, "a spirit of persecution began again to manifest itself against us in the neighborhood where I now resided, which was commenced by a man of the Methodist persuasion, who professed to be a minister of God. This man had learned that my father-in-law and his family had promised us protection, and were friendly, and inquiring into the work; and knowing that if he could get him turned against me, my friends in that place would be but few, he visited my father-in-law, and told him falsehoods concerning me of the most shameful nature, which turned the old gentleman and his family so much against us, that they would no longer promise us protection nor believe our doctrines." (HC 1:108.)

It was on this discordant note that the Prophet separated from his in-laws and left the area, never again to return except for short visits. Isaac Hale, already advanced in age, became progressively more bitter and antagonistic. Urged on by Joseph's enemies four years later, this senile old man signed an affidavit against the Prophet obtained and likely prepared by apostate Philastus Hurlburt. This, with numerous other questionable or false affidavits, was used by the vitriolic editor Eber D. Howe in publishing the progenitor of all anti-Mormon books, *Mormonism Unvailed.*

As the Prophet left Harmony, he was conscious of having reached a pivotal point in his life. Now that the Book of Mormon had been published, the Church had been organized, and thriving congregations were being established by enthusiastic and able disciples, he realized that he must enlarge the scope of his activities and change his base of operations. For the time being, he decided to take up residence at Fayette. His trusted and faithful friend Joseph Knight provided the wagon in which he transported his meager belongings there.

Chapter Ten

Kirtland, Ohio: The First "Gathering Place"

Upon his return to Fayette, the Prophet began preparing for the first general conference of the Church, to be held in September. First, however, two immediate problems of some importance gave him concern. The first problem was the residual effect upon Oliver Cowdery and the Whitmer family of Oliver's presumptuous command to Joseph to alter one of the revelations. The other, a new challenge to his authority and to the prescribed order of the Church, came from Hiram Page, one of the eight witnesses and a son-in-law of Peter Whitmer, Sr. To his consternation, the Prophet found that Page had been purporting to receive revelations through the medium of a "peep" stone or "seer" stone that had come into his possession. Furthermore, Oliver and the Whitmers appeared to accept these as divinely inspired and were prepared to act upon them, and they seemed to expect the entire church, including the Prophet, to act upon them.

The reaction of the Prophet to this new difficulty was typical—and predictable. He sought the Lord in fervent prayer for direction, and in answer he received a revelation that resolved both problems. In it Oliver was directed that he should not "write by way of commandment, but by wisdom," and that only Joseph had been appointed "to receive commandments and revelations" for the Church. As to Page, Oliver was instructed to "take thy brother, Hiram Page, between him and thee alone, and tell him that those things which he hath written from that stone are not of me and that Satan deceiveth him." (D&C 28.) Oliver followed this direction and was able to convince Hiram of his error. Furthermore, Oliver became convinced of the impropriety of attempting to give direction to the head of the Church by way of commandment and sought forgiveness from the Prophet, which was readily granted. Thus a confrontation with some of Joseph's most ardent early supporters was averted and the way was cleared for a conference free of dissension or controversy.

Out of this conference and several key revelations received in connection with it emerged three vital concepts that were to absorb much of the time and energies of the Prophet and the Church during the ensuing decade. These were the concepts of gathering, evangelism among the Indians and others, and the establishment of the city of Zion.

A revelation given to Joseph Smith in September 1830 in the presence of six elders contained this significant direction: "And ye are called to bring to pass the gathering of mine elect; for mine elect hear my voice and harden not their hearts; Wherefore the decree hath gone forth from the Father that they shall be gathered in unto one place upon the face of this land, to prepare their hearts and be prepared in all things against the day when tribulation and desolation are sent forth upon the wicked." (D&C 29:7-8.) In an earlier revelation given through the Prophet, Oliver was instructed to "go unto the Lamanites and preach my gospel unto them" and was told that no man knew the location of the city of Zion, but that it would be "on the borders by the Lamanites." (D&C 28:8-9.) A revelation given during the conference designated Peter Whitmer, Jr., as Oliver's companion on his mission to the Lamanites, and later Parley P. Pratt and Ziba Peterson were directed to join them. There was great excitement and anticipation among the Saints as these four prepared to leave in October 1830 for their mission. None of them, with the possible exception of the Prophet, foresaw the far-reaching effects and historic significance of that undertaking.

It was doubtless the presence in this group of Parley P. Pratt that caused them to follow the route west that took them through the Kirtland, Ohio, area near Cleveland. Pratt had lived there for some time as a minister in a minor Protestant sect, and the missionary party spent some time proselyting among his old acquaintances and others. The result was that within two or three weeks, 127 were converted and baptized "and this number soon increased to one thousand." (Parley P. Pratt, *Autobiography* [1874], p. 48.) Among these converts were Sidney Rigdon, the pastor of a small congregation at Mentor, Ohio; Edward Partridge, W. W. Phelps, Frederick G. Williams, Newel K. Whitney, and Lyman Wight, prosperous farmers or merchants in the area; and scores of others. The largest number of these new converts resided in or near Kirtland and belonged to an independent sect, headed by Lyman Wight, which practiced a communal type of living as part of their religious beliefs. Before the missionaries left to continue their journey westward, they ordained Rigdon, Partridge, Wight, and others to the priesthood and left them "to take care of the churches and to minister the gospel." (Ibid.)

The accounts of Joseph Smith and his spiritual attainments given by Oliver Cowdery and Peter Whitmer, Jr., who knew him intimately, created in the new converts at Kirtland a great desire to see the Prophet and to receive personal direction from him. Impelled by this desire, Sidney Rigdon and Edward Partridge traveled to Fayette in December 1830. Both of these men were twelve years older than the Prophet, better educated than he, and much more experienced in the affairs of the world. Yet they accepted without question the instructions he gave to them. Shortly after their arrival, Joseph received a revelation for each of them. In one revelation, Edward Partridge, who was described by the Prophet as being "a pattern of piety," was instructed to proclaim the gospel "as with the voice of a trump." (D&C 36:1.)

Sidney Rigdon was told that without knowing it, he had acted as a harbinger for the message that the Prophet brought by the emphasis given in his teachings to the principles of faith, repentance, and baptism. He was instructed to act as a protector and a spokesman for the Prophet, and to "write for him; and the scriptures shall be given, even as they are in my own bosom." (D&C 35:20.) This latter instruction launched the Prophet and Sidney on the ambitious project of revising the scriptures, as directed by the Spirit, which occupied their time intermittently for many years.

Furthermore, the Lord revealed to Joseph what he referred to as the "doings of olden times, from the prophecy of Enoch." (HC 1:133.) This was prompted by inquiries from Joseph's followers about scriptures referred to in the Bible that could not be found, particularly the "Prophecy of Enoch" referred to in the book of Jude. The resulting revelation, now printed in the Pearl of Great Price as chapters 2 through 8 in the book of Moses, represented one of the most remarkable and wide-ranging revelations ever received by the Prophet, covering, among others, the subjects of creation, the fall, the atonement, the necessity of opposition in all things, free agency, repentance, justification, and sanctification.

The final revelation received by the Prophet during Sidney's visit consisted of only four short verses. However, it had a more direct and far-reaching effect upon the young church than all the others combined. It commanded that the "church . . . should assemble together at the Ohio, against the time that my servant Oliver Cowdery shall return unto them." (D&C 37:3.) This was the first explicit direction given to the Saints to gather together in one place.

The principal object of the gathering was to concentrate the power and influence of the Church into a single locality. This would simplify the problems of administration, give the members a sense of unity and strength that could never be achieved were they to remain scattered, and bring most of the membership of the Church under the direct influence of Joseph Smith. The spectacularly successful proselyting efforts had brought into the Church a diverse, highly independent assortment of persons whose primary commitment was their inner conviction that Joseph's story about the Book of Mormon and the restoration of the priesthood was true. They yet had to learn the full import and scope of that story, which could best be accomplished by direct contact with the teacher.

By the end of January 1831, Joseph and Emma had completed arrangements to move to Ohio. They traveled in company with Sidney Rigdon, Edward Partridge, and others. At Kirtland they went directly to Newel Whitney's store, where the Prophet greeted him with the words, "Newel Whitney, thou art the man; you have prayed me here, now what do you want of me." When Newel had recovered from the shock of this unorthodox greeting and had learned the identity of the stranger, he invited the Prophet and Emma to stay in his home. His offer of hospitality was accepted, and the Prophet and Emma remained there for several weeks until they were able to make more permanent arrangements.

Within the next few months several hundred of the Prophet's followers were to make their way to the Kirtland area from Palmyra, Manchester, Fayette, Colesville, and other communities in the East. It is easy at this remote point in time to minimize the magnitude of that undertaking and to equate it with the ease and comfort with which such a journey can be made today. But this exodus was accomplished only with great travail and hardship. One of the best accounts of the journey was left by Lucy Mack Smith, the Prophet's mother. Her company, which consisted of eighty persons, rented a flatboat and floated down the Erie Canal to Buffalo. As they were en route, the canal broke, causing confusion and upset, especially among the thirty children aboard the boat. At Buffalo they found the harbor ice locked and tourist traffic had piled up there, making it almost impossible to find lodging or to book passage on a boat going west. Through great effort and much prayer, Lucy found lodging for the children and was able to book deck passage on a boat out of Buffalo that almost miraculously was able to clear the harbor by a narrow opening in the ice flow. The water was choppy, producing great sickness among most of the company huddled together on the deck for protection against the cold March winds. The travelers finally disembarked at Fairport, not far from Cleveland, for the last leg of their journey to Kirtland by land.

The travail through which this group passed was repeated time and again by other groups of migrating Saints. Most of them arrived in Kirtland in about the same disorganized, disheveled condition—tired, hungry, and not a little anxious, with no homes, little food or money, and few prospects of getting any. Most of them, therefore, had to rely upon the kindness and hospitality of the local members until they were able to reestablish themselves on farms or in businesses or trades. This imposed an exceedingly heavy burden upon the local members. It was in these dire circumstances that the first bishop of the Church was appointed by revelation. His chief duty was to see that the needy were properly cared for: "And again, I have called my servant Edward Partridge; and I give a commandment, that he should be appointed by the voice of the church, and ordained a bishop unto the church, to leave his merchandise and to spend all his time in the labors of the church." (D&C 41:9.) This is all that was required for prosperous Edward Partridge to leave a thriving business and take up the onerous, sometimes thankless, task of caring for the needs of the flood of new converts who were to inundate Kirtland within the next few months obedient to the command to gather.

With a man as able and dedicated as Edward Partridge to assume the principal responsibility of attending to the physical needs of the Saints, the Prophet was freed to attend to the spiritual needs of his followers. He continued with the engrossing task of revising the scriptures, assisted by Sidney Rigdon. He administered to the needs of those who were afflicted. He gave counsel and instruction to the many who sought him out. And it was during this period that he received several key revelations that further expanded the scope of the doctrines and aims of the Church.

We are greatly indebted to Parley P. Pratt for the insights he left to us of Joseph Smith at work at this critical time. He was present on the occasion when the Prophet received the revelation that defined the moral law of the gospel. In that revelation, now identified as section 42 of the Doctrine and Covenants, members of the Church were instructed in the principles of chastity, cleanliness, simplicity in dress, the care of the poor and the sick, and personal and public offenses. He was also present a few days later when the Prophet received a revelation, now known as section 43, which gave warning and instructions about false spirits and spurious revelations. Parley wrote the following account of the circumstances under which this last-mentioned revelation was received:

"Feeling our weakness and inexperience, and lest we should err in judgment concerning these spiritual phenomena, myself, John Murdock, and several other Elders, went to Joseph Smith, and asked him to inquire of the Lord concerning these spirits or manifestations.

"After we had joined in prayer in his translating room, he dictated in our presence the following revelation. . . . [Each] sentence was uttered slowly and very distinctly, and with a pause between each, sufficiently long for it to be recorded, by an ordinary writer, in long hand.

"This was the manner in which all his written revelations were dictated and written. There was never any hesitation, reviewing, or reading back, in order to keep the run of the subject; neither did any of these communications undergo revisions, interlinings, or corrections. As he dictated them so they stood, so far as I have witnessed; and I was present to witness the dictation of several communications of several pages each." (Pratt, pp. 61-62.)

One can imagine the powerful impact exerted upon those who witnessed one of these episodes. Here was one who, like the prophets of old, spoke authoritatively in the name of God. His whole demeanor, the substance of his declarations, the corroborating testimony of those who had been personal witnesses of some of his divine manifestations, and the solid achievements he had attained against heavy odds all combined to surround the Prophet with an aura of charismatic excitement. As the word spread through determined and resourceful missionaries that God had spoken and was speaking again through a living man, and as they learned of the commandment to gather in Ohio, the converts flocked to Kirtland. Almost invariably the first request of each one was to see the Prophet. Many were content merely to gaze upon him; others were desirous to hear him speak or to expound the scriptures, while others, more bold and aggressive, sought personal direction from the Lord through the Prophet as to their course of action. Some few were disappointed when they met Joseph because his appearance and demeanor did not correspond with their preconceived notions of how a prophet should look and act. These few were surprised to find him engaged in the normal pursuits that occupied a good part of the time of any man on the frontier: sawing or splitting logs, tending farm animals, cultivating the land, or performing necessary chores around the house. Nor were these few prepared for the Prophet's sunny disposition, his easy and friendly way with acquaintances, or his fun-loving bent for sports activities, good-natured repartee, or harmless practical jokes. However, those who faulted the Prophet for these qualities did not detract from his stature or influence, but merely betrayed their own narrow views and understanding of the role of a prophet. Brigham Young, who arrived in Kirtland in September 1832, left this revealing account of his first contact with the Prophet: "We proceeded to Kirtland and stopped at John P. Greene's, who had just arrived there with his family. We rested a few minutes, took some refreshments and started to see the Prophet. We went to his father's house and learned that he was in the woods chopping. We immediately repaired to the woods, where we found the Prophet, and two of his three brothers, chopping and hauling wood. Here my joy was full at the privilege of shaking the hand of the Prophet of God, and receiving the sure testimony, by the spirit of prophecy, that he was all that any man could believe him to be as a true prophet. He was happy to see us and bid us welcome. We soon returned to his house, he accompanying us." (HC 1:297.)

Later that evening in the Prophet's home, Brigham Young was asked to offer prayer. While praying, he spoke in an unknown tongue, which was unintelligible to all in the circle except Joseph. At the conclusion, the others watched the Prophet intently to see if he condemned Brigham, for not long before he had reprimanded some of Saints in Kirtland for babbling incoherently in what they erroneously assumed was an unknown tongue. This time, however, the Prophet commended Brigham and advised those present that he had spoken in the pure Adamic language. It is reported that Joseph afterward confided to some of those present that Brigham Young would one day stand as the president of the Church. (CHC 1:289.)

Remarkable incidents of this kind appear to have been almost a daily occurrence in the early days of Kirtland. Parley P. Pratt left this account of the miraculous healing of a member:

"About this time a young lady, by the name of Chloe Smith, being a member of the Church, was lying very low with a lingering fever. . . . Many of the Church had visited and prayed with her, but all to no effect; she seemed at the point of death, but would not consent to have a physician. This greatly enraged her relatives, who had cast her out because she belonged to the Church, and who, together with many of the people of the neighborhood, were greatly stirred up to anger, saying, 'these wicked deceivers will let her lie and die without a physician, because of their superstitions; and if they do, we will prosecute them for so doing.' Now these were daily watching for her last breath, with many threats.

"Under these circumstances, President Smith and myself, with several other Elders, called to see her. . . . We kneeled down and prayed vocally all around, each in turn; after which President Smith arose, went to the bedside, took her by the hand, and said unto her with a loud voice 'in the name of Jesus Christ arise and walk!' She immediately arose, was dressed by a woman in attendance, when she walked to a chair before the fire, and was seated and joined in singing a hymn. The house was thronged with people in a few moments, and the young lady arose and shook hands with each as they came in; and from that minute she was perfectly restored to health." (Pratt, pp. 66-67.)

As Bishop Edward Partridge became involved in the monumental task of finding accommodations and caring for the physical wants of the many members who thronged into Kirtland, he became acutely aware of the need for more detailed instructions. Section 51 of the Doctrine and Covenants partly filled this need. In it, he was directed to "appoint unto this people their portions, every man equal according to his family, according to his circumstances and his wants and needs." The revelation then spelled out the details for transferring to each man his "portion," which was to be secured by a "writing." Provision was also made for the creation of a bishop's storehouse into which were to be placed "all things both in money and in meat, which are more than is needful for the wants of this people." This, taken in conjunction with another revelation given about this same time (D&C 41), established the principle of stewardship in the Church. According to this concept, each member was responsible for and had full control over the property in his charge. He was to keep that portion of the yield necessary to maintain his family and turn over the balance to the bishop. Later this concept was modified by the institution of the law of tithing, which required a contribution of one-tenth of a person's annual increase.

There is only a superficial similarity between these concepts and the communistic design of producing an equitable distribution of goods and services. Both seek the laudable goal of eliminating want and poverty, but they differ radically in the means used to achieve that end. The first is based upon common consent and the uncontrolled determination of the individual as to what constitutes a tithe or what portion of the production from a stewardship is required to maintain the steward and his family. The second depends for its success upon the dictatorial and coercive control of all the means of production and distribution in a society.

It was made clear to the travel-weary Saints who poured into Kirtland that their stay there would be temporary. They knew that the Zion which had been promised and which they earnestly sought lay farther to the west. While the precise location had not been designated, they knew that the promised land was somewhere "on the borders of the Lamanites," which was understood to mean the Missouri. But even though they knew that Kirtland was little more than a waystation, they commenced to build and to plant their roots as if they intended it to be their permanent home. In this they were obedient to counsel. "And I consecrate unto them this land for a little season," declared a revelation given to the Prophet in May 1831, "until I, the Lord, shall provide for them otherwise, and command them to go hence; And the hour and the day is not given unto them, wherefore let them act upon this land as for years, and this shall turn unto them for their good." (D&C 51:16-17.) Thus were Joseph's followers taught a lesson in patience and forbearance, one which was to sustain them in the years ahead as they moved from place to place in search of peace and rest.

In June 1831 the Prophet presided at a conference of the Church in Kirtland, with approximately two thousand persons in attendance. Gathered together in this way, where they could feel the dedication and enthusiasm of each other, many of the Saints commenced to see for the first time the strength and the potential of the church they had embraced. As Joseph looked out over this vast congregation, he too marveled at the phenomenal growth and success of the Church since its organization just fourteen months before. Now there sat before him two thousand members, most of whom had been uprooted from their homes and who were prepared to do whatever else was required of them. And, even as the conference met, many missionaries were out proselyting others into the Church.

Chapter Eleven

A Vanguard Moves to Missouri

The day following the 1831 conference in Kirtland, the Prophet received a revelation that directed that the next conference be held in Missouri, and instructed him and Sidney Rigdon and several other brethren to go there in pairs. It also promised that, contingent upon their faithfulness, the land of their "inheritance" would be designated. (D&C 52.)

The Prophet commenced immediately to make preparations to leave for Missouri. Because of the arduous nature of the trip, Emma was to remain in Kirtland with the Newel K. Whitneys. He left in her charge his valuable papers, including the manuscript of the revision of the scriptures on which he had been working intermittently for several months.

In the interval before his departure, the Prophet received several other revelations, which came in response to specific inquiries from individual groups as to their duty or conduct. Thus, Algernon Sidney Gilbert was directed to accompany the Prophet and Sidney Rigdon to Missouri. (D&C 53.) Newel Knight was told to lead the Colesville Branch to Missouri in search of a new place to settle. (D&C 54.) William W. Phelps was also instructed to go to Missouri to assist Oliver Cowdery in the selection, writing, and printing of books for schools in the Church. (D&C 55.) Similarly, Thomas B. Marsh and Selah J. Griffin were counseled to go "speedily to the land of Missouri." (D&C 56.)

Their preparations all completed, the Prophet and his party left Kirtland on June 19, 1831. Their first stop was Cincinnati, which they reached by means of wagons, canal boats, and stages. While waiting for a steamer to take the party to Louisville, Kentucky, the Prophet had an interview with the Reverend Walter Scott, one of the founders of the Campbellite or Newlight Church, the church with which both Sidney Rigdon and Parley P. Pratt had been affiliated prior to their conversion. Many had followed these and other Campbellite leaders into the new church, and the infectious enthusiasm of these converts, coupled with an aggressive evangelism with their families and friends, created the unsettling possibility that the flow of membership from one church to the other would not only continue but would grow in size and intensity. Thus the meeting was understandably tense. The Reverend Scott rejected out of hand the account of the spiritual experiences of the Prophet and his followers. In recording the interview in his journal, Joseph later observed: ". . . he manifested one of the bitterest spirits against the doctrine of the New Testament (that 'these signs shall follow them that believe' as recorded in Mark the 16th chapter,) that I ever witnessed among men." (HC 1:188.)

Eleven years of ridicule and opposition for his religious beliefs had conditioned the Prophet to accept rejection as almost a matter of course. As always, he did not permit the rejection to alter his views; neither did he find it necessary to explain himself or to demean his critic. In this we see one of Joseph's great strengths and a reason why he exerted such a strong influence upon his followers. Not only did he hold himself out as a prophet; he acted like a prophet. His followers found no uncertainty in him; no tendency to explain, argue, or rationalize. He stated his views with positive finality, without dogmatism or pomposity. Yet it was precisely this quality of positiveness that, while attracting and impressing his followers, repelled and antagonized his detractors.

The journey from Cincinnati to Louisville and from Louisville to St. Louis was covered in the comparative luxury of river steamers. Never before had Joseph been a passenger on one of these. Until then, the smaller canal boats that plied the Erie Canal had been the largest water conveyances he had seen. The leisurely, comfortable ride on the river gave him time for unhurried reflection on the past. It also permitted him to give prayerful consideration to his future course.

Accompanied by four of his brethren, the Prophet covered the last leg of the journey from St. Louis to Independence on foot, which enabled him to observe the landscape and to gauge the spirit and attitudes of the inhabitants. He was struck by the openness of the country and by the "rolling prairies," which, he recorded, "lie spread out like a sea of meadows . . . decorated with a growth of flowers so gorgeous and grand as to exceed description." He noted that unlike the heavily forested lands in the eastern United States, timber here was to be found only along the water courses. He also observed the richness of the soil and the abundance of wild game.

(HC 1:197.) He could envision this rich, bountiful land inhabited by Latter-day Saints whose thrift, industry, and dedication to Christian principles would make of it a literal Zion, a place of beauty where the pure in heart would dwell and which would be a fit abode for the Savior at his second coming.

These thoughts were jarred and shaken when the Prophet observed the scruffy character of the people who inhabited the land. In one of his most scathing denunciations, he said of the people who then occupied Missouri: ". . . how natural it was to observe the degradation, leanness of intellect, ferocity, and jealousy of a people that were nearly a century behind the times, and to feel for those who roamed about without the benefit of civilization, refinement, or religion." (HC 1:189.)

Within a few days after the Prophet's party arrived in Independence, he received a revelation that answered dual questions that had been uppermost in the minds of his followers for many months. Where was the ultimate place of gathering to be, and where was the temple to be built? The revelation specified "the land of Missouri" as "the land which I have appointed and consecrated for the gathering of the saints." Furthermore, Independence was designated "the center place" and the site where the temple was to be constructed. (D&C 57:1-3.) This revelation also admonished the Saints to purchase as much land as their resources would permit; appointed Edward Partridge to act as bishop; and directed Sidney Gilbert to open a store and William W. Phelps and Oliver Cowdery to establish a printing shop.

The great disparity between the grandeur of the Zion to be and the squalid frontier village Joseph's followers now saw before them caused some to have doubts and anxieties. Consequently, the Prophet sought for and received a revelation that elaborated upon the future of the land and city of Zion and the role of those who were to participate in establishing them. The revelation first cautioned the Saints not to be impatient about the fulfillment of the great promises concerning the city of Zion and the temple. "Ye cannot behold with your natural eyes," it said, ". . . the design of your God concerning those things which shall come hereafter, and the glory which shall follow after much tribulation. For after much tribulation come the blessings. . . ." (D&C 58:3-4.) There followed an explanation of the reasons for the arduous trip to Missouri and the designation of the ultimate place of gathering that some considered to be premature: "I have sent you—that you might be obedient, and that your hearts might be prepared to bear testimony of the things which are to come; And also that you might be honored in laying the foundation, and in bearing record of the land upon which the Zion of God shall stand." (D&C 58:6-7.) Reemphasis was given to the need for those who had been specifically designated to settle in the land, as well as encouragement to those who might "desire it through the prayer of faith." All others, however, were given significant direction: "And now, verily, I say concerning the residue of the elders of my church, the time has not yet come, for many years, for them to receive their inheritance in this land. . . ." (D&C 58:44.)

The obvious effect of this revelation was to minimize the short-range importance of Missouri in the eyes of the Saints. While they realized that Independence ultimately would be the center of church power and influence, most also knew that this condition would not exist "for many years" and only "after much tribulation." Even those who realized there would be a delay in the ultimate gathering mistakenly believed that it would occur during their lifetimes.

On August 2, Joseph helped the Colesville Branch "lay the first log, for a house, as a foundation of Zion in Kaw township, twelve miles west of Independence." Symbolically, this log was carried by twelve men representing the twelve tribes of Israel. Sidney Rigdon then consecrated and dedicated the land of Zion "for the gathering of the Saints." (HC 1:196.) The following day, the Prophet, in the presence of six of his brethren, dedicated the temple site.

With the dedication of the temple site and the dedication and consecration of the land of Zion, the Prophet had completed the essential work that had brought him to the land of Missouri. He therefore commenced to make preparations for the return trip to Kirtland, giving final instructions to those who were to remain in Missouri and directing the plans of those who were to return to Kirtland. In a revelation received shortly before their departure, the returning brethren were instructed to travel in pairs and to expound the doctrines of the restored faith in the "congregations of the wicked." (D&C 60:8.)

On August 6, 1831, the Prophet and ten elders shoved off from the Independence landing in canoes. They paddled downstream for three days, pulling to shore only to rest and to eat and sleep. They encountered much turbulence, accentuated by the small size of their canoes, which were tossed about like corks on the angry river. On the third night out of Independence, while they were camped at McIlwaine's Bend, William W. Phelps "in open vision by daylight, saw the destroyer in his most horrible power, ride upon the face of the waters." The Prophet reported that "others heard the noise, but saw not the vision." (HC 1:203.) The following morning the Prophet received a revelation, which warned about the great dangers lurking upon the waters and which instructed the Saints coming to Zion to avoid the waterways except for the placid canals. "Nevertheless," the revelation continued, "unto whom is given power to command the waters, unto him it is given by the Spirit to know all his ways; Wherefore, let him do as the Spirit of the living God commandeth him, whether upon the land or upon the waters, as it remaineth with me to do hereafter." (D&C 61:27-28.)

Shortly after his return to Kirtland, the Prophet received two additional revelations that further elaborated the present and future status of the land of Zion in Missouri: the Church was to acquire land there by purchase, a few were directed to go to the land of Zion to settle, and the general body of the Church was counseled to defer moving there until some future time. These revelations and those received by the Prophet while he was in Missouri effectively convinced his followers of the subordinate role Missouri was to play in the development of the Church within the immediate future. At the same time, they tacitly recognized the ultimate importance and preeminent role of that land.

In Kirtland Joseph found a strong undercurrent of opposition, fault-finding, and apostasy at work. These problems were complicated by a difficult family problem. Since their arrival in Kirtland in January, Joseph and Emma had lived as guests in the home of Newel K. Whitney, the Kirtland merchant. While they had been made to feel welcome, the Whitney home was not large, and the crowded conditions created strains upon both families. These were heavily increased in the spring when, following a difficult pregnancy, Emma lost twins, a boy and a girl, within three hours after their birth. The almost inconsolable grief she experienced after losing her second and third children was eased when nine days later she took in the motherless twins of John Murdock, who were born the same day as her own. (HC 1:260). But though they lifted part of Emma's load of grief, the Murdock twins added a significant burden on the already overtaxed facilities of the Whitney household. Thus the Prophet had commenced to look for other housing accommodations for his family. The pressing duties that rested upon him as the head of the Church made it impossible for him to devote time personally to building a home or to earn money with which to buy one. Therefore, he had to look to members of the Church or to the Church itself to satisfy this need. His problem was solved when John Johnson of nearby Hiram offered him the use of a bungalow located on the large and thriving Johnson farm.

At Hiram, the Prophet found the seclusion and leisure necessary to enable him to continue with the task of revising the Bible. Sidney Rigdon, who had lodgings nearby, served as his scribe. Through the months of October and November 1831, they devoted themselves almost exclusively to this work except for a number of conferences held in the area to give instruction and inspiration to the Saints. The most important was one held on November 1 at Hiram, where a decision was made to compile and publish 10,000 copies of the commandments and revelations received by the Prophet since the commencement of his ministry. During the course of the conference, he received a revelation that was designated as the Preface of the Book of Commandments and that is now identified as the first section of the Doctrine and Covenants. This revelation was directed not only to the members of the Church, but also to nonmembers throughout the world. Its tone was bold and authoritative. ". . . the voice of warning," it said, "shall be unto all people, by the mouths of my disciples, whom I have chosen in these last days. And they shall go forth and none shall stay them, for I the Lord have commanded them. Behold, this is mine authority, and the authority of my servants, and my preface unto the book of my commandments, which I have given them to publish unto you, O inhabitants of the earth." (D&C 1:4-6.) Herein lies the key to the vigorous spirit of evangelism that has characterized the exponents of Mormonism from the beginning. They consider themselves to be the only sect on earth empowered by God to perform the saving ordinances and to speak and act authoritatively in his name. While acknowledging that there are elements of truth in all churches and that God is no respecter of persons and is as willing to hear and bless the non-Mormon as well as the Mormon, the Saints maintain that theirs is the "strait and narrow way" through which any truth seeker must pass in his search for the ultimate good or happiness. It was because of this that the Mormon missionaries were as aggressive in proselyting among Protestants and Catholics as among non-Christians. In fact, they preferred and gave greater emphasis to proselyting among other Christian sects because they found that their familiarity with the basic tenets of Christianity made them more likely candidates for conversion to Mormonism. The almost phenomenal success the missionaries had among some Protestant sects also produced a violent reaction that was to cause great trouble and upset for the Saints for years to come.

At this same conference, Oliver Cowdery was appointed to take charge of the final arranging, proofreading, and publication of the Book of Commandments. The printing would be done on the Church press, which was to be set up in Missouri under the direction of W. W. Phelps. For nearly two weeks after the conference the Prophet carefully reviewed the revelations with Oliver, who then left with John Whitmer for Missouri.

Following the conference some of the Prophet's disciples became involved in a discussion about the manner in which revelations from the Lord are received. Some of the brethren apparently entertained doubts as to whether the revelations the Prophet had received for the Church actually represented the mind and will of the Lord or were merely an expression of fugitive thoughts that came into Joseph's mind. Chief among the questioners was William E. M'Lellin. It is a mark of the Prophet's method of dealing with men that no attempt was made to resolve this dispute by argument or debate. Instead, he appealed to the Lord for guidance, and in response, he received a revelation that said, in part, "Your eyes have been upon my servant Joseph Smith, Jun., and his language you have known, and his imperfections you have known; and you have sought in your hearts knowledge that you might express beyond his language; this you also know. Now, seek ye out of the Book of Commandments, even the least that is among them, and appoint him that is the most wise among you; Or, if there be any among you that shall make one like unto it, then ye are justified in saying that ye do not know that they are true." (D&C 67:5-7.) M'Lellin accepted the challenge and made a futile attempt to compose a so-called revelation. Joseph could scarcely conceal his sense of jubilation at M'Lellin's failure when he made this comment about the incident: "After the foregoing was received, William E. M'Lellin, as the wisest man, in his own estimation, having more learning than sense, endeavored to write a commandment like unto one of the least of the Lord's, but failed; it was an awful responsibility to write in the name of the Lord. The Elders and all present that witnessed this vain attempt of a man to imitate the language of Jesus Christ, renewed their faith in the fulness of the Gospel, and in the truth of the commandments and revelations which the Lord had given to the Church through my instrumentality; and the Elders signified a willingness to bear testimony of their truth to all the world." (HC 1:226.)

The Prophet's comparatively short stay at Hiram proved to be one of the most prolific periods from a literary standpoint of any in his career. Thirteen revelations were received there. In addition, a good part of his work on the revision of the Bible was performed at Hiram. For this reason, the Johnson bungalow later came to be known as the "revelation house." Among the revelations received there was one regarded by many as the most significant one he ever received. His journal contains this explanation of the conditions under which it was received:

"From sundry revelations which had been received, it was apparent that many important points touching the salvation of man, had been taken from the Bible, or lost before it was compiled. It appeared self-evident from what truths were left, that if God rewarded every one according to the deeds done in the body the term 'Heaven,' as intended for the Saints' eternal home must include more kingdoms than one. Accordingly, on the 16th of February, 1832, while translating St. John's Gospel, myself and Elder Rigdon saw the following vision." (HC 1:245.)

There then followed a revelation 119 verses long that elaborated in great detail the condition of men and women in the life after death. It affirmed the universality of the resurrection: that all who have lived or who will yet live will be resurrected with tangible bodies of flesh and bone, and that upon resurrection they will be assigned to that degree of afterlife which their lives on earth have merited. It specified three degrees of glory likened unto the sun, moon, and stars, called the celestial, terrestrial, and telestial degrees. It also specified degrees of afterlife not considered to be degrees of glory. Those who hoped to attain the highest degree were expected to live according to the strictest standard of conduct, to be baptized into The Church of Jesus Christ of Latter-day Saints, to receive the gift of the Holy Ghost, and by faith and continuing repentance from improper conduct to become absolutely perfect through the atoning blood of Jesus Christ.

This revelation, perhaps more than any other received by the Prophet, rescued the Church from any valid charge of bigotry or overzealousness in its proselyting efforts. The message was clear and reasonable. God, who is no respecter of persons, had provided for the resurrection of all through the atoning sacrifice of the Savior and by that same means had made it possible for sinful man to be reconciled to God's perfection through obedience to the principles Jesus taught. Thus, salvation was dependent not only upon the great vicarious sacrifice wrought by the Savior, but also upon the diligent effort of each individual. The message this revelation provided the elders as they proselyted among other Christian sects was that of a better way of life. In essence they said, "Bring all that is good and true with you from your present religion and follow us to higher ground."

An unfortunate side effect of the concepts taught by this revelation was that they gave a small handful of the members an unwarranted feeling of superiority. Because the Church was considered to be the gateway into the celestial kingdom, this minority felt that membership in it gave them special status, leading to an unfortunate feeling of condescension toward nonmembers. Negative reaction against this feeling on the part of outsiders produced much of the friction and unrest that existed between the Church and others in those early days.

The reaction of the Prophet toward this revelation is significant. "Nothing could be more pleasing to the Saints," Joseph wrote, "upon the order of the kingdom of the Lord, than the light which burst upon the world through the foregoing vision. Every law, every commandment, every promise, every truth, and every point touching the destiny of man, from Genesis to Revelation, where the purity of the scriptures remains unsullied by the folly of men, go to show the perfection of the theory [of different degrees of glory in the future life] and witnesses the fact that that document is a transcript from the records of the eternal world. The sublimity of the ideas; the purity of the language; the scope for action; the continued duration for completion, in order that the heirs of salvation may confess the Lord and bow the knee; the rewards for faithfulness, and the punishments for sins, are so much beyond the narrow-mindedness of men, that every honest man is constrained to exclaim: *'It came from God.'* " (HC 1:252-53.)

Chapter Twelve

The Challenges of Apostasy and Violence

The spirit of apostasy and opposition that had been festering in Ohio came to a head in the spring of 1832, producing the first and only act of overt violence against the Prophet or the Church in Ohio. For weeks before the tragic event occurred, the Prophet saw ominous signs of its coming. The ranks of the apostates were swelled with a number of embittered former members, including three of the sons of the Prophet's host, John Johnson. The Prophet's enemies and detractors outside the Church rallied around this small center of apostates, joining in their blind hatred of him and feeding on false stories and innuendos.

So loud and insistent had the opposition become that by March, Joseph began to use pseudonyms in the revelations he received. Thus he was referred to as Enoch, Newel K. Whitney as Ahashdah, and Sidney Rigdon as Pelagoram. (See D&C 78.) This device prevented enemies within and outside the Church from knowing of special instructions given to certain members.

The storm finally broke on a spring evening as Joseph dozed while tending one of the twins, who had been sick with the measles. Emma was in the bedroom with the healthier twin, trying to get some much-needed sleep. The first sign of danger was a light tapping on a windowpane. Shortly afterwards the front door burst open and within seconds the room was filled with a horde of angry, shoving men, who grabbed the Prophet and carried him outside. As they did so, he managed to free one of his legs and to violently kick one of the mobbers. This act only infuriated the mob, which overpowered him and swore they would kill him unless he submitted to them. This threat quieted him. The man whom the Prophet had kicked thrust a blood-covered hand into his face, mauling and roughing him. Another choked him so violently that he momentarily lost consciousness. On reviving, he saw Sidney Rigdon stretched out on the ground and, thinking him dead, commenced to plead for his own life. He was told to call on God for help, as the mob intended to show no mercy.

At this point the mob seemed uncertain as to what they should do. While some of them held him, others stood nearby discussing their next move. Finally he was stripped naked, except for his shirt collar, and his body was scratched all over by a man who fell upon him like a wild animal. Then he was tarred and feathered, beaten senseless, and left for dead.

When he revived, he struggled back to the house, where several friends and neighbors, attracted by the commotion, had assembled. The sight of his tar-daubed body caused Emma to think he had been fatally injured, and she fainted. He was given a blanket to cover his nakedness, and friends and family spent most of the night painfully scraping the tar and feathers from his body.

The attack occurred on a Saturday night. The next day Joseph spoke at Sabbath day services despite his bruised appearance. In the audience were several of the mobbers, including the leaders, who were amazed at his recuperative powers and daring.

On Monday, Joseph called at the home of Sidney Rigdon, where he found his scribe badly lacerated and delirious from the mobbing. Upon seeing the Prophet, he demanded his razor so he could kill him; when his wife left the room he demanded his razor again so he could kill her. His temporary derangement was caused when the mobbers dragged him from his home by the heels, permitting his head to bump over the steps and rocky ground. Older and less resilient than Joseph, Sidney carried the emotional scars of this ordeal through the remainder of his life.

Joseph was not deterred by this act of violence, although it brought great sorrow into his home. One of the twins, already weakened by the measles, contracted a cold while exposed during the mobbing and died shortly thereafter. The death and burial of a fourth baby within a few short years rendered Emma almost inconsolable, especially when added to the trauma produced by the beating administered to her husband. She too was permanently affected by this tragedy and ever after was filled with terror and anxiety when thoughts of that dreadful night were called to mind. Those inclined to fault Emma for her failure to remain loyal to the Church and its leaders after Joseph's martyrdom should consider these and other countless tragedies and privations she was called upon to endure for the sake of her husband.

Any calculation by the mobbers that their act of violence would deter or impede the Prophet in his work wholly failed to assess the depth of his belief in the truth and importance of what he was doing. It was the same kind of error in judgment that caused those responsible for his martyrdom to believe that death would remove his influence and result in the demise of the church he had established. As a matter of fact, this mobbing served to fuel his energies and determination. It also revealed the extent of the bitterness and enmity his teachings had aroused and made him more wary and cautious in his future dealings with those both in and out of the Church.

Prior to the outbreak of this violence, the Prophet had been considering another trip to Missouri. Reports of dissension within the Church and conflicts with Gentiles had given him concern, and he was anxious to be there to help resolve these difficulties. He was also interested in expediting completion of the Church-owned press in Independence and publication of the Book of Commandments. The mobbing accelerated his time schedule and he made immediate plans to depart.

At the time of this second trip to Missouri, Joseph was only twenty-six years old. Facing him were decisions of great magnitude and complexity affecting the well-being and the very lives of hundreds of Saints who looked to him for guidance. No experience or training in the past seemed to qualify him to solve the knotty problems of finance, economics, and organization that now confronted him and his followers. Previously, his practical experience had been limited to farming and working as a hired hand. In addition, of course, were the phenomenal spiritual experiences he had enjoyed and the mental discipline derived from his work in translating the Book of Mormon, in revising the scriptures, and in dictating the revelations he had received. But all this scarcely qualified him for the arduous task of directing the business affairs of a rapidly growing church and of counseling its members about their most intimate personal problems.

It was a mark of the Prophet's character that he showed no hesitancy about moving into areas of activity about which he knew very little. His technique was to see the need, to decide to satisfy it, and then to marshal the necessary means to achieve the end. In this we see a parallel to the character of one of the main figures in the Book of Mormon. Nephi, commanded by his father to obtain a valuable historical record from a wealthy and powerful prince, accepted the task without question and without knowledge of the means of accomplishment, declaring, "I will go and do the things which the Lord hath commanded, for I know that the Lord giveth no commandments unto the children of men, save he shall prepare a way for them that they may accomplish the thing which he commandeth them." (1 Nephi 3:7.)

This analogy becomes more convincing in view of the fact that this second trip to Missouri was actually undertaken because of a revelation he had received in March 1832. The language of that revelation is vital to an understanding of what transpired in Independence at that time: "For verily I say unto you, the time has come, and is now at hand; and behold, and lo, it must needs be that there be an organization of my people, in regulating and establishing the affairs of the storehouse for the poor of my people, both in this place and in the land of Zion . . . for a permanent and everlasting establishment and order unto my church, to advance the cause, which ye have espoused, to the salvation of man, and to the glory of your Father who is in heaven; That you may be equal in the bonds of heavenly things, yea, and earthly things also, for the obtaining of heavenly things. . . . For if you will that I give unto you a place in the celestial world, you must prepare yourselves by doing the things which I have commanded you and required of you." (D&C 78:3-7.) Using the pseudonyms, the revelation then commanded Joseph, Sidney Rigdon, and Newel K. Whitney to "sit in council with the saints which are in Zion" and "to prepare and organize" to the end "that the church may stand independent above all other creatures beneath the celestial world." (Vv. 9-14.)

Obedient to this revelation, the Prophet called a general council of the Church shortly after his arrival in Missouri. His preeminent position of leadership in the Church was ratified by this council when he was sustained as the "President of the High Priesthood of the Church." Between the morning and afternoon sessions, a controversy that had developed between Sidney Rigdon and Edward Partridge was resolved. These were two of the most able men in the Church at that time, and to have them at odds with each other was a great embarrassment to the Prophet, especially since it gave some credence to the gossip that Zion and Kirtland were working against each other. A revelation received at the afternoon session heralded the reconciliation between the two old friends in these opening words: "Verily, verily, I say unto you, my servants, that inasmuch as you have forgiven one another your trespasses, even so I, the Lord, forgive you." (D&C 82:1.)

The revelation also established what came to be known as a central board of control "to manage the affairs of the poor, and all things pertaining to the bishopric both in the land of Zion and in the land of Shinehah [Kirtland]." (V. 12.) The effect of this organizational change was to divest Bishop Partridge of the absolute control he had theretofore exerted over welfare matters in the land of Zion; it also increased the prominence in Zion of two of the scribes and witnesses to the Book of Mormon, Oliver Cowdery and Martin Harris.

The revelation then went on to enunciate the principles vital to the success of the cooperative kind of living the Prophet had advocated: "And you are to be equal, or in other words, you are to have equal claims on the properties, for the benefit of managing the concerns of your stewardships, every man according to his wants and his needs, inasmuch as his wants are just—And all this for the benefit of the church of the living God, that every man may improve upon his talent, that every man may gain other talents, yea, even an hundred fold, to be cast into the Lord's storehouse, to become the common property of the whole church." (Vv. 17-18.)

Concurrent with the creation of the central board of control, the Prophet and his associates brought into existence a single firm to control the mercantile activities of the Church in Zion and Kirtland. Each branch of the firm was to operate under a separate name: in Zion, as Gilbert, Whitney and Company, and in Kirtland, as Newel K. Whitney and Company. (CHC 1:285.)

To provide adequate operating capital for the firm, the council authorized it to negotiate a loan of up to $15,000 with 6% annual interest. The firm of Newel K. Whitney and Company was directed to negotiate this loan.

Other major business transacted by the general council related to the Church press. Because of lack of funds and supplies, the first edition of the Book of Commandments was reduced from 10,000 to 3,000 copies. Also, W. W. Phelps was directed to correct and publish the selection of hymns that had been collected by Emma Smith. Furthermore, the Prophet gave necessary directions about the forthcoming publication of the Church's first periodical, the *Evening and Morning Star,* to be edited by W. W. Phelps and Oliver Cowdery and printed on the Church's press at Independence.

The first issue of this publication came off the press just a few months after the Prophet and his party returned to Kirtland. Upon receiving it Joseph reflected about it in his journal:

"In July we received the first number of *The Evening and Morning Star,* which was a joyous treat to the Saints. Delightful, indeed, was it to contemplate that the little band of brethren had become so large, and grown so strong, in so short a time as to be able to issue a paper of their own, which contained not only some of the revelations, but other information also,—which would gratify and enlighten the humble inquiries after truth.

"So embittered was the public mind against the truth, that the press universally had been arrayed against us; and although many newspapers published the prospectus of our paper, yet it appeared to have been done more to calumniate the editor, than give publicity to the forthcoming periodical. Editors thought to do us harm, while the Saints rejoiced that they could do nothing against the truth but for it." (HC 1:273.)

In the establishment of this periodical, the Prophet recognized the power of the written word and the need for an official organ through which the Saints could be given uniform instructions and by which the aims and doctrines of the Church could be accurately represented to the world. The power and effectiveness of the *Star* was attested to only a year after the publication of its first issue when enemies of the Church, incensed by a misinterpretation of an article that appeared in it, burned the print shop and scattered the type.

On the return trip to Kirtland, the Prophet reflected with some satisfaction upon the solid achievements of his few weeks in Independence. His position of unquestioned leadership in the Church in Zion had been reaffirmed. Troublesome enmities between some of the leading disciples had been resolved. The organization to care for the needs of the poor who were flocking to Zion had been broadened and strengthened. A commercial arm of the Church had been established, and arrangements had been made to print the Book of Commandments and a hymnbook and to commence the publication of an official organ of the Church.

More significant, perhaps, than all of these achievements was the fact that the chief responsibility for carrying them on had been vested in others. Joseph was never one to become involved in the complicated details of the great enterprises he set in motion.

Rather, he was prone to delegate extensively to others while retaining the ultimate authority in his own hands. He was the initiator and motivator, the final arbiter of what was or was not to be done. To an extent, therefore, everyone in the Church became instruments through whom his will and designs were executed. Yet, in all this, there was no sense of authoritarianism in his leadership, nor was there a tendency on his part to aggrandize himself. Each member seemed imbued with the desire to excel in the management of his own stewardship, exercising a high degree of independence and imagination.

Underlying all this, however, was the recognition by the Prophet and his followers that the earthly organization of the Church was, in fact, controlled and directed from beyond the veil and that its actual head was Jesus Christ, whose name it bore. Joseph, therefore, was merely regarded as an agent of the Savior, just as the members were agents of the Savior, albeit the nature of their respective duties and authority differed. The members of the Church saw themselves collectively as "the body of Christ," with each fulfilling a vital and indispensable role. This "body" was made up of many interdependent parts, the loss of any one of which greatly impaired the efficient and healthful functioning of the whole.

While the Prophet's party was en route to Kirtland, Newel K. Whitney suffered a painful injury when he jumped from a stage being pulled at full speed by frightened horses. His foot caught in the wheel as he jumped, throwing him violently to the ground. In the process, his leg and foot were broken in several places. While Sidney Rigdon went on alone to Kirtland, Joseph stayed to nurse and to care for Newel. During this time, the Prophet was almost fatally poisoned. "While at this place," he later wrote, "I frequently walked out in the woods, where I saw several fresh graves; and one day when I rose from the dinner table, I walked directly to the door and commenced vomiting most profusely. . . . so great were the muscular contortions of my system, that my jaw in a few moments was dislocated. This I succeeded in replacing with my own hands, and made my way to Brother Whitney (who was on the bed), as speedily as possible; he laid his hands on me and administered to me in the name of the Lord, and I was healed in an instant, although the effect of the poison was so powerful, as to cause much of the hair to become loosened from my head.

Thanks be to my Heavenly Father for His interference in my behalf at this critical moment. . . ." (HC 1:271.)

The combination of spiritual fervor, sincerity, and simple faith that characterized the Prophet are clearly evident in this brief account. It is interesting to note that when faced with a grave crisis involving a question of life or death, he turned instinctively to God for assistance. Nor was it sufficient for him merely to implore God in his own behalf. Instead, he went to his ailing companion "as speedily as possible" to seek a blessing at his hands. It is significant also that his companion knew immediately what was expected of him and, without any hesitancy or coaching, proceeded to bless the Prophet authoritatively "in the name of the Lord." It is one thing to express faith and confidence in God and to expound the principles he has given to men in the scriptures. It is quite another thing to speak and to act in his name as an authorized agent, exercising Godly power. Yet this is precisely what Newel K. Whitney did, believing full well that God, through priesthood delegation, had invested him with that power.

Chapter Thirteen

Growth of the New Church

By the time the Prophet arrived back in Kirtland, the bitter spirit of hostility and persecution that had produced the mobbing at Hiram had largely dissipated. This made it possible for him to resume the task of revising the scriptures. Using a variety of scribes, but most frequently Sidney Rigdon, he remained at this precise and demanding task most of the summer.

As autumn approached, some of the missionaries who had been sent to proselyte in the eastern United States began returning to Kirtland and presenting "the histories of their several stewardships in the Lord's vineyard." (HC 1:286.) On the whole, these brethren reported a phenomenal degree of success in their labors. Many branches had been organized and the new converts were reportedly imbued with a great desire to share the message with others and ultimately to gather with the Saints either in Kirtland or Independence. The harvest of converts at this time was one of the most fruitful of any comparable period in terms of the impact the converts had upon the history of the Church. This harvest included Brigham Young, who later became a member of the first Quorum of Twelve Apostles and the second president of the Church, succeeding Joseph; George Albert Smith, a son of John Smith and the Prophet's first cousin, who years later became an apostle and a member of the First Presidency; Heber C. Kimball, who became one of the original members of the Twelve and a long-time confidant and counselor to his cousin, Brigham Young; and Joseph Young, Brigham's older brother, who later served as the presiding officer of the First Council of the Seventy. In time these men began to assume positions of importance in the Church, overshadowing some of the earlier converts who, for the moment, were in the forefront, including such men as Sidney Rigdon, Oliver Cowdery, and David Whitmer, who gradually faded into the background or apostatized. The eclipse of these early leaders demonstrated the inconstant nature of many men, a fact with which the Prophet was to become intimately acquainted as he saw first one and then another of his most trusted aides turn away from him in times of stress or difficulty. While imprisoned in the Liberty, Missouri, jail many years later, he wrote:

"Behold, there are many called, but few are chosen. And why are they not chosen? Because their hearts are set so much upon the things of this world, and aspire to the honors of men, that they do not learn this one lesson—That the rights of the priesthood are inseparably connected with the powers of heaven, and that the powers of heaven cannot be controlled nor handled only upon the principles of righteousness."

Continuing, he observed: "We have learned by sad experience that it is the nature and disposition of almost all men, as soon as they get a little authority, as they suppose, they will immediately begin to exercise unrighteous dominion. Hence many are called, but few are chosen." (D&C 121:34-36, 39-40.)

During September 1832 the Prophet received a significant revelation that elaborated on the role and function of the Aaronic and Melchizedek priesthoods. To him who receives both of these priesthoods and who magnifies his callings therein, the revelation holds out this awesome prospect: " . . . all that my Father hath shall be given unto him." (D&C 84:34.) Stated in theological terms, this means that those who satisfy these criteria will become joint heirs with Christ, to share fully with him all that the Father has. This concept, added to the fast-growing arsenal of new ideas and doctrines expounded by the Prophet, provided fresh incentives for the Saints in their vigorous quest for perfection.

In the early fall the Prophet, accompanied by Bishop Newel K. Whitney, made a hurried trip to Albany, New York City, and Boston to negotiate loans persuant to the decision reached at the general council in Independence. Not only was this trip successful in providing funds for the Church's ecclesiastical and commercial activities, but it also broadened the scope of the Prophet's vision and understanding. This was his first trip to the financial and cultural centers of the United States, and not only was he able to see the marvelous fruits of industry and commerce, but he was also able to compare himself with men of education, means, and worldly achievement. A letter he wrote to Emma while he was in New York City provides a revealing insight into his reactions to this exposure:

"This day I have been walking through the most splendid part of the city of New York. The buildings are truly great and wonderful to the astonishment of every beholder, and the language of my heart is like this. Can the great God of all the earth, maker of all things magnificent and splendid, be displeased with man for all these great inventions sought out by them? My answer is no it can not be, seeing these great works are calculated to make men comfortable, wise, and happy, therefore not for these works can the Lord be displeased. Only against man is the anger of the Lord kindled because they give him not the Glory. Therefore their iniquities shall be visited upon their heads and their works shall be burned up with unquenchable fire. . . .

"Oh how long, O Lord, shall this order of things exist and darkness cover the people. After beholding all that I had any desire to behold I returned to my room to meditate and calm my mind and behold, the thoughtful home of Emma and Julia rushes upon my mind like a flood and I could wish for a moment to be with them. My breast so fills with all the feelings and tenderness of a parent and husband, and could I be with you I would tell you many things. Yet when I set foot upon this great city like Ninevah . . . my bowels are filled with compassion towards them. . . .

"I prefer reading and praying and holding communion with the holy Spirit and writing to you than walking the streets and beholding the distractions of men. . . ."

Absent from this letter, which he signed "Your affectionate husband until death," are all the trivia and banalities one might expect in the letter of a twenty-seven-year-old visiting the big city for the first time. Rather than talking about buildings, personalities, vehicles, shops, industry, or entertainment, he dwells on God and his relationship to men. One must not wrongly infer from this, however, that Joseph was aloof or stuffy. Among his family and friends he was cheery and outgoing. But there was always an undertone of sincerity and of seriousness, as is clearly evident in this letter.

The Prophet's tender references to Emma and Julia, the surviving twin, take on new meaning when it is known that at the time Emma was in the last stages of pregnancy. Just before the Prophet returned from his trip she gave birth to their fourth child, Joseph Smith III. After the anguish of losing three children at birth, along with the male twin who died following the mobbing at Hiram, young Joseph came as a great joy to his parents. At the same time, his arrival imposed greater burdens on them, especially Emma, who now had two babies to care for and who was almost camping out until Joseph could arrange for suitable and permanent housing for his family. Within a short while he was able to acquire a house for them, though we find little reference in his journal to this significant event. He was so preoccupied with the burdens of giving direction to the fast-growing church and of counseling his brethren about the myriad of problems facing them that he seemed to have little time for his own personal affairs. Yet this preoccupation should not be misinterpreted as representing a lack of concern or love for his own family, as the intimate letter to Emma demonstrates.

During the latter part of 1832 the Prophet received many discouraging reports from Missouri. Because of their lack of experience in administering the affairs of the Church and because of the lack of means and the rapid influx of new converts, the leaders there were experiencing difficulties in allocating stewardships and in making provision for all. Under date of November 27, 1832, Joseph wrote to William W. Phelps in Independence, unburdening himself of strong feelings he had about the situation there. Since the letter states that some of the views expressed in it had been given to him "by a vision from heaven," a segment of it was later adopted as part of the Doctrine and Covenants. After the usual courtesies and preliminaries, the Prophet wrote:

". . . I have many things which I wish to communicate . . . which are lying with great weight on my mind. . . .

"Brother William, in the love of God, having the most implicit confidence in you as a man of God, having obtained this confidence by a vision of heaven, therefore I will proceed to unfold to you some of the feelings of my heart, and to answer the question.

"Firstly, it is the duty of the Lord's clerk, whom He has appointed, to keep a history, and a General Church Record of all things that transpire in Zion, and of all those who consecrate properties and receive inheritances legally from the Bishop; and also the manner of life, their faith, and works and also of the apostates who apostatize after receiving their inheritances. It is contrary to the will and commandment of God, that those who receive not their inheritance by consecration . . . should have their names enrolled with the people of God; neither is their genealogy to be kept, or to be had where it may be found on any of the records or history of the Church; their names shall not be found neither the names of the fathers, nor the names of the children written in the book of the law of God, saith the Lord of hosts. Yea, thus saith the still small voice, which whispereth through and pierceth all things, . . . all they who are not found written in the book of remembrance, shall find none inheritance in that day but they shall be cut asunder, and their portion shall be appointed them among unbelievers, where are wailing and gnashing of teeth. These things I say not of myself; therefore, as the Lord speaketh, He will also fulfil. And they who are of the High Priesthood, whose names are not found written in the book of the law, or that are found to have apostatized, or to have been cut off from the Church; as well as the lesser Priesthood, or the members, in that day, shall not find an inheritance among the Saints of the Most High. . . .

"Now, Brother William, if what I have said is true, how careful men ought to be what they do in the last days, lest they are cut short of their expectations, and they that think they stand should fall, because they keep not the Lord's commandments; whilst you, who do the will of the Lord and keep His commandments, have need to rejoice with unspeakable joy, for such shall be exalted very high, and shall be lifted up in triumph above all the kingdoms of this world. . . ." (HC 1:297-99.)

As the year 1832 drew to a close, the Prophet received two unusual and contrasting revelations within a period of three days. The first one, received on Christmas day, was a somber prediction about a devastating and bloody war that was to afflict the United States and that was to "terminate in the death and misery of many souls." (D&C 87:1.) The second (D&C 88), received on December 27, was designated by the Prophet as the Olive Leaf. In transmitting a copy of this revelation to William W. Phelps in January, Joseph alluded to it as "the Lord's message of peace to us" which he had "plucked from the Tree of Paradise." (HC 1:316.) The kaleidoscopic quality of the Prophet's mind is shown no more clearly than by a study of these revelations dealing with war and peace.

The first was undoubtedly prompted by a political crisis that arose in the United States in 1832 as a result of the protective tariff law passed by Congress in 1828. Additional import duties imposed under that law in 1832 produced a violent reaction among residents of the agrarian southern states, who had little industry and who were almost wholly dependent upon the import of manufactured goods to sustain their economy. In the forefront of the bitter opposition to this measure was South Carolina, whose state convention declared the additional duties unconstitutional and asserted that any attempt to enforce them would be resisted by arms or by secession from the Union. Accounts of this crisis filled the press of the day and the subject was a favorite topic of conversation during the Prophet's trip to New York in October.

While meditating upon this grave crisis on Christmas day, Joseph received one of the most startling and specific revelations of his career. It predicted that the "rebellion of South Carolina" would be the beginning of a series of wars that would be "poured out upon all nations." It dwelt in some detail upon a war between the northern states and the southern states who, it was foretold, would call on another nation, "even the nation of Great Britain, as it is called, and they shall also call upon other nations, in order to defend themselves against other nations; and then war shall be poured out upon all nations." It also revealed that "after many days, slaves shall rise up against their masters, who shall be marshaled and disciplined for war." Then the revelation figuratively erupts into a description about the terror and destruction of war: "And thus, with the sword and by bloodshed the inhabitants of the earth shall mourn; and with famine, and plague, and earthquake, and the thunder of heaven, and the fierce and vivid lightning also, shall the inhabitants of the earth be made to feel the wrath, and indignation, and chastening hand of an Almighty God, until the consumption decreed hath made a full end of all nations." (D&C 87:3-6.)

The historical facts of the Civil War and the subsequent involvement of Great Britain dramatically attest to the prophetic nature of this revelation. Neither can its luster be dimmed by critics who argue that the rebellion alluded to was the rebellion of 1832, not the one that commenced at Fort Sumter, or who may infer some deceitfulness from the fact that the revelation was not published until 1852, twenty years after it was received. The fact remains that the Civil War did commence with the rebellion of South Carolina, and that the commencement of that war occurred some eight years after the revelation was published and twenty-eight years after the Prophet first received it.

When the Olive Leaf was received two days later, there was no hint of the gloomy, pessimistic spirit that seemed to pervade the Prophet's thinking on Christmas day. Now instead of dwelling upon the terror of war and the cataclysmic events the world was to face before the end, his mind was turned toward eternal things and great philosophical concepts. The revelation affirmed the eternal nature of the soul and the universality of the resurrection. It also affirmed the governance of law in the universe, the limitlessness of space and God's creations, and the indestructability of matter. It acknowledged the influence of God throughout the universe by means of His Holy Spirit, thus differentiating between God the person and the influence and power of God. Most importantly, perhaps, the revelation dwelled upon the gradations which would exist in the hereafter and the conditions to be met by those who aspired to the highest of those grades, the celestial kingdom. Those who hoped to attain that kingdom were admonished to seek "diligently and teach one another words of wisdom" and to seek learning "out of the best books." They were told to cease from all "light speeches," laughter, lustful desires, pride, lightmindedness, and wicked doings. They were admonished to love one another and to share. Finally they were enjoined: "Cease to be idle; cease to be unclean; cease to find fault one with another; cease to sleep longer than is needful; retire to thy bed early, that ye may not be weary; arise early, that your bodies and your minds may be invigorated. And above all things, clothe yourselves with the bond of charity, as with a mantle, which is the bond of perfectness and peace. Pray always, that ye may not faint, until I come." (See D&C 88:118-26.)

In early 1833 the Prophet's mind turned to a serious problem that had developed within the ranks in Missouri. Correspondence from some of the leaders there, especially W. W. Phelps and Sidney Gilbert, betrayed a spirit of cynicism and defection that greatly troubled Joseph. If the leaders in Zion reacted in this way, he thought, then what attitudes were developing among the lay members? Determined to head off any incipient rebellion among the brethren, the Prophet wrote a blunt letter to Phelps, telling him to change. "Our hearts are greatly grieved," he wrote, "at the spirit which is breathed both in your letter and that of Brother Gilbert's, the very spirit which is wasting the strength of Zion like a pestilence; and if it is not detected and driven from you, it will ripen Zion for the threatened judgments of God. . . . Brother, suffer us to speak plainly, for God has respect to the feelings of His Saints, and He will not suffer them to be tantalized with impunity. Tell Brother Gilbert that low insinuations God hates; but He rejoices in an honest heart, and knows better who is guilty than he does. We send him this warning voice, and let him fear greatly for himself, lest a worse thing overtake him."

In a postscript, the Prophet added this word of admonition: "It is vain to try to hide a bad spirit from the eyes of them who are spiritual, for it will show itself in speaking and in writing, as well as in all our other conduct. It is also needless to make great pretensions when the heart is not right; the Lord will expose it to the view of His faithful Saints."

As if this were not enough to bring Brother Phelps to a recognition of his failings, the Prophet concluded with this criticism: "We wish you to render the *Star* as interesting as possible, by setting forth the rise, progress, and faith of the Church, as well as the doctrine; for if you do not render it more interesting than at present, it will fall, and the Church suffer a great loss thereby." (HC 1:317.)

In order to add strength to this stinging rebuke, the Prophet caused to have written on the same day an epistle to "the Bishop, his Council and the Inhabitants of Zion" representing the decision of a conference of twelve high priests held in Kirtland, which reemphasized and elaborated on what the letter to Brother Phelps had said: "Brother Gilbert's letter . . . has been received and read attentively, and the low, dark, and blind insinuations, which were in it, were not received by us as from the fountain of light, though his claims and pretensions to holiness were great. . . . We are aware that Brother Gilbert is doing much, and has a multitude of business on hand; but let him purge out all the old leaven, and do his business in the spirit of the Lord, and then the Lord will bless him, otherwise the frown of the Lord will remain upon him." Continuing in its denunciating tone, the letter said: "Brother Phelps' letter of December 15th is also received and carefully read, and betrays a lightness of spirit that ill becomes a man placed in the important and responsible station that he is placed in." (HC 1:319.)

The last paragraph of this same letter noted in passing that "the School of the Prophets will commence, if the Lord will, in two or three days." This signaled an undertaking that hardly has a parallel in modern ecclesiastical history. As the name implies, the school represented a deliberate effort on the part of its members to cultivate and develop their spiritual powers. This was done both through study and through a practical application of the principles of spirituality. This discipline, commenced by the Prophet, has continued among the leadership of the Church to this present day, although the format of the meetings has changed over the years and the name of the school has not always been used.

Within a few days after the school was commenced, a spiritual phenomenon of the most unusual nature occurred. It represented the first occasion on which the gift of tongues was exercised by the Prophet. Fourteen leaders of the Church and a number of other members were assembled in conference at Kirtland. "I spoke to the conference in another tongue," recorded the Prophet, "and was followed in the same gift by Brother Zebedee Coltrin, and he by Brother William Smith, after which the Lord poured out His Spirit in a miraculous manner, until all the Elders spake in tongues, and several members, both male and female, exercised the same gift. Great and glorious were the divine manifestations of the Holy Spirit. Praises were sung to God and the Lamb; speaking and praying, all in tongues, occupied the conference until a late hour at night, so rejoiced were we at the return of these long absent blessings." (HC 1:323.)

This unusual spiritual phenomenon continued on the following day, where there was "much speaking, singing, praying, and praising God, all in tongues." Then followed the ancient but seldom performed ordinance of the washing of feet, which was instituted by the Savior during his earthly ministry. The Prophet recorded the event in these words: "Each Elder washed his own feet first, after which I girded myself with a towel and washed the feet of all of them, wiping them with the towel with which I was girded."

This signal day was concluded by partaking of the Lord's supper, with the emblems of the bread and wine blessed by the Prophet and then passed to those in attendance.

Such occasions of high spiritual excitement did more than almost anything else to spread a spirit of enthusiasm and commitment throughout the entire church. Those who were present related to others the circumstances of these spiritual outpourings, and they, in turn, repeated the story. And so the news spread like wildfire. As would be expected, there were some exaggerations and some unintended misrepresentations. Some inferred that the speaking in tongues was the kind of wild, undisciplined, and pointless gibberish that the Prophet had previously condemned and which, in the future, he was to condemn again and again. Taking license from this unfounded inference, some members commenced to revert to their old sectarian ways and to engage in shoutings and bodily contortions in church meetings. This unfortunate development later caused the Prophet to be exceedingly cautious in exercising the gift of tongues. But many who were close to the Prophet came under the influence of this gift and used it intermittently throughout their lives—although frequently it was manifested only in small, intimate groups. Eliza R. Snow, for example, who conducted a school in Nauvoo attended by Joseph's children, was blessed with this gift throughout her life. But when it was manifested, it was done to convey a message of warning or of blessing or to provide a spiritual uplift.

The Prophet completed his revision of the New Testament on February 2, 1833. An entry under that date revealed that he had "sealed it up, no more to be opened till it arrived in Zion." (D&C 1:324.) The destruction of the press in Zion a few months later, and the hectic condition of the Church leader's life thereafter, prevented him from publishing an approved, verified version of this work during his lifetime.

Chapter Fourteen

The Prophet
as Adminstrator

With the completion of the monumental work of revising the New Testament, Joseph turned his energies to more mundane activities. During the next few months, he devoted considerable time to planning the City of Zion. An elaborate plat was prepared and forwarded to the brethren in Zion in June 1833. The spirit of mobocracy that erupted in Independence during the following months, and which continued almost unabated for several years, prevented the Saints from using this enlightened city plan in Missouri to any great extent. However, the basic plan was used in the development of Nauvoo, and later, when the Mormons were driven west, it was used for hundreds of communities established in the Rocky Mountains from Mexico to Canada. A description that accompanied the plat enables one easily to identify it with cities like Salt Lake, Provo, Ogden, and Logan, Utah, and Mesa, Arizona:

"The city plat is one mile square, divided into blocks containing ten acres each. . . . The streets will be eight rods wide, intersecting each other at right angles. The center tier of blocks forty by sixty rods will be reserved for public buildings, temples, tabernacles, school houses, etc.

"All the other blocks will be divided into half acre lots, a four rod front to every lot, and extending back twenty rods. . . . All of the houses are to be built of brick or stone; and but one house on a lot, which is to stand twenty five feet back from the street, the space in front being for lawns, ornamental trees, shrubbery, or flowers according to the taste of the owners; the rest of the lot will be for gardens, etc."

The far-seeing, practical, and civic-minded nature of the Prophet's plan is further revealed by these provisions:

"Lands on the north and south of the city will be laid off for barns or stables in the city among the homes of the people.

"Lands for agriculturalists sufficient for the whole plat are also to be laid off on the north and south of the city plat, but if sufficient land cannot be laid off without going too great a distance, then farms are to be laid off on the east and west also; but the tiller of the soil as well as the merchant and the mechanic will live in the city. The farmer and his family, therefore, will enjoy all the advantages of schools, public lectures and other meetings. His home will no longer be isolated, and his family denied the benefits of society, which has been, and always will be, the great educator of the human race; but they will enjoy the same privileges of society, and can surround their homes with the same intellectual life, the same social refinement as will be found in the home of the merchant or banker or professional man." (CHC 1:311-12.)

The Prophet made it clear that it was never intended that this would be the plan for a single city; rather, it was intended to be the prototype of the kind of city that would fill up the earth in the latter days. "When this square is thus laid off and supplied," he wrote, "lay off another in the same way, . . . and so fill up the world in these last days, and let every man live in the city, for this is the city of Zion." (CHC 1:312.)

A principal feature of the city of Zion was to be the temple, a subject with which the Prophet's mind was preoccupied during the early part of 1833. It was during this period that his attention was drawn to the subject of a temple to be constructed in Kirtland. As he considered the matter and wrestled in prayer about it, he was led to take concrete steps toward that end by appointing a building committee comprised of Hyrum Smith, Reynolds Cahoon, and Jared Carter. Under date of June 1, 1833, this committee directed a circular letter to all the churches, inviting subscription toward the construction of the Kirtland Temple. (HC 1:349.)

On the same date the Prophet received a revelation that chastised those in the Church who had been negligent in keeping the commandments, that drew a sharp distinction between those who had been "called" and those who were "chosen," and that gave explicit instructions about the construction of the temple. "Now here is wisdom," the revelation said, "and the mind of the Lord; let the house be built, not after the manner of the world, for I give not unto you that ye shall live after the manner of the world; Therefore let it be built after the manner which I shall show unto three of you, whom ye shall appoint and ordain unto this power. And the size thereof shall be fifty and five feet in width, and let it be sixty-five feet in length, in the inner court thereof.

And let the lower part of the inner court be dedicated unto me for your sacrament offering, and for your preaching, and your fasting, and your praying, and the offering up of your most holy desires unto me, saith your Lord. And let the higher part of the inner court be dedicated unto me for the school of mine apostles, saith . . . Jesus Christ your Lord." (D&C 95:13-17.)

Thus was undertaken the first major building effort on the part of the Church, an effort that was to culminate less than three years later amid one of the most dramatic spiritual outpourings ever experienced. The temple was constructed almost entirely with volunteer labor and donated materials, establishing a pattern of cooperative building that was followed by the Saints for many years and that extended not only to the construction of temples and chapels, but also to public buildings and private dwellings. As the economy has become more diversified and complex, the practice of donating labor and materials has been supplanted largely by the donation of money, but the same dedication and liberality that characterized those who built the Kirtland Temple is evident among the members of the Church at this writing. To a great extent, the same kind of organizational structure used to build that temple, directed by a building committee, is used now in constructing church buildings.

Two significant events that occurred in the life of the Prophet during the first half of 1833 were to have a vital, lasting effect on the Church. The first was the receipt of the revelation known as the Word of Wisdom; the second was the organization of the highest governing body of the Church, the First Presidency.

The Word of Wisdom, received on February 27, 1833, embodies a comprehensive code of health, representing another significant step in extending the influence of the Church into every phase of the lives of its members. The object of all this was to produce a community of perfect, "celestial" beings, since the health of the body has a direct if not a controlling effect upon the health and vitality of the spirit.

What commenced as a sound code of health, not given by way of "commandment" or "constraint," later took on a new and different role. In a country where alcohol and tobacco were used extensively, the abstainer was marked as being different or peculiar, especially when it was learned that his abstinence was based upon a revelation from God. Thus the Word of Wisdom quite soon readily identified members of the Church and set them apart from their fellows. Within the Church, it also became a means of recognizing those who were wholeheartedly committed to its principles. In time it produced a powerful cohesive force among the membership not unlike that produced among the Jews as a result of their much stricter, more comprehensive dietary laws. More to the point, however, it helped to produce, in time, a society of people noted for long lives, general good health, confident optimism, and ability to endure hardship and persecution.

Prior to March 1833 the organization of the Church had been rudimentary in character. Until then, all authority and responsibility had been vested in the Prophet, who, subject to the principle of common consent, had been empowered to act alone in all matters pertaining to church government. It is true that Edward Partridge and Newel K. Whitney had been called as bishops, and the governing board previously mentioned had been formed to set policy in local temporal affairs. But at the general church level, the Prophet stood alone in giving direction to the entire church in matters both temporal and spiritual. Of course, he often sought counsel of others, but these counselors held no official position.

This condition was changed on March 8, 1833, when the Prophet received a revelation that brought into being the highest governing quorum of the Church, the First Presidency. After affirming Joseph's position as the ultimate earthly authority of the Church, holding the "keys," the revelation provided: "And again, verily I say unto thy brethren, Sidney Rigdon, and Frederick G. Williams, their sins are forgiven them also, and they are accounted as equal with thee in holding the keys of this last kingdom; As also through your administration the keys of the school of the prophets, which I have commanded to be organized; That thereby they may be perfected in their ministry for the salvation of Zion. . . ." (D&C 90:6-8.) Then followed a general charge to the First Presidency and a description of the scope and purpose of their ministry: "And now, verily I say unto you, I give unto you a commandment that you continue in the ministry and presidency. And when you have finished the translation of the prophets, you shall from thenceforth preside over the affairs of the church and the school; And from time to time, as shall be manifested by the Comforter, receive revelations to unfold the mysteries of the kingdom; And set in order the churches, and study and learn, and become acquainted with all good books, and with languages, tongues, and people. And this shall be your business and mission in all your lives, to preside in council, and set in order all the affairs of this church and kingdom." (D&C 90:12-16.)

Ten days later the Prophet completed the organization of the First Presidency by ordaining Sidney Rigdon and Frederick G. Williams as his counselors, positions to which they had been called by revelation. (HC 1:334.)

This incident reveals clearly the pragmatic nature of Joseph's leadership and of the organization he headed. Innovation and change were dictated by the needs of the moment. Like a vibrant, living organism, the Church acquired new parts and capabilities as it grew toward maturity. Two years later, the second governing body, the Quorum of Twelve Apostles, was added. Subsequently the seventies came into being, and during the tenure of some of Joseph's successors, other church offices were created as the needs required. But need was not the only criterion justifying these additions; they were and are made only after diligent prayer and as a result of revelation.

With the addition of two able men to help shoulder the ever-increasing burden of church administration, Joseph was freed somewhat to devote himself to the higher aspects of the work: to regulate and set in order all the affairs of the Church, to counsel, and to broaden the scope of his understanding.

The formation of the First Presidency also accelerated an unfortunate process that had commenced some time before. Oliver Cowdery and David Whitmer, who were caught up in the complicated web of Missouri affairs, saw in this change a further decline in their status and influence. These early confidants of the Prophet, who had shared some of his most sacred and important experiences, now felt ostracized, not only by the long distance that separated Kirtland and Independence, but also by what they considered to be an organizational gulf between them and their leader. As they fed on these and other imagined slights or provocations, they became more and more out of harmony with the Prophet and other leaders of the Church.

Had a conspiracy of some kind existed between the Prophet and these associates, as some critics are wont to assume, this likely would have been the point at which a scandalous rupture would have occurred. With their exclusion from the now formalized governing body of the Church, these men, had they been conspirators, would have seen the fruits of the conspiracy, whether money, power, or notoriety, slipping away from them. In that event, it would have been logical for them to have exposed the Prophet, to have attempted to wrest leadership of the Church from him, or to have bolted the Church and to set up a rival organization. None of these alternatives occurred. Instead, they continued their membership, for the time being at least, and nursed their hurt feelings at having been passed over.

Not long after the First Presidency was organized, the first apostate of any consequence appeared on the scene in the person of "Doctor" Philastus Hurlburt. This man, who was later to prove to be such a nemesis to the Church, was not a medical doctor. His title derived from his being the seventh son in his father's family and from "the old folk-lore superstition that the seventh son would possess supernatural qualities that would make him a physician." He had had a checkered career before joining the Mormons, having been previously excluded from the Methodist Church for immoralities. He was described by one of his contemporaries as being a man of fine physique, very pompous, good looking, and very ambitious, with some energy, though of poor education." (HC 1:355.)

Ordained an elder on March 18, 1833, the same day on which Sidney Rigdon and Frederick G. Williams were set apart as counselors in the First Presidency, he was excommunicated on June 3, 1833, for "unChristian conduct with women, while on a mission to the east." (HC 1:352.) After a rehearing on June 21, he was forgiven and reinstated "because of the liberal confession which he made." (HC 1:354.) However, only two days later, he was again cut off from the Church because of additional corroborating testimony brought against him.

Hurlburt, enraged by the acts of discipline imposed upon him by the Church, immediately took it in his mind to retaliate against those who had thus humiliated and offended him. He concluded that the most effective way to get back at the Church was to deliver a crippling blow against its leader, Joseph Smith. So it was that he commenced an insidious campaign to gather information with which to blacken the reputation of the Prophet and to impugn his character and motives. What Hurlburt lacked in integrity and veracity, he compensated for in diligence and single mindedness. He set about to interview former acquaintances of the Prophet and his family in various areas where they had lived. If he could not find those who had been personally acquainted with the Smiths, he was content to find those who had heard about them. He deliberately ignored friends of the Smiths or those who had anything good to say about them, and concentrated strictly upon their enemies and detractors. From roughly a hundred of these, he obtained so-called affidavits, all of which supported his preconceived notion that the Prophet was a fraud and charlatan. These affidavits, which all appear to have a common authorship, deal almost exclusively with hearsay and speculative conclusions.

It was during his activities in seeking out the critics of the Prophet that Hurlburt heard rumor that the Book of Mormon was a plagiarism of what has since been known as the Spaulding manuscript. According to these rumors, the Prophet had come into the possession of an old manuscript written by a man named Solomon Spaulding, which reportedly contained an account of the origin of the American Indians and the migration of their ancestors to the American continent many centuries ago. The rumor purported that Joseph had then altered the manuscript in minor details, had invented the story of the Angel Moroni, and had either conspired with the eleven witnesses or duped them. Hurlburt undertook an eager search for the Spaulding manuscript, even going to the expense of making a trip to Massachusetts to interrogate Spaulding's widow. He was directed by her to eastern New York, where he ultimately found the manuscript in the attic of an old farmhouse. One of the Prophet's most severe critics commented thus on Hurlburt's disappointment in finding this theory to be without foundation: "Now to his bitter chagrin he found that the long chase had been in vain; for while the romance did concern the ancestors of the Indians, its resemblance to the Book of Mormon ended there. None of the names found in one could be identified in the other; the many battles which each described showed not the slightest similarity with those of the other, and Spaulding's prose style, which aped the eighteenth century British sentimental novelists, differed from the style of the Mormon Bible as much as *Pamela, or Virtue Rewarded* differed from the New Testament." (Brodie, p. 144.)

Although the so-called Spaulding theory was exploded almost before it had taken root, it has nevertheless been advanced again and again over the years by enemies or critics of the Prophet who eagerly grasp at anything that offers to explain away Joseph's claim of divine influence in the translation of the Book of Mormon.

As before mentioned, the Hurlburt affidavits were later made available to Eber D. Howe, a local editor, who included them in his book *Mormonism Unvailed* along with the series of critical letters written by Ezra Booth. All of the derogatory books written since that time about the Church or Joseph Smith have been based upon these affidavits and the other anti-Mormon materials gathered by Howe. Most authors whose object it is to attack the Prophet or the Church have accepted these materials at face value and have used them uncritically and as authoritative. It is curious that able people, who in most other things are objective and fair, would place credence in a man like Philastus Hurlburt, an admitted adulterer who was expelled from two religious societies for unchristianlike conduct, in preference to Joseph Smith, the founder and chief leader of a sect whose moral and ethical standards rank among the highest of any known today.

The case of Philastus Hurlburt illustrated a facet of the newly founded church that came into prominence at that time, namely, the use of ecclesiastical sanctions to enforce discipline among its members. The Church had been in existence at that time for approximately three years, and numerous converts had been brought into the fold with an almost unbelievable variety of beliefs and practices. Thus the Prophet and his associates were faced with the gigantic task of molding the membership into a society that was homogenous in its acceptance and observance of fundamental principles. To those who had braved the ridicule and rejection of family and friends to join the unpopular sect, there was nothing more to be feared than to have their fellowship with the Church severed. But when the leaders found a person in violation of these tenets, one who stubbornly refused to repent and conform, they were not at all reluctant to cut him off by means of excommunication or disfellowshipment. A letter from the First Presidency dated July 2, 1833, gives insight into the disciplinary machinery at that time. Writing about the transgressions of a father and son named John and Eden Smith, the First Presidency wrote: "We feel to rebuke the Elders of that branch of the Church of Christ, for not magnifying their office, and letting the transgressor go unpunished. We, therefore, enjoin upon you, to be watchful on your part, and search out iniquity, and put it down wherever it may be found. You will see by this, brethren, that you have authority to sit in council on the Smiths; and if found guilty, to deal with them accordingly." (HC 1:371.)

While this policy of church discipline may seem unduly severe, it becomes more logical and reasonable when viewed in light of the purpose it sought to achieve. Unlike criminal sanctions imposed under civil law, the object of church discipline is not to exact retribution; rather, it is to bring about a reclamation of the transgressor through repentance. Once the trangressor has brought his life back into conformity with the tenets of the Church and has demonstrated over a sufficiently long period of time that the change is genuine, then he is accepted back into full fellowship, as though the transgression had not occurred.

Consequently, in disciplining a transgressor, the object and hope of the Church court is that the sanction imposed will be the means of cleansing the transgressor and rectifying his breach of the rules, thus making it possible for him to live at peace with himself and within the society of the Church.

Chapter Fifteen

Storm Clouds Over the Missouri Saints

The internal troubles faced by Joseph Smith in Kirtland in 1833 were inconsequential when compared with the external troubles confronting the Saints in Missouri. Pressures had been building up there that were soon to explode into mobbings, plunder, arson, and rapine. Many of the causes of these difficulties lay in the rapid influx of the Mormons, their distinctive religious beliefs, their aggressive proselyting, and their cohesiveness, which some outsiders interpreted as clannishness. Perhaps more disturbing to the old settlers than almost anything else was the belief of the Latter-day Saints that Missouri was their promised land. This, coupled with the confident, oft-expressed, expectation that the Saints would one day possess the land to the exclusion of all others, created a sense of anxiety and concern. When these ideas were first advanced, the Missourians either ignored them or passed them off as the fantasies of a deluded but harmless cult. But when the Saints' ranks began to swell and when the native settlers discovered that the Saints were intelligent and industrious, were in dead earnest about their religion, and were directed by imaginative and enterprising leaders, they became fearful and began to seek ways to combat these incursions on their security.

Many leaders of non-Mormon sects in the area were in the vanguard of the initial attack on the Church. Especially prominent in his efforts to arouse feelings against the Saints in Independence was a Reverend Pixley. Of him, Newel Knight observed: "[He] did not content himself in slandering us to the people of Jackson county, but also wrote to eastern papers telling horrible lies about us, with the evident intention of rousing a spirit of hatred against us. His talk was of the bitterest kind, his speeches perfectly inflammatory; and he appeared to have an influence among the people to carry them with him in his hellish designs. Nor did he confine his actions to the white settlers, but tried to stir up the Indians against us, and use every means in his power to accomplish his purposes. . . . the public mind became so excited that on the 20th of July a meeting was called and largely attended by not only the rabble of the county, but also the men holding official positions." (HC 1:372.)

The Reverend Pixley wrote a tract entitled "Beware of False Prophets." The lead article in the July 1833 issue of the *Evening and Morning Star* bore the same title and attempted to clarify some of the distortions or falsehoods in the minister's pamphlet, but it was considered by non-Mormons to be an attack on their churches.

A second article appearing in that issue of the *Star* produced an even more violent reaction among the Gentile community. Entitled "Free People of Color," it was intended to warn the Saints against encouraging free blacks to migrate to Missouri; however, in the biased minds of enemies of the Church, it was interpreted to have an opposite meaning. Slave-holders in the area were especially agitated by reports that the Mormons were openly encouraging free blacks to enter the state in violation of Missouri law. Control of their slaves was difficult even under the most favorable circumstances, and they could foresee endless trouble in the morale of their slaves if free blacks were admitted to the community.

Once the false rumor was in circulation that the Mormons were striking at the foundation of their slave economy, it spread like wildfire among the old settlers. Hurried and well-attended meetings were called to discuss how to cope with this new threat to their peace and prosperity. Old grievances and enmities against the Church were exhumed and aired at these meetings, which became progressively more acrimonious and hostile in tone.

Then an ultimatum was issued to the Latter-day Saints that was variously called the "Manifesto," the "Constitution," or "The Secret Constitution." Its authors attempted to give the document an air of legality and respectability by couching it in formal language and by mimicking the phraseology of the Declaration of Independence. For example, it concluded with these words: "We each pledge to each other our bodily powers, our lives, fortunes and sacred honor." Astonishingly enough, the manifesto frankly acknowledged that its object was an illegal one. It bluntly said, ". . . the arm of the civil law does not afford us a guarantee, or at least a sufficient one, against the evils which are now inflicted upon us, and seem to be increasing." The signatories wrote that they were determined to rid themselves of the society of the Mormons "peaceably if we can, forcibly if we must." They found justification for what they intended to do in "the laws of nature" and "the law of self preservation." The Saints were accused of "tampering" with the slaves of the old settlers and of "endeavoring to sow dissensions and raise sedition among them . . . [by] inviting free negroes and mulattos from other states to become 'Mormons' and remove and settle among us." Finally, the Church and its members were accused of blasphemy because of their belief in modern revelation as well as their teachings that Jackson County was the land of promise and the place where the City of Zion and the great temple of the Saints would be built.

Publication of the so-called Manifesto created a violent reaction among the other non-Mormons at Independence, who rallied to the cause of the mob that had drawn it up and joined with them in demanding the immediate departure of the Saints.

Although the leaders of the Church in Missouri were aware of the unfriendly feelings toward them, they scarcely realized the depth and bitterness of these feelings until the Manifesto was published. Then they acted promptly to try to resolve the difficulties. On July 16, 1833, an extra issue of the *Evening and Morning Star* was published, calling attention to the misinterpretation that had been placed on the article "Free People of Color" and explaining that its intention "was not only to stop free people of color from emigrating to this state, but to prevent them from being admitted as members of the Church." (HC 1:379.)

An objective reading of the *Star* makes it patently clear that the Church was trying to deter its members from encouraging free blacks to migrate to Missouri. However, the statement about preventing blacks from joining the Church was inaccurate and merely represented the editor's frightened reaction to the furor his original article had produced. In fact, there were some black members of the Church at that time. No special effort had been made to proselyte them, but neither had an attempt been made to exclude them. Nevertheless, the attitude and policy of the Church toward blacks was at the core of the difficulties the Saints faced in Missouri.

It is a paradox of history that the Church was bitterly attacked in Missouri in the 1830s because of its alleged liberal attitude toward blacks, while today, in the 1970s, it is attacked because of its alleged discriminatory policy toward the blacks. The paradox is all the more striking in view of the fact that the Church policy has remained unchanged over the years. It is the public attitude toward blacks that has altered radically.

The extra issue of the *Star* was an exercise in futility insofar as it was intended to stanch the flow of bitterness toward the Church. The ringleaders of the anti-Mormon faction in Missouri were determined that the unwanted newcomers leave their midst. Four days later a surly, boisterous mob of from three to five hundred persons assembled in Independence and demanded that the Church newspaper be discontinued, that the store be closed, and that all Mormon workers discontinue their labors. When these demands were rejected by the Church leaders, the mob promptly destroyed the press and then proceeded to tar and feather several of the brethren, including Bishop Partridge. It was only the agreement of Sidney Gilbert to close the store that prevented the mob from running totally rampant.

The Saints had no legal or practical recourse against the attacks, since many, if not most, of the civil officials to whom they ordinarily would have appealed were members of the mob. Thus it became necessary for the Saints to submit to all of its demands. On July 23, leaders of the Church entered into a treaty with the mob. Under the treaty's terms, Oliver Cowdery, W. W. Phelps, William M'Lellin, Edward Partridge, Lyman Wight, Simeon Carter, Peter and John Whitmer, and Harvey H. Whitlock agreed to move from the county with their families before the first of the following January. In addition, they agreed to use their influence to persuade the rest of the Saints then in Jackson County to leave, half by the following January and the remainder by the following April, and to use their influence to deter other members from migrating to Missouri. John Corrill and Algernon Sidney Gilbert were allowed to remain as agents of the Church to wind up its affairs, although it was stipulated that the store could purchase no new stock but could only sell the merchandise then on the shelves. Finally, it was agreed that publication of the *Star* would be discontinued.

As soon as the so-called treaty between the mobbers and the Saints had been signed, Oliver Cowdery left for Kirtland to seek counsel from the Prophet and other leaders of the Church. The news he brought jolted the Prophet as had few things. Joseph was greatly concerned about the prospect that the Saints in Missouri would lose their homes, farms, and businesses. And he was even more concerned about the possibility some of them would suffer bodily harm or might even lose their lives. He immediately called a council of the brethren in Kirtland to solicit their views and recommendations. Prayerful man that he was, he also importuned God for spiritual direction. He was fortified by a revelation he had received on August 2 that contained these significant words: ". . . ye shall forsake all evil and cleave unto all good, that ye shall live by every word which proceedeth forth out of the mouth of God. For he will give unto the faithful line upon line, precept upon precept; and I will try you and prove you herewith. And whoso layeth down his life in my cause, for my name's sake, shall find it again, even life eternal. Therefore, be not afraid of your enemies, for I have decreed in my heart . . . that I will prove you in all things, whether you will abide in my covenant, even unto death, that you may be found worthy. For if ye will not abide in my covenant ye are not worthy of me." (D&C 98:11-15.)

It was not, therefore, in a spirit of dejection or defeat that the Prophet appraised the tragic events at Independence.

Shortly after Oliver Cowdery arrived in Kirtland, the Prophet sent Orson Hyde and John Gould to Missouri with advice for the Saints there. The Church members were to exercise restraint and forbearance and, through the normal processes of law, to endeavor to obtain redress for the damages they had suffered.

Since there was little, if anything, the Prophet could do for the Saints in Missouri than had already been done, he turned his attention to the affairs of the Church in Kirtland and elsewhere. If the future of the Saints in Missouri looked bleak and uncertain for the moment, quite the opposite was true in Kirtland. This little community was figuratively bursting with activity and high expectation. The anti-Mormon feeling that had flared into violence not long before had subsided for the moment. On July 23, only three days after the mob action had erupted in Missouri, the Saints in Kirtland laid the cornerstone of the temple there. This had infused them with almost unbounded optimism. The temple was not only the place where they expected to receive great spiritual blessings, but it also represented the first tangible object that was to symbolize the unity and the high purpose of the Church. That purpose was nothing short of absolute perfection—of godhood—for men and women. The temple was to house the School of the Prophets, where the principles leading to perfection or exaltation were to be expounded and where the Saints expected to receive further light and knowledge from heaven.

One of the critical problems that arose out of the Independence episode was the destruction of the Church press. The Prophet was acutely aware of the need for the Church to have a public voice, sharpened by his observance of the almost miraculous results that had followed the publication of the Book of Mormon. Accordingly, he immediately began to make arrangements to acquire another press. On September 11, a council convened in Kirtland and established a new press, which was to publish a periodical called the *Latter-day Saints Messenger and Advocate.* Not long after, representatives were sent east to purchase the press and other necessary equipment.

While the Prophet had considerable ability as an administrator, his real forte was as a teacher and motivator. He was never more content than when he was expounding the principles of the gospel and bearing personal witness of the reality and power of God. It was in this spirit that he, Sidney Rigdon, and Freeman Nickerson undertook a mission to the eastern states and into Canada in October 1833. They held meetings along the way and bore testimony of the truthfulness of the Book of Mormon and the restoration of the gospel. Most impressive to his listeners were Joseph's personal testimony of the appearances to him of divine, resurrected beings and the spiritual manifestations he had experienced through the power of the Holy Ghost.

The Prophet kept a diary of this trip, which reveals something about his character and inner life. On October 6, following a meeting at Springfield, Ohio, he recorded: "Brother Sidney spoke to the people, etc., and in the evening held a meeting at Brother (John) Reed's. Had a great congregation, paid good attention. Oh God, seal our testimony to their hearts." A few days later he recorded a nagging concern he had for his family: "I feel very well in my mind. The Lord is with us, but have much anxiety about my family." This anxiety was removed when that night he received a revelation (D&C 100), which assured him that his family was well and which directed that he and Sidney were to "continue your journey and let your hearts rejoice."

Frequent entries implored God's blessings on him, the work, and his family. On October 13 he noted, "The Lord gave His spirit in marvelous manner for which I am thankful to the God of

Abraham. Lord bless my family and preserve them." A few days later he recorded, "We find that conviction is resting on the minds of some. We hope that great good may yet be done in Canada, which O Lord grant for thy name's sake."

From the standpoint of proselyting success, the highlight of the trip occurred on October 26 when, following a Sunday service, twelve persons were baptized. Of that occasion, the Prophet wrote: "We broke bread, laid on hands for the gift of the Holy Spirit. Had a good meeting, the spirit was given in great power to some and the rest had great peace. May God carry on his work in this place till all shall know him, Amen."

Five days later, the missionaries arrived back in Kirtland after an absence of about a month. In a spirit of gratitude, the Prophet made a final entry about this journey: "Found my family all well according to the promise of the Lord, for which blessing I feel to thank his holy name. Amen." (Diary entries quoted in Dean C. Jessee and William G. Hartley, "Joseph Smith's Missionary Journal," *New Era,* February 1974, pp. 34-36.)

The Prophet's return from Canada coincided almost exactly with the start of the final eruption in Jackson County, Missouri, which ended with the expulsion of the Saints from that place. Not content with the agreement the Saints had previously made to leave after the first of the year, the mob moved on October 31 to expedite their departure. On that night some fifty men, filled with liquor and hatred, attacked a colony of the Saints west of the Big Blue. They tore the roofs off ten homes, beat several of the brethren, and frightened the women and children into fleeing into the surrounding wilderness. While the attack was brutal and terrifying, it was a mere prelude to what happened the next day. A two-pronged attack on that day, apparently preplanned and coordinated, completely demoralized the Saints and destroyed any capability or will they might have had to resist the aggressions of the mob. That night a portion of the mob invaded a prairie settlement of the Saints about twelve miles west of Independence. Almost simultaneously, another segment of the mob commenced an attack on the Saints in Independence, stoning and ransacking houses, strewing furniture and other contents about the street, and driving many from their homes. The following day, those Saints who had not been driven from their homes the night before left hurriedly through fear of further violence.

Some of the brethren went to Esquire Silver on Sunday to attempt to obtain a peace warrant. He refused because of fear of reprisals from the mob. Their efforts to obtain protection from the law having failed, the next day the Saints mustered a group of thirty men armed with seventeen guns. Another group of about one hundred volunteers was organized from among outlying branches of the Church. This contingent was camped outside Independence when word came that the state militia was being sent into the area to protect the Saints in their rights. Relying on these representatives, the members of the Church gave in to demands that they relinquish their arms. Once the mobbers learned the Saints were without weapons, the pressure upon them to leave became even more savage and relentless.

As the situation in Missouri worsened, the pleas to Kirtland for help became more frequent and insistent. The Prophet's heavy responsibilities and commitments in Kirtland made it impossible for him to leave at the moment, so the directions he gave to the Saints in Missouri had to be sent by post or relayed through subordinates. Unavoidable delays in communication and a lack of reliable knowledge about the conditions there heightened the difficulties while reducing the Prophet's capacity to deal with them.

At the same time, concerns had developed about conditions in and around Kirtland. The vigor with which the Saints had commenced building the temple, accelerated plans to build new homes and businesses, and the constant influx of new converts gave rise to grave apprehension among the Gentile community. These evoked threats from enemies there and raised the unpleasant spectre of a forced move from that place also. This dilemma was expressed in a letter from the Prophet to Bishop Partridge at Liberty, Missouri, on December 5, 1833:

"We know not what we shall be called to pass through," it said, "before Zion is delivered and established; therefore, we have great need to live near to God, and always to be in strict obedience to all His commandments, that we may have a conscience void of offense toward God and man. It is your privilege to use every lawful means in your power to seek redress for your grievances from your enemies, and prosecute them to the extent of the law; but it will be impossible for us to render you any temporal assistance, as our means are already exhausted, and we are deeply in debt, and know of no means whereby we shall be able to extricate ourselves.

"The inhabitants of this county threaten our destruction, and we know not how soon they may be permitted to follow the example of the Missourians; but our trust is in God, and we are determined, His grace assisting us, to maintain the cause and hold out faithful unto the end, that we may be crowned with crowns of celestial glory, and enter into the rest that is prepared for the children of God." (HC 1:450.)

But while the Prophet was beset on all sides by great difficulties, he went forward with his work. On the day following the gloomy letter to Bishop Partridge, the new press was dedicated in Kirtland. The expectations of Joseph for this press and the main purpose for which it was established are expressed in his journal entry for December 6, 1833: "Being prepared to commence our labors in the printing business, I ask God in the name of Jesus, to establish it for ever, and cause that His word may speedily go forth to the nations of the earth, to the accomplishing of His great work in bringing about the restoration of the house of Israel." (HC 1:451.)

The sad plight of his people in Missouri kept returning to the Prophet's mind like a bad dream. He was at a loss to understand why they had been so brutally treated and why the plans for the establishment of Zion had been frustrated. In a letter dated December 10, 1833, and addressed to several of the brethren in Zion, he frankly acknowledged his dilemma and his ignorance of what had gone wrong and why. "Now, there are two things of which I am ignorant," he wrote, "and the Lord will not show them to me, perhaps for a wise purpose in Himself—I mean in some respects—and they are these: Why God has suffered so great a calamity to come upon Zion, and what the great moving cause of this great affliction is; and again, by what means He will return her back to her inheritance, with songs of everlasting joy upon her head. These two things, brethren, are in part kept back that they are not plainly shown unto me; but there are some things that are plainly manifest which have incurred the displeasure of the Almighty. . . . I am aware that I ought not to murmur, and do not murmur, only in this, that those who are innocent are compelled to suffer for the iniquities of the guilty; . . . it is with difficulty I can keep from complaining and murmuring against this dispensation; but I am sensible that this is not right, and may God grant that notwithstanding your great afflictions and sufferings, there may not anything separate us from the love of Christ." (HC 1:454.)

The Prophet then repeated the counsel he had consistently given to the Missouri Saints since the outbreak of the difficulties there. ". . . retain your lands," he wrote, "even unto the uttermost, and employ every lawful means to seek redress of your enemies; and pray to God, day and night, to return you in peace and in safety to the lands of your inheritance: and when the judge fail you, appeal unto the executive; and when the executive fail you, appeal unto the president; and when the president fail you, and all laws fail you, and the humanity of the people fail you, and all things else fail you but God alone, and you continue to weary Him with your importunings, as the poor woman did the unjust judge, He will not fail to execute judgment upon your enemies, and to avenge His own elect that cry unto Him day and night." (HC 1:455.)

Finally, the Prophet returned to a theme that appears again and again in his correspondence—the need for a press. Despite the fact that a new press had been set up recently in Kirtland, he urged the brethren in Missouri to establish another one there as soon as possible, in order to disseminate information about the Church and its teachings and to plead before the public the cause of the Saints in the Missouri difficulties. The precise location of the press seemed unimportant to him. While he suggested that it might be established in Liberty, he hastened to add, "God will be willing to have it in any place where it can be established in safety." (HC 1:456.)

Still greatly agitated in his mind about the perils and uncertainties facing his people in Missouri and troubled about the causes that had produced them, Joseph prayed fervently to the Lord for enlightenment and direction. In answer, he received a revelation (D&C 101) on December 16, 1833, which attributed the difficulties in Missouri to the neglect and transgressions of the people. ". . . there were jarrings, and contentions, and envyings, and strifes, and lustful and covetous desires among them; therefore by these things they polluted their inheritances. They were slow to hearken unto the voice of the Lord their God; therefore, the Lord their God is slow to hearken unto their prayers, to answer them in the day of their trouble." The revelation looked beyond the immediate difficulties facing the Saints, to the millennial peace and glory that were to be the reward of those who keep the commandments and do the Lord's bidding: ". . . and all things shall become new that my knowledge and glory may dwell upon all the earth." Then came the promise to those who would survive and overcome all difficulties: "And all they who suffer persecution for my name, and endure in faith, though they are called to lay down their lives for my sake yet shall they partake of all this glory." (D&C 101:6-7, 25, 35.)

Chapter Sixteen

The March
of Zion's Camp

Joseph Smith's brilliant and resourceful mind was seldom at rest. It moved with rapidity from subjects as grave and portentous as the threatened destruction of a humble, God-fearing people on the American frontier to those as simple and commonplace as a leak in the roof of Emma's kitchen. When his mind was on a particular subject, he focused upon it his full attention and energies. He would doggedly cling to that subject until its possibilities had been exhausted; then he would move to something else upon which he would bestow the same kind of relentless concentration.

He faced the year 1834 with some feeling of ambivalence. Viewed from a long-range vantage point, he and the Church had taken giant strides. The Saints were established in two major centers, however tenuously. Emissaries of the Church continued to proselyte aggressively and with great success. Most of the converts were genuinely committed to the principles of the gospel, including the one of gathering, and were loyal and subordinate to the Prophet. As a result, his influence and power were increased almost daily as converts continued to pour into the Kirtland area. Work on the temple was being pushed, a new press had been established, and the sleepy little town of Kirtland had fully come to life and was bustling with activity. Considering all this, he could not help but feel a certain sense of exultation, especially in view of the exciting prospects ahead. After all, the achievements of the Church to this time were but a minor prelude to what was anticipated in the future, for Joseph and his followers confidently believed that theirs was the enviable task of creating a perfect society, suitable for the habitation of the Savior.

But a close range view of the Church gave the Prophet some cause for concern. The most immediate pressing problem was the sad plight of the Saints in Missouri. Until now, he had attempted to resolve the complicated difficulties there through letters or personal couriers. This had proved to be unsatisfactory, however, for the long delays between the dispatch of a letter or messenger and the time of its arrival often made the counsel inapplicable to the changed conditions that had arisen in the interim. What the Saints faced in Missouri was akin to a war, and the Prophet knew that it was not feasible for a general to formulate and execute strategy and deploy his forces from a command post hundreds of miles from the front. Thus there commenced to form in his mind the idea of organizing a para-military force, which he would lead to Missouri to help the embattled Saints. He had come to the reluctant conclusion that the only possible way in which the rights of the Missouri Saints could be protected was by self help. The law enforcement machinery in that state was in the hands of avowed enemies of the Church, and any expectation that the Saints could obtain relief from that source was mere wishful thinking.

But the Missouri crisis was only one of a number of grave concerns facing Joseph Smith at the beginning of 1834. Equally serious was an internal eruption in the Church at Kirtland, brought on by the rebellion of some of the members. With an aggressive proselyting campaign such as the one waged by the Church, it was only natural that converts of every imaginable kind would be brought into the fold, including many complainers and troublemakers.

During January the Prophet met with other leaders in Kirtland to draft a procedure to govern the Church's high council in handling cases of church discipline. Joseph later reviewed and corrected the minutes of that meeting, which were, on February 19, "read three times and unanimously adopted and received for a form and constitution of the High Council of the Church" by a group of sixty-two men convened for this purpose. (HC 2:31. See also D&C 102.)

A number of important cases were heard by the council, including the trial of Martin Harris, who was accused of slanderous statements against the Prophet. When he was brought before the council, Martin "confessed that his mind was darkened, and that he had said many things inadvertently, calculated to wound the feelings of his brethren, and promised to do better." The record of the trial reveals that "the council forgave him, with much good advice." (HC 2:26.) Another important case brought before the council—one that would have far-reaching effects on the Prophet and the Church—was that of Philastus Hurlburt, who, after his excommunication, redoubled his efforts to embarrass and destroy Joseph Smith and the Church through questionable affidavits and theories on the origin of the Book of Mormon. (See Chapter 14.)

It is revealing of the Prophet's character to see how he reacted to the great pressures exerted upon him during this period. Violent attacks upon his people, dissensions within the Church, and threats upon his life by aggressive and determined apostates did not produce feelings of bitterness or fear or retaliation. Rather, they produced in him increased feelings of humility and reliance upon the Lord. One is struck in reading his journal entries of this period by the frequency with which he implored the Lord for help and guidance in all aspects of his temporal and physical responsibilities, ranging from pleas for protection for the Saints, to economic affairs and concerns for his family and personal associates.

On February 24, 1833, the thought Joseph had had previously about sending a para-military force to aid the Missouri brethren crystallized in his mind. On that date he received a revelation which contained this key statement: "Behold, I say unto you, the redemption of Zion must needs come by power; Therefore, I will raise up unto my people a man, who shall lead them like as Moses led the children of Israel. For ye are the children of Israel, and of the seed of Abraham, and ye must needs be led out of bondage by power, and with a stretched-out arm. And as your fathers were led at the first, even so shall the redemption of Zion be." (D&C 103:15-18.)

The revelation added some specific instructions about the procedure to be followed in preparing for this undertaking. Joseph was directed to assemble the necessary manpower: ". . . say unto the strength of my house, my young men and the middle aged— Gather yourselves together unto the land of Zion, upon the land which I have bought with money that has been consecrated unto me." (V. 22.)

The revelation also placed a limitation on the size of the force to be taken to Missouri. Parley P. Pratt and Lyman Wight were directed to recruit "companies to go up unto the land of Zion, by tens, or by twenties, or by fifties, or by an hundred, until they have obtained to the number of five hundred of the strength of my house. . . . if you cannot obtain five hundred, seek diligently that peradventure you may obtain three hundred. And if ye cannot obtain three hundred, seek diligently that peradventure ye may obtain one hundred. But verily I say unto you, a commandment I give unto you, that ye shall not go up into the land of Zion, until you have obtained a hundred of the strength of my house, to go up with you unto the land of Zion." (Vv. 30, 32-34.)

Armed with these instructions, the Prophet and his associates fanned out in different directions to find manpower, weapons, money, and supplies for the expedition, which came to be known as Zion's Camp.

With Parley P. Pratt as his companion, Joseph went into western New York, speaking along the way, laying before the brethren what had happened to the members of the Church in Zion, and apprising them of "the prophecies and revelations concerning the order of the gathering to Zion, and the means of her redemption." (HC 2:41.)

While the principal object of this mission was to enlist volunteers for the march to Zion, every opportunity was taken also to preach the gospel to nonmembers. At a small hamlet named Freedom, the Prophet and Parley P. Pratt preached "to an overflowing house." Such an interest was shown that they stayed over to hold another meeting the following day. As a result of this proselyting effort, a young Methodist by the name of Heman T. Hyde was baptized. The cumulative effect of this single conversion is seen from the following account written later by Parley P. Pratt: ". . . his parents were Presbyterians, and his mother, on account of the strength of her traditions, thought that we were wrong, and told me afterwards that she would much rather have followed him to an earthly grave than to have seen him baptized. Soon afterwards, however, herself, her husband, and the rest of the family, with some thirty or forty others, were all baptized and organized into a branch of the Church—called the Freedom branch—from which nucleus the light spread and souls were gathered into the fold in all the regions round. Thus mightily grew the word of God, or the seed sown by that extraordinary personage, the Prophet and Seer of the nineteenth century." (Pratt, pp. 109-10.)

On March 17, a conference was held at Avon, Livingston County, New York, with a number of priesthood holders in attendance. There the goals to raise money and to recruit men for Zion's Camp were discussed and assignments were made. Two fund-raising groups were appointed to work in assigned areas, and it was decided that the Prophet, with Sidney Rigdon and Lyman Wight, would return to Kirtland, preaching and soliciting funds on the way. "Arrived home at Kirtland on the 28th of March," Joseph recorded in his journal, "finding my family all well. The Lord be praised for this blessing!" (HC 2:45.)

By the first part of May, the Prophet and his aides had assembled about two hundred men with teams, baggage, provisions, and arms. Ahead of them lay an arduous march of a thousand miles to carry supplies to the afflicted and persecuted Saints in Missouri, to reinforce and strengthen them, and, if possible, to influence the governor of the state to call out sufficient additional force to cooperate in restoring their rights to them.

Manifesting again his penchant for organization, Joseph divided the camp into groups of twelve. Instead of appointing a leader of each group, however, he permitted the members to select their own leader by popular vote. While this democratic method gave the members of the camp a greater sense of responsibility, it was hardly calculated to promote the kind of tight organization and discipline normally found in an army. The group leaders, in the final analysis, felt more responsibility toward those who had elected them than toward the leaders of the entire camp. But this was precisely the result the Prophet had set out to achieve. It was not an army and never was intended to be one. It was a loosely knit camp whose general direction and purpose were guided by those at the top but whose everyday functions and housekeeping chores were to be performed independently within each twelve-man group. Each group had two cooks, two firemen, two tent-men, two watermen, two wagoners and horsemen, one runner, and one commissary. The comfort and well-being of the groups depended on the foresight and resourcefulness of their immediate leaders, not Joseph Smith. Thus, groups headed by men of the calibre of Brigham Young were well cared for. Others did not fare so well, and when something went wrong within a group, the tendency was to blame the Prophet rather than the immediate leaders.

The aggressive, open effort the Prophet and his associates made to enlist men and gather money and supplies for Zion's Camp generated countless rumors about its objectives. There was speculation as to whether Joseph had designs of empire. His enemies claimed that he looked upon himself as a modern Mahomet, bent on coercing all into his beliefs and way of life. In the eyes of some of his avowed enemies, Zion's Camp represented a bold attempt to advance his ambition of dominance by force. Starting from this false premise, it is understandable why opposition to the camp became so extreme and bitter. This, in turn, heightened concern for the safety of the camp and produced unusual countermeasures to mask its identity and purpose. Thus the men were very secretive and reluctant to divulge their destination or the purpose of their journey to those who inquired. Wilford Woodruff recorded a typical conversation with an outsider: " 'My boy, where are you from?' 'From the East.' 'Where are you going?' 'To the West.' 'What for?' 'To see where we can get land cheapest and best.' 'Who leads the camp?' 'Sometimes one, sometimes another.' 'What name?' 'Captain Wallace, Major Bruce, Orson Hyde, James Allred,' etc." (HC 2:67.)

The trumpet in the camp became the signal that called the brethren to prayer night and morning. It sounded just before bedtime when, in their respective tents, the men presented their "thank-offerings with prayer and supplication," and it sounded again early the next morning, usually at four A.M., when "every man was again on his knees before the Lord, imploring His blessing for the day." (HC 1:64-65.)

The scant provisions with which the travelers commenced their journey were insufficient to last them the entire trip, so the commissaries were kept very busy, scrounging for food as they ranged out in front and to the sides of the route of march. These men also doubled as recruiters who encouraged able-bodied Saints along the way to join the march to bring relief to the beleaguered members in Missouri. Because of this, the size of the camp was augmented from time to time as it moved slowly toward its destination.

The Prophet's little band was not long on the trail before a characteristic emerged among some of its members that is typical of any similar group: a spirit of griping, complaining, and fault-finding. To such persons there is no good condition that cannot be made bad and no bad condition that cannot be made worse by their sour and negative attitude.

A standout among the complainers was Sylvester Smith, apparently no relation of the Prophet's. He became embroiled in several controversies, including an altercation over the Prophet's dog, which he threatened to kill. Once he openly refused to follow an order given by the Prophet and afterward "manifested very refractory feelings." (HC 2:101.) These feelings on Sylvester's part continued throughout the entire duration of the march, and finally, in August 1834, a lengthy high council court was conducted to air charges made by him against the Prophet of "criminal conduct during his journey to and from Missouri this spring and summer." (HC 2:142.) The court exonerated the Prophet of the charges and condemned Sylvester, who at first accepted the decision but who later retracted a statement acknowledging his error on the ground he had signed it "for fear of punishment." (HC 2:159.) Within two months, however, he voluntarily wrote a letter to the Church periodical, the *Messenger and Advocate,* which puts in proper perspective the difficulties in which he had been embroiled:

"Having heard that certain reports are circulating abroad, prejudicial to the character of Brother Joseph Smith, Jun., and that said reports purport to have come from me, I have thought proper to give the public a plain statement of the facts concerning the matter. It is true, that some difficulties arose between Brother Joseph Smith Jun., and myself, in our travels the past summer to Missouri; and that on our return to this place I laid my grievances before a general council, where they were investigated in full, in an examination which lasted several days, and the result showed to the satisfaction of all present, I believe, but especially to myself, that in all things Brother Joseph Smith, Jun., had conducted worthily, and adorned his profession as a man of God, while journeying to and from Missouri. And it is no more than just that I should confess my faults by saying unto all people, . . . that the things that I accused Brother Smith of were without foundation. . . . I am now perfectly satisfied that the errors of which I accused [him] before the council, did not exist, and were never committed by him. . . . I hope that the disclosure of this truth . . . will put a final end to all evil reports and censurings which have sprung out of anything that I have said or done." (HC 2:160.)

Having thus unburdened himself of these guilt feelings, Sylvester added a thought about the Prophet's work that typifies an attitude the Prophet's disciples have had from the beginning: "I wish still further to state for the relief of my own feelings, which you must be sensible are deeply wounded in consequence of what has happened, that I know for myself, because I have received testimony from the heavens that the work of the Lord, brought forth by means of the Book of Mormon, in our day through the instrumentality of Brother Joseph Smith Jun., is eternal truth, and must stand, though the heavens and the earth pass away."

Central to this attitude is a clear delineation between the Prophet as an individual and the Prophet's work. Joseph was looked upon essentially as a conduit through which the Lord did *His* work and made *His* will known, so the work far transcended the man. To the true disciple, nothing the man might do would ever diminish or obscure the magnitude of the work he produced.

Joseph was not a man to nurse a grudge. Though he could and did speak out boldly, sometimes harshly, against those who opposed or injured him, he was prone to forgive and forget once an antagonist showed signs of relenting and changing. Only a few months after the members of Zion's Camp returned to Kirtland, Sylvester was called and ordained as one of the seven presidents of the First Quorum of Seventies. In the early part of 1836 Joseph selected him to serve temporarily as his personal secretary and scribe. In this position he was privy to the most intimate and confidential dealings of the head of the Church and was charged with keeping Joseph's private journal. It is difficult to believe that this was the same person who, less than two years earlier, had shrieked at Joseph in a moment of uncontrolled rage, "You have stamped out liberty of speech! You prophesy in the name of the Lord! You've got a heart corrupt as hell." (As quoted in Brodie, p. 153.)

While most of the members of Zion's Camp were young and virile and accustomed to the rigors of farm life, they were ill prepared for the physical endurance such a march entailed. Added to their physical burdens were the uncertainties about what might beset them on the way in the form of illness or attack from their enemies, and the concern about what lay at the end of the trail. It is little wonder, then, that there were irritations along the way. But considering the circumstances, the inexperience of the marchers, the fatigue they suffered, the paucity of their food, and their inferior equipment, the marvel is that they fared as well as they did. The Prophet's detractors are prone to dwell on the negative aspects of the march and to apply unrealistically a standard of performance that might be expected of a well-provisioned and equipped, disciplined and experienced military force.

It is fortunate that the camp included among its members an

able and precise diarist, Wilford Woodruff, who wrote: "We pitched our tents at night and had prayers night and morning. The Prophet gave us our instructions every day. We were nearly all young men brought together from all parts of the country, and were therefore strangers to each other. We soon became acquainted and had a happy time in each others association. It was a great school for us to be led by a Prophet of God a thousand miles through cities, towns, villages, and through the wilderness. . . ." (Matthias F. Cowley, *Wilford Woodruff* [Salt Lake City: Bookcraft, 1964], p. 40.)

Many incidents occurred along the line of march that demonstrated the Prophet's superior ability as a teacher and exemplar. He seldom missed an opportunity to illustrate a principle. One of the most dramatic experiences arose from the camp's frequent and sometimes terrifying encounters with rattlesnakes. Joseph had observed the savage reaction of his brethren upon seeing a snake. The usual, almost instantaneous response was to reach for some instrument with which to kill the snake. One sultry evening in late May while the brethren were pitching their tents on the prairie, they found three prairie rattlesnakes. As they prepared to kill them, the Prophet intervened, saying, " 'Let them alone—don't hurt them! How will the serpent ever lose his venom while the servants of God possess the same disposition, and continue to make war upon it? Men must become harmless, before the brute creation; and when men lose their vicious dispositions and cease to destroy the animal race, the lion and the lamb can dwell together, and the sucking child can play with the serpent in safety.' The brethren took the serpents carefully on sticks and carried them across the creek. I exhorted the brethren not to kill a serpent, bird, or an animal of any kind during our journey unless it became necessary in order to preserve ourselves from hunger." (HC 2:71-72.)

Not long after this incident, the Prophet took occasion to determine whether the lesson had been fully understood: "I had frequently spoken on this subject," he wrote, "when on a certain occasion I came up to the brethren who were watching a squirrel on a tree, and to prove them and to know if they would heed my counsel, I took one of their guns, shot the squirrel and passed on, leaving the squirrel on the ground. Brother Orson Hyde, who was just behind, picked up the squirrel, and said, 'We will cook this, that nothing may be lost.' I perceived that the brethren understood what I did it for, and in their practice gave more heed to my precept than to my example, which was right." (HC 2:72.)

One can imagine the anxious concern with which the Prophet made this perilous trip. Ill-provisioned and staffed, inexperienced in the arts of military discipline and management, and unsure about the danger that lay at the end of the trail, Joseph realized the need for help from a power beyond his own. He sought that help constantly through fervent prayer. It was not uncommon for him to leave the company in order to find a quiet, secluded place where he could pour out his soul to the Lord in vocal, secret prayer.

Given the Prophet's implicit faith in the reality and power of God, his vast knowledge of spiritual things and the means by which spiritual powers can be invoked and controlled, and his energetic and persistent seeking for spiritual guidance, it is no wonder that the long march of Zion's Camp was punctuated by events of an almost miraculous nature. Critics and detractors have referred to these in a sneering, condescending way, stating or implying that they were the product of superstition or a hyperactive imagination or a malign intent to mislead and deceive. But this attitude is not unusual, since the miraculous experiences of prophets in all ages have been viewed with skepticism and disbelief by some.

The Prophet affirmed in his account of the march that the camp was attended by angels. He said, "We know that the angels were our companions, for we saw them." (HC 2:73.) Parley P. Pratt recorded this singular experience: "On one occasion, I had travelled all night to overtake the camp with some men and means, and having breakfasted with them and changed horses, I again started ahead on express to visit other branches, and do business to again overtake them. At noon I had turned my horse loose from the carriage to feed on the grass in the midst of a broad, level plain. . . . I sank down overpowered with a deep sleep, . . . so completely was I exhausted for want of sleep and rest; but I had only slept a few moments . . . when a voice, more loud and shrill than I had ever before heard, fell on my ear, and thrilled through every part of my system; it said: *'Parley, it is time to be up and on your journey'*. In the twinkling of an eye I was perfectly aroused; I sprang to my feet so suddenly that I could not at first recollect where I was, or what was before me to perform. I related the circumstance afterwards to brother Joseph Smith, and he bore testimony that it was the angel of the Lord who went before camp, who found me overpowered with sleep, and thus awoke me." (Pratt, pp. 114-15.)

Part of the country through which the camp passed was characterized by large mounds left by a civilization that had inhabited the land anciently. While digging in one of these mounds, several men found the skeleton of a man. There then followed one of those visionary experiences for which the Prophet became noted. When the brethren inquired about the skeleton, he replied, ". . . the visions of the past [were] opened to my understanding by the Spirit of the Almighty. I discovered that the person whose skeleton was before us was a white Lamanite, a large, thick-set man, and a man of God. His name was Zelph. He was a warrior and chieftain under the great prophet Onandagus, who was known from the Hill Cumorah, or eastern sea to the Rocky mountains. The curse was taken from Zelph, or, at least, in part—one of his thigh bones was broken by a stone flung from a sling, while in battle, years before his death. He was killed in battle by the arrow found among his ribs, during the last great struggle of the Lamanites and Nephites." (HC 2:79-80.)

This account is reminiscent of instances in the early days of Joseph's prophetic career while he was translating the Book of Mormon. So intimate and detailed was his knowledge of the early American Indian culture that he commented on conditions, events, and personalities as if he had lived among that people for years. With Joseph, the veil between this life, the past, the future, and the unseen world of spirits was so thin that he moved easily and almost at will from one realm to the other. In doing so, he reported to his amazed followers what he saw and felt. These incidents occurred so often and the reported results had proved to be so accurate that Joseph's followers instinctively looked to him for an explanation of any event they did not fully understand.

Ordinarily, the Prophet's outlook was positive and optimistic. But occasionally, when provoked or when moved upon by the Spirit, his words could be harsh and condemnatory. One such occasion occurred on June 3, 1834, when, exasperated by the contentions among the brethren of the camp, he mounted a wagon and said that the Lord had revealed to him that "a scourge would come upon the camp in consequence of the fractious and unruly spirits that appeared among them, and they should die like sheep with the rot." (Cowley, p. 43.)

This prophecy saw literal fulfillment several weeks later when the camp was striken by cholera. Heber C. Kimball recorded the incident in his journal: "When the Cholera first broke out in the camp, Brother John S. Carter was the first who went forth to rebuke it, but [he] himself, was immediately seized by it, and . . . was the first who was slain. In about thirty minutes after his death, Seth Hitchcock followed him; and it appeared as though we must sink under the destroyer with them. We were not able to obtain boards to make coffins, but were under the necessity of rolling [those who died] up in their blankets, and burying them in that manner. . . . Our hopes were that no more would die, but while we were uniting in a covenant to pray once more with uplifted hands to God, we looked at our beloved brother, Elder Wilcox, and he was gasping his last. . . . Those only who witnessed it can realize anything of the nature of our sufferings. . . . We felt to sit and weep over our brethren, and so great was our sorrow that we could have washed them with our tears, to realize that they had traveled one thousand miles through so much fatigue to lay down their lives for our brethren—and who hath greater love than he who is willing to lay down his life for his brethren? . . . About 12 o'clock at night we placed Brother Wilcox on a small sled, which we drew to the place of interment, with one hand hold of the rope, and in the other we bore our firelocks for our defense. While one or two were digging the grave, the rest stood with their arms to defend them. This was our situation, the enemies around us, and the destroyer in our midst. Soon after we returned another brother was taken away from our little band; then it continued until five . . . were taken away. . . . Brother Joseph, seeing the sufferings of his brethren, stepped forward to rebuke the destroyer, but was immediately seized with the disease himself; and I assisted him a short distance from the place, when it was with difficulty he could walk. All that kept our enemies from us was the fear of the destroyer which the Lord so sent among us. . . ." (*Times and Seasons* 6:839.)

This epidemic raged for four days, during the course of which sixty-eight men were afflicted and fourteen died. The disease was finally abated to an extent by the use of one of those homemade remedies which would boggle the mind of a modern physician. The cure consisted of "dipping the persons afflicted in cold water, or pouring it upon them, and giving them whisky thickened with flour to the consistency of starch." (HC 2:119.) One cannot help but wonder whether a person having undergone this treatment once would feign recovery or die rather than be subjected to it a second time.

By June 16, 1834, the camp had reached and ferried across the Grand River. In a sense this marked the end of the traveling phase of Zion's Camp, for the marchers were now in Missouri, not far from their beleaguered brethren in Clay County. Aware that Joseph's band was near, the Missouri Saints had opened up negotiations with Governor Dunklin and with the mobbers in early June in an attempt to regain possession of their Jackson County lands or to obtain just compensation for them. Under the date of June 5, the principal leaders of the Missouri community of Saints dispatched a letter to Governor Dunklin in which they asked for a military guard to escort them on their return to Jackson County. They also asked for an appropriation to cover their ferriage and other expenses. In a letter dated June 6, addressed to a Colonel I. Thornton, the governor outlined several bases upon which an accommodation might be reached between the Saints and the Jackson County mobbers. First, he suggested that the Saints sell their Jackson County lands provided that they could get a fair price for them. Second, he would try to persuade the mob to abide the law and permit the Saints to occupy their land in peace. Third, he proposed that there be a segregation of the lands owned by the two factions so that the chance of friction between them would be minimized. He then indicated that should all these alternatives fail, it would be necessary to resolve the matter strictly on the basis of the legalities involved. The tone of his letter implied that he was sympathetic to the position of the Saints. However, it contained a significant sentence, which doubtless exerted a strong influence on the Prophet to disband Zion's Camp a few days later. The Governor wrote: "Indeed, the Mormons have no right to march to Jackson County in arms, unless by order or permission of the commander in chief; men must not 'levy war' in taking possession of their rights, any more than others should in opposing them in taking possession." (HC 2:86.)

The Prophet officially disbanded Zion's Camp on June 23, 1834. On the day before, he received a revelation that chided his followers for their disobedience, gave counsel to the Saints about their conduct in the midst of their enemies, and looked forward to "an endowment from on high" for those who were to be "chosen." The shortcomings of the Saints were capsuled in this scathing indictment: "But behold, they have not learned to be obedient to the things which I required at their hands, but are full of all manner of evil, and do not impart of their substance, as becometh saints, to the poor and afflicted among them; And are not united according to the union required by the law of the celestial kingdom." The revelation predicted that the Saints would be "chastened until they learn obedience, if it must needs be, by the things which they suffer." (D&C 105:3-4, 6.)

One cause of the difficulties of the Saints in Missouri was the injudicious tendency of some to be extravagant in predicting that the land comprised the central gathering place of the Saints and would ultimately be controlled and governed by them. These predictions unfortunately were sometimes made with a tinge of arrogance, alarming the older settlers and causing them to draw false inferences about the objectives of the Saints and their means of obtaining them. The revelation focused on this problem: "And let all my people who dwell in the regions round about be very faithful, and prayerful, and humble before me, and reveal not the things which I have revealed unto them, until it is wisdom in me that they should be revealed. Talk not of judgments, neither boast of faith nor of mighty works, but carefully gather together, as much in one region as can be, consistently with the feelings of the people; And behold, I will give unto you favor and grace in their eyes, that you may rest in peace and safety, while you are saying unto the people: Execute judgment and justice for us according to law, and redress us of our wrongs." (D&C 105:23-25.)

Finally, the revelation pointed toward a great spiritual "endowment" to be conferred upon "the first Elders" in the temple to be built at Kirtland. Those who were to receive this endowment were to be "chosen" through the Prophet "by the voice of the Spirit." (Vv. 33, 35-36.)

As Joseph appraised the conditions in Missouri in light of this revelation, he was struck with the realization that the time for the "redemption" of the land of Zion lay in the remote future. Plans for building up the center stake of Zion and erecting the beautiful temple would have to be shelved for the time being. For now, the brethren would have to be content to wage a delaying action, designed to retain a foothold in Missouri while salvaging everything possible from the Jackson County expulsion. In order to strengthen the local brethren and provide more direct control of their affairs, the Prophet organized the Missouri Saints in the same manner that the Saints at Kirtland had been organized, with a presidency of three and a high council of twelve. David Whitmer was appointed "President of the Church in Zion" with W. W. Phelps and John Whitmer as assistants. The Prophet later recorded the instructions given to the leaders in Zion on this historic occasion: "After singing and prayer, I gave the Council such instructions in relation to their high calling, as would enable them to proceed to minister in their office agreeable to the pattern heretofore given; read the revelation on the subject; and told them that if I should now be taken away, I had accomplished the great work the Lord had laid before me, and that which I had desired of the Lord; and that I had done my duty in organizing the High Council, through which council the will of the Lord might be made known on all important occasions, in the building up of Zion, and establishing truth in the earth." (HC 2:124.)

Having done all within his power to strengthen the Saints in Zion against the terrible ordeal that still faced them there, the Prophet and other followers departed for Kirtland on July 9, 1834. By this time he had become a seasoned traveler according to the standards of the day, and the thousand miles between Zion and Kirtland were easily negotiated by teams, by foot, and by canal and river boats. The three-week trip afforded him an opportunity to appraise the successes and failures of Zion's Camp and to reflect upon his future course.

The most beneficial aspect of Zion's Camp was the experience in discipline and privation afforded to its members. Those who endured the fatigue and uncertainties of the trip were never quite the same afterward. The fact that they had responded willingly and had survived under the most trying conditions gave them a sense of self-confidence and resiliency, which would sustain them in facing the many trials and difficulties that lay ahead. The reaction of Brigham Young to the trek was typical of the more dedicated members of the camp. Upon his return to Kirtland, he was asked, "Well, what did you gain on this useless journey to Missouri with Joseph Smith?" "All we went for," Brigham replied. "I would not exchange the experience I gained in that expedition for all the wealth of Geauga county." (CHC 1:370-71.) Though he didn't know it then, Zion's Camp was Brigham Young's training for the great exodus westward he was to lead a few years later. The problems of supply, organization, and discipline he observed in the camp were to appear again in the westward trek, except on a magnified scale. Instead of the responsibility of leading a few hundred healthy young men through an area with well-defined and heavily traveled roads and waterways to a predetermined place, he would lead thousands of men, women, and children of all ages, healthy and ill alike, through an uncharted desert country toward a destination which, at the outset, was uncertain. And perhaps without ever consciously intending to do so, Brigham marked with care every detail of Joseph's mode of operation against the time when he would have a similar responsibility in an entirely different setting.

The joy of the Prophet in returning to Kirtland was overshadowed by the unpleasantness of answering the malignant charges leveled against him by Sylvester Smith. Once that difficulty was resolved, the Prophet's life settled into a comfortable routine for a short season. It was a welcome change to enjoy the love and companionship of his family and to give direction to the local affairs of the Church. The most pressing ecclesiastical matter at the moment was the construction of the temple. While a building committee had the chief responsibility for carrying this project forward, Joseph was an active participant in practically all phases of the work. He recorded under the date of September 1, 1834: "I continued to preside over the Church, and in forwarding the building of the house of the Lord in Kirtland. I acted as foreman in the Temple stone quarry, and when other duties would permit, labored with my own hands." (HC 2:161.)

Chapter Seventeen

Calling of the Twelve and the Seventy

Matters of doctrine and procedure were constantly brought to the attention of the Prophet for interpretation and direction. The practice of speaking in tongues at church meetings was becoming quite widespread, and Joseph, concerned that many members were being misled into an essentially unproductive habit, took occasion to define more precisely the purposes of the gift. He explained that it had been given "for the preaching of the Gospel to other nations and languages, but it was not given for the government of the Church." Focusing on a particular case, in which the content of a speech delivered in tongues was used as testimony in a church court proceeding, the Prophet directed that this was "contrary to the rules and regulations of the Church, because in all our decisions we must judge from actual testimony." He advised that the Saints speak in their "own language in all such matters, and then the adversary cannot lead our minds astray." (HC 2:162.)

In October 1834 the Church commenced the publication of the *Messenger and Advocate* under Joseph's leadership. This explanation was given of the relationship with the earlier church periodical published in Missouri and the origin of the name: "As the *Evening and Morning Star* was designed to be published at Missouri, it was considered that another name would be more appropriate for a paper in this place [Kirtland], consequently, as the name of this Church has lately been entitled the Church of the Latter-day Saints, and since it is destined, at least for a season, to bear the reproach and stigma of this world, it is no more than just that a paper disseminating the doctrines believed by the same, and advocating its character and rights should be entitled *The Latter-day Saints Messenger and Advocate*." (HC 2:167.)

The comparatively muted voice of the new Church-sponsored publication was hardly a match for the loud, incessant, and usually inaccurate anti-Mormon press, which almost daily spewed forth a stream of half truths or outright fabrications against this resilient and ever-growing young sect. To a large extent, this campaign of vilification was instigated and promoted by sectarian clergymen who were alarmed by the heavy inroads on their membership being made by the vigorous proselyting of the Mormons. While on a trip to Michigan with several of the brethren in October 1834, the Prophet encountered a man named Ellmer who illustrated well the way in which rumor feeds on error and lies. While crossing the lake on a steamer, this man engaged Oliver Cowdery in conversation during the course of which he said that he was "personally acquainted with Joe Smith," that he was "a dark complexioned man," that he had heard Joseph "preach his lies . . . in Bainbridge Chenango county, New York," that Joseph was then dead, and the man "was glad" of it. Later the Prophet wrote in his journal these comments: "I concluded that he learned it from the popular priests of the day, who, through fear that their craft will be injured, if their systems are compared with the truth, seek to ridicule those who teach the truth, and thus I am suffering under the tongue of slander for Christ's sake, unceasingly. God have mercy on such, if they will quit their lying. I need not state my complexion to those that have seen me, and those who have read my history thus far, will recollect that five years ago I was not a preacher, as Ellmer represented; neither did I ever preach in Bainbridge." (HC 2:68-69.)

No sooner had Joseph returned from his trip than he began to prepare to teach the elders in a special school. He prepared and delivered a series of "Lectures on Theology," which were later published in the Doctrine and Covenants under the title "Lectures on Faith." These were more than a mere doctrinal treatment of an important subject. They were intended to motivate the Prophet's followers to practice the powerful principles they expounded. Illustrative of this is the following statement on faith that the Prophet made early in his ministry: "It is the privilege of every Elder to speak of the things of God; and could we all come together with one heart and one mind in perfect faith the veil might as well be rent today as next week, or any other time, and if we will but cleanse ourselves and covenant before God, to serve Him, it is our privilege to have an assurance that God will protect us at all times." (*Teachings of the Prophet Joseph Smith* [Deseret Book, 1976], p. 9.)

The Prophet also taught that "faith comes by hearing the word of God, through the testimony of the servants of God." He added that such a testimony "is always attended by the Spirit of prophecy and revelation." (HC 3:379.)

In stressing the principle of faith, Joseph did not have in mind a sterile memorization of the recorded scriptures on the subject. Rather, he intended that the Saints would use it as a principle of power and achievement. He was wont to remind them that through faith "the worlds were framed by the word of God" (Hebrews 11:3), and that the church and kingdom of God were to be built up in the latter day by the same means. He never tired of recalling the great achievements of the prophets of old, accomplished through the exercise of this fundamental principle. It was his aim to imbue the elders of the Church with the same dauntless courage and iron will manifested by the saints in the early days.

The School of the Prophets was not merely a forum where the students were taught theological concepts. It was a place where they learned the practical application of the principles, which they then taught to others. It was not until later that the Prophet articulated, in a formal way, the basic tenets of the Church. At this time, therefore, the concept of faith had not been officially ranked as the first fundamental principle of the gospel. However, one cannot read the scriptures prayerfully or reflect upon life's purpose and meaning without recognizing that this concept lies at the root of all spiritual development. The essence of the force of faith that the Prophet sought to convey to his followers is embodied in this journal entry made in the latter part of 1834: "No month ever found me more busily engaged than November; but as my life consisted of activity and unyielding exertions, I made this my rule: *When the Lord commands, do it.*" (HC 2:170.)

At this time the Prophet and the Church were beset with heavy financial obligations. Construction of the temple, aid to the poor, financing of the printing press and other church enterprises, assistance to the Saints who were struggling for survival in Missouri, and a myriad of other demands for money made him especially conscious of the vital need to be solvent and to have the necessary means to do his work. Having received the sum of $430 from some of the brethren in the East, which helped to ease the financial burdens, the Prophet joined with Oliver Cowdery in a special prayer on November 29, 1834 "for the continuance of blessings." After "rejoicing before the Lord on this occasion," they entered into the following covenant with the Lord, which had far-reaching implications not only for them and their families, but also for the entire membership of the Church at that day and in the years ahead. "That if the Lord will prosper us in our business and open the way before us that we may obtain means to pay our debts; that we be not troubled nor brought into disrepute before the world, nor His people; after that, of all that He shall give unto us, we will give a tenth to be bestowed upon the poor in His church, or as He shall command; and that we will be faithful over that which He has entrusted to our care, that we may obtain much; and that our children after us shall remember to observe this sacred and holy covenant; and that our children, and our children's children, may know of the same, we have subscribed our names with our own hands." (HC 2:174-75.)

Perhaps more striking even than this unusual covenant was a prayer the Prophet later composed and included in his record, pertaining to this significant event: "And now, O Father, as Thou didst prosper our father Jacob, and bless him with protection and prosperity wherever he went, from the time he made a like covenant before and with Thee; as Thou didst even the same night, open the heavens unto him and manifest great mercy and power, and give him promises, wilt Thou do so with us his sons; and as his blessings prevailed above his progenitors unto the utmost bounds of the everlasting hills, even so may our blessings prevail like his; and may Thy servants be preserved from the power and influence of wicked and unrighteous men; may every weapon formed against us fall upon the head of him who shall form it; may we be blessed with a name and a place among Thy saints here, and Thy sanctified when they shall rest. Amen."

This incident opens a window into the innermost recesses of the Prophet's soul. We see there a man with a childlike faith in the reality and power of God and with confidence that God would deal with him in the same way He had dealt with the great prophets of the Old Testament.

Whatever Joseph's motivation and intentions may have been, there can be no doubt about the import to himself of what he did. He made a solemn pledge that thereafter he would pay a tenth "of all that He shall give unto us" for the benefit of "the poor in His Church" or "as He shall command." He also pled that his children after him would remember to observe "this sacred and holy covenant."

This private covenant was actually the precursor of a general covenant, obligatory upon all members of the Church, which was given by revelation a few years later. There had been previous allusions to the ancient law of tithing in modern revelations given to Joseph, but it was not until 1838 at Far West, Missouri, that it was given to the Saints in Zion as "a standing law unto them forever," and to be "an ensample unto all the stakes of Zion." (D&C 119.)

The involvement of Oliver Cowdery in this significant occurrence presaged his return to a position of high leadership in the Church. A revelation received in April 1830 when the Church was officially organized had called Oliver "the second elder" of the Church. (D&C 20:3.) In the interim, he had spent most of his time in Missouri, far removed from the center of power that naturally gravitated around the Prophet. Now it was like old times to find these two young men together again, joining in solemn covenant to obey the ancient law of tithing and invoking the great blessings for compliance that God had promised to the prophets of an earlier time. Their joint participation in this event doubtless evoked many memories of past, almost transcendent experiences they had shared, epic events that had bound them together with special, enduring bonds no one else could share. Nothing save their own disobedience could sever those bonds. Yet even while serving with selfless dedication amidst the severe trials of Missouri, Oliver must have wondered about his status in the Church when the Prophet selected Sidney Rigdon and Frederick G. Williams as his counselors. Any question Oliver may have entertained in this respect was answered on December 5, 1834, when, without any warning or preliminaries, the Prophet ordained him as an assistant president of the Church. The minutes of the meeting at which this event took place make it plain that the failure of the Prophet to bring Oliver into the inner circle of the Church sooner resulted solely from Oliver's absence in Missouri. (HC 2:176.)

If the events that the Prophet and Oliver viewed in retrospect were inspiring and novel, the ones that faced them in the months ahead were calculated to produce feelings of awe and amazement.

Joseph faced the year 1835 with optimism. The difficulties in Missouri were, for the time being, quiescent. Work on the holy temple in Kirtland was moving forward satisfactorily, and the enthusiastic acceptance of the gospel by throngs of new converts portended another year of growth and expansion. This last aspect of the Church had inspired many hours of meditative and prayerful reflection on the part of the Prophet. He accurately foresaw that the ready acceptance of the elders' message in the United States would also occur with varying degrees of success anywhere in the world where the missionaries were given an audience. He was also conscious of the burdensome charge given to him to see to it that the restoration message was broadcast to the ends of the earth.

It became obvious that the fulfillment of this heavy responsibility would require a more formalized and elaborate organizational structure than the one theretofore used in proselyting. To this time missionaries had been sent out on a somewhat casual basis, without specific direction or training, and reported to the head of the Church or his designee upon their return. With ever-increasing burdens being placed upon him, the Prophet sought a solution that would enable him to retain ultimate control of a worldwide proselyting effort but would impose upon others the details of its formulation and execution.

The answer lay in a revelation he received almost a year before the Church was organized (D&C 18), which declared: " . . . there are others who are called to declare my gospel, both unto the Gentile and unto Jew; Yea, even twelve; and the Twelve shall be my disciples, and they shall take upon them my name." The revelation also declared that the Twelve were to be ordained of God and were, in turn, to "ordain priests and teachers; to declare my gospel, according to the power of the Holy Ghost." (D&C 18:26-27, 32.)

The three witnesses to the Book of Mormon—Oliver Cowdery, David Whitmer, and Martin Harris—were directed to seek out and find the Twelve. The main criteria for identifying the first members of this body were also found in the revelation: " . . . the Twelve are they who shall desire to take upon them my name with full purpose of heart." (V. 27.)

For over five and half years this revelation had lain dormant, insofar as it pertained to the Twelve, largely because the need did not yet exist for the special services of such a body. The Prophet was certain now, however, that the call of the Twelve was both expedient and necessary, and he went forward with preparations to put it into effect. In the formation of both the Quorum of the Twelve and the Quorum of the Seventy, which occurred at about the same time, he referred not only to section 18, but also to visions he had received on the subject. (HC 2:182, 202.)

As the time drew near for calling the Twelve, attention was focused on those who comprised Zion's Camp. Where else in the entire church could be found men who, by their deeds, had manifested a greater desire to serve with full purpose of heart? It was from this group, then, that the following twelve men were selected for membership in this quorum: Thomas B. Marsh, David W. Patten, Brigham Young, Heber C. Kimball, Orson Hyde, William E. M'Lellin, Parley P. Pratt, Luke S. Johnson, William B. Smith, Orson Pratt, John F. Boynton, and Lyman E. Johnson. Marsh, the oldest member of the group, was thirty-five at the time of the call. Lyman Johnson, the youngest, was not yet thirty. Little did these Twelve realize the great pressures to which they would be subjected and the trials they would be called upon to endure. Only three of them, David W. Patten, Brigham Young, and Heber C. Kimball, were to remain unfalteringly true to the high standards of the apostleship set for them at the time of their call; and David W. Patten was to suffer a martyr's death within four years, so that only the two stalwarts, Brigham Young and Heber Kimball, who were later to lead the exodus westward, endured to the end.

On February 14, 1835, the Prophet convened a special meeting in Kirtland where the Twelve were chosen, ordained, and instructed. Joseph promised that though weak and insignificant at the moment, those chosen ultimately would be "powerful and mighty," and that great things would be accomplished by them "from this hour." (HC 2:182.)

The three witnesses were called upon to pray in order. Then they were blessed "by the laying on of the hands of the Presidency," following which they called up, ordained, and blessed the Twelve. An insight into the fervor manifested on this occasion is gained from this excerpt of the blessing conferred upon Brigham Young: "He shall go forth from land to land and from sea to sea; and shall behold heavenly messengers going forth; and his life shall be prolonged; and the Holy Priesthood is conferred on him, that he may do wonders in the name of Jesus; that he may cast out devils, heal the sick, raise the dead, open the eyes of the blind, go forth from land to land and from sea to sea; and that heathen nations shall even call him God himself, if he do not rebuke them." (HC 2:187-89.)

In a general charge delivered to the Twelve, Oliver Cowdery reviewed some of the circumstances behind their selection and commented on some of the special challenges with which they would be confronted in the years ahead: "It is known to you that previous to the organization of this Church in 1830, the Lord gave revelations, or the Church could not have been organized. . . . Those who embarked in this cause were desirous to know how the work was to be conducted. They read many things in the Book of Mormon concerning their duty, and the way the great work ought to be done; but the minds of men are so constructed that they will not believe, without a testimony of seeing or hearing. The Lord gave us a revelation that, in process of time, there should be twelve men chosen to preach His Gospel to Jew and Gentile. Our minds have been on a constant stretch, to find who these twelve were; when the time should come we could not tell; but we sought the Lord by fasting and prayer to have our lives prolonged to see this day, to see you. . . . You have many revelations put into your hands—revelations to make you acquainted with the nature of your mission; you will have difficulties by reason of your visiting all the nations of the world. You will need wisdom in a tenfold proportion to what you have ever had; you will have to combat all the prejudices of all nations." (HC 2:194-95.)

He went on to urge the Twelve to obtain a personal knowledge of God's existence and power if, indeed, they then lacked such knowledge; to avoid an aspiring, ambitious spirit; and to be zealous and constant in their labors. In conclusion, he took each one by the hand and asked: "Do you with full purpose of heart take part in this ministry, to proclaim the Gospel with all diligence, with these your brethren, according to the tenor and intent of the charge you have received?" (HC 2:198.) They all responded in the affirmative.

The reactions of the Twelve to this impressive ceremony were as the Prophet had anticipated. His long experience with spiritual beings and events had demonstrated the fervor and the enthusiasm that they produce. He had also learned by experience, however, that this natural exuberance had to be tempered with discipline and system in order for it to produce lasting good. In reviewing his own experiences, he noted that he had been dilatory in some respects, especially in keeping accurate records of important events. A striking example of this neglect was the fact that he had failed to record the exact date upon which the resurrected apostles Peter, James, and John had conferred the Melchizedek Priesthood upon him and Oliver Cowdery. While he retained a bright recollection of the incident itself and of the important things that transpired during the course of it, his memory was vague about the precise date when it occurred. Years later, when pressed to provide some of the specifics, the best he could do was to report that it had occurred some time in the late spring or early summer of 1829. (It should be noted parenthetically that his failure to designate a specific date on which this visitation occurred lends credence to his account. Had he been of a disposition to mislead or misrepresent, it would have been simple to have picked a date at random—any date—in order to satisfy his critics. But the fact was that he had forgotten it, and since he had failed to make a record at the time, his only recourse was to deal in generalities.) It was, therefore, with this and other similar events in mind that the Prophet felt constrained to impart some words of counsel to the newly selected members of the Twelve.

In the minutes of the meeting it is recorded that he said: "It is a fact, if I now had in my possession, every decision which had been had upon important items of doctrine and duties since the commencement of this work, I would not part with them for any sum of money; but we have neglected to take minutes of such things, thinking, perhaps, that they would never benefit us afterwards. . . . now we cannot bear record to the Church and to the world, of the great and glorious manifestations which have been made to us with that degree of power and authority we otherwise could, if we now had these things to publish abroad.

"Since the Twelve are now chosen, I wish to tell them a course which they may pursue. . . . If they will, every time they assemble, appoint a person to preside over them during the meeting, and one or more to keep a record of their proceedings, and on the decision of every question or item, be it what it may, let such decision be written, and such decision will forever remain upon record, and appear an item of covenant of doctrine. . . .

"Here is another important item. If you assemble from time to time, and proceed to discuss important questions, and pass decisions upon the same, and fail to note them down, by and by you will be driven to straits from which you will not be able to extricate yourselves, because you may be in a situation not to bring your faith to bear with sufficient perfection or power to obtain the desired information; or, perhaps, for neglecting to write these things when God had revealed them, not esteeming them of sufficient worth, the Spirit may withdraw and God may be angry. . . ."

The Prophet then added this significant prophecy: "Here let me prophesy. The time will come, when, if you neglect to do this thing, you will fall by the hands of unrighteous men. Were you to be brought before the authorities, and be accused of any crime or misdemeanor, and be as innocent as the angels of God, unless you can prove yourselves to have been somewhere else, your enemies will prevail against you; but if you can bring twelve men to testify that you were in a certain place, at that time, you will escape their hand." (HC 2:198-99.)

Recordkeeping among Joseph's followers was to be greatly stimulated a few months later when he was visited by the prophet Elijah, who restored the keys of what Joseph called the "sealing power." The mission of this revered patriarch, as the Old Testament records, was to "turn the heart of the fathers to the children, and the heart of the children to their fathers." (Malachi 4:6.) Elijah's appearance and the portentous effect of his mission had vast implications, for it greatly accelerated and fed the already lively interest of the Saints in keeping records. Convinced that their own happiness and success depended upon the secure status of their ancestors and their descendants, Joseph's followers launched a massive program of genealogical research and personal recordkeeping.

Shortly after the Twelve were called and ordained, the Prophet organized the First Quorum of the Seventy from among those who had accompanied him to Missouri in Zion's Camp. The seventies were "to constitute traveling quorums, to go into all the earth, whithersoever the Twelve Apostles shall call them." (HC 2:202.)

With the organization of these two quorums, the Prophet had a corps of able, disciplined men to spearhead the ambitious project of taking the gospel message to the ends of the earth. At that time the jurisdiction and responsibility of these quorums was limited to proselyting among nonmembers and to establishing branches of the Church in areas where there were sufficient numbers of converts. Affairs in the established stakes were administered by local leaders who were answerable directly to the Presidency of the Church and who were, for the most part, free from the control of the Twelve. Later this pattern was changed and the Twelve were given jurisdiction and authority with respect to administration within the stakes.

In this as in other matters pertaining to the Church, the Prophet acted as the needs of the moment required. This method of operation was demonstrated again with respect to a major revelation on priesthood, part of which he received on March 28, 1835. It was prompted by a request on that day from the Twelve: ". . . we therefore feel to ask of him whom we have acknowledged to be our Prophet and Seer, that he inquire of God for us, and obtain a revelation, (if consistent) that we may look upon it when we are separated, that our hearts may be comforted. . . . We have unitedly asked God our heavenly Father to grant unto us through His Seer, a revelation of His mind and will concerning our duty the coming season, even a great revelation, that will enlarge our hearts, comfort us in adversity, and brighten our hopes amidst the powers of darkness." (HC 2:21.)

The Prophet records that pursuant to this request he "inquired of the Lord" and received the revelation on priesthood now known as section 107 of the Doctrine and Covenants. Later, some other miscellaneous items were added to this document. This revelation clearly defines the relationship between the Aaronic and Melchizedek priesthoods, specifies the duties of the different offices in these priesthoods, and outlines the procedures to be followed in conducting their affairs.

The call and ordination of the Twelve and the Seventy relieved the Prophet and the First Presidency of the heavy load of responsibility for the Church's proselyting activities. Furthermore, sharing these responsibilities tended to strengthen and enlarge the abilities of subordinates and to produce in them greater commitment and dedication to the Church.

Joseph Smith now had two strong arms to facilitate the work of the Church. The first was the newly created proselyting arm comprised of the Twelve and the Seventy, whose responsibility was to carry the message of the restoration to the nations of the earth. To their proselytes went the admonition to gather to Zion, which, in its broader interpretation, included Kirtland as well as Missouri. At these places of gathering was found the other arm: local presidencies, high councils, and bishops, who were charged with the responsibility to integrate the new members into the Church, to teach them the details of church doctrine and procedure, and to give them counsel and, where necessary, assistance to satisfy their physical needs.

The separate and distinct roles of these two arms were clearly enunciated by the Prophet at a special meeting held on May 2, 1835. The minutes of that meeting read in part: "President Joseph Smith then stated that the Twelve will have no right to go into Zion, or any of its stakes, and there undertake to regulate the affairs therof, where there is a standing high council; but it is their duty to go abroad and regulate all matters relative to the different branches of the Church. When the Twelve are together, or a quorum of them, in any church, they will have authority to act independently, and make decisions, and those decisions will be valid. But where there is not a quorum, they will have to do business by the voice of the Church. No standing High Council has authority to go into the churches abroad, and regulate the matters thereof, for this belongs to the Twelve." (HC 2:220.)

Chapter Eighteen

The Publication of New Scripture

As Joseph Smith's mind turned from the problems of organization and administration, it commenced to focus upon doctrinal matters. Paramount in his thinking was the publication of a compilation of revelations he had received over the years. The compilation, made by a committee chaired by the Prophet, culminated on August 17, 1835, at a general assembly in Kirtland when the volume was accepted to "become a law and a rule of faith and practice to the Church." (HC 2:243.)

Not only was there a general acceptance of the book by the assembly, but leaders of every branch of the Church hierarchy bore witness of the divine origin of the revelations it contained. Typical of these testaments was one given by the Quorum of the Twelve: "We therefore feel willing to bear testimony to all the world of mankind, to every creature upon the face of all the earth, that the Lord has borne record to our souls, through the Holy Ghost shed forth upon us, that these Commandments were given by inspiration of God, and are profitable for all men, and are verily true." (HC 2:245.)

Also included in the book were the lectures on faith, which the Prophet had delivered to the elders, a statement on the Church's attitude toward marriage, and a statement of government and laws.

With the publication of this volume and its distribution throughout the Church, Joseph now had a powerful tool for bringing about a uniformity of understanding with respect to doctrine and procedures among the Saints. Most of the revelations had already been previously published, but only a small percentage of the members subscribed to the periodicals in which they appeared and a still smaller percentage took the trouble to cut out and preserve them for future reference. Now the revelations, conveniently bound together, could be purchased and retained by the Saints for frequent use in the years ahead. They also became a vital tool in the hands of the missionaries. Here was objective evidence to support their contention that a modern-day prophet had been raised up who, in the tradition of Israel's ancient prophets, spoke authoritatively in the name of God.

Even as the Doctrine and Covenants was accepted along with the Book of Mormon, events were combining to usher in the third volume Joseph Smith was to contribute to the body of ecclesiastical literature. On July 3, 1835, a man named Michael Chandler arrived in Kirtland with an exhibit of four ancient mummies that had been exhumed from their gravesite in Egypt. With these mummies were found several papyrus scrolls inscribed with a curious hieroglyphic writing. Having heard of the Prophet's widespread reputation as a translator of ancient writings, Mr. Chandler brought a sample of the hieroglyphics to him for inspection. When the Prophet produced his translation or interpretation of these writings, Mr. Chandler furnished him a certificate that read: "This is to make known to all who may be desirous, concerning the knowledge of Mr. Joseph Smith, Jun., in deciphering the ancient Egyptian hieroglyphic characters in my possession, which I have, in many eminent cities, showed to the most learned; and, from the information that I could ever learn, or meet with, I find that of Mr. Joseph Smith, Jun., to correspond in the most minute matters." (HC 2:235.) The rather involved syntax of the certificate evoked an apologetic footnote from the Prophet: "Mr. Chandler is responsible for the English of the above certificate, and I do not feel at liberty to edit it."

The facility with which Joseph translated these characters prompted a group of the Saints in Kirtland to purchase the mummies and the scrolls and to present them to him, and he immediately commenced to translate the writings, using Oliver Cowdery and W. W. Phelps as scribes. The Prophet soon discovered to his surprise that the scrolls included accounts of the lives and ministries of Abraham and Joseph of old. He translated the account of Abraham in its entirety, and it was later included in the third volume of latter-day scripture, the Pearl of Great Price. With the published version of this writing, he included a copy of some of the hieroglyphics found in the scrolls along with his English translation or interpretation, thereby deliberately providing the means by which scholars of his day or of some remote time could appraise his abilities as a translator. (In November 1967 some of the scrolls acquired by the Prophet in 1835 came into the possession of the Church. Parts of these have since been translated by a noted scholar, who has uncovered evidence corroborating Joseph's prophetic and linguistic claims.)

The writings of Abraham elaborate upon the concept of a preexistent state. One especially striking passage alludes to the "intelligences" that existed before the world was formed and confirms that Abraham was one of a select group from among these and was chosen for a leadership role before he was born. (Pearl of Great Price, Abraham 3:22-23.) The writing also tells about Abraham's personal life, including the circumstances under which he obtained priesthood authority from God. Finally, it touches on the subject of celestial astronomy and makes reference to the sphere on which God dwells.

Concurrent with the work of translating the papyrus scrolls during the summer of 1835, Joseph was engaged in writing a series of letters to the elders of the Church through the pages of the *Messenger and Advocate*. By this means he was able to elaborate on Church doctrine and to answer questions on policies and procedures that were being encountered by the missionaries in the field. For example, the first of these letters explained the concept of gathering and the difficulties in Missouri, and discussed the doctrines of faith and repentance.

In another letter, the Prophet wrote: "But we pause here and offer a remark upon the saying which we learn has gone abroad, and has been handled in a manner detrimental to the cause of truth, by saying, 'that in preaching the doctrine of gathering, we break up families, and give license for men to leave their families, women their husbands, children their parents and slaves their masters, thereby deranging the order and breaking up the harmony and peace of society.' " This was a most serious charge for enemies of the Church to level at a group of people who prided themselves upon being family-oriented and who taught the need for filial and civil obedience. In his response, the Prophet enunciated what he considered to be the first principles of the gospel: "We shall here show our faith, and thereby, as we humbly trust, put an end to these false and wicked misrepresentations, which have caused, we have every reason to believe, thousands to think they were doing God's service, when they were persecuting the children of God; whereas, if they could have enjoyed the true light, and had a just understanding of our principles, they would have embraced them with all their hearts, and been rejoicing in the love of the truth. And now to show our doctrine on this subject, we shall commence with the first principles of the Gospel, which are faith, repentance, and baptism for the remission of sins, and the gift of the Holy Ghost by the laying on of hands." (HC 2:255.)

In a subsequent letter Joseph developed his concept of the gathering in some detail. His basic premise was that the gathering of the Lord's chosen people had been foretold by many ancient prophets and that it was a prerequisite to the Second Coming. He explained that the Church was the kingdom of God upon the earth, and that it would not be displaced or removed until the Savior returned to claim it.

He also took occasion in his letters to defend the Church against the bitter attacks then being made by its enemies. At the time, Howe's *Mormonism Unvailed* [*sic*] was being widely circulated and other clamorous voices were being raised against the Church. Toward these enemies, the Prophet turned the full force of his rhetoric: "The Kingdom of heaven is like unto a mustard seed. Behold, then is not this the Kingdom of heaven that is raising its head in the last days in the majesty of its God, even the Church of the Latter-day Saints, like an impenetrable, immovable rock in the midst of the mighty deep, exposed to the storms and tempests of Satan, but has, thus far, remained steadfast, and is still braving the mountain waves of opposition, which are driven by the tempestuous winds. . . ; urged onward with redoubled fury by the enemy of righteousness, with his pitchfork of lies, as you will see fairly represented in a cut contained in Mr. Howe's *Mormonism Unveiled?*" (HC 2:268.) Having thus excoriated one of his chief detractors, he administered a final blow that at once showed his disdain for Mr. Howe and his competitive nature: "And we hope that this adversary of truth will continue to stir up the sink of iniquity, that the people may the more readily discern between the righteous and the wicked." Thus was Mr. Howe put in the position of having attacked truth, not Joseph Smith. Furthermore, the Prophet made it clear that any future attacks by Mr. Howe or those of like mind not only would fail, but would also be welcomed as a means of insuring the victory of the Church's cause.

Chapter Nineteen

The Prophet as a Leader

In appraising the life and work of Joseph Smith, it is significant to see that the differences between him and his associates who later became disaffected were based strictly upon personal conflicts and not in any way upon the substance of the work he brought forth nor upon the validity of the spiritual manifestations he experienced.

Events that transpired during the autumn of 1835 provide an interesting view into some of the domestic challenges the Prophet faced. It has already been seen that a high sense of loyalty and unity generally characterized his relationships with members of his family. From the time he first told them of visitations to him by divine beings, they had given him unwavering support. Had he experienced rejection or ridicule from them in those early stages of his spiritual development, it is likely that his achievements would have been far less noteworthy.

But although the Smiths presented a united front with respect to their contacts with others, their internal relationships were not entirely without friction. At the root of this friction was the volatile William Smith, one of the Prophet's younger brothers, who had recently been appointed to the Quorum of the Twelve Apostles.

The difficulty between Joseph and William at this time arose out of charges of the maltreatment of a child that William had brought against a member named Elliot. In the course of the trial, the Prophet objected to evidence sought to be introduced through his mother, declaring that it related to a matter that had already been settled by the court. William exploded at this, charging the Prophet with "invalidating or doubting" his mother's testimony. The Prophet ruled William to be out of order and asked him to sit down. William refused. The stormy scene that followed was described by the Prophet: "I repeated my request. He became enraged. I finally ordered him to sit down. He said he would not, unless I knocked him down. I was agitated in my feelings on account of his stubbornness, and was about to leave the house, but my father requested me not to do so. I complied, and the house was brought to order after much debate on the subject, and we proceeded to business." (HC 2:295.)

Not satisfied with the outcome of the trial, William confronted the Prophet later, seeking some vindication. Their brother Hyrum was invited in to arbitrate the dispute when another tempestuous scene occurred: ". . . Brother Hyrum began to make some remarks in the spirit of meekness," the Prophet wrote. "He [William] became enraged. I joined Brother Hyrum in trying to calm his stormy feelings, but to no purpose, he insisted that we intended to add abuse to injury, his passion increased, he arose abruptly, declared that he wanted no more to do with us. He rushed out at the door. We tried to prevail on him to stop, but all to no purpose. He went away in a passion, and soon after sent his license to me. He went home and spread the leaven of iniquity among my brothers, and especially prejudiced the mind of Brother Samuel. I soon learned that he was in the street exclaiming against me, and no doubt our enemies rejoiced at it. And where the matter will end I know not, but I pray God to forgive him and them, and give them humility and repentance." (HC 2:297.)

This disagreement with William was even more serious than another one that brought them to blows because of the way in which William went about afterwards tearing down the Prophet. Of particular concern was the way in which William's venomous anger infected the inner circle of the Smith family, especially Samuel, who theretofore had been one of the Prophet's staunchest supporters.

While this rift ultimately healed over, it left deep scars. For William it heralded the time when, a decade later and following the Prophet's martyrdom, he would be excommunicated from the Church for his recalcitrance. Meanwhile, in 1839 he was dropped from the Twelve for insubordination; he was reinstated afterward only upon strong entreaties of relatives.

It was during the period of turmoil over William's disaffection that another incident occurred that showed an entirely different side of the relationships within the Smith family. The Prophet's father suffered a serious illness, and on a Wednesday in early October 1835 Joseph called upon him and "administered some wild herbs, agreeably to the commandment." In the Prophet's summary of that visit, he included this supplication: "May God grant to restore him immediately to health for Christ the Redeemer's sake. Amen." (HC 2:288.)

During the next three days, the Prophet waited on his father. On the fifth day, there occurred one of those unusual spiritual experiences for which the Prophet by now had become noted. Despairing at the way in which his father's condition had been worsening, he went to that source whence he had always found help in the past. Of the events of that day he wrote: "Waited on my father again, who was very sick. In secret prayer in the morning, the Lord said, 'My servant, thy father shall live.' I waited on him all this day with my heart raised to God in the name of Jesus Christ, that He would restore him to health, that I might be blessed with his company and advice. . . . At evening Brother David Whitmer came in. We called on the Lord in mighty prayer in the name of Jesus Christ, and laid our hands on him, and rebuked the disease. And God heard and answered our prayers—to the great joy and satisfaction of our souls. Our aged father arose and dressed himself, shouted, and praised the Lord. Called Brother William Smith, who had retired to rest, that he might praise the Lord with us, by joining in songs of praise to the Most High." (HC 2:289.)

Another incident a few days later again demonstrated the Prophet's love and concern for his family. He wrote: "In the morning I was called to visit at Brother Samuel Smith's. His wife was confined and in a dangerous condition. Brother Carlos went to Chardon after Dr. Williams. I went out into the field and bowed before the Lord and called upon Him in mighty prayer in her behalf. And the word of the Lord came unto me, saying, 'My servant Frederick shall come, and shall have wisdom given him to deal prudently, and my handmaid shall be delivered of a living child, and be spared'. The doctor came in about one hour afterwards, and in the course of two hours she was delivered, and thus what God had manifested to me was fulfilled every whit." (HC 2:292-93.)

While Joseph often conferred blessings upon his family and friends, he was not averse to being critical or even condemnatory when the circumstances appeared to require it. He reproved one of his followers, Reynolds Cahoon, through a revelation that contained these harsh words: "Mine anger is kindled against my servant Reynolds Cahoon, because of his iniquities, his covetous and dishonest principles, in himself and family, and he doth not purge them away and set his house in order. Therefore, if he repent not, chastisement awaiteth him, even as it seemeth good in my sight, therefore go and declare unto him these words." (HC 2:299.)

Through another revelation, he delivered this scornful reproof to the Twelve: "Behold they are under condemnation, because they have not been sufficiently humble in my sight, and in consequence of their covetous desires, in that they have not dealt equally with each other in the division of the monies which came into their hands, nevertheless, some of them dealt equally, therefore they shall be rewarded; but verily I say unto you, they must all humble themselves before me, before they will be accounted worthy to receive an endowment, to go forth in my name unto all nations." (HC 2:300.)

Joseph was always forthright with the Brethren, almost to the point of bluntness, so that they knew precisely where they stood in his estimation. He never dissembled or temporized with them, but always spoke out boldly regardless of the consequences.

The strong rebuke that the Prophet administered to the Twelve had an interesting effect upon them. Their reactions were a good indication of their character and their sense of dedication to the work and to the Prophet. In light of subsequent events, one wonders whether the rebuke was in part a deliberate attempt by the Prophet to test his followers, to find out for a surety upon whom he could rely.

A significant entry in his journal in November 1835 reveals clearly the character of three of the original members of the Twelve based upon their reactions to the stinging rebuke. This entry noted: "William E. M'Lellin and Orson Hyde came in and desired to hear the Revelation concerning the Twelve. My scribe read it to them. They expressed some little dissatisfaction, but after examining their own hearts, they acknowledged it to be the word of the Lord, and said they were satisfied. After school, Brigham Young came in, and desired also to hear it read; after hearing it, he appeared perfectly satisfied." (HC 2:302.)

These reactions seemed to foreshadow what lay ahead of each of these men in their respective roles in the Church. Within a few years Orson Hyde was to be dropped from the Quorum of Twelve because of a disaffection from the Prophet and William E. M'Lellin was to be excommunicated. While Orson Hyde was later reinstated in the Twelve and thereafter rendered long and faithful service until the time of his death, his disaffection prevented him from becoming the head of the Church.

By the end of 1835, the Prophet had acquired almost a celebrity status in the area. It was a great novelty among the people then, as it is now, for a man to claim not only to be in direct communication with God, but also to have the authority to speak and to act in His name. While there were others who made pretentious claims to being prophets, none had credentials like Joseph's to support their claims. His fellowmen could point to two volumes of religious literature he had produced, to the testimonies of reliable people who had witnessed miraculous things performed by him, and to several thriving communities comprised largely of his followers. These measureable evidences aroused a great curiosity about the character and personality of the man who produced them, and this curiosity drew scores of people to Kirtland to see and to hear for themselves the man who was revered by his followers as a prophet of God.

One such visitor who came from the East expressed a view that was quite commonly held among those who were unacquainted with spiritual things. Of him the Prophet wrote: "After hearing my name, he remarked that I was nothing but a man, indicating by this expression that he had supposed that a person to whom the Lord should see fit to reveal His will, must be something more than a man. He seemed to have forgotten the saying that fell from the lips of St. James, that Elias was a man subject to like passions as we are, yet he had such power with God, that He, in answer to his prayers, shut the heavens that they gave no rain for the space of three years and six months; and again, in answer to his prayer, the heavens gave forth rain, and the earth gave forth fruit. Indeed, such is the darkness and the ignorance of this generation, that they look upon it as incredible that a man should have any intercourse with his Maker." (HC 2:303.)

That same month, the Prophet was visited by a man from New York who first identified himself as "Joshua, the Jewish Minister" but who, in fact, turned out to be a notorious character named Matthias who was suspected of having committed serious crimes. The Prophet spent several days with the man, informing him about the Church and listening to his strange views on the meaning of the biblical prophecies and on various doctrines, including the resurrection. When Joshua (or Matthias) finally advanced the strange doctrine of the transmigration of the soul or spirit from father to son, claiming that he was a direct descendant of the apostle Matthias and that Matthias's spirit was resurrected in him, the Prophet abruptly terminated the relationship. "I told him that his doctrine was of the devil," he wrote, "that he was in reality in possession of a wicked and depraved spirit, although he professed to be the Spirit of truth itself; and he said also that he possessed the soul of Christ." The Prophet then concluded his entry with one of those wry comments for which he was noted: "He tarried until Wednesday, 11th, when, after breakfast, I told him, that my God told me, that his god was the devil, and I could not keep him any longer, and he must depart. And so I, for once, cast out the devil in bodily shape, and I believe a murderer." (HC 2:307.)

On another day, Joseph entertained another visitor with quite the opposite result: "This afternoon, Erastus Holmes, of Newbury, Ohio, called on me to inquire about the establishment of the Church, and to be instructed in doctrine more perfectly. I gave him a brief relation of my experience while in my juvenile years . . . ; also the revelation that I received afterwards concerning the Book of Mormon, and a short account of the rise and progress of the Church up to this date. He listened very attentively, and seemed highly gratified, and intends to unite with the Church." (HC 2:312.)

And so an almost endless stream of people made their way to Kirtland to see the Mormon prophet in person. Among them were believers and unbelievers, scoffers and adulators, the righteous and the wicked. Their appraisals of the Prophet were as diverse as their own personalities, but upon one point they were all in agreement: they had been in the presence of an unusual man who did not fit into the common mold.

Judging alone from the frequency and the extent of the Prophet's interviews with visitors during this period, one might infer that he had time for little else. But in reality these merely represented the mortar that bound together the more important and enduring duties claiming his attention. His journal reveals that in the midst of all this he continued to give constant and effective direction to the rapidly growing church he headed. He was studying Hebrew, teaching grammar to his family, continuing with the translation of the papyrus scrolls, writing for the church publications, participating in debating societies, and constantly blessing and exhorting his family and his brethren and sisters in the Church.

With all his heavy responsibilities, the Prophet manifested again and again a spirit of prayer and contrition. On Sunday, December 20, 1835, he recorded in his journal: "Took solid comfort with my family. Had many serious reflections. Brothers Palmer and Taylor called to see me. I showed them the sacred records to their joy and satisfaction. O! may God have mercy upon these men, and keep them in the way of everlasting life."

The following Tuesday, he noted: "At home. Continued my studies. O may God give me learning, even language; and endue me with qualifications to magnify His name while I live. I also delivered an address to the Church, this evening. The Lord blessed my soul. My scribe is unwell. O may God heal him. And for his kindness to me, O my soul, be thou grateful to him, and bless him. And he shall be blessed of God for ever, for I believe him to be a faithful friend to me, therefore my soul delighteth in him. Amen." (HC 2:344.)

These entries provide another revealing insight into Joseph's character and his unwavering knowledge of the existence of God and of the fact that God hears and answers the fervent prayers of his children on earth. The Prophet knew how to use prayer as a tool in attaining righteous objectives and in learning the mind and will of the Lord. Nothing was too insignificant for him to make a matter of prayer. In fact, as his understanding matured and his experiences multiplied, he became even more reliant upon the Lord through prayer. This had two significant results. First, the longer Joseph served in the ministry, the clearer it became to him that he was an agent, not a principal. Therefore, it became incumbent upon him to ascertain in each instance what his principal, the Lord, would have him do. And second, through long experience and from a study of the scriptures, he became absolutely convinced of the essential partnership that must exist between God and man. On the one hand, he recognized that God is omniscient and all powerful, the Creator of the earth and the Father of our spirits. Yet, he knew also that earth life is a testing or proving ground for man, and that out of God's great respect for the integrity and independence of his children, he does not or will not intervene in their lives without invitation. It was intended from the beginning that men would have their free agency, and that the condition upon which God would enter their lives was that they would invite him in. Joseph understood this principle well and he applied it frequently and effectively. He recognized that God, through his omniscience and his infinite love for men, was better able than he to chart a safe course through any difficulty. And knowing that God would not upbraid or criticize him for asking, Joseph continued to the end his life-long practice of imploring him for guidance or solace. It is significant that his last reported words, uttered just before he fell from the second-story window of the Carthage jail where he was fatally shot, were "O Lord, My God." (HC 6:618.)

Chapter Twenty

The Kirtland Temple Is Completed

As the year 1836 began, the Saints were feverishly completing work on the temple at Kirtland. The outside plastering was completed about this time, and the Brethren commenced to use the upper room for a variety of gatherings. During this period they were busily engaged in studying a number of subjects, including Hebrew and music, and they often used the temple for classroom space.

While the temple filled an urgent, practical need in providing additional space for the ever-growing activities of the Church, the Prophet had in mind much higher and more important uses for it. To him it belonged in the same category as the temples built by ancient Israel, which were special, sanctified edifices where ordained priests engaged in the higher ordinances and rituals and where, on occasion, divine revelations were received and heavenly beings appeared. Joseph had already had enough experience with spiritual things to know that communication with the unseen world did not depend upon the existence of any special buildings or, for that matter, upon the existence of any buildings at all. Indeed, most of the major divine manifestations he had received had occurred out of doors, including the appearance of the Father and the Son in the first vision, and later appearances of John the Baptist and Peter, James, and John. So in building the temple Joseph labored under no illusion about the conditions that must precede direct contact with the unseen world. He knew that these essential conditions were spiritual, not physical, in nature; that they depended upon the inner qualities of faith and humility; and that, therefore, God or other heavenly beings could speak to man out of the burning bush, as in the case of Moses, or on the highway, as in the case of Paul, or in the grove, as in his own experience. Yet he also recognized that beautiful, refined surroundings tend to induce feelings of reverence, and a temple would, therefore, help to create the conditions necessary for direct communion with the spiritual world.

As the work neared completion, Joseph commenced to prepare his own mind and the minds of the Brethren for the events that were to accompany the temple's dedication. Toward this end, a special meeting, attended by most of the high leaders of the Church, was held on Wednesday, January 13, 1836. At that time there were discussions about the "endowment" the worthy members of the Church were soon to receive. There were instructions about the demeanor of the Brethren in their council meetings, and numerous organizational changes were made, following which blessings of ordination or setting apart were conferred. Special prayers were also offered in behalf of certain persons who were ill or afflicted.

The events of the day had a most profound effect upon the Prophet, who wrote: "This has been one of the best days that I ever spent; there has been an entire union of feeling expressed in all our proceedings this day; and the spirit of the God of Israel has rested upon us in mighty power, and it has been good for us to be here in this heavenly place in Christ Jesus, and although much fatigued with the labors of the day, yet my spiritual reward has been very great indeed." (HC 2:368.)

On Thursday, January 21, a series of meetings commenced in the Kirtland Temple that were almost without parallel in the history of religion. That day Joseph and other leading brethren were at their studies early, as was their practice. The school continued until about three P.M., when Joseph undertook a procedure that had been revealed to him previously and about which he had prayed and meditated earnestly. In the attic area of the printing office, near the temple, the brethren "attended the ordinance of washing [their] bodies in pure water." Then they "perfumed [their] bodies and heads, in the name of the Lord." (HC 2:379.)

Following these preliminaries, the Presidency, the Prophet's father, Joseph Smith, Sr., and the councils of Kirtland and Zion met in the upper room of the temple "at early candle-light." The Presidency, Joseph's father, and a few others went into the west upper room, where they blessed and consecrated holy oil to be used in the proceedings that were to follow. Joseph Smith, Sr., was anointed first with the oil and was blessed in turn by each of those present. Then he, as the patriarch, anointed and blessed each member of the Presidency. The Prophet recorded that on this occasion his father sealed upon him "the blessings of Moses, to lead Israel in the latter days, even as Moses led him in days of old; also the blessings of Abraham, Isaac, and Jacob."

After the other members of the Presidency joined with Joseph's father in laying their hands upon the Prophet, there occurred an electrifying experience. "The heavens were opened," the Prophet wrote, "and I beheld the celestial kingdom of God, and the glory thereof, whether in the body or out I cannot tell. I saw the transcendent beauty of the gate through which the heirs of that kingdom will enter, which was like unto circling flames of fire; also the blazing throne of God, whereon [were] seated the Father and the Son. I saw the beautiful streets of that kingdom, which had the appearance of being paved with gold. I saw Fathers Adam and Abraham, and . . . my brother, Alvin, that has long since slept, and marvelled how it was that he had obtained an inheritance in that kingdom, seeing that he had departed this life before the Lord had set His hand to gather Israel the second time, and had not been baptized for the remission of sins."

The sight of Alvin in the celestial kingdom startled the Prophet, who could not reconcile it with his understanding of the scriptures at that time. The answer came to him by way of revelation:

"All who have died without a knowledge of this Gospel, who would have received it if they had been permitted to tarry, shall be heirs of the celestial kingdom of God; also all that shall die henceforth without a knowledge of it, who would have received it with all their hearts, shall be heirs of that kingdom, for I, the Lord, will judge all men according to their works, according to the desires of their hearts." (HC 2:380. See also Pearl of Great Price, Joseph Smith—Vision of the Celestial Kingdom.)

The fact that the Prophet marveled upon seeing Alvin in his vision betrayed a common misconception that existed at that time that entrance into the celestial kingdom required baptism during mortality. The rationale for this doctrine lay in the Savior's injunction to Nicodemus, "except a man be born of water and of the Spirit, he cannot enter into the kingdom of God." (John 3:5.) To one who does not believe in a continuity of life between bodily death and the resurrection, it is logical to believe that this directive requires baptism during mortality. But it is quite otherwise to one who believes that the spirit in man is eternal and continues to live despite the death of its mortal cloak. To such a believer, it is logical that after the death of his mortal body, his spirit, which possesses intelligence and reasoning powers, can comprehend and apply the principles of faith and repentance. If, then, the earthly ordinances of baptism and confirmation can be performed here vicariously, the requirements of the Savior's statement to Nicodemus will be met.

It was later revealed to the Prophet that vicarious baptism and confirmation are indeed basic principles of the gospel. In light of this, certain obscure passages in the New Testament take on new meaning. No longer is it necessary to speculate about the import of the statement in 1 Peter that following the Savior's bodily death "he went and preached unto the spirits in prison" who were disobedient in the days of Noah. (1 Peter 3:19-20.) Nor are we left in darkness about this statement: "For for this cause was the gospel preached also to them that are dead, that they might be judged according to men in the flesh, but live according to God in the spirit." (1 Peter 4:6.)

In Paul's first epistle to the Corinthian saints he wrote extensively about the doctrine of vicarious work for the dead and the universality of the resurrection, including this statement: "Else what shall they do which are baptized for the dead, if the dead rise not at all? why are they then baptized for the dead?" (1 Corinthians 15:29.)

These and other scriptures supporting the doctrine of vicarious work for the dead were not made clear to the Prophet until some time after his vision of the celestial world. From this emerges another important facet of his genius: that none of the basic truths and doctrines he revealed were arrived at by empirical means. In other words, a significant fact of truth was first revealed to him by extrasensory means, and later the corroborating scriptures were found to support it.

The presence of Alvin in the celestial world was only a part of the vision opened to the Prophet at the Kirtland Temple. In addition, he saw the apostles who had served with the Savior during his earthly ministry; he saw Brigham Young "standing in a strange land, in the far south and west, in a desert place"; he saw the Twelve in the celestial kingdom; and he beheld the redemption of Zion "and many things which the tongue of man cannot describe in full." (HC 2:381.)

When those who had joined the Prophet in the west upper

room had received their anointings, the high councils of Kirtland and Zion were invited to join them. Wrote the Prophet, "The visions of heaven were opened to them also. Some of them saw the face of the Savior, and others were ministered unto by holy angels, and the spirit of prophecy and revelation was poured out in mighty power; and loud hosannas, and glory to God in the highest, saluted the heavens, for we all communed with the heavenly host." (HC 2:382.)

On the following day the Twelve and the Seventy received their washings and anointings with similar results. The Prophet wrote: "The heavens were opened, and angels ministered to us." (HC 2:283.) Thus, within two days the highest leaders of the Church had received the endowments toward which they had looked with such eager anticipation. For some, it was their first exposure to spiritual phenomena; for others, such as the Prophet, Oliver Cowdery, and Sidney Rigdon, it was an exciting confirmation of knowledge they had gained by similar means in the past.

In subsequent days the Prophet continued to confer the endowment upon other worthy priesthood holders. Concurrently, the work on the lower floors of the temple went forward at a rapid pace.

By February 22 the lower room of the temple was ready for painting, and the next day "the sisters met again at the Temple to work on the veil," white canvas curtains which, when lowered, divided the main floor into four compartments. (HC 2:399.)

Nearly everyone played some role in construction of the temple; and having invested their labor and money in its construction, they naturally entertained a proprietary attitude toward it. At the same time they felt, almost without exception, that this lovely edifice, while it represented the fruits of their industry, was not really theirs. It was the House of the Lord, the loving title they conferred upon it. Though they were in reality the proprietors, they considered themselves as guests in the building.

By Sunday, March 27, 1836, all was in readiness for the temple dedication. The members began to assemble at seven A.M., a full hour before the doors were scheduled to open. The sun rising over Kirtland that beautiful spring morning reminded the Saints of their sacrifice as its rays glistened on the pieces of glass and crockery that had been mixed into the outside plaster. To them this was symbolic of the twinkling heavens on a starry night and heightened their expectations of the celestial outpourings they confidently expected would attend the dedication.

The main floor of the Kirtland Temple is arranged with identical pulpits in the east and west ends of the building facing each other. Between the pulpits are pews with movable benches so that the occupants, by moving the benches one way or the other, can face either pulpit, depending on the location of the speaker. The stand on the west is for the leaders of the high or Melchizedek Priesthood, while the stand on the east accommodates the leaders of the lower or Aaronic Priesthood.

On this historic occasion, members of the First Presidency acted as ushers, assisted by doorkeepers who were stationed at both the inner and outer doors. Prior to the opening of the doors at eight o'clock, the First Presidency, in the presence of other priesthood leaders, "dedicated the pulpits, and consecrated them to the Lord." (HC 2:410.)

According to the Prophet's calculation, some nine hundred to a thousand persons were seated inside the temple. Many who could not gain admittance were taken to a nearby schoolhouse, where a separate meeting was held. Still others had to be turned away, and so a second dedicatory session was held later in the week.

Today's generation, accustomed to meetings not longer than two hours in duration, is intrigued by the fact that the dedicatory session started officially at nine A.M. and adjourned at four P.M., the congregation "having manifested the most quiet demeanor during the whole exercise." (HC 2:428.) The speakers included the Prophet, Sidney Rigdon, Oliver Cowdery, Hyrum Smith, Don Carlos Smith, Brigham Young, and David W. Patten.

A choir directed by M. C. Davis sang several numbers. Most of the lyrics were written by either W. W. Phelps or Parley P. Pratt. Two of these songs, "Now Let Us Rejoice" and "The Spirit of God Like a Fire Is Burning," have, over the intervening years, become special favorites of Latter-day Saint congregations. The last of these two songs was sung immediately following the dedicatory prayer, a precedent that has been followed since at the dedication of other temples.

In addition to these items, the agenda of the meeting included the sustaining of the principal officers of the Church, the celebration of the Lord's Supper, and the rendition of the "Hosanna Shout" led by Sidney Rigdon.

Some of those attending this meeting experienced unusual spiritual phenomena. Frederick G. Williams, for example, "arose and testified that while President Rigdon was making his first prayer, an angel entered the window and took his seat between Father Smith and himself, and remained there during the prayer." The same record states that "President David Whitmer also saw angels in the house." (HC 2:427.)

While these and other spiritual occurrences were a great source of inspiration to the Saints, equally satisfying was the sense of peace and contentment that came into the hearts of all because they had contributed willingly of their time and means to construct the House of the Lord. The essence of this feeling was embodied in the following excerpt from the dedicatory prayer: "For Thou knowest that we have done this work through great tribulations; and out of our poverty we have given of our substance, to build a house to Thy name, that the Son of Man might have a place to manifest Himself to His people." (HC 2:431.)

A noteworthy characteristic of the Latter-day Saints always has been their penchant for meetings. It comes as no surprise, therefore, to learn that despite the seven-hour dedicatory service, the Prophet announced that a special meeting for the brethren of the priesthood would be held that evening to give them instruction "respecting the ordinance of washing of feet, which they were to attend to on Wednesday following." At the same time, the Prophet "gave them instructions in relation to the spirit of prophecy, and called upon the congregation to speak, and not to fear to prophesy good concerning the Saints, for," said he, "if you prophesy the falling of these hills and the rising of the valleys, the downfall of the enemies of Zion and the rising of the kingdom of God, it shall come to pass. Do not quench the Spirit, for the first one that opens his mouth shall receive the Spirit of prophecy." (HC 2:428.)

Obedient to this instruction, the Prophet's nineteen-year-old cousin George A. Smith arose and began to prophesy. The words of this fervent, dedicated young man, who was to become an apostle and later a counselor to President Brigham Young, triggered a spiritual outpouring almost unmatched in ecclesiastical history. No sooner had he commenced to speak than "a noise was heard like the sound of a rushing mighty wind, which filled the

Temple, and all the congregation simultaneously arose, being moved upon by an invisible power; many began to speak in tongues and prophesy; others saw glorious visions; and I beheld the Temple was filled with angels, which fact I declared to the congregation. The people of the neighborhood came running together (hearing an unusual sound within, and seeing a bright light like a pillar of fire resting upon the Temple), and were astonished at what was taking place. This continued until the meeting closed at eleven p.m." (HC 2:428.)

Unusual as these occurrences were, they were to be overshadowed to some extent by the events of the ensuing week.

One acquainted with the Prophet's extensive and varied experiences in spiritual matters might erroneously assume that they occurred without apparent effort on his part. Quite the contrary was true. Communication with the unseen world was an exhausting and demanding experience that required great concentration and mental and physical exertion, including fervent prayer. It was not uncommon for these prayer episodes to be preceded by fasting as a means of focusing all thought and energy on a certain object.

So it was that the Prophet and his counselors, Frederick G. Williams, Sidney Rigdon, Hyrum Smith, and Oliver Cowdery, met "in the most holy place in the Lord's House" shortly before noon on Tuesday and "sought for a revelation from [God] concerning the authorities of the Church going to Zion, and other important matters." The outcome of this petition was recorded by the Prophet: "After uniting in prayer, the voice of the Spirit was that we should come into this place three times, and also call the other presidents, the two Bishops and their counselors, each to stand in his place, and fast through the day and also the night, and that during this, if we would humble ourselves, we should receive further communications from Him. After this word was received we immediately sent for the other brethren, who came." (HC 2:429.)

After commencing their fast, they decided to remain in the temple all night. In preparation for the events of the next day, the Prophet gave the brethren instruction in the ordinance of washing of feet, and the sacrament was administered. "The Holy Spirit rested down upon us," he wrote, "and we continued in the Lord's House all night, prophesying and giving glory to God." (HC 2:430.)

The following morning, Wednesday, approximately three hundred members of the priesthood assembled in the temple at eight A.M. The procedure followed by the smaller group the previous night was then repeated with the ordinances of washing of feet and the sacrament. These were interspersed throughout the day with many instructions and prophesyings. Since the Prophet and his inner circle had been in the temple since noon the previous day and were responsible for conducting a second dedicatory session on Thursday, they departed from the temple Wednesday night, leaving the Twelve in charge of the meeting. Of the events that occurred after he departed, the Prophet wrote: "The brethren continued exhorting, prophesying, and speaking in tongues until five o'clock in the morning. The Savior made His appearance to some, while angels ministered to others, and it was a Pentecost and an endowment indeed, long to be remembered, for the sound shall go forth from this place into all the world. . . ." (HC 2:432-33.)

The second dedicatory session was held on Thursday to accommodate those who were unable to attend the first session on Sunday. The Prophet noted that "the services of the day were commenced, prosecuted and terminated in the same manner as at the former dedication, and the Spirit of God rested upon the congregation, and great solemnity prevailed." (HC 2:433.)

The thrilling events of the week built toward a climax on Sunday, April 3, 1836. Following an afternoon service where the sacrament was administered, the Prophet and Oliver Cowdery retired to the pulpit, "the veils being dropped," and engaged in "solemn and silent prayer." As they arose from prayer, four visions were opened to their minds when, in succession, the Savior, Moses, Elias, and Elijah appeared to them. The description of the Savior as he appeared on that occasion is as detailed as any ever given. The Prophet recorded: "We saw the Lord standing upon the breastwork of the pulpit, before us; and under his feet was a paved work of pure gold, in color like amber. His eyes were as a flame of fire; the hair of his head was white like the pure snow; his countenance shone above the brightness of the sun, and his voice was as the sound of the rushing of great waters. . . ." (D&C 110:2-3.)

Referring to the temple the Savior said: ". . . I have accepted this house, and my name shall be here; and I will manifest myself to my people in mercy in this house. Yea, I will appear unto my servants, and speak unto them with mine own voice, if my people will keep my commandments, and do not pollute this holy house. Yea the hearts of thousands and tens of thousands shall greatly rejoice in consequence of the blessings which shall be poured out, and the endowment with which my servants have been endowed in this house. And the fame of this house shall be spread to foreign lands; and this is the beginning of the blessing which shall be poured out upon the heads of my people." (D&C 110:7-10.)

The purpose of Moses' visit was to commit "the keys of the gathering of Israel from the four parts of the earth, and the leading of the ten tribes from the land of the north." Elias "committed the dispensation of the gospel of Abraham," and Elijah committed the keys of the dispensation "to turn the hearts of the fathers to the children, and the children to the fathers." (D&C 110:11-12, 15.)

With the culmination of the events surrounding the dedication of the Kirtland Temple, there came to the Prophet a feeling of assurance similar to the one he experienced after the Angel Moroni appeared to the three witnesses. There were now several hundred brethren who were bound to the Church and to the Prophet by solemn covenants. Because of the spiritual outpouring that had taken place, many of these brethren had also been filled with a fire and determination that would not be quenched. It was their obligation to carry the message abroad; to gather the elect from the four quarters of the earth; to act as the binding link between the generations past and those yet unborn; and to prepare for the second coming of the Savior and the establishment of the kingdom of God upon the earth. The Prophet took comfort from the knowledge that these men now shared his goals and were under solemn obligation to obtain them.

Chapter Twenty-one

Missionary Work Is Accelerated

Soon after the temple was dedicated, the brethren fanned out in many directions to proselyte and bear testimony of the things they had witnessed. Aroused by the happenings at Kirtland, the brethren close to the Prophet had taken to heart his counsel that they not stifle the Spirit and that they act upon the whisperings that would come.

A striking example of the prophetic gift aroused in Heber C. Kimball occurred just a few weeks after the temple dedication. One evening he and several others went to the home of Parley P. Pratt. Because of a heavy debt and the need to build a house for his wife, who was ill, Elder Pratt had been hesitant to leave on a mission. Elder Pratt later recorded what happened after he had admitted the nocturnal visitors: "Elder Heber C. Kimball . . . being filled with the spirit of prophesy . . . blessed me and my wife, and prophesied as follows: 'Brother Parley, thy wife shall be healed from this hour, and shall bear a son, and his name shall be Parley. . . . Arise, therefore, and go forth in the ministry, nothing doubting. Take no thoughts for your debts, nor the necessaries of life, for the Lord will supply you with abundant means for all things. Thou shalt go to Upper Canada, even to the city of Toronto, the capital, and there thou shalt find a people prepared for the fulness of the Gospel, and they shall receive thee, and thou shalt organize the church among them, and it shall spread thence into the regions round about, and many shall be brought to the knowledge of the truth and shall be filled with joy; and from the things growing out of this mission, shall the fulness of the Gospel spread into England, and shall cause a great work to be done in that land.' " (Orson F. Whitney, *Life of Heber C. Kimball,* p. 96.)

This unusual and explicit prophecy was fulfilled in every particular. Parley's wife, who had been barren for ten years and had been an incurable consumptive for six years, did indeed conceive and bear a son, who was named Parley. Within a few weeks, Parley found himself in Toronto, where, by unusual means, he came in contact with John Taylor, the head of a group of Bible students who were unaffiliated with any Christian sect and who were earnestly seeking for truth. Most of this group and others in the vicinity joined the Church through Parley's ministry. Among those converts were many from Great Britain, including John Taylor and his wife, and Joseph Fielding and his two sisters. One of the sisters, Mary Fielding, was later to marry Hyrum Smith and to bear him a son, Joseph F. Smith, who became the sixth president of the Church; his son, Joseph Fielding Smith, became the tenth president of the Church. No sooner had these natives of Great Britain joined the Church than they began to write to their relatives to tell them about their conversion to a church that was led by a man who claimed to be a prophet and whose words and works supported his claims. These letters excited great interest among their British kin, and it was out of this circumstance that the third part of Elder Kimball's prophecy was fulfilled. When he and his associates went to Great Britain a few months later on the first foreign mission for the Church, they found many interested listeners who were prepared to give them a friendly audience and to show them hospitality.

One cannot read with an open mind the journals of such men as Heber C. Kimball, Brigham Young, Parley P. Pratt, Orson Pratt, and Wilford Woodruff, who were intimately acquainted with Joseph Smith, without being impressed by two significant things. First, they were imbued with the same spiritual qualities possessed by the Prophet. They prophesied and spoke in tongues; they healed the sick and cast out devils; they had dreams and visions; and they followed unquestioningly what they referred to as "the whisperings of the Spirit." Although they were men of intellect who were forceful and independent by nature, they invariably yielded their will to the inner promptings or impressions they received. The other facet in their lives that deserves special attention is their constancy of purpose and loyalty to Joseph. These men routinely left family and friends, crossed mountains, plains, and oceans, endured hunger, thirst, and fatigue, and suffered every known hardship and privation in order to fulfill their ministry—all without monetary reward and at great personal sacrifice. Nor was it merely a one-time effort, but rather a continuing, lifelong occupation, which they pursued with enthusiasm and zeal.

Aside from the frequent promptings they received through the veil, the chief moving force that inspired these men was the personal influence of the Prophet Joseph Smith. They emulated him and sought constantly to perform in such a way as to receive his approval. Nothing he asked of them was ever declined or considered as being extreme or unreasonable. Their loyalty to him was absolute and unquestioning.

Against this background, the phenomenal growth and vitality of the Church and the towering influence of the Prophet Joseph Smith among his disciples becomes understandable. But even while the Church basked in the warmth of the spiritual outpouring at Kirtland and tasted the fruit of unprecedented growth, the seeds of turmoil were being sown among the Saints by forces that were beyond their control.

During this period, the entire United States was caught up in a wave of false prosperity, generated in large part by extensive speculations in land and the absence of a sound, controlled banking system. The banking laws of Ohio and other states were exceedingly loose, permitting the formation of banks without adequate safeguards. Once formed, these banks issued what seemed to be unlimited quantities of notes that, more often than not, were secured by land whose value had been inflated all out of proportion. In an effort to provide a convenient medium of exchange among the Saints and to permit them to share to a greater extent in what later proved to be an entirely false prosperity, the Prophet and other leading brethren in Kirtland organized the Kirtland Safety Society Bank in November 1836. On the assumption that the Ohio legislature would grant them a charter as it had done in numerous other cases, the organizers of the bank proceeded to have its banknotes engraved and to take other preliminary steps to prepare for business. By this time, however, a powerful anti-Mormon feeling had crept into the government of Ohio, which resulted in a denial of the application. The Prophet noted that "because we were Mormons, the legislature raised some frivolous excuse on which they refused to grant us those banking privileges they so freely granted to others." (Brodie, p. 196.) Reacting to this discriminatory treatment, he and his associates took what later proved to be an ill-conceived step that at once showed their contempt for the officials who had unfairly ruled against them and their spunky attitude toward adversity. On January 2, 1837, the day after they had received word of the legislature's decision, the

Prophet converted the Kirtland Safety Society Bank into the Kirtland Safety Society Anti-Banking Company. The banknotes, which had been rendered useless by the legislature's decision, were salvaged by the simple expedient of printing the prefix "anti" before and the suffix "ing" after the word "bank."

The careless, off-hand way in which this transaction was handled was an accurate reflection of the spirit of the times, though the Prophet's detractors have sought to use this incident to show a malignant quality in his character. To do this is to ignore the circumstances that brought it forth and to apply to him a rigid standard of business conduct that, during an era of chicanery and deceit, finds few parallels in our history.

The business enterprise was doomed to failure from the start. The lack of a sound banking system, coupled with the unbridled spirit of speculation that gripped the entire country, created a disastrous situation. Bank failures and panic became commonplace when banks were unable to convert their principal asset, land, into cash in order to redeem the notes and bonds presented for payment. The number of failures in May 1837 totaled 800 banks, with $120 million in deposits.

The failure of the Kirtland Safety Society was a devastating blow to the Prophet and to those who had invested in it. Those of shallow belief could not understand how a man who had communed with eternal beings through the veil could have failed so badly in a business venture. These critics did not understand that a man, though a prophet, is not immune from the economic or other difficulties that confront us all. They also drew wrong inferences from the incident, being ignorant of the broad scope of the economic ills that were afflicting the entire country.

Almost overnight the attitude in Kirtland changed from one of hope and love to one of hatred and despair. The Prophet wrote concerning the radical change that took place at this time: "As the fruits of this spirit, evil surmisings, fault finding, disunion, dissension, and apostasy followed in quick succession, and it seemed as though all the powers of earth and hell were combining their influence in an especial manner to overthrow the Church at once, and make a final end." (HC 2:487.)

Caught up in the maelstrom created by the panic of 1837, many members and some high leaders lost their moorings and became disaffected from the Prophet and the Church. Others were infected with an apostate spirit that caused them to attack and deride Joseph in a most vicious way. Heber C. Kimball wrote: "This order of things increased during the winter to such an extent that a man's life was in danger the moment he spoke in defense of the Prophet of God." (Whitney, p. 101.)

Conditions deteriorated to the point that on a particular Sunday, a group of malcontents met in the temple and bitterly attacked Joseph. The dissidents were led by the Prophet's erstwhile scribe and close associate, Warren Parrish, who embezzled large sums of money from the Kirtland Safety Society and was ultimately excommunicated from the Church. Others close to the Prophet, including some of the Twelve, similarly became disaffected.

In late June or early July, the Prophet formally severed all connection with the Kirtland Safety Society. In doing so he wrote: "Some time previous to this I resigned my office in the 'Kirtland Safety Society,' disposed of my interest therein, and withdrew from the institution; being fully aware, after so long an experiment, that no institution of the kind, established upon just the righteous principles for a blessing not only to the Church but the whole nation, would be suffered to continue its operations in such an age of darkness, speculation and wickedness. Almost all banks throughout the country, one after the other, have suspended specie payment, and gold and silver have risen in value in direct ratio with the depreciation of paper currency. The great pressure of the money market is felt in England as well as America, and bread stuffs are everywhere high." (HC 2:497.)

The failure of the Kirtland Safety Society and the accompanying turmoil and dissension presented to the Prophet one of the greatest challenges to his leadership he had ever faced. His economic woes were compounded by numerous disaffections occurring among the brethren, including some in the highest circle of leadership. All this posed a real threat that the Church, which only a short year before had seemed impregnably secure, would be brought down and its hopes for a utopian society buried in the shambles.

In the midst of all these difficulties the Prophet suffered a debilitating illness that brought him near to death. Thus it was especially galling to him to hear rumors that his illness was a retribution visited upon him by God for alleged wrong doing. Of this he wrote with some bitterness: "While I was thus afflicted, the enemy of all righteousness was suggesting, apostates reporting, and the doubtful believing that my afflictions were sent upon me, because I was in transgression, and had taught the Church things contrary to godliness." Manifesting again the supreme confidence he always had in himself and in the certitude of his cause, he concluded with an entry that was both condescending and disdainful in its tone: "but of this the Lord judge between me and them, while I pray my Father to forgive them the wrong they do." (HC 2:493.)

A normal tendency for one confronted with great, unexpected difficulty is to retreat, to indulge in self-justification or self-condemnation, or to seek pity and support. However, we search in vain for the presence of any of these negative qualities in the Prophet following the adversities of 1837. On the contrary, we see him struggling to find something that would reverse the backward momentum and put him and the Church on the offensive.

The answer came in the early part of June 1837. ". . . God revealed to me that something new must be done for the salvation of His Church," the Prophet wrote. "And on or about the first of June, 1837, Heber C. Kimball, one of the Twelve, was set apart by the spirit of prophecy and revelation, praying and laying on of hands, of the First Presidency, to preside over a mission to England, to be the first foreign mission of the Church of Christ in the last days." (HC 2:489.)

The way in which this call was extended provides fresh insight into the unorthodox, inspirational manner in which the Prophet gave leadership to the Church. "On Sunday, the 4th of June, 1837," wrote Elder Kimball, "the Prophet Joseph came to me, while I was seated in front of the stand, above the sacrament table, on the Melchizedek side of the Temple, in Kirtland, and whispering to me, said 'Brother Heber, the Spirit of the Lord has whispered to me: "Let my servant Heber go to England and proclaim my Gospel, and open the door of salvation to that nation." ' " (Whitney, pp. 103-4.)

This was the first step in a long journey that was to end in the conversion of thousands in the British Isles and northern Europe. And it was these converts, impelled by the spirit of gathering, who immigrated to the United States in a constant stream and provided the support for the westward exodus of the Saints.

Those who do not believe in God's existence and the reality

and power of spiritual forces are inclined to explain this incident and the almost unbelievable consequences that flowed from it on the basis of Joseph's genius or his shrewdness. But Joseph candidly acknowledged that his course of action had been revealed to him by God and that Heber had been set apart "by the spirit of prophecy and revelation, prayer and laying on of hands."

Although startling in its effect, the call received by Elder Kimball was not wholly unexpected. Some months before, in a conversation with Willard Richards, he had, in a spirit of prophecy, predicted for himself a mission to the shores of Europe. " 'Shall I go with thee,' enquired Willard. 'Yea, in the name of the Lord, thou shalt go with me when I go,' Heber replied." (Whitney, pp. 106-7.)

This was a recurring phenomenon with Joseph and his followers. It was as if they were all plugged in to a central communication system, receiving and relaying messages other than through the physical senses. The answer is found in the theology revealed and taught by the Prophet Joseph Smith:

First, all who have lived or who will live are influenced from birth by the light of Christ, which proceeds forth from the presence of God to fill "the immensity of space." Anyone may avail himself of the vast benefits of this light by living the principles taught in the scriptures, and everyone who is attuned to this light will have similar perceptions, regardless of their locality, even as persons separated by distance have similar perceptions of the sun.

Second, those who comply with the basic teachings of faith in Christ, repentance from sin, and baptism by immersion by one authorized of God may receive the gift of the Holy Ghost, which equips them with extraordinary spiritual powers and perception. The Prophet is reported to have said that the possession of the Holy Ghost by the Latter-day Saints was the chief factor that differentiated them from all others.

It is clear from the lives of Heber C. Kimball and other disciples of the Prophet that this teaching about the Holy Ghost was not an idle piece of rhetoric. Rather it was something that entered into every facet of their lives.

For an understanding of the ecclesiastical reasons behind the overseas missionary effort commenced by the Prophet in 1837, one must focus upon an event that accompanied the dedication of the Kirtland Temple the year before. This was the appearance to Joseph Smith of the biblical prophet Moses, who conferred the keys of the gathering. It was understood by Joseph and his followers from the beginning that by the authority that accompanied these keys, the Prophet, acting in the role of Moses, would lead modern Israel out of the world to a promised land even as the ancient Moses led the children of Israel out of captivity in Egypt.

The Prophet's private journal during this period betrays his preoccupation with the progress of Elder Kimball's missionary force and the unfolding of the work in England. He duly noted the departure of Elders Kimball, Orson Hyde, and Willard Richards and Joseph Fielding, a priest, from Kirtland on Tuesday, June 13, 1837. These brethren were joined in New York by three missionaries from Canada: John Goodson, Isaac Russell, and John Snyder. The seven men arrived in Liverpool on July 20 and, moving thence inland to Preston, immediately commenced their ministry, resulting in the first fruits of this ministry—the baptism of nine persons—on July 30. On August 4 the baptism and confirmation of Jennetta Richards, a daughter of the Reverend John Richards, took place. Jennetta was later to become the bride of Willard Richards. The circumstances of Jennetta's baptism and subsequent marriage to Willard Richards demonstrates the remarkable spiritual perception of these first missionaries. On the day of her baptism and confirmation, Heber remarked to Willard, "I baptized your wife today."

Two entries from Willard's diary tell the rest of the tale. In March 1838 he recorded: "I took a tour through the branches and preached. While walking in Thornly I plucked a snowdrop, far through the hedge, and carried it to James Mercer's and hung it in his kitchen. Soon after, Jennetta Richards came into the room, and I walked with her and Alice Packer to Ribchester, and attended meeting with Brothers Kimball and Hyde at Brother Clark's. While walking with these sisters, I remarked, 'Richards is a good name; I never want to change it; do you Jennetta?' 'No, I do not' was her reply, 'and I think I never will.' "

The second entry concludes the story: "Sept. 24. 1839, I married Jennetta Richards. . . . Most truly do I praise my Heavenly Father for His great kindness in providing me a partner according to his promise. I receive her from the Lord, and hold her at his disposal. I pray that he may bless us forever. Amen." (Whitney, p. 144.)

The Prophet made due note of the extension of the work from Preston to other communities in England. He seemed to take great satisfaction in the progress of the brethren there, assuming an almost paternal attitude toward them. He gloried in their successes and anguished in their setbacks. He took particular note of a powerful manifestation of satanic forces that occurred on the eve of the first baptisms in England. "About daybreak Sunday, July 30th, Elder Isaac Russell, who had been appointed to preach on the Obelisk in Preston market place that day, and who slept in the second story of their lodgings in Wilford street, went up to the third loft where Elders Hyde and Kimball were sleeping, and called upon them to pray for him, that he might be delivered from the evil spirits that were tormenting him to such a degree that he felt he could not live long unless he obtained relief. They immediately arose and laid hands on him and prayed that the Lord would have mercy on His servant and rebuke the devil. While thus engaged Elder Kimball was struck with great force by some invisible power and fell senseless on the floor; and the first thing Elder Kimball recollected was being supported by Elders Hyde and Russell beseeching the throne of grace in his behalf. They then laid him on the bed but his agony was so great he could not endure it, and arose, fell on his knees and prayed; then he arose and sat upon the bed while the brethren distinctly saw the evil spirits, who foamed and gnashed upon them with their teeth, by legions for the space of some minutes; Elder Richards was present the latter part of the time." (HC 2:503.)

Elder Kimball's account of this experience provides further insight into the spiritual strugglings through which he and his associates passed in order to fulfill the mandate given to them by the Prophet: "I then arose and sat upon the bed, when a vision was opened to our minds, and we could distinctly see the evil spirits, who foamed and gnashed their teeth at us. We gazed upon them about an hour and a half (by Willard's watch). We were not looking towards the window, but towards the wall. Space appeared before us and we saw the devils coming in legions, with their leader, who came within a few feet of us. . . . I shall never forget the vindictive malignity depicted on their countenances as they looked me in the eye. . . . I felt excessive pain, and was in the greatest distress for some time. I cannot even look back on the scene without feelings of horror; yet by it I learned the power of the adversary, his enmity against the servants of God, and got some understanding of the invisible world. We distinctly heard those spirits talk and express their wrath and hellish designs against us. However, the Lord delivered us from them, and blessed us exceedingly that day." (Whitney, pp. 130-31.)

The Prophet commented on this report: "When I heard of it, it gave me great joy, for I knew that the work of the Lord had taken root in that land. It was this that made the devil make a struggle to kill you." (Ibid., p. 132.)

Heber's experience called to the Prophet's mind his own terrible exposure to the power of evil as he knelt in the grove seventeen years earlier. On that occasion, the most powerful manifestation of satanic influence occurred just before the appearance of the Father and the Son. So it was that the incredible experience of Heber C. Kimball and his brethren in Preston occurred just a few hours before the first converts were baptized in England. This group of nine converts was the vanguard of an army numbered in tens of thousands who embraced the gospel, immigrated to America, and helped significantly to establish the Latter-day Saints in the mountainous West.

It was his experience in the grove and Heber C. Kimball's confrontation with Satan in Preston that prompted the Prophet's oft-quoted statement: "The nearer a person approaches the Lord, a greater power will be manifested by the adversary to prevent the accomplishment of His purposes." (HC 2:511.)

Chapter Twenty-two

The Saints Depart from Kirtland

While the Prophet's main focus of interest during the late 1830s was the progress of the missionary efforts in England, many other activities and problems were competing for his attention. In early August 1837 plans were laid for construction of a temple in Far West, Missouri. The August issue of the *Messenger and Advocate* contained a prospectus for a new Church-sponsored paper to be published at Kirtland, the *Elders' Journal.*

Joseph also undertook a mission to Canada to proselyte and to check on the small branches that had sprung up there. His first attempt to go to Canada was aborted to Painesville, Ohio, when he was "detained all day by malicious and vexatious law suits." He wrote of this incident with understandable irritation: "About sunset I got into my carriage to return home to Kirtland; at this moment the sheriff sprang into the carriage, seized my lines, and served another writ on me, which was sworn out by a man who had a few weeks previously brought a new fashioned cooking stove to Kirtland, and prevailed upon me to put it up in my kitchen, saying it would give credit to his stove, wishing to have it tested by our people; and now he thought would be a good time to get pay for it. I gave my watch to the officer for security and we all returned home." (HC 2:502.)

A task ever present in these early days of the Church was that of maintaining discipline and order among the members. Drawn from many areas and having divergent social, political, and religious backgrounds, these converts presented special problems of administration. The Prophet's task was magnified by the inherent independence and aggressiveness that characterized most Americans of the day. Occasionally, harsh measures were required to bring some of the more recalcitrant brethren into line; and sometimes even these failed, as was true with Oliver Cowdery. In one unsuccessful attempt to subdue Oliver, whose headstrong propensities seemed always to keep him in hot water, the Prophet resorted to the unusual expedient of broadcasting his failings through a printed, public announcement. "Oliver Cowdery," wrote the Prophet, "has been in transgression, but as he is now chosen as one of the presidents or counselors, I trust that he will yet humble himself and magnify his calling, but if he should not, the Church will soon be under the necessity of raising their hands against him; therefore pray for him." In the same announcement, which came after the numerous defections that accompanied the financial problems of 1837, the Prophet wrote: "David Whitmer, Leonard Rich, and others have been in transgression, but we hope that they may be humble and ere long make satisfaction to the Church, otherwise they cannot retain their standing; therefore we say unto you, beware of all disaffected characters, for they come not to build up, but to destroy and scatter abroad." (HC 2:511.)

This instance of strong, even harsh, chastisement by the Prophet was not an isolated case. He often used it deliberately as the means of bringing about the necessary discipline within the ranks of the Church. Once, in an introspective mood, he analyzed with some detachment his use of this disciplinary tool. "I frequently rebuke and admonish my brethren," he said, "and that because I love them, not because I wish to incur their displeasure, or mar their happiness." With blunt but refreshing realism, he then acknowledged the result of such conduct: "Such a course of conduct is not calculated to gain the good will of all, but rather the ill will of many; therefore, the situation in which I stand is an important one; so, you see, brethren, the higher the authority, the greater the difficulty of the station; but these rebukes and admonitions become necessary, from the perverseness of the brethren, for their temporal as well as spiritual welfare. They actually constitute a part of the duties of my station and calling. Others have other duties to perform, that are important, and far more enviable, and may be just as good, like the feet and hands, in their relation to the human body—neither can claim priority, or say to the other, I have no need of you." (HC 2:478.)

As word of the first conversions in England filtered back to his headquarters, the Prophet commenced to appraise the effect upon the Church of a large and continuous flow of converts from abroad. He had seen what had happened in Kirtland shortly after the Church was organized when the flood of converts from the eastern United States literally swamped the facilities of that small town. Now he had every confidence that this experience would be repeated, except on a magnified scale. Consequently, his mind commenced to focus more and more upon the subject of the gathering and the needs of the thousands of converts who would soon throng into the central gathering place of the Church. At a conference held in Kirtland on September 17, 1837, he spoke on the subject of the gathering "and the duties of the different quorums in relation thereto." The conclusion reached at the conference was of far-reaching significance: "It appeared manifest to the conference that the places appointed for the gathering of the Saints were at this time crowded to overflowing, and that it was necessary that there be more stakes of Zion appointed in order that the poor might have a place to gather to, 'wherefore it was moved, seconded, and voted unanimously that President Joseph Smith, Jun., and Sidney Rigdon be requested by this conference to go and appoint other stakes, or places of gathering.' " (HC 2:513-14.)

Ten days later, in company with Sidney Rigdon, his brother William Smith, and his trusted friend Vinson Knight, the Prophet departed from Kirtland "to fulfill the mission appointed . . . in establishing places of gathering for the Saints." (HC 2:518.) Traveling via Terre Haute, Indiana, they arrived at Far West, Missouri, around the first of November. After studying the conditions there for several days and conferring with the local brethren, Joseph convened a meeting on November 6 where it was decided to petition the trustees of Far West to alter the plat of the townsite so as to provide for four acres in each block, divided into four lots. The council also concluded "that there is sufficient room in this country for the churches to continue gathering from abroad." (HC 2:521.)

The Prophet envisioned that the Saints would literally fill up the land with each householder having an acre of ground from which to produce many of the necessities of life. He also recognized that the prospect of immigrating to a fertile, productive area would be a powerful lure to the converts from abroad and would help soften the impact of leaving home and family to gather to a new land.

While Joseph was optimistic about the prospects in Missouri, he was also a realist. He knew that the uneasy truce between the Saints and the Missouri mobocrats was, at best, very fragile. This fact, however, in no way deterred him from going ahead to encourage a rapid migration of his people to that area.

The Prophet returned to Kirtland to find a powerful group of erstwhile supporters in open rebellion against him and the Church. Led by Warren Parrish, John F. Boynton, Luke S. Johnson, and Joseph Coe, this group had publicly renounced Joseph and set up a new religious cult, which they called the "Church of Christ." So belligerent and aggressive were the dissenters that they had become a dominent force in Kirtland, intimidating those who remained loyal to the Prophet. In the forefront of the rapidly diminishing group who remained steadfast was Brigham Young, but even his iron will could not withstand the violent spirit of apostasy that prevailed, and he was forced to leave Kirtland a few days before Christmas.

The hostile climate finally caused the Prophet to leave in mid-January. Accompanied by Sidney Rigdon, he fled on horseback at night, in order to "escape mob violence, which was about to burst upon us." (HC 3:1.) Destitute of means, they traveled only as far as Dublin, Ohio, where they sought employment at cutting and sawing wood. Unable to acquire the means to continue with the journey, the Prophet one day both shocked and complimented Brigham Young, who was also in Dublin at the time. Approaching Brigham, Joseph said, "You are one of the Twelve who have charge of the kingdom in all the world; I believe I shall throw myself upon you, and look to you for counsel in this case." Brigham at first doubted that the Prophet was in earnest. But being assured he was, Brigham responded: "If you will take my counsel it will be that you rest yourself, and be assured you shall have money in plenty to pursue your journey." Soon after, a Brother Tomlinson in Dublin was able to sell his farm because of counsel given by Elder Young. In gratitude, and at the suggestion of Elder Young, he gave the Prophet three hundred dollars, which enabled him to continue his journey to Missouri. (HC 3:2.)

Learning of the Prophet's approach, the brethren in Far West sent out a welcoming party. Joseph could not help but contrast the warm reception he received from these brethren with the bitterness and enmity that characterized those whom he had recently left in Kirtland. He noted with satisfaction that they received him "with open arms" and provided "teams and money to help me forward." (HC 3:8.) The party arrived in Far West on March 14, 1838, where occurred a repetition of the earlier welcome.

While he was genuinely pleased by the warm reception he had

been given, Joseph was not a little troubled by a bitter schism that had opened up between two quarreling factions within the Church at Far West. As he pieced the facts together, it was made to appear that on February 5, 1838, a "Committee of the whole," moderated by Thomas B. Marsh, had rejected the presidency of the Church in Zion, consisting of David Whitmer, W.W. Phelps, and John Whitmer. The controversy arose out of the sale of certain lands in Missouri, the alleged misuse of church funds, and, as to David Whitmer, his "persisting" in the use of tea, coffee, and tobacco. (HC 3:3-4.) In a meeting of the high council held on March 10, "it was decided that William W. Phelps and John Whitmer be no longer members of the Church of Christ of Latter-day Saints, . . . until they learn to blaspheme no more against the authorities of God, nor fleece the flock of Christ." (HC 3:8.)

In addition to these problems facing the Prophet in Missouri, there was the ever-present threat of further violence from non-member enemies of the Church. The uneasy truce that had emerged from the shambles of the Jackson County expulsion was tenuous at best, and the Prophet knew that the anxieties of the nonmembers in Missouri toward the burgeoning growth of the Church would be greatly heightened by his move there and the prospect of a flood of new converts from abroad.

Not long after his arrival in Missouri, the Prophet composed a "political motto" for the Church. Following a principle of leadership that he often employed, he gained wider support for this pronouncement by obtaining the approving signatures of seven other brethren, including four members of the Twelve. He also published the answers to a number of theological questions that had been put to him. Under date of March 29, 1838, he directed a long and newsy letter to the Church in Kirtland advising the members there, among other things, of his safe arrival in Missouri, the warmth of the reception he had been accorded, and the excommunication of W.W. Phelps and John Whitmer. He transmitted with his letter a copy of the political motto, which contained this significant passage: ". . . woe to tyrants, mobs, aristocracy, anarchy, and toryism, and all those who invent or seek out unrighteous and vexatious law suits, under the pretext and color of law, or office, either religious or political." This statement takes on added meaning when it is viewed in light of the following sentence, which appeared in the body of the letter: "We have heard of the destruction of the printing office, which we presume to believe must have been occasioned by the Parrish party, or more properly the aristocrats or anarchists." (HC 3:9, 11.)

The above-quoted statement from the political motto also contained a veiled reference to Oliver Cowdery, who, by this time, had become irreconcilably disaffected from the Church and had turned to the practice of law. Formal charges were preferred against him on April 11, 1838, to which he made no defense, saying only, "I shall lay them carefully away, and take such a course with regard to them, as I may feel bound by my honor, to answer to my rising posterity." Because of his failure to defend himself against the charges, a church court entered a judgment on April 12, 1838, that "he was considered no longer a member of the Church of Jesus Christ of Latter-day Saints." (HC 3:17-18.)

The disfellowshipment of his old and beloved friend was a traumatic experience for the Prophet. For over nine years they had been intimately associated in the ministry and had shared some of the most unusual experiences ever enjoyed by mortals. Those of the Prophet's detractors who attempt to explain him on a conspiratorial basis stand baffled at the decline and fall of Oliver Cowdery. Had there been a conspiracy between the two men to deceive their associates and the public, had their stories about the translation of the Book of Mormon and the appearance of divine beings been fabricated, had they deliberately set about to gain power and influence through fraud and misrepresentation, then evidence to this effect would have surfaced at the time Oliver was disfellowshipped. But the records are devoid of any such evidence. On the contrary, the records indicate that the points of difference between Oliver and Joseph were personal ones, wholly unrelated to the facts and principles upon which the Church was founded. The letter Oliver filed with the church court makes this clear: "I beg you, sir," it said, "to take no view of the foregoing remarks, other than my belief in the outward government of this Church. I do not charge you, or any other person who differs with me on these points, of not being sincere, but such difference does exist, which I sincerely regret." (HC 3:18.) Never, after leaving the Church, did Oliver deny the reality of the things to which he had testified, nor did he ever question the principles expounded by the Prophet Joseph Smith.

A decade after his disfellowshipment, and four years after Joseph's martyrdom, Oliver returned to the Church. Samuel W. Richards recorded the substance of a conversation he had with Oliver following his rebaptism, which reveals his true feelings and attitudes: "In what had now transpired with him," Brother Richards wrote, "he felt to acknowledge the hand of God, in that he had been preserved; for if he had been with the church he would have undoubtedly been with Joseph in his days of trial and shared a like fate with him; but being spared, he now desired to go to the nations and bear testimony of this work which no other living man could bear. . . . Before taking his departure he wrote and left with the writer of this, the following statement, which we believe to be his last living testimony, though oft repeated, of the wonderful manifestations which brought the authority of God to men on the earth: 'While darkness covered the earth and gross darkness the people; long after the authority to administer in holy things had been taken away, the Lord opened the heavens and sent forth His word for the salvation of Israel. In fulfillment of the sacred scripture, the everlasting gospel was proclaimed by the mighty angel (Moroni) who, clothed with the authority of his mission, gave glory to God in the highest. This gospel is the "stone taken from the mountain without hands" John the Baptist, holding the keys of the Aaronic Priesthood; Peter, James and John, holding the keys of the Melchizedek Priesthood, have also ministered for those who shall be heirs of salvation, and with those administrations, ordained men to the same Priesthoods. These Priesthoods, with their authority, are now, and must continue to be, in the body of the Church of Jesus Christ of Latter-day Saints. Blessed is the Elder who has received the same, and thrice blessed and holy is he who shall endure to the end. Accept assurances, dear brother, of the unfeigned prayer of him who, in connection with Joseph the Seer, was blessed with the above ministrations, and who earnestly and devoutly hopes to see you in the celestial glory.' " (Preston Nibley, *The Witnesses of the Book of Mormon* [Deseret Book, 1953], p. 52.)

While the Prophet genuinely regretted the disaffection of Oliver Cowdery, he did not permit it to interfere with the ongoing activities of the Church. Characteristically, he turned with vigor and enthusiasm to the many other activities that needed his attention. On April 26, 1838, he received an important revelation which, among other things, fixed the official name of the church as

The Church of Jesus Christ of Latter-day Saints; commanded the construction of a temple at Far West, Missouri; and directed "that the city of Far West . . . be built up speedily by the gathering of my Saints." (D&C 115.)

The diverse nature of his interests at this period reveal again that Joseph was no ivory-tower prophet-leader. His activities ranged from the sublime act of declaring God's will by revelation to the menial task of plowing his garden. One day might be occupied in studying English grammar, while on the next Joseph would be engaged in discussing issues and personalities with local politicians.

It was during this period that he commenced in earnest the monumental task of writing a history of the Church. He recognized that in large part this would revolve around his own activities. As a result, his history consisted mostly of an auto-biographical chronology. Since only he knew the intimate details of these events, he was anxious to record them so that future generations would have a clear understanding of the unusual happenings that accompanied the organization and rise of the Church.

Some of the Prophet's detractors see in all this an attempt to alter history rather than to record it. One of the most agile of these critics premised a book in part upon the theory that Joseph invented the story of his first vision in the late 1830s as a means of shoring up his image as a prophet. This same author embarrassedly acknowledged in a supplement to her work published in 1971 that "important newly released evidence from the manuscript archives of the Mormon church in Salt Lake City does indicate that late in 1830 or early in 1831 Joseph Smith began to write and to talk with some freedom among his fellowmen about a great vision in his youth." (Brodie, p. 406.) This author attempted to cover her oversight and to save face by declaring, "Despite dedicated searching of early newspapers and manuscripts during the past twenty-five years, no one has yet found any documents written before the publication of the Book of Mormon in 1830 which mention Joseph Smith's first vision of God and Jesus Christ, though these are indeed evidences of his claims that he had seen an angel or angels in connection with his discovery of the gold plates." (Ibid.) The implication from this is that since "dedicated searching" failed to uncover such a document, it does not exist, implying that the Prophet's account is a fabrication.

Special attention has been drawn to these statements to underscore again the accuracy of the comment of the Prophet that his name would be had for good and for evil throughout the earth. (See HC 1:11.) There is a suspicion that no objective evidence, regardless of its probity, would convince the Prophet's critics and detractors that he was anything but a charlatan or imposter, so if a pre-1830 document mentioning the first vision were found, those critics would merely shift ground and point to another real or imagined defect or inconsistency to support their preconceived notion that he was a fraud. At the same time, it is doubtful that any negative disclosure about him would convince Joseph's disciples and followers that he was or is anything other than what he represented himself to be—a prophet of the living God.

And so, the controversy about Joseph Smith, and what or who he really was, continues unabated, and will to the end of time. He was perfectly conscious of this fact when he commenced dictating his history of the Church in 1838, and he was aware, too, that in doing so, he was also heaping fuel upon the fire of controversy that had swirled around him from the very beginning.

The Gathering in Missouri

The most urgent concern of the Prophet at the time of the exodus from Kirtland was to prepare for the flood of converts from abroad that he confidently expected would come. Toward this end, he left Far West on May 18, 1838, with a large group of brethren "for the purpose of visiting the north country, and laying off a stake of Zion; making locations, and laying claims to lands to facilitate the gathering of the Saints, and for the benefit of the poor." (HC 3:34.) They spent about two weeks exploring the area northward along the Grand River and its tributaries. During this trip, Joseph selected a townsite that he named Adam-ondi-Ahman, shortened to Diahman by the Saints. This unusual name had its origin in a revelation received by the Prophet (D&C 107), which disclosed that three years before the death of Adam, the patriarchs Seth, Enos, Cainan, Mahalaleel, Jared, Enoch, and Methuselah, together with all their righteous posterity, assembled in that place, at which time Adam conferred a final blessing upon them. On that occasion, the heavens were opened and the Lord appeared to them, blessing Adam and saying, "I have set thee to be the head; a multitude of nations shall come of thee, and thou art a prince over them forever." (D&C 107:55.)

Diahman occupied a place of special significance in the eyes of the Saints, especially since they were told that this singular meeting would be repeated in the latter days, augmented by other patriarchs and their progeny raised up in the interim. On June 28, 1838, a stake was organized there with John Smith, the Prophet's uncle, as the president, and Reynolds Cahoon and Lyman Wight as his counselors. The Prophet's close friend and supporter, Vinson Knight, who was later to play a key role in the ecclesiastical and civil government of Nauvoo, was chosen as the acting bishop *pro tempore*. (HC 3:38.)

A nagging worry of the Prophet during this period was the lack of means to carry on the work of the Church. The financial collapse in Kirtland had literally bankrupted the Church and its principal leaders, and since their expulsion from Jackson County, the Saints in Missouri had few, if any, surplus resources. The Prophet realized that the survival of the Church required a viable, continuing method of financing. In his search for a solution, he reached for the tool that had extricated him from so many difficulties in the past: prayer. In answer, he received what has since been identified as section 119 of the Doctrine and Covenants. After requiring that all surplus properties be placed in the hands of the bishop immediately, the revelation declared: "And this shall be the beginning of the tithing of my people. And after that, those who have thus been tithed shall pay one-tenth of all their interest annually; and this shall be a standing law unto them forever, for my holy priesthood, saith the Lord." (D&C 119:3-4.)

This revelation tried the faith of some of the Saints, who couldn't understand how they could survive financially by giving any meager surplus they had to the Church and thereafter donating one-tenth of their annual increase. However, the great majority of them accepted and lived the principle without hesitation. Those who questioned or doubted the efficacy of this law were referred to the promise in the scriptures held out to those who complied with it, and were encouraged to put the scriptures to the test. Joseph knew that the doubters and questioners could not be persuaded by argument or logic, but only by actual experience. He knew also that were a person to be convinced of the truth of a principle through personal experience, he would probably become an advocate of it and would bring others to his views.

On the same day he received the revelation on tithing, Joseph received three other revelations, which show a pattern whose objective was to consolidate the central power of the Church in Missouri while accelerating the missionary work abroad. The first was directed to several leading brethren in Kirtland, instructing them to wind up their affairs there immediately and to move to Missouri. (D&C 117.) The second outlined steps to be taken to fill vacancies in the leading councils caused by those who had become disaffected, and also directed that the Twelve were to prepare to "go over the great waters, and there promulgate my gospel, . . . and bear record of my name." (D&C 118.) The last revelation received that day designated the First Presidency, the bishop, and the high council to serve as a special council to direct the disposition of the tithes. (D&C 120.)

By the latter part of July 1838 the expected flood of immigrants to Missouri had commenced to crest. In an entry on July 28, the Prophet noted with some satisfaction: "I left Far West for Adam-ondi-Ahman, in company with President Rigdon, to transact some important business, and to settle some Canadian brethren in that place, as they are emigrating rapidly to this land from all parts of the country." (HC 3:48.)

To help provide necessary cohesion among the Saints who were flocking to Far West and the newly established communities on the Grand River, the Prophet commenced to edit the *Elders' Journal,* which was printed and published by Thomas B. Marsh, president of the Quorum of the Twelve. The third number of the *Journal,* published in July, contained a lengthy article by David W. Patten of the Twelve, which considered the restoration and gathering in great detail. The last sentence of this article was a clarion call for the Saints to gather to the land of Zion, or Missouri. ". . . for the time is at hand," it concluded; "therefore gather up your effects, and gather together upon the land which the Lord has appointed for your safety." (HC 3:54.)

The best evidence of the continuing influence the Prophet exerted over his followers is the almost instantaneous way in which they responded to his call to gather. The obedient faithfully settled their private affairs, uprooted their families, and moved, bringing with them few belongings and grand hopes for the future. This was no ordinary man whose call they heeded. He was a man whose concepts and methods were reminiscent of Moses of old, a man who had roused them from lives of complacency and had aimed them toward goals that, at best, most people only dream about.

And, like a Moses, Joseph was constantly on the move during these days, trying to find accommodations for the thousands of Saints who thronged to Missouri at his call. A brief entry under date of August 1, 1838, reveals some of the harassing nature of the Prophet's life during this period: "I tarried at home with my family, also the 2nd and 3rd, to refresh myself after my many late fatigues and arduous duties which I had been called upon to perform." (HC 3:55.) And not only were these duties arduous and fatiguing, but they were also sometimes unpleasant and worrisome. Human nature being what it is, one would expect that some among the thousands who crowded into Missouri at this time would come grumbling and complaining. A group from Canada was especially difficult. Its members were unwilling to settle in the area designated for them and instead selected another site. The way this touchy situation was handled shows the iron grasp in which Joseph held the reins of leadership: "This morning my council met me at my house," he recorded, "to consider the conduct of certain Canada brethren, who had settled on the forks of Grand river, contrary to counsel. On investigation, it was resolved that they must return to Adam-ondi-Ahman, according to counsel, or they would not be considered one with us." (HC 3:55.)

The incident also reveals an interesting facet of the society Joseph brought into existence. Few, if any, groups are as open-armed toward strangers as are the Latter-day Saints. They will balk at no expense or inconvenience to proselyte others to their beliefs; and once a proselyte is admitted, he is accepted in fellowship and becomes entitled to the same rights and privileges enjoyed by those who preceded him into the Church. But a person's continued good standing depends on how he adheres to the standards of the Church.

Any significant failure to measure up, coupled with a refusal to change, may result in official censure, in disfellowshipment, or, in extreme cases, in excommunication. These sanctions continue in effect until the individual has, through acknowledgment of his transgressions, proper contrition, and forsaking for a suitable period of time, demonstrated his willingness to conform. It is by this means that the Church maintains proper discipline among its members and insures that a minimum standard of good conduct will be met. However, unlike sanctions imposed by civil law, the object of church discipline is reformation, not retribution. So a church sanction is imposed not to punish the transgressor, but to help him reform.

Some critics of the Prophet and the Church condemn this practice as being both uncharitable and undemocratic. However, such criticism ignores the reality that often the most charitable thing one can do for a person who is a recalcitrant is to impose loving, but firm, discipline. It also ignores the fact that the Church's government is theocratic and not democratic in nature, that it is an ecclesiastical government headed by God, whose earthly agents merely do his bidding and execute his will. It is true, of course, that many reject the premise that the church Joseph established is headed by God or that its leaders execute God's will. But that is another issue, unrelated to the criticism that the Church's system of discipline is undemocratic.

As it turned out, the problems Joseph Smith had of settling the difficulties with headstrong Church members who did not follow counsel was insignificant compared to the ominous threat posed by nonmember and apostate enemies of the Church. Foreseeing that the political control of local government would inexorably shift to the newcomers as they gained numerical superiority, the old settlers decided to draw the line of battle with the Mormons at the ballot box. They devised a scheme to prohibit the Saints from voting at the election scheduled in Gallatin on August 6, 1838.

Judge Morin, who was friendly to the Saints, leaked word of this scheme to John D. Lee and Levi Stewart, and of the plan to elect William P. Peniston, the reputed leader of the mob, in Clay County. Judge Morin also advised the Saints to go to the polls "prepared for an attack, to stand their ground, and have their rights." (HC 3:56.) This warning went unheeded.

During the morning of election day, candidate Peniston delivered a highly emotional speech intended to inflame the already smouldering passions against the Saints, declaring that "the Mormon leaders are a set of horse thieves, liars, counterfeiters, and you know they profess to heal the sick, and cast out devils, and you all know that is a lie." At that moment Richard Welding, the mob bully, picked a fight with Samuel Brown, who, with about a dozen of the brethren, was at the polls to vote. This sparked a vicious brawl that resulted in several serious injuries. Although outnumbered by about ten to one, the brethren defended themselves vigorously, but they were soon forced to withdraw. In recording the event, the Prophet noted wryly, "Very few of the brethren voted." (HC 3:58.)

When the report of this incident reached the Prophet at Far West, he assembled fifteen to twenty men and left immediately for Gallatin. They were joined by other brethren from different areas, some of whom also had been intimidated by threats of the mob. When distorted reports of the size and aim of the group reached the mob, it reacted with unusual belligerence. An incident then occurred which, of itself, seemed innocuous when compared with the scenes of brutality and intimidation to which the Saints were subjected almost daily. However, it was magnified all out of proportion by enemies of the Saints and became one of the prime factors in producing later savage attacks upon them.

An obscure justice of the peace named Adam Black had sold a farm to the Prophet's trusted associate Vinson Knight and had received part payment for it. Black had then joined with the mob to exclude the Saints from Daviess County. Angered by such conduct on the part of an elected official, the Prophet and a small group of men accosted Black at his home one day, demanding an explanation and seeking assurance that their rights would be respected in the future. Black signed a statement declaring that he was bound to support the Constitution of the United States and the state of Missouri and that he would refrain from associating with the mob in the future. Later he swore in an affidavit that Joseph and the others threatened him with instant death if he did not sign the statement.

William Peniston also executed an affidavit in which he referred to the Adam Black incident and declared that the Mormons had assembled an army of five hundred and had threatened his life and "to do the same to all the old settlers and citizens of Daviess county." (HC 3:61.) Based upon these fabricated affidavits, Judge King, an outspoken enemy of the Saints, issued a warrant for the arrest of the Prophet and his follower Lyman Wight.

The harassment and intimidation these contrived charges produced were negligible in comparison with the frenzied reaction they caused among the Gentiles and even among some of the Prophet's erstwhile supporters. In such a climate, every known or imagined defect of Joseph Smith and his loyal followers was magnified all out of proportion, and they were made to appear as militant aggressors rather than as a group of citizens who had been goaded into defensive action by a mob that threatened their lives, their liberty, and their property.

When word of the difficulties reached Governor Lilburn Boggs, he ordered several generals of the state militia to increase their forces. It was unfortunate for the Saints, and for the reputation of the state of Missouri, that Governor Boggs, who was also commander in chief of the Missouri militia, had an ingrained hatred toward the Latter-day Saints. That hatred, as later events proved, blinded him to reality and caused him to misconstrue the goals of the Saints and to use the powerful forces at his command as an instrument of unlawful oppression and violence.

The mob, goaded on by its leaders and by false reports of the size, conduct, and intentions of the Mormon forces, engaged in repeated and indiscriminate acts of violence against the Saints. Any acts of retaliation or defense on the part of the Saints were interpreted as aggressions that endangered the peace.

The skirmishes occurred intermittently over several counties during the autumn of 1838. Finally a full-scale confrontation occurred at the little riverport town of De Witt. Located on the Grand River near its confluence with the Missouri River, De Witt had been settled by a number of Latter-day Saint families. Through the summer they had been subjected to several threats which, for the most part, they had ignored. In the latter part of September, however, the threats became more frequent and ominous. They reached a crescendo when forces of the resident mobbers were augmented by a group from Carroll County, and on September 20 over a hundred armed men invaded De Witt and threatened the Saints with death if they did not leave the state. The mob set a deadline of October 1 for the departure, and they blockaded the town, placing guards at all of the main access roads. The Saints in De Witt appealed to Governor Boggs, requesting that the militia quell the mob and protect their rights as citizens. His answer was received with shocked disbelief. He declared that "the quarrel was between the Mormons and the mob," and that it would be necessary for them to "fight it out." (HC 3:157.)

As soon as Joseph learned of the siege at De Witt, he went immediately to comfort and give direction to the Saints there. He managed to gain access to the town only by using unfrequented roads. "I found my brethren," Joseph wrote, "who were only a handful in comparison to the mob by which they were surrounded, . . . and their provisions [were] nearly exhausted, and no prospect of obtaining any more." (HC 3:153.)

The plea of the De Witt Saints was carried to Governor Boggs by several respected nonmembers who lived in the vicinity and who voluntarily told of the ill treatment the Saints had received at the hands of the mob. It was this fact that caused the Prophet to view the governor's blunt response with alarm and that presented him with one of the most agonizing dilemmas of his career. The highest executive officer of the state apparently did not intend to protect the rights of his people; on the contrary, it appeared that he was in sympathy with the mob. This left the Prophet with only two alternatives. Either he could yield to the mob and leave Missouri, or he could follow Governor Boggs' unusual suggestion and enforce the rights of his people by self-help.

As he returned to Far West, the Prophet weighed these unpleasant alternatives. If the first were adopted, where would the Saints go? At that moment, no place seemed very hospitable. They had tasted the bitter fruit of bigotry and mobocracy wherever they had lived—in New York, in Pennsylvania, in Ohio, and now in Missouri. Perhaps the problem could be solved if the Saints were to move to a remote, uninhabited area. This consideration likely caused Joseph to eye the vast wilderness to the west as a place of temporary refuge, but the circumstances were not ripe yet. (Later he prophesied that his followers would ultimately be driven to the Rocky Mountains, where they would become a powerful people, prior to their return to Missouri.)

For the moment, the better of the two questionable alternatives seemed to be for the Saints to remain in Missouri and protect their rights as best they could. It was with this intention that the Prophet arrived in Far West to help arrange for the defense that Governor Boggs had refused to provide.

Considering the repeated wrongs the Saints had suffered at the hands of their enemies, it is understandable that feelings ran high when the Prophet reported on the fall of De Witt and the governor's cold response to the plea for help. Some of the brethren, blessed with more bravado than good sense, made extreme statements that have since been unduly magnified. Some of these have been attributed to the Prophet and from them have been drawn many wrong inferences. It is claimed, for example, that Joseph delivered a fiery speech at this time, likening himself to Mohammed and declaring he would rule by the sword. (Brodie, p. 229.) Through the retelling and embellishing of this false story, Joseph has been made to appear as a reckless, flamboyant, and quite incompetent leader who, while surrounded by heavily armed and numerically superior enemies, declared an intention to do something that was both beyond reason and at variance with his character and past conduct. This story gained currency because at about this time Thomas B. Marsh and Orson Hyde, members of the Twelve, apostatized and made the same charge. In an affidavit executed October 24, 1838, Elder Marsh declared: "I have heard the Prophet say that he would yet tread down his enemies, and walk over their dead bodies; and if he was not let alone, he would be a second Moham-med to this generation, and that he would make it one gore of blood from the Rocky Mountains to the Atlantic ocean; that like Mohammed, whose motto in treating for peace was, 'the Alcoran or the Sword.' So should it be with us, 'Joseph Smith or the Sword.' " (HC 3:167.) In a "me-too" affidavit, Orson Hyde merely said, "The most of the statements in the foregoing disclosure I know to be true; the remainder I believe to be true." Of the in-cident, John Taylor, third president of the Church, later said: "Testimonies from these sources are not always reliable, and it is to be hoped, for the sake of the two brethren, that some things were added by our enemies that they did not assert, but enough was said to make this default and apostasy very terrible. I will here state that I was in Far West at the time these affidavits were made. . . . And I know that these things, referred to in the affidavits, are not true." (HC 3:168.)

Another false charge made against the Prophet at this time was that he had organized a secret band called the Danites who were oathbound to do the bidding of the Prophet "whether right or wrong." The Marsh affidavit referred to the Danites and laid the responsibility for them at the Prophet's door.

In fact, an aspiring man named Sampson Avard organized the Danites and falsely represented that he had done so on the au-thority of the Church leaders. His object was to overthrow the Church, which, according to the Prophet, "he tried to accomplish by his smooth, flattering, and winning speeches, which he frequently made to his associates, while his room was well guarded by some of his followers, ready to give him the signal on the ap-proach of anyone who would not approve of his measures." (HC 3:179.)

Avard formed his band into tens and fifties along the lines of the organization the Prophet had created for the defense of his people. In the beginning, his plans seemed harmless enough, and so he carried along with him many of the brethren. As his speeches became more militant, however, some of the brethren grew suspi-cious and uneasy. They found he advocated concepts at variance with the doctrines taught by the Prophet. Their suspicions were confirmed when Avard called a secret meeting of his captains and laid before them his plans. "Know ye not, brethren," he declared, "that it soon will be your privilege to take your respective companies and go out on a scout on the borders of the settlements, and take to yourselves spoils of the goods of the ungodly Gentiles? for it is written, the riches of the Gentiles shall be consecrated to my people, the house of Israel; and thus you will waste away the Gentiles by robbing and plundering them of their property; and in this way we will build up the kingdom of God, and roll forth the little stone that Daniel saw cut out of the mountain without hands, and roll forth until it filled the whole earth. For this is the very way that God destines to build up His kingdom in the last days. If any of us should be recognized, who can harm us? for we will stand by each other and defend one another in all things. If our enemies swear against us, we can swear also. . . . Why do you startle at this, brethren? As the Lord liveth, I would swear to a lie to clear any of you; and if this would not do, I would put them or him under the sand as Moses did the Egyptian; and in this way we will consecrate much unto the Lord, and build up His kingdom; and who can stand against us? And if any of us transgress, we will deal with him amongst ourselves. And if any one of this Danite society reveals any of these things, I will put him where the dogs *cannot bite him.*" (HC 3:180-81.)

This speech was too much even for the most gullible of the brethren to accept, and when Avard had finished, the room literally erupted in violent rejection of what he had said. With his mask ripped away, the brethren for the first time recognized Avard for what he was: a conspiring, vicious, and unprincipled man who, in the name of religion, was attempting to use the same evil tools wielded by the ancient secret orders so much condemned in the Book of Mormon. When word of the affair reached the First Presidency, he was promptly excommunicated "and every means proper used to destroy his influence." (HC 3:181.) He reacted by joining the mobbers and spreading false and malicious rumors about the Prophet and his followers.

In retrospect, it is apparent that the apostasy of Thomas B. Marsh and Orson Hyde was brought about in large part by the lies and misrepresentations of Sampson Avard. These two inexperienced apostles lacked the discernment to see through Avard, to withstand the terrible pressures built up by the mob spirit, which was all around them, and by their own inherent weaknesses. To their credit, it must be acknowledged that they later saw their error and returned to the Church, and Orson Hyde was even reinstated as a member of the Twelve. However, through this apostasy, he lost his place of seniority and thereby failed to succeed to the presidency of the Church upon the death of Brigham Young.

One can only imagine the feelings of betrayal and frustration Joseph experienced at this time. The dangers arising from the mobbings and the indifference of Governor Boggs were intensified by these defections within the ranks. At times, it seemed to the Prophet that the only place of refuge for him was within the depths of his own soul, where, shielded from the mobs that hemmed him in and from false and misled brethren, he could commune with God. As always, these moments of prayerful introspection produced within Joseph a great sense of peace and an attitude of detachment toward all that he did. This was shown in a conversation between him and one of his followers during this period. When the man asked what he should do in light of the precarious, uncertain condition the Saints faced in Missouri, Joseph counseled him to settle upon the land and to plant, to till, and to harvest "as if for years."

It was in this spirit that the Prophet set about to prepare for the defense of his people. Parley P. Pratt has left us this account of what took place: "After the evacuation of De Witt, when our citizens were officially notified that they must protect themselves, and expect no more protection from any department of the State Government, they assembled in Far West to the number of one thousand men, or thereabout, and resolved to defend their rights to the last. A call was made upon every person who could bear arms to come forward in defence of our houses, homes, wives and children, and the cause of our country and our God." (Pratt, p. 176.)

In the meantime, the mobs, secure in the knowledge they would be unhampered by the state, left a devastating trail of murder, rapine, and arson over the countryside. In the midst of this chaos, word was received in Far West that a large force led by a Captain Bogart, one of the bitterest enemies of the Church, had taken prisoner several of the brethren and had made ominous threats about driving the Saints from the state. Fearing that Far West would be jeopardized were this force not checked, Elias Higbee, the highest elected official in the county, ordered Lt. Colonel George M. Hinkle, the commanding officer, to dispatch a company to scatter the mob and retake the prisoners. The two forces met under cover of night in a fateful skirmish later called the Battle of Crooked River. The Far West company lost three men in the attack, including Elder David W. Patten of the Twelve. Several were wounded. The casualties among the mob were comparable. Although the mob fought from a favored defensive position, they were put to flight by Patten's men, who fought with a terrible fury, believing that their families, their homes, and their very lives were at stake.

As Bogart's men scattered, they carried with them fanciful stories of what had happened. Some represented themselves as the sole survivors of an awful carnage, inflicted by an overwhelming force of heavily armed Mormons. Such tales, combined with the false reports about the Danites and the Prophet's supposed ambition to be a second Mohammed, spread terror and confusion. A letter to Governor Boggs from Sashiel Woods, a sectarian preacher and long-time enemy of the Saints, illustrates the kind of propaganda that brought the downfall of Joseph and his followers in Missouri: "Sir:—We were informed last night by an express from Ray County, that Captain Bogart and all his company, amounting to between fifty and sixty men, were massacred at Buncombe, twelve miles north of Richmond, except three. This statement you may rely on as being true, and last night they expected Richmond to be laid in ashes this morning. We could distinctly hear cannon, and we knew the 'Mormons' had one in their possession. Richmond is about twenty-five miles west of this place, on a straight line. We know not the hour or minute we shall be laid in ashes— our county is ruined—for God's sake give us assistance as soon as possible." (B. H. Roberts, *The Missouri Persecutions* [Salt Lake City: George Q. Cannon & Sons Co., 1900], p. 225.)

Another message to Governor Boggs from Amos Rees and Wiley C. Williams called for aid to "put a stop to the devastation which is menaced by these infuriated fanatics, and they *must go prepared, and with a full determination to exterminate or expel them from the State en masse.*" (Ibid, p. 226.)

The governor's reaction to these messages was instantaneous. Without checking the accuracy of the facts, and ignoring the declaration of neutrality he had made when the Saints were expelled from De Witt, he issued an order to General John B. Clark that has no parallel in American history for executive irresponsibility: ". . . I have received . . . information of the most appalling character, which changes the whole face of things and places the 'Mormons' in the attitude of open and avowed defiance of the laws, and of having made open war upon the people of this State. Your orders are, therefore, to hasten your operations and endeavor to reach Richmond, in Ray County, with all possible speed. The 'Mormons' must be treated as enemies and *must be exterminated* or driven from the State, if necessary for the public good. Their outrages are beyond description. If you can increase your force, you are authorized to do so to any extent you may think necessary." (Ibid., pp. 228-29.)

This order sealed the doom of the Latter-day Saints in Missouri. It was a signal to the bigots and Mormon-haters that the law and other civilized restraints were to be suspended until they were rid of Joseph Smith and his followers. More than that, it put the executive power of the state, including the militia, squarely behind the mobs.

The governor's exterminating order galvanized several corps of state militia into action to build up their forces, chiefly through recruitment of the mobbers. This made it possible for the enemies of the Saints not only to fight them under color of law, but also to receive pay for it.

Within a few days after it was issued, Governor Bogg's extermination order bore its first bitter fruit. On October 30, 1838, a mob numbering over two hundred attacked a small Mormon settlement called Haun's Mill, a few miles from Far West. On learning of the approach of the mob, the women and girls fled into the woods while most of the defenseless men and boys sought refuge in an old blacksmith's shop. As the mob reached the clearing, a Latter-day Saint named David Evans ran toward them waving his hat, shouting "Peace! Peace!" The cold-blooded answer was a fusillade of shots fired at the blacksmith's shop and at those who were fleeing into the woods. The mob then approached the shop and fired round after round into it through the cracks between the logs. When the carnage was ended, the terrified survivors counted nineteen dead and more than twelve wounded.

The savagery of the attack was typified by the death of Thomas McBride, an aged Revolutionary War veteran, who was shot down while pleading for his life and whose body was then mutilated with a corn cutter. Almost more sickening was the death of twelve-year-old Sardius Smith, who was dragged from his hiding place and shot in the head at point-blank range; his eight-year-old brother was shot through the hip.

Within hours word of the massacre reached the Prophet in Far West. He was devastated by the news. Knowing of the governor's extermination order and seeing in the massacre precisely what the consequences of the order would be to his beloved people, Joseph knew instinctively the time had come to capitulate and accede to the demands to leave the state. But before he could convey his feelings to those who led the troops garrisoned at Far West, Colonel Hinkle of the Caldwell County militia, a member of the Church, took it upon himself to open negotiations with Generals Samuel D. Lucas and Alexander Doniphan, who commanded several thousand troops ringing Far West. Assuming an authority over the civilian population that he never possessed, Colonel Hinkle entered into a four-part agreement with the generals that required that the Prophet and other church leaders be surrendered, tried, and punished; that the property of all the Saints who had taken up arms in their own defense be appropriated to pay their debts and to indemnify their enemies for any losses they had suffered; that the Saints not to be imprisoned leave the state as soon as directed by the commander-in-chief; and that the Saints relinquish all their arms.

The Prophet and his associates received word of Colonel Hinkle's betrayal in shocked disbelief. Under the terms of this agreement, they were to be placed in the hands of their avowed enemies; their property was to be confiscated without any semblance of due process; and their families and followers were to be left leaderless and unprotected, subject to the whims of an executive who already had ordered their extermination.

But under the stressful circumstances, there was little the Prophet could do but go with the tide, since the troops committed to the defense of Far West had linked hands with the troops that surrounded it. And in view of the butchery at Haun's Mill, Joseph knew that any resistance to the demands of General Lucas likely would bring about the brutal deaths of many more of his loyal followers.

Faced with these hard realities, the Prophet yielded to the inevitable. And in the process, there seemed to settle upon him a mantle of stoic serenity that was to remain with him for the rest of his days.

Parley P. Pratt, who was taken prisoner along with the Prophet and other leaders of the Saints, wrote: "The haughty general rode up, and without speaking to us, ordered his guard to surround us. They did so very abruptly, and we were marched into camp surrounded by thousands of savage looking beings, many of whom were dressed and painted like Indian warriors. These all set up a constant yell, like so many bloodhounds let loose upon their prey. . . . If the vision of the infernal regions could suddenly open to the mind, with thousands of malicious fiends, all clamoring, exulting, deriding, blaspheming, mocking, railing, raging and foaming like a troubled sea, then could some idea be formed of the hell which we had entered." (Pratt, pp. 186-87.)

The first night of this captivity brings to mind the mocking, blasphemous spirit of the Savior's tormentors at the crucifixion. "The guards during the whole night," Parley wrote, "kept up a constant tirade of mockery, and the most obscene blackguardism and abuse. They blasphemed God; mocked Jesus Christ; swore the most dreadful oaths; taunted brother Joseph and others; demanded miracles; wanted signs, such as: 'Come, Mr. Smith, show us an angel.' 'Give us one of your revelations.' 'Show us a miracle.' 'Come, there is one of your brethren here in camp whom we took prisoner yesterday in his own house, and knocked his brains out with his own rifle, which we found hanging over his fireplace; he lays speechless and dying; speak the word and heal him, and then we will all believe.' 'Or, if you are Apostles or men of God, deliver yourselves, and then we will be Mormons.' Next would be a volley of oaths and blasphemies; then a tumultuous tirade of lewd boastings of having defiled virgins and wives by force, etc., much of which I dare not write; and, indeed, language would fail me to attempt more than a faint description." (Ibid.)

Chapter Twenty-four

Expulsion from Missouri

With Joseph and other Church leaders in custody, the militia in Far West relinquished their arms, according to the Hinkle agreement, which left the city defenseless. On the following day, General Lucas's men ransacked the city on the pretext of looking for concealed weapons. One historian recorded that in the process, "the people were robbed of their most valuable property, insulted and whipped. . . . The chastity of a number of women was defiled by force; some of them were strapped to benches and repeatedly ravished." (Roberts, p. 244.)

On the second night, a court-martial was held, during which Joseph and the other prisoners were sentenced to be shot the following morning in the public square at Far West, as an example to Joseph's followers. Had it not been for the bold stand of General Doniphan, these executions likely would have been carried out. General Doniphan, recognizing that the prisoners were civilians and thus not subject to the jurisdiction of a military court, bluntly told General Lucas that the executions would be cold-blooded murder. He also warned that if General Lucas went forward, he would remove his troops before the executions, as he did not intend to witness them nor have anything to do with them. General Lucas, recognizing that this action could pave the way for later criminal charges against him, rescinded the order. Instead, he decided to take the prisoners to Independence, to exhibit them as trophies of his conquest.

The scene in which the Prophet and the other prisoners bade farewell to their families in Far West was charged with high emotion. The Prophet wrote: "Myself and fellow prisoners were taken to the town, into the public square, and before our departure we, after much entreaty, were suffered to see our families, being attended all the while by a strong guard. I found my wife and children in tears. . . . When I entered my house, they clung to my garments, their eyes streaming with tears, while mingled emotions of joy and sorrow were manifested in their countenances. I requested to have a private interview with them a few minutes, but this privilege was denied me by the guard. I was then obliged to take my departure. Who can realize the feelings which I experienced at that time, to be thus torn from my companion, and leave her surrounded with monsters in the shape of men, and my children, too, not knowing how their wants would be supplied. . . . My partner wept, my children clung to me, until they were thrust from me by the swords of the guards. I felt overwhelmed while I witnessed the scene, and could only recommend them to the care of that God whose kindness had followed me to the present time, and who alone could protect them, and deliver me from the hands of my enemies, and restore me to my family." (HC 3:193.)

The town square was crowded as the prisoners departed under heavy guard. Having said goodbyes to their wives and children in the privacy of their homes, they now bid farewell to their friends and other relatives in public. ". . . hundreds of the brethren crowded around us," Parley P. Pratt recorded, "anxious to take a parting look, or a silent shake of the hand; for feelings were too intense to allow of speech." He also noted the touching scene as Joseph bid farewell to his parents: "In the wagon sat Joseph Smith, while his aged father and venerable mother came up overwhelmed with tears, and took each of the prisoners by the hand with a silence of grief too great for utterance." (Pratt, p. 190.)

The trip to Independence took on the aspect of a triumphal procession for the militia, whose officers proudly exhibited their prisoners at every stop along the route. False stories about the Prophet had so poisoned the minds of most nonmembers that they expected to find some kind of a monster of depraved appearance and conduct. For these, it came as a distinct shock to find, instead, a handsome, powerfully built, mild-mannered man.

General Moses Wilson, who commanded the brigade that escorted the prisoners to Independence, was profoundly affected by his prisoners' demeanor. Parley P. Pratt had written this scathing denunciation of General Wilson for his conduct after the fall of Far West: "I went to Gen. Moses Wilson in tears, and stated the circumstances of my sick, heart-broken and destitute family in terms which would have moved any heart that had a latent spark of humanity yet remaining. But I was only answered with an exultant laugh, and a taunt of reproach by this hardened murderer." As the trip wore on and General Wilson became better acquainted with the Prophet and his brethren, his attitudes softened until, at the end, he had feelings of congeniality toward them.

Of this radical change, Parley noted: "Indeed, it was now evident that he was proud of his prey, and felt highly enthusiastic in having the honor of returning in triumph to Independence with his prisoners, whom his superstition had magnified into something more than fellow citizens—something noble or supernatural, and worthy of public exhibition." (Pratt, pp. 190, 192.)

One day during the course of the trip to Independence, General Wilson, in a relaxed, expansive mood, made an almost clinical analysis of the difficulties between the Latter-day Saints and their nonmember neighbors in Missouri. Said he: "We know perfectly that from the beginning the Mormons have not been the aggressors at all. As it began in '33 in Jackson County, so it has been ever since. You Mormons were crowded to the last extreme, and compelled to self-defence; and this has been construed into treason, murder and plunder. We mob you without law; the authorities refuse to protect you according to law; you then are compelled to protect yourselves, and we act upon the prejudices of the public, who join our forces, and the whole is legalized, for your destruction and our gain. Is not this a shrewd and cunning policy on our part, gentlemen?

"When we drove you from Jackson County, we burned two hundred and three of your houses; plundered your goods; destroyed your press, type, paper, books, office and all—tarred and feathered old Bishop Partridge, as exemplary an old man as you can find anywhere. We shot down some of your men, and, if any of you returned the fire, we imprisoned you, on your trial for murder, etc. Damn'd shrewdly done, gentlemen; and I came damn'd near kicking the bucket myself; for, on one occasion, while we were tearing down houses, driving families, and destroying and plundering goods, some of you good folks put a ball through my son's body, another through the arm of my clerk, and a third pierced my shirt collar and marked my neck. No blame, gentlemen; we deserved it. And let a set of men serve me as your community had been served, and I'll be damn'd if I would not fight till I died." (Ibid., p. 191.)

The stoical attitude of the Prophet had prepared him for either life or death, for his confidence remained absolutely unshaken that whether he lived or died, he would ultimately prevail over all of his enemies, either in time or in eternity.

On the night of November 2, 1838, he enjoyed one of those unusual spiritual experiences of his life, one that convinced him that his life would be spared. Parley P. Pratt recorded that on the following morning, the Prophet, speaking in a "cheerful and confidential tone," told him and the others: "Be of good cheer, brethren; the word of the Lord came to me last night that our lives should be given us, and that whatever we may suffer during this captivity, not one of our lives should be taken." (Ibid., p. 192.)

The prisoners and their escort arrived at Independence in a torrential rainstorm. Despite this, hundreds lined the streets to gaze with curiosity at them as they slowly passed by to the accompaniment of a drum and bugle corps. General Wilson, peacock-proud of his role as captor, introduced the prisoners one by one, calling them by name. With this pageantry over, the prisoners were taken to a vacant house and placed under guard.

Joseph and his brethren were mildly surprised at the humanitarian treatment they received during their confinement at Independence. By comparison with the treatment they had received at Far West, they were comfortable and well off. The extreme hatred of the Jackson County residents toward the Saints had subsided following the bloody expulsion a few years before. In the meantime, many new settlers had come to the area who were essentially untainted by the hostile feelings that previously existed. They were especially curious about the man who was accepted as a prophet who had conversed with heavenly beings. Ever alert to any chance to proselyte, Joseph and the others took occasion to preach and to explain the policies and doctrines of the Church to the great numbers of people who came to look at them.

Within a short while, the surveillance over the prisoners was relaxed to the extent that they were permitted to walk the street alone without guards. Ultimately they were allowed to move to a comfortable hotel, although they were required to pay for their own accommodations.

When the residents saw the mild and harmless character of the prisoners and realized that the stories being circulated about them were unfounded, the tide of public opinion turned in their favor. This was enhanced by the courteous, almost deferential, respect shown by community leaders who invited the men to their homes on a social basis. It was found after such an exposure that the prisoners were not dangerous, but were men of intelligence with broad interests, practical experience, and high moral and spiritual qualities.

But this relatively pleasant interlude was not destined to last. The enemies to the north were clamoring for the return of the prisoners to subject them to their own special brand of kangaroo-court "justice." Not content with subjugating the Mormon community and imprisoning their leaders, the mob was determined to spill the blood of the Prophet and his chief aides, and they intended to accomplish this under the guise of law. Thus General Clark made repeated demands that the prisoners be sent to Richmond for trial and tried to get volunteers to take the prisoners there. But these efforts failed, because by then the sympathies in Independence ran in favor of the prisoners. Some even disobeyed orders to take them to Richmond. "At last a colonel and two or three officers started with us, with their swords and pistols," wrote Parley P. Pratt, "which were intended more to protect us than to keep us from escaping." (Ibid., p. 197.)

For the prisoners, their entry into Richmond was another descent into the foul maelstrom from which they had been rescued when they were moved to Independence. At the direction of General Clark, they were chained together and imprisoned in a ramshackle, vacant house, with the windows boarded up, and guarded by a group of illiterate, profane men.

Confident that the prisoners were secure and would not escape, General Clark turned his attention to the trial that lay ahead. Despite the abortive attempt at a military trial at Far West, he opted for that procedure—it would be much speedier and far less cumbersome than a civil trial. In fact, he had reached his decision even before the military court was convened, and was overheard making assignments to the firing squad before the trial was brought to order.

When word of General Clark's intent was leaked to friends of the Prophet, they confronted the general in the same way General Doniphan had confronted General Lucas at Far West. When it was pointed out to him that the military probably lacked jurisdiction to try the prisoners for the offenses of which they stood accused, he postponed the trial and sent to Fort Leavenworth for a military code of laws. After poring over these for about a week, he came to the reluctant conclusion that he lacked the authority to try the prisoners. Thus he relinquished jurisdiction to the local civil judge, Austin A. King, an avowed enemy of the Church, who had recently published a letter in the *Missouri Argus* accusing the Mormons of arson and murder.

While General Clark wrestled with his jurisdictional question, the Prophet and his fellows were kept imprisoned in their dark, foul-smelling jail, almost incessantly subjected to the vile, profane cursing and tauntings of their guards, who took special pleasure in recounting stories of the rape and degradation of Mormon women. The scene was worsened by the delirium and fainting spells of Sidney Rigdon, who had taken ill and was out of his head much of the time. During this trying period occurred a much-publicized incident. Unable to tolerate the guards' profanities any longer, Joseph stood erect and, in a loud, authoritative voice, commanded them to be silent, or either he or they would die immediately. There was such a tone of finality in his words, such an air of commanding authority in his bearing, that the guards instantly fell silent.

The incident had such a powerful effect upon Parley P. Pratt that years later when he wrote his autobiography, he said of it, ". . . dignity and majesty have I seen but once, as it stood in chains, at midnight, in a dungeon in an obscure village in Missouri." (Pratt, p. 211.)

The proceeding before Judge King was in the nature of a preliminary hearing to determine whether there was sufficient evidence to justify a full-scale criminal trial. Involved were the prisoners who had been with Joseph since the first arrests at Far West and about fifty other brethren who had been arrested later and taken directly to Richmond. This larger group was kept under guard in an open, unfinished courthouse, which exposed them to the biting cold of a Missouri November.

The prisoners were accused of treason, murder, arson, larceny, theft, and stealing. The star witness was the apostate Sampson Avard. He was joined by over forty others, including several men who had once stood close to the Prophet—William W. Phelps, John Whitmer, John Corrill, and George N. Hinkle.

For fifteen weary days the prisoners listened to a seemingly endless parade of perjured and suborned witnesses. Each night the Prophet was returned to his cell and shackled to his fellow prisoners. Questioning of the prosecutors failed to produce any probative evidence to support a criminal charge. Joseph, for example, was bound over for trial on a charge of treason based principally upon the testimony of a witness who answered yes when asked whether the Mormons professed to believe in the twenty-seventh verse of the seventh chapter of Daniel. This, together with Avard's false story about the Prophet's involvement with the Danites, caused Judge King to declare grandly to his clerk, "Put that down; that is a strong point for treason!" (Roberst, p. 260.)

Once the prosecution had ended its tedious presentation, the defendants were asked to submit a list of potential witnesses to testify in their behalf. They complied by submitting a list of forty or fifty men. To their dismay, this was turned over to their old enemy, Captain Bogart, who himself had been a witness for the prosecution. Bogart proceeded to arrest and charge every man on the list whom he could find. This charade was repeated a second time with the same result.

Almost miraculously, seven witnesses, four men and three women, were finally able to evade Captain Bogart's dragnet and the intimidations of the court, and to testify in behalf of the prisoners. An eighth witness for the defense did not fare so well. Of him the Prophet wrote: "We saw a man at the window by the name of Allen, and beckoned him to come in, and had him sworn, but when he did not testify to please the court, several rushed upon him with their bayonets, and he fled the place; three men took after him with loaded guns, and he barely escaped with his life." With that, the prisoners gave up all hope of making any reasonable defense to the fabricated charges against them. The Prophet noted: "It was of no use to get any more witnesses, even if we could have done so." (HC 3:211.)

In light of the farcical nature of the proceedings, it came as no surprise that the Prophet, his brother Hyrum, Sidney Rigdon, and three other men were bound over for trial on the charge of treason and sent to the jail in nearby Liberty. Parley P. Pratt and four others were bound over for trial on the charge of murder and were left in Richmond in the filthy quarters where the Prophet and the others had been shackled during the trial. All the other prisoners were released.

The Prophet left this biting summary of the court's decision:

"Our treason consisted of having whipped the mob out of Daviess county, and taking their cannon from them; the murder, of killing the man in the Bogart battle." (HC 3:212.)

Even as Judge King gaveled the preliminary hearing to a close, the Prophet's mind was at work trying to formulate a plan of action. He had seen that legal learning and skill were useless in the presence of a biased or dishonest judge, and he came to realize that the assertion of legal rights depended upon adequate machinery of government and the qualifications of those operating it. Thus his mind began to turn away from the study of law toward the architecture of government. In the future he would be more interested in whether a forum was properly structured and directed by men of integrity than in a knowledge of the technical rules governing it. The genesis of the unusual governmental structure he was to bring into being in Nauvoo, Illinois, a few months later can be found in the bitter experiences of Far West, Richmond, and Liberty.

Confined for several months in jail, and faced with the uncertainty of the outcome of the formal trial that still lay ahead, the Prophet was greatly concerned about the safety of his family and about the leadership of the Church members, most of whom were baffled by the dramatic turn of events that had put their prophet-leader behind bars. Many turned away from him at this time, either because of indifference or because they had been infected by the apostate spirit that had taken many others out of the Church.

However, there was still a large number of the Saints who would, the Prophet knew, follow him to the death if necessary. It was upon these stalwart members that he fixed his attention once he had settled down in the cold, dimly lighted quarters of the Liberty jail. Rather than wasting time bemoaning his fate, he set about to use the weapons at hand. A stream of letters commenced to flow from him to members of his family and the brethren. These letters were devoid of even a hint of pessimism or self-pity; on the contrary, they breathed a spirit of buoyant self-confidence, even truculence. In a letter addressed to the Church at large in December 1838 he wrote: "Dear brethren, do not think that our hearts faint, as though some strange thing had happened unto us, for we have seen and have been assured of all these things beforehand, and have an assurance of a better hope than that of our persecutors. Therefore God hath made broad our shoulders for the burden. We glory in our tribulation, because we know that God is

with us, that He is our friend, and that He will save our souls."
(HC 3:227.)

He was scornful and derisive in the letter of the brethren who
had apostatized and turned on him. Of the leading apostates he
wrote: ". . . in fine, we have waded through an ocean of tribulation
and mean abuse, practiced upon us by [men] . . . who are so very
ignorant that they cannot appear respectable in any decent and
civilized society, and whose eyes are full of adultery, and cannot
cease from sin. . . . whose hearts are full of corruption, whose cloak
of hypocrisy was not sufficient to shield them or to hold them up
in the hour of trouble, who after having escaped the pollutions of
the world through the knowledge of their Lord and Savior Jesus
Christ, became again entangled and overcome—their latter end is
worse than the first. But it has happened unto them according to
the word of the Scripture: 'The dog has returned to his vomit, and
the sow that was washed to her wallowing in the mire.' " (HC
3:232.) Some hint of the reasons that impelled the Prophet to
speak out in such strong language is seen in another excerpt
from this same letter: "We have learned also since we have been
prisoners, that many false and pernicious things, which were calculated to lead the Saints far astray and to do great injury, have been
taught by Dr. Avard as coming from the Presidency, and we have
reason to fear that many other designing and corrupt characters
like unto himself, have been teaching many things which the
Presidency never knew were being taught in the Church by any-
body until after they were made prisoners. . . . Thus we find that
there have been frauds and secret abominations and evil works of
darkness going on, leading the minds of the weak and unwary into
confusion and distraction, and all the time palming it off upon the
Presidency, while the Presidency were ignorant as well as innocent
of those things which those persons were practicing in the Church
in their name." (HC 3:231.)

Because of the powerful impact of his writings, the Prophet's
enemies found him almost as formidable while imprisoned as while
free. In fact, his imprisonment added another element of
authenticity to his already impressive credentials as a prophetic
man of God. Words sent from the Liberty jail were read avidly by
his disciples and told and retold through the efficient Mormon
grapevine, and these served to stiffen the backbones of many of the
loyal Saints who may have wavered.

By the spring of 1839 the Prophet's words had lost much of the strident quality that characterized the earlier letters. This was attributable to the mellowing, sobering effect of his vile surroundings and to the knowledge that the earlier letters had produced the desired effect of strengthening the resolve of his followers. Now the stridency was replaced by a philosophical, poetic tone. In a letter dated March 25, 1839, addressed to the Church at Quincy, Illinois, "and scattered abroad," the Prophet seemed to reach the pinnacle of his literary attainment. In fact, some of the excerpts from this letter were later considered to be of such surpassing merit that they were included in the Doctrine and Covenants. One of these, often quoted, posed a rhetorical question about the sad plight of the Saints and the duration of their suffering: "O God, where art thou? And where is the pavilion that covereth thy hiding place? How long shall thy hand be stayed, and thine eye, yea thy pure eye, behold from the eternal heavens the wrongs of thy people and of thy servants, and thine ear be penetrated with their cries? Yea, O Lord, how long shall they suffer these wrongs and unlawful oppressions, before thine heart shall be softened toward them, and thy bowels be moved with compassion toward them?" (D&C 121:1-3.) The answer to this question appears later, in between comments about the vagaries of the law and the problems of settlement of the Saints. "My son," it commenced, "peace be unto thy soul; thine adversity and thine afflictions shall be but a small moment; And then, if thou endure it well, God shall exalt thee on high. . . ." (D&C 121:7-8.)

Still later, this answer is elaborated upon in language that shows again the implacable will of the Prophet and the unshakeable confidence he had in his ultimate triumph over all his enemies: "The ends of the earth shall inquire after thy name, and fools shall have thee in derision, and hell shall rage against thee; While the pure in heart, and the wise, and the noble, and the virtuous, shall seek counsel, and authority, and blessings constantly from under thy hand. And thy people shall never be turned against thee by the testimony of the traitors. And although their influence shall cast thee into trouble, and into bars and walls, thou shalt be had in honor; and but for a small moment and thy voice shall be more terrible in the midst of thine enemies than the fierce lion, because of thy righteousness; and thy God shall stand by thee forever and ever." (D&C 122:1-4.)

Taken in its entirety, this letter mirrors the basic qualities in the Prophet's character that at once endeared him to his friends and enraged his enemies. To his friends he manifested love and concern for their welfare, and his words inspired confidence in the rightness of his position and in his ability to lead. To his enemies, he threw down the gauntlet, offering or seeking no quarter, and manifesting what to them was an irritating certainty in his ultimate triumph and supremacy. As was true with almost everything the Prophet did or said, the letters that flowed from the Liberty jail forged a powerful two-edged sword that cleared the path of leadership before him while undercutting his position in the eyes of the world.

But writing these letters comprised only a fraction of the Prophet's literary output and activities during his confinement in the Liberty jail. From there he directed an aggressive campaign to alter the public attitudes toward the Latter-day Saints and their leaders, producing a veritable flood of letters to the state officials, editors, and other leading citizens. The Prophet noted the results of this effort with some satisfaction. "As nigh as we can learn," he wrote in a letter dated March 25, 1839, "the public mind has been for a long time turning in our favor, and the majority is now friendly; and the lawyers can no longer browbeat us by saying that this or that is a matter of public opinion, for public opinion is not willing to brook it; for it is beginning to look with feelings of indignation against our oppressors, and to say that the 'Mormons' were not in the fault in the least." (HC 3:292.)

The tide of public opinion favorable to the Saints, particularly from influential voices outside the state, finally seeped into the consciousness of the Missouri officialdom, and Governor Boggs and his associates began to grope for a way out. The effect at the executive level was to produce more leniency toward Joseph and the other prisoners. At the legislative level, it produced the usual vacuous debates over what could or should be done. Expressions of regret over what had happened to the Saints were shown to be more pretended than real when the legislature eventually voted two thousand dollars as reparations for the Saints in Caldwell County, coupled with an appropriation of two hundred thousand dollars "to defray the expenses incurred in driving the 'Mormons' from the State, and dispossessing them of their property." (Roberts, p. 269.)

The relaxed surveillance of the guards enabled Joseph to give more constant and effective leadership to his people. The Liberty jail became, in effect, the command post from which he directed the exodus to Illinois. A stream of visitors to the jail brought him reports about what was going on, and he gave the visitors instructions to be relayed to his followers. Fortunately, Brigham Young had eluded the mob and had remained free. With the apostasy of Thomas B. Marsh, Brigham had succeeded to the presidency of the Twelve Apostles. In this capacity he directed the movement of the Saints to Illinois, following the general directions of the Prophet and using imaginative innovation where the circumstances required it.

An insight into the loose yet firm control the Prophet exerted over his followers while he was imprisoned is gained from this excerpt from one of his letters: "Now, brethren, concerning the places for the location of the Saints, we cannot counsel you as we could if we were present with you; and as to the things that were written heretofore, we did not consider them anything binding, therefore we now say once for all, that we think it most proper that the general affairs of the Church, which are necessary to be considered, while your humble servant remains in bondage, should be transacted by a general conference of the most faithful and the most respectable of the authorities of the Church, and a minute of those transactions may be kept, and forwarded from time to time to your humble servant; and if there should be any corrections by the word of the Lord, they shall be freely transmitted, and your humble servant will approve all things whatsoever is acceptable unto God. If anything should have been suggested by us, or any names mentioned, except by commandment, or thus saith the Lord, we do not consider it binding; therefore our hearts shall not be grieved if different arrangements should be entered into. Nevertheless we would suggest the propriety of being aware of an aspiring spirit, which spirit has oftentimes urged men forward to make foul speeches, and influence the Church to reject milder counsels, and has eventually been the means of bringing much death and sorrow upon the Church." (HC 3:295.)

So preoccupied was he with the condition of his family and, followers that Joseph, in a way, seemed oblivious to the subhuman conditions under which he and his fellow prisoners lived. Except for the incident when he rebuked the profane guards at Richmond, he appears to have taken the inconvenience of his imprisonment in stride and to have endured it with stoic silence. Consequently, we must look to others for an account of the squalid conditions under which the prisoners were confined.

We learn that the outside measurements of the Liberty jail were only 22½ by 22 feet. The walls were of double construction, with the four-foot space between the outer stone wall and the inner oak wall being filled with loose rock. Inside were two levels, each about 14 feet square. The only ventilation came from two small windows with iron bars. The beds consisted of hewn logs covered with straw. The food was described as "very coarse, and so filthy that we could not eat it until we were driven to it by hunger." (Ivan J. Barrett, *Joseph Smith and the Restoration* [Brigham Young University Press, 1973], p. 423.)

But amid the confusion, the harassment, and the endless inconvenience of prison life, Joseph maintained a basic composure and serenity. His main concerns were his family, his followers, and whether his imprisonment would jeopardize his ability to lead. All these are mirrored in a touching letter he wrote to Emma in his own hand on March 21, 1839. Manifesting the lonesome feelings of any man separated from his family, he pleaded for news from home. "I want you to try to gain time and write to me a long letter and tell me all you can and even if old major [a favorite family pet] is alive yet and what those little pratlers say that cling around your neck."

Toward the end of the letter, in a rare introspective mood, he raised questions about the effect of his imprisonment upon his family and his friends. "I feel like Joseph in Egypt," he wrote, almost as if talking to himself in a reverie. "Doth my friends yet live[?] [I]f they live do they remember me[?] [H]ave they regard for me[?] [I]f so let me know it. . . ." Focusing then upon his beloved wife, he asked, "Dear Emma do you think that my being cast into prison by the mob renders me less worthy of your friendship[?]" Answering his own question, he concluded, "No I do not think so." (N. B. Lundwall, *The Fate of the Persecutors of the Prophet Joseph Smith* [1952], pp. 112-14.)

When Joseph was not busy writing letters to his family and friends, or writing memorials for a redress of grievances, or conferring with the lawyers about his defense, he was devising schemes to escape. Several of these were tried but failed. As the weight of public opinion shifted more and more toward the Saints, his captors seemed almost as anxious for his escape as was he, but the timing was as important as were the appearances.

Sidney Rigdon had been released on bail February 25, 1839, because of his failing health. Sometime later Joseph and the others petitioned the court for their release. Three weeks later, Judge Turnham responded and came to visit them in jail. He explained that if he were to admit them to bail too, it would cost him his life. He went on to say, however, that the governor was "heartily sick" of the affair and that he had "arranged a plan for their escape." (Roberts, p. 271.)

This plan came to fruition in April 1839. During that month the prisoners were moved to Daviess County. En route, the party, which consisted of the prisoners, a sheriff, and four guards, stopped at Diahman, where the prisoners were permitted to purchase two horses. What followed is best told in the words of Hyrum Smith: ". . . we bought a jug of whisky, with which we treated the company, and while there the sheriff . . . said that Judge Birch told him never to carry us to Boone county . . . and, said he, I shall take a good drink of grog, and go to bed, and you may do as you have a mind to. Three other of the guards drank pretty freely of the whisky, sweetened with honey. They also went to bed, and were soon asleep and the other guard went along with us, and helped to saddle the horses." Concluding his account of the escape, Hyrum noted wryly: "Two of us mounted the horses, and the other three started on foot, and we took our change of venue for the State of Illinois; and in the course of nine or ten days arrived safely in Quincy, Adams county, where we found our families in a state of poverty, although in good health." (HC 3:321.)

Months after his flight to Illinois, the Prophet found the time to prepare a detailed summary of the persecutions he and his people endured while in Missouri. Excerpts from that summary provide a helpful insight into those events as seen through his eyes. Speaking of the expenses he incurred in defending himself he wrote: "Before leaving Missouri I had paid the lawyers at Richmond thirty-four thousand dollars in cash, lands, etc.; one lot which I let them have, in Jackson county, for seven thousand dollars, they were soon offered ten thousand dollars for it, but would not accept it. For other vexatious suits which I had to contend against for the few months I was in this state, I paid lawyers' fees to the amount of sixteen thousand dollars, making in all about fifty thousand dollars, for which I received very little in return; for sometimes they were afraid to act on account of the mob, and sometimes they were so drunk as to incapacitate them for business. But there were a few honorable exceptions."

After listing those who were his chief antagonists, he said: "I was in their hands, as a prisoner, about six months; but notwithstanding their determination to destroy me, with the rest of my brethren who were with me, and although at three different times (as I was informed) we were sentenced to be shot, without the least shadow of law (as we were not military men), and had the time and place appointed for that purpose, yet through the mercy of God, in answer to the prayers of the Saints, I have been preserved and delivered out of their hands, and can again enjoy the society of my friends and brethren, whom I love, and to whom I feel united in bonds that are stronger than death. . . ."

Of the confidence he had that he would survive and of the feelings he entertained during his confinement he wrote: "During the time I was in the hands of my enemies, I must say, that although I felt great anxiety respecting my family and friends, who were so inhumanly treated and abused . . . I felt perfectly calm, and resigned to the will of my Heavenly Father. . . . from my first entrance into the camp, I felt an assurance that I, with my brethren and our families, should be delivered. Yes, that still small voice, which has so often whispered consolation to my soul, in the depths of sorrow and distress, bade me be of good cheer, and promised deliverance, which gave me great comfort. And although the heathen raged, and the people imagined vain things, yet the Lord of Hosts, the God of Jacob was my refuge; and when I cried unto Him in the day of trouble, He delivered me; for which I call upon my soul, and all that is within me, to bless and praise His holy name. For . . . I was 'troubled on every side, yet not distressed; perplexed, but not in despair; persecuted, but not forsaken; cast down, but not destroyed.' "

The Prophet paid special tribute to those who had stood by him and who had befriended him while he was imprisoned. Of them he wrote: "Their attention and affection to me, while in prison, will ever be remembered by me; and when I have seen them thrust away and abused by the jailer and guard, when they came to do any kind offices, and to cheer our minds while we were in the gloomy prisonhouse, gave me feelings which I cannot describe; while those who wished to insult and abuse us by their threats and blasphemous language, were applauded, and had every encouragement given them."

With frank realism and perhaps with some foreboding, Joseph recognized that the Saints had not seen an end to persecution. In fact, he held it out to his followers as a way of life. Wrote he: "We shall therefore do well to discern the signs of the times as we pass along, that the day of the Lord may not 'overtake us as a thief in the night.' Afflictions, persecutions, imprisonments, and death, we must expect, according to the scriptures, which tell us that the blood of those whose souls were under the altar could not be avenged on them that dwell on the earth, until their brethren should be slain as they were."

The Prophet concluded this remarkable account by severely castigating those who were responsible for the abuse and persecution that had been heaped upon the Latter-day Saints. "If these transactions had taken place among barbarians," he wrote, ". . . then there might have been some shadow of defense offered. But can we realize that in a land which is the cradle of liberty and equal rights . . . a persecution the most unwarrantable was commenced, and a tragedy the most dreadful was enacted, by a large portion of the inhabitants of one of those free and sovereign states which comprise this vast Republic." (HC 3:327-31.)

Chapter Twenty-five

The Founding of Nauvoo

It was with feelings of ambivalence that Joseph turned his back on Missouri. He was gratified to leave behind the stench and squalor of the filthy jails that had been his home for many months. He was relieved to be free of the malignant neighbors who for years had harassed and intimidated and murdered his people. And he was overjoyed with the prospect of again having the love and companionship of his family and friends and of getting on with the vital work of building up the Church. At the same time, he could not help but feel regret over the blasted hopes and the apparent failures left behind. Gone temporarily was the hope of a utopian society fit to receive the Savior at his second coming. Vanished for the moment were the plans to build the holy temple to which the Savior was to return. And the founding of the city of Zion would now have to be postponed to some indefinite time in the future. The Prophet knew from the revelations he had received that these failures had come about in large part through the disobedience and the stiffneckedness of the Saints. As a responsible and conscientious leader, he could not help but wonder about the extent to which these failures could be ascribed to deficient leadership on his part.

But these reflections were only of a fleeting nature. It was foreign to the Prophet's character to brood over the past or to permit past failures to hinder his performance either in the present or the future. In this, Joseph was an apt practitioner of the second fundamental principle of the gospel, repentance, which is founded on the premise of man's fallibility and of his power to change and improve.

Thus, while Joseph recognized there were deficiencies in the conduct of his people and in his own conduct while in Missouri, he was determined to profit from them. And despite failures there, the revelations and teachings about Zion had implanted in the minds of his followers the idea that they, or their descendants, would return to Missouri one day to claim what they considered to be their own.

The Prophet arrived in Quincy, Illinois, on April 22, 1839, "amidst the congratulations of my friends, and the embraces of my family, whom I found as well as could be expected, considering what they had been called to endure." (HC 3:327.)

The Saints had been warmly received in Quincy following their expulsion from Missouri. The citizens of that community, and especially a group known as the Democratic Association, had met there the previous February to consider the plight of the exiles and the ways in which they might be assisted. Out of that meeting came a resolution that stated: "Resolved, That the strangers recently arrived here from the state of Missouri, known by the name of the 'Latter-day Saints,' are entitled to our sympathy and kindest regard, and that we recommend to the citizens of Quincy to extend all the kindness in their power to bestow on the persons who are in affliction." (HC 3:269.)

Without demeaning the sincerity of those who extended this welcome to the Saints, it should be noted that at the time, the state of Illinois was heavily in debt; and the chief hope in avoiding public bankruptcy lay in attracting new settlers to the area, thus broadening the tax base. So the kindness reflected in this resolution was not founded entirely upon Christian charity. There was a good deal of self-interest mixed up in it. It should be noted too that at that time, there existed in Illinois in large numbers many of the irreligious, hard-drinking old settlers of the kind whom the Saints had known, to their sorrow, in Ohio and Missouri. This element would surface in the years ahead to harass and ultimately kill the Prophet.

Joseph hardly had time to say hello to his family and followers before he was caught up in the monumental task of finding a suitable location for the permanent settlement of the Saints. Three days after his arrival in Quincy, he had crossed the river into Iowa to examine potential sites. Their traumatic experiences in Missouri and Ohio had convinced Joseph and the other brethren of the desirability of establishing a separate community of their own rather than moving into an area that had been settled previously by others. Thus, the brethren were looking for a sizeable tract that would accommodate a town site with nearby agricultural land sufficient to sustain a population of fifteen to twenty thousand people. It was not their intention to preclude nonmembers from living in their midst. Quite the contrary. But it was their intention to structure a community in a way that would make life there wholly compatible with their customs and ideals.

The Prophet, Bishop Vinson Knight, and Alanson Ripley had been appointed as the committee to select the gathering place of the exiled Saints. On May 1 this committee purchased 135 acres of swampland on the Illinois side of the river from Hugh White for five thousand dollars and forty-seven acres of improved land from Isaac Galland for nine thousand dollars. A few huts stood on the land and comprised what was then known as Commerce, Illinois. Of this purchase, the Prophet recorded: "When I made the purchase of White and Galland, there were one stone house, three frame houses, and two block houses, which constituted the whole city of Commerce. Between Commerce and Mr. Davidson Hibbard's, there was one stone house and three log houses, including the one that I live in, and these were all the houses in this vicinity, and the place was literally a wilderness. The land was mostly covered with trees and bushes, and much of it so wet that it was with the utmost difficulty a footman could get through, and totally impossible for teams. Commerce was so unhealthful, very few could live there; but believing that it might become a healthful place by the blessing of heaven to the Saints, and no more eligible place presenting itself, I considered it wisdom to make an attempt to build up a city." (HC 3:375.)

After these initial purchases, the Saints made other purchases on both the Illinois and the Iowa sides of the river. The lands were extensive enough to enable the Prophet to project the building of a city of somewhat grand proportions. The novel ideas that had been incorporated in the Prophet's plat of the city of Zion some years before were to find practical expression in building the new city. Sites in the center of the town were to be reserved for public buildings and for the temple. Residential lots were to be large enough to accommodate homes and associated buildings and to enable the residents to raise truck gardens, poultry, and barnyard animals. Industrial and business activities were to be segregated, and the surrounding farm land was near enough to make commuting easy and convenient. This particular site also had the advantage of being adjacent to a large, navigable river, which would enhance its value as a commercial center and would facilitate access to it by the thousands of Latter-day Saints who would flock there from the surrounding areas and from the fruitful missions abroad.

After the necessary property acquisitions, the Prophet arranged for a survey of the area and the subdivision of lots within the townsite. These lots were then sold for five hundred dollars each, although those Saints who had suffered the most during the Missouri persecutions were given their lots free.

As the Prophet reflected upon the plans for the city, it occurred to him that the name Commerce was wholly unsuited for the kind of city he had projected in his mind. Calling upon his Hebrew studies some years before in Kirtland, he came up with a name for the city that more nearly coincided with the image he had conceived for it. It would be known as Nauvoo, or, as it was often referred to later, Nauvoo the Beautiful. This Hebrew name literally signified "a beautiful situation" and, according to the Prophet, carried with it "the idea of rest."

Once the preliminaries of property acquisitions and surveys had been completed, the Saints began to gather to Nauvoo, where they set about with characteristic vigor and enthusiasm to build anew. The terrible losses in property and life they had suffered in Kirtland and in Missouri had in no way dampened their ardor. On the contrary, they seemed only to fuel the Saints' energies and their determination to show the world the fruits of their religion.

On Friday, May 10, 1839, Joseph moved his family into a small log cabin on the bank of the Mississippi River in Commerce. It was from these unpretentious quarters that the settlement of the Prophet's last city of residence was to be directed. He entertained no illusions about the permanence of his stay there. Stirring within were vague impressions about the short time left for him to complete his earthly mission. He was also conscious of the rough road that lay ahead for him and the Saints.

Joseph did not permit the endless responsibilities of building a new city to interfere with his basic life-style. Once he had clarified the objectives, delegated authority to his subordinates, and set the wheels of progress in motion, he turned to the spiritual and intellectual pursuits that always took precedence with him, including the monumental task of continuing to write his history. As urgent matters arose that could not be postponed, he would lay aside his literary efforts or other intellectual tasks that claimed his attention, do what had to be done at the moment, and then pick up and continue his study or dictation where he had left off.

We see in this practice a pattern that was evident from the

very beginning of his ministry. He was never able to devote long, uninterrupted periods of time to these pursuits, but he had mastered the law of particles, and he almost literally completed his writing, translating, and editing tasks line upon line, as he could squeeze out a moment here or there. Also, ever present was a scribe or secretary to assist him—Emma, Oliver Cowdery, Sidney Rigdon, one of the Whitmer boys, a member of the Twelve, or whoever was available. When it was feasible, though, he would employ someone who could be with him constantly during his working hours, to record or make note of whatever was important at the moment. During the early part of his ministry in Nauvoo James Mulholland was his principal scribe. Later, the English convert William Clayton filled this role.

Several reasons seem to explain why the Prophet was so habituated to the use of a scribe or secretary. He thought more clearly while he spoke, and being freed from the mechanical necessity of recording his thoughts, they flowed more smoothly and logically. Also, when he was moved upon by the Spirit as revelations came, he could focus all his attention upon the substance of the things being shown or told him and upon their translation or explanation; to have to record them manually would have greatly impeded his work. In addition, because of his limited opportunities for formal schooling, his handwriting was almost illegible, his spelling was poor, and he knew practically nothing about punctuation. Being keenly aware of his scholastic deficiencies, Joseph was, therefore, prone to gather around him those who possessed the mechanical skills he sorely lacked.

A final reason for his use of a scribe appears to be that the Prophet, whether unconsciously or deliberately, seemed always to want a witness or witnesses to what he did, and a sure way to achieve this was to always have a scribe at hand.

As the Prophet found opportunity to do so, he preached to the Saints around Nauvoo to build them up in their confidence and faith, to give them instructions, and, when necessary, to correct his subordinates to prepare them for the challenges which lay ahead. An indication of the enthusiasm with which his words were received is found in this account of a sermon he delivered on June 23, 1839: "Went to Brother Wilcox's and preached to a very crowded congregation; and so eager were they to hear, that a part of them stood out in the rain during the sermon. In general they expressed good satisfaction as to what they heard." (HC 3:378.)

By this time, most of the Twelve had gathered in Nauvoo. In the latter part of April several of them, headed by Brigham Young, had returned to Far West to lay the cornerstone of the temple in fulfillment of an earlier prophecy, in defiance of a boast by the mob that it would never take place. There Wilford Woodruff and George A. Smith had been ordained apostles, in accordance with an earlier decision. In June, Orson Hyde, who had repented after his defection in Missouri, was received back into fellowship and restored to his place in the Quorum. While the energies and ability of these leaders would have provided a tremendous impetus toward the building up of Nauvoo, the Prophet had his eye on a more distant goal. The Twelve were to be about their task of warning the world of impending judgment, of calling it to repentance, and of fueling the energies of Nauvoo with a stream of new converts from abroad. Joseph had observed the impact upon the Church of the first harvest of converts from England, and he foresaw that while keeping the Twelve at home might be beneficial temporarily in helping to build up Nauvoo, in the long run their labors abroad would be vastly more productive as they multiplied the working capacity of the Saints through conversions.

In anticipation of the departure of the Twelve for England to continue their proselyting efforts, in June 1839 the Prophet commenced to give them detailed and explicit instructions, including the exposition of Church doctrines and directions on personal conduct. In a journal entry he noted that he had "taught the brethren at considerable length on the following subjects": faith, repentance, baptism, the gift of the Holy Ghost, tongues, and the resurrection. On the subject of revelation, he told them: "A person may profit by noticing the first intimation of the spirit of revelation; for instance, when you feel pure intelligence flowing into you, it may give you sudden strokes of ideas, so that by noticing it, you may find it fulfilled the same day or soon; (i.e.) those things that were presented unto your minds by the Spirit of God, will come to pass; and thus by learning the Spirit of God and understanding it, you may grow into the principle of revelation, until you become perfect in Christ Jesus." (HC 3:381.)

On July 2, 1839, Joseph called a meeting of the Twelve and some of the Seventy to give them final instructions before they departed for their missions abroad. The First Presidency blessed

Wilford Woodruff and George A. Smith, ratifying the ordinations they had received under the hands of the Twelve in April in Far West.

The instructions given on this occasion reveal the depth of the Prophet's maturity and his understanding of human nature. He summarized his remarks as being "calculated to guard them against self-sufficiency, self-righteousness, and self-importance; touching upon many subjects of . . . value to all who wish to walk humbly before the Lord, and especially teaching them to observe charity, wisdom and fellow-feeling, with love one towards another in all things, and under all circumstances." (HC 3:383.)

The Prophet spoke on the subject that to him was of overriding importance to those commissioned to speak and to act in the name of God—communication with the unseen world. Said he: "We may look for angels and receive their ministrations, but we are to try the spirits and prove them, for it is often the case that men make a mistake in regard to these things. God has so ordained that when He has communicated, no vision is to be taken but what you see by the seeing of the eye, or what you hear by the hearing of the ear. When you see a vision, pray for the interpretation; if you get not this, shut it up; there must be certainty in this matter. An open vision will manifest that which is important. Lying spirits are going forth in the earth. There will be great manifestations of spirits, both false and true."

He then went on to give his disciples explicit instructions about the appearance and conduct of angels, the power of the devil, and the gift of tongues: "An angel of God never has wings. Some will say that they have seen a spirit; that he offered them his hand, but they did not touch it. This is a lie. First, it is contrary to the plan of God: a spirit cannot come but in glory; an angel has flesh and bones; we see not their glory. The devil may appear as an angel of light. Ask God to reveal it; if it be of the devil, he will flee from you; if of God, He will manifest Himself, or make it manifest. . . .

"Every spirit, or vision, or singing, is not of God. The devil is an orator; he is powerful. . . . The gift of discerning spirits will be given to the Presiding Elder. Pray for him that he may have this gift. Speak not in the gift of tongues without understanding it, or without interpretation. The devil can speak in tongues. . . . Let no one speak in tongues unless he interpret, except by the consent of the one who is placed to preside; then he may discern or interpret, or another may."

In conclusion, the Prophet set before his brethren examples of spiritual giants to emulate: "Let us seek for the glory of Abraham, Noah, Adam, the Apostles, who have communion with [knowledge of] these things, and then we shall be among that number when Christ comes." (HC 3:391-92.)

Instructions of this kind had not been heard on the earth for centuries. Following Christ's advent, religious leaders had drifted into a sort of spiritual limbo, expressing belief in the unseen world but never speaking authoritatively about it from firsthand knowledge. What they knew about God, angels, and the devil was mere hearsay, gleaned from books; and lacking direct knowledge of these things, they spoke about them vaguely and with uncertainty. But here we find the Prophet Joseph Smith treating these subjects with an almost clinical matter-of-factness. To him the existence of extraterrestrial beings was not a subject for speculation and debate, but was a reality to be reckoned with in day-to-day living. It was not a question of whether these things existed, but rather how one should conduct himself to gain the favor of the one while avoiding the influence of the other. Because of the vast experience he had had with the unseen world, he was anxious to prepare the minds of his disciples against the spiritual onslaughts he knew they would face when they went abroad again to proselyte.

Some idea of the effect of Joseph's instructions upon his disciples can be gained from Heber C. Kimball's account of his and Brigham Young's departure for their mission: "President Brigham Young left his home at Montrose to start on the mission to England. He was so sick that he was unable to go to the Mississippi, a distance of thirty rods, without assistance. After he had crossed the river he rode behind Israel Barlow on his horse to my house, where he continued sick until the 18th. He left his wife sick with a babe only three weeks old, and all his other children were sick and unable to wait upon each other. . . . On the 17th, Sister Mary Ann Young got a boy to carry her up in his wagon to my house, that she might nurse and comfort Brother Brigham to the hour of starting.

"September 18th, Charles Hubbard sent his boy with a wagon and span of horses to my house; our trunks were put into the wagon by some brethren; I went to my bed and shook hands with my wife who was then shaking with a chill, having two children lying sick by her side; I embraced her and my children, and bade them farewell. . . .

"It was with difficulty we got into the wagon, and started down the hill about ten rods; it appeared to me as though my very inmost parts would melt within me at leaving my family in such a condition. . . . I asked the teamster to stop, and said to Brother Brigham, 'This is pretty tough, isn't it; let's rise up and give them a cheer.' We arose, and swinging our hats three times over our heads, shouted, 'Hurrah, hurrah for Israel.' Vilate, hearing the noise, arose from her bed and came to the door. She had a smile on her face. Vilate and Mary Ann Young cried out to us: 'Goodbye, God bless you.' We returned the compliment, and then told the driver to go ahead. After this I felt a spirit of joy and gratitude, having had the satisfaction of seeing my wife standing upon her feet, instead of leaving her in bed, knowing well that I should not see them again for two or three years." (Whitney, pp. 265-66.)

This same dedication and tough-minded endurance characterized all that the Twelve and their associates did during this mission to the British Isles. They became the instruments by which thousands of British converts were brought into the fold of the Church. They diligently applied the principles of spirituality that the Prophet had taught them prior to their departure. They prophesied, healed the sick, cast out devils, and spoke in tongues. They instantly heeded any whispering or spiritual impression that came to them.

On the eve of one of his most successful missionary efforts, apostle Wilford Woodruff announced in the midst of a speech that he would be leaving for another field of labor on the morrow, despite the fact that he had scheduled several meetings ahead in that locality. This came about because of a spiritual impression he had received that he should leave. He did not know at the time exactly where he should go, but he departed in confidence that the details would be made clear to him as he went along. Later he recorded the results of this impromptu proselyting effort: ". . . I note the remarkable fact that I had been led by the spirit . . . through a densely populated country . . . and chose no part of it for my field of labor until I was led by the Lord to the house of John Benbow, at Frome's Hill, where I preached for the first time on the 5th of March, 1840; now, on the 22nd of June, I was going to the Manchester conference, to represent this fruitful field of my labors with thirty-three organized churches numbering 541 members, 300 of whom received the ordinance of baptism under my hands." (Cowley, p. 149.)

The Prophet secretly yearned to accompany the Twelve on their mission to the British Isles. This is evident from the avid way in which he watched and recorded in his journal every aspect of their journeys and ministry. Each obstacle they encountered and each success they experienced was duly noted. This keen interest was rooted not only in his responsibilities as the head of the Church, but also in his family loyalties. It was two hundred years before, in 1638, that his paternal ancestor, Robert Smith, had immigrated to America from England. Other ancestors had also originated in the British Isles, and he knew that many of his blood relatives still lived in that land. Moreover, he knew that many of the inhabitants of that land were of Israelite descent and that the process of ferreting these out and gathering them to Zion, or America, was an essential prerequisite to the second coming of the Savior.

When the Saints first settled there, Nauvoo was a sickly place, swampy and heavily infested with mosquitoes and other insects. Because of this, some of the Saints came reluctantly, being persuaded only by the assurances of their prophetic leader that the Lord would temper the elements and modify the adverse conditions.

In July 1839, prolonged rain, interspersed with hot, muggy days, had converted the area into a literal pesthole. The fever ran rampant among the Saints, and many of them died or were near death. Those who were not sick enough to be in bed were lethargic and barely able to move around. Under these conditions, all work and most other activities practically came to a standstill.

The Prophet himself fell prey to the fever and was confined to his quarters for many days. As he awakened on the morning of July 22, 1839, he was imbued with a great desire to be up and about his work. Praying to God for strength and guidance, he became filled with the electric energy that was always evident in him when he acted under inspiration. Wilford Woodruff recorded what then happened: ". . . he arose from his bed and commenced to administer to the sick in his own house and door-yard, and he commanded them in the name of the Lord Jesus Christ to arise and be made whole; and the sick were healed upon every side of him. Many lay sick along the bank of the river; Joseph walked along up to the lower stone house, occupied by Sidney Rigdon, and he healed all the sick that lay in his path. . . . After healing all that lay sick upon the bank of the river as far as the stone house, he called upon Elder Kimball and some others to accompany him across the river to visit the sick at Montrose. . . . Among the number were several of the Twelve. On his arrival the first house he visited was that occupied by Elder Brigham Young, the President of the Quorum of the Twelve, who lay sick. Joseph healed him, then he arose and accompanied the Prophet on his visit to others who were in the same condition."

Many miraculous healings were recorded as the Prophet, accompanied by various members of the Twelve, visited the homes of the sick and blessed them. At the home of Elijah Fordham, it was reported that he "spoke in a very loud voice, saying, 'Brother Fordham, I command you, in the name of Jesus Christ, to arise from this bed and be made whole.' His voice was like the voice of God, and not of man. . . . Brother Fordham arose from his bed, and was immediately made whole." (See HC 4:3-5.)

When the Prophet could not go in person to bless the sick and afflicted, he empowered the Twelve to go in his stead, and many were healed.

The effects of the epidemic were evident among the Saints for weeks after the epidemic abated. Many of those who were blessed by the Prophet experienced only a temporary recovery; after the powerful effect of his presence and the commanding force of his words wore off, they reverted to their previous condition. Others were permanently healed and thereafter went about their tasks with customary and even renewed vigor. Still others, though not healed even temporarily, were so motivated by the Prophet's energetic example that they left their beds, determined to keep working as long as life remained.

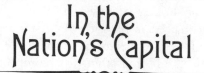

Chapter Twenty-six

In the Nation's Capital

With the Twelve gone into the mission field, the Prophet felt the added weight of responsibility that rested upon him to motivate and direct the thousands of Latter-day Saints who were pouring into Nauvoo in a seemingly endless stream. With the herculean task of building a new civilization facing him, his teaching took on a new dimension. Shelved for the time being were the themes of broad, eternal scope and in their place appeared down-to-earth exhortations about the conduct of life and how to survive in a turbulent world. The notes of a sermon delivered in late September illustrate this significant change in focus: "Held a meeting at my own house. After others had spoken I spoke and explained concerning the uselessness of preaching to the world about great judgments, but rather to preach the simple Gospel. Explained concerning the coming of the Son of Man; also that it is a false idea that the Saints will escape all the judgments, whilst the wicked suffer; for all flesh is subject to suffer, and 'the righteous shall hardly escape;' still many of the Saints will escape, for the just shall live by faith; yet many of the righteous shall fall a prey to disease, to pestilence, etc., by reason of the weakness of the flesh, and yet be saved in the Kingdom of God. So that it is an unhallowed principle to say that such and such have transgressed because they have been preyed upon by disease or death, for all flesh is subject to death; and the Savior has said, 'Judge not, lest ye be judged.' " (HC 4:11.)

A few days later, Joseph admonished the brethren "to be careful in speaking on those subjects which are not clearly pointed out in the word of God, which lead to speculation and strife." (HC 4:13.)

In these and other similar exhortations of the Prophet, we see him trying to channel the energies of the Saints toward more conventional and productive goals and to avoid the excessive and sometimes impractical enthusiasms that occasionally took hold of some of his followers. He was the first to recognize that some of the difficulties inflicted upon the Saints in Missouri came about because of the unwise and overzealous conduct of a few of them. It was his hope that a repetition of this unfortunate consequence could be avoided, and so at this time he began a determined effort to bridle the people and to teach them discipline and wisdom.

In the meantime, the Saints were experiencing the same difficulty in adjusting to their new environment and in accommodating themselves to changed circumstances as did any other group of pioneers. Inevitably there were jarrings and misunderstandings. Most of these were settled amicably, in good faith, by honest people whose chief object was to build a society worthy of the companionship of the Savior. Occasionally, however, those involved in controversy lost sight of their objective or permitted selfish interests to override the common good. In these instances, the ecclesiastical authorities were not reluctant to take prompt and, if necessary, stern measures to preserve the peace and prevent a breakdown of law and order. Thus, during this era will be found many cases decided by the church courts which involved issues quite foreign to the usual matters handled by these tribunals.

At this point, the local civil government was only in its incipient stage of development and not equipped to handle efficiently most kinds of conflicts between individuals. The Church instinctively moved into this vacuum and for a while provided the sanctions and discipline necessary to ensure good order. Later, as the civil government assumed the responsibilities that rightfully belonged to it, the Church withdrew and, for the most part, left the field to those who were elected by the political process. But this withdrawal was, of necessity, a gradual thing. And as the authority shifted from the Church to the civil government, it tended to remain vested in the same group of men who acted simultaneously in both church and civil capacities. It is understandable, therefore, that the line dividing ecclesiastical and civil authority became blurred in the minds of the general membership of the Church. To a lesser but still substantial degree, a similar blurring occurred also in the minds of most of the leaders of the Church, a circumstance that was to be a source of great difficulty for many years to come.

For the time being, though, the great anxiety of the Prophet was not that the Saints would usurp the prerogatives of the law, but that the law would continue to turn a deaf ear to their cries for a redress of the grievances arising out of the depredations inflicted upon them in Missouri. Ever since these barbarities had commenced, the Prophet had been directing a stream of protest aimed at officials in Missouri and at the general public through the communications media. The first efforts had had little effect except in producing the climate that brought about the Prophet's release from custody. Later efforts had been much more successful and had produced a radical change in the attitudes of the general public toward the Latter-day Saints. Whereas originally they had been looked upon as a sect of radical, unorthodox malcontents, they were now regarded by many as a group of unfortunate religionists who had been unjustly maligned and oppressed.

The Prophet Joseph Smith, ever alert to the tides of public opinion, was determined to capitalize on this favorable turn of events. So, in the fall of 1839, he decided to put the Church's case before the federal government in Washington, D.C. His decision was based upon a feeling that the Saints' position was right and that in a land noted for its commitment to liberty and freedom, there must be a forum where wrongs of such magnitude could be righted. Having pleaded without success before every other known tribunal, he felt some assurance of a receptive audience in Washington.

Accompanied by two experienced advisers, Sidney Rigdon and Elias Higbee, and his rough-hewn friend and bodyguard, Orrin Porter Rockwell, the Prophet left Nauvoo in a two-horse carriage on October 29, 1839, bound for the nation's capital. The party stopped in Quincy for a few days to put their papers in order. While there, Elder Rigdon became ill. They continued their journey to Springfield, where Dr. Robert O. Foster, a member of the Church, prescibed some medicine for Elder Rigdon. When this did not bring about the desired cure, Dr. Foster joined the party and administered other medicines along the way.

The rest of the trip passed routinely except for an exciting incident near its end. At one of the regular stops, the coachman left the team untended while he took his grog in a nearby tavern. In his absence, something frightened the horses, causing them to bolt and run full-speed downhill over a tortuous, rocky trail. The terrified passengers were tossed about violently by the lurching of the driverless coach. One woman passenger was so terrified that she was about to throw her baby out the window in the irrational hope that it might be spared the crushing death she foresaw at the end of their wild ride, but the Prophet managed to restrain her from doing so. After trying to calm the other passengers, he commenced a perilous maneuver that has since become a trademark of western movies. Carefully opening the coach door, he found a handhold on the outside by which, with the exertion of his powerful arm muscles, he pulled himself slowly upward into the driver's seat. Grasping the reins of the stampeding team, he managed to bring it under control and finally to a snorting halt. No sooner had the coach made its final squeaking lurch than the disheveled passengers piled out, their fears now turned to exuberant, almost incoherent joy. When the flood of elation had subsided, they turned their attention to Joseph. "My course was spoken of in the highest terms of commendation," he wrote, "as being one of the most daring and heroic deeds, and no language could express the gratitude of the passengers, when they found themselves safe, and the horses quiet. There were some members of Congress with us, who proposed naming the incident to that body, believing they would reward such conduct by some public act; but on inquiring my name, to mention as the author of their safety, and finding it to be Joseph Smith the 'Mormon Prophet,' as they called me, I heard no more of their praise, gratitude, or reward." (HC 4:23-24.)

The cold, negative attitude of these people toward the Prophet presaged the general reception he was to receive at the hands of official Washington. He soon learned that the shift in public opinion toward the Saints meant no more than that the public deplored the barbaric treatment they had received. It did *not* mean that the public was prepared to accord them more sympathetic understanding than that to which any underdog would be entitled. To most people of the day, the Latter-day Saints and their leader were merely misguided fanatics who were deserving of no more than the common civilities due to any human being, and once that concession had been made, they were entitled to nothing else.

The Prophet and his party checked into a second-rate hotel at the corner of Missouri and Third streets. Their pinched finances made it necessary for them to economize at every turn, and so they avoided the finer hotels and restaurants. Having established their headquarters and having again reviewed the voluminous protests, appeals, and memorials they had brought with them, Joseph and the others set about the monumental task of trying to persuade the national government to right the wrongs their people had suffered in Missouri. It took but a short while for them to learn that their influence in the federal government was practically nonexistent. There was no one there to plead their cause. The representatives from Ohio and Missouri, whom they had helped to elect, felt no sense of obligation to them because of the exodus to Illinois, and the Illinois representatives did not owe their election to the influence of the Saints in any sense.

The Prophet's chances of getting some relief for the Saints were also doomed by a legal philosophy prevailing at the time. It was generally acknowledged that the U.S. Constitution offered no protection to its citizens from acts committed by a state or by other citizens. The remedy for anyone so aggrieved was to seek redress by appeal to the legislature of the state involved or to the local courts. Since the halls of Congress and the federal executive departments were filled with lawyers who had been brought up with this concept, the reaction toward the pleas of Joseph and his associates was automatic and final. "You're in the wrong forum," they would be told time and time again. "Don't talk to us; go back to the legislature or to the courts in Missouri." While this answer may have been sufficient—and honestly so—for one trained in the technicalities of the prevailing legal system, it was hardly satisfying to those who had endured the mobbings, the burnings, and the scourgings that the Saints had endured.

The most disappointing rejection came from President Martin Van Buren. Joseph felt that if he could get the ear of the President and make him see the terrible plight of the Saints, some means would be found to give them assistance. It came as a crushing blow, therefore, that after the whole matter had been laid before President Van Buren, his response was, "Gentlemen, your cause is just, but I can do nothing for you." (HC 4:80.) The Prophet, of course, knew better. While recognizing the deterring effect of the prevailing legal views, he knew that if Mr. Van Buren were really of a mind to help the embattled Saints, he could do so through the exercise of the enormous executive power he wielded. In recounting the details of the interview, Joseph turned the full force of his scorn and invective upon Mr. Van Buren: ". . . the President . . . treated me very insolently, and it was with great reluctance he listened to our message. . . . His whole course went to show that he was an office-seeker, that self-aggrandizement was his ruling passion, and that justice and righteousness were no part of his composition. I found him such a man as I could not conscientiously support at the head of our noble Republic." (HC 4:80.) Later, Joseph made this prophetic comment about President Van Buren: "On my way home I did not fail to proclaim the iniquity and insolence of Martin Van Buren, toward myself and an injured people, which will have its effect upon the public mind; and may he never be elected again to any office of trust or power, by which he may abuse the innocent and let the guilty go free." (HC 4:89.)

An interesting footnote to this episode is that Martin Van Buren was the Democratic party candidate for reelection in 1840 and was soundly defeated by the Whig candidate, William Henry Harrison. Van Buren was again a presidential candidate in 1848, being the nominee of the Free Soil party. Opposed by Lewis Cass, the Democratic party candidate, and Zachary Taylor, a Whig, he did not receive a single electoral vote.

Consistent with his habits, the Prophet used his spare time to good advantage while he was in Washington. Whenever possible he accepted invitations to speak, both to member and nonmember groups. Invariably those who heard Joseph speak left with an entirely different impression of the man than they carried with them to the meeting. A principal reason for this, aside from his persuasive eloquence and personal magnetism, was the distorted, caricatured image of the man that had been projected to the public by his enemies. So gross and inaccurate was this caricature that almost any quality the Prophet may have projected would have cast him in a more favorable light. Not only did those who came to hear him find a man with an improved character over what they had been led to expect, but they also found a man with superior qualities who was deserving of careful study and attention. His discourse was reasonable and devoid of all cant and posturing. It consisted, for the most part, of an earnest, down-to-earth declaration of faith in a living God, with reasons and explanations given to support that faith. His delivery was not studied nor polished, but was conversational in tone; and the illustrations and analogies he used were of a kind to enable his listeners to grasp his meaning immediately and to relate it to their own experience.

One meeting the Prophet attended and spoke at in Washington stands out above all others merely because a good record of it has come down to us. The meeting was held in early February 1840 and was attended by many educated nonmembers, including Congressman Mathew S. Davis, a skilled observer and writer. The day following the meeting, while the memory of it was still fresh in his mind, Mr. Davis wrote a lengthy letter to his wife, describing the Prophet and recording the substance of his talk, which occupied more than two hours. These comments are of interest, revealing as they do the development of the Prophet's doctrinal conceptions at that time as understood by a perceptive nonmember.

"He commenced by saying," Congressman Davis wrote, "that he knew the prejudices which were abroad in the world against him, but requested us to pay no respect to the rumors which were in circulation respecting him or his doctrines. . . . He said, 'I will state to you our belief, so far as time will permit.' 'I believe,' said he, 'that there is a God, possessing all the attributes ascribed to Him by all Christians of all denominations; that He reigns over all things in heaven and on earth, and that all are subject to His power.' . . . He then took up the Bible. 'I believe,' said he, 'in this sacred volume. In it the "Mormon" faith is to be found. We teach nothing but what the Bible teaches. We believe nothing but what is to be found in this book. I believe in the fall of man, as recorded in the Bible; I believe that God foreknew everything, but did not foreordain everything; I deny that foreordain and foreknow are the same thing. He foreordained the fall of man; but all merciful as He is, He foreordained at the same time, a plan of redemption for all mankind. I believe in the Divinity of Jesus Christ, and that He died for the sins of all men, who in Adam had fallen.' He then entered into some details, the result of which tended to show his total unbelief of what is termed *original sin*. He believes that it is washed away by the blood of Christ, and that it no longer exists. As a necessary consequence, he believes that we are all born pure and undefiled. That *all* children dying at an early age (say *eight* years) not knowing good from evil, were incapable of sinning; and that all such assuredly go to heaven. 'I believe,' said he, 'that a man is a moral, responsible, free agent; that although it was foreordained he should fall, and be redeemed, yet after the redemption it was not foreordained that he should again sin. In the Bible a rule of conduct is laid down for him; in the Old and New Testaments the law by which he is to be governed, may be found. If he violates that law, he is to be punished for the deeds done in the body.

" 'I believe that God is eternal. That He had no beginning, and can have no end. Eternity means that which is without beginning or end. I believe that the *soul* is eternal; and had no beginning; it can have no end.' . . . He said very little of rewards and punishments; but one conclusion, from what he did say, was irresistible— he contended throughout, that everything which had a *beginning* must have an *ending;* and consequently if the punishment of man *commenced* in the next world, it must, according to his logic and belief have an *end*." (HC 4:78-79.)

It is not clear how a copy of this letter fell into the hands of the Prophet. Possibly Mr. Davis gave it to him. However gratifying it may have been to Joseph to observe how the attitude of this man toward him and the Saints had been changed by his talk, it provided no comfort to see that neither Mr. Davis nor others who heard him speak stepped forward to aid the Saints in obtaining redress for their grievances.

When it became apparent that his efforts in Washington would be fruitless, Joseph decided to return home. He departed in the latter part of February 1840 and arrived in Nauvoo on March 4. The results of his four-month absence from home were summed up in a journal entry made on that date: "I arrived safely at Nauvoo, after a wearisome journey . . . having witnessed many vexatious movements in government officers, whose sole object should be the peace and prosperity and happiness of the whole people; but instead of this, I discovered that popular clamor and personal aggrandizement were the ruling principles of those in authority; and my heart faints within me when I see, by the visions of the Almighty, the end of this nation, if she continues to disregard the cries and petitions of her virtuous citizens, as she has done, and is now doing." (HC 4:89.)

We can only surmise the impact of the Prophet's visit to Washington on his inner views and his future actions. Perhaps on this occasion was planted in Joseph's mind the seed that came to flower several years later when he decided to run as a candidate for United States President. Through contact with the principal leaders of the national government, he had the opportunity to make comparisons that convinced him he was more able than they and that his motives and aspirations were of a higher order than theirs. But as always, his concern about a problem and his approach toward a solution entailed more than a mere intellectual analysis of it. That was always accompanied by an appeal to heaven for clarification and guidance. Subsequent events were to confirm this fixed habit in the Prophet when he announced his candidacy and commenced one of the most novel presidential campaigns in U.S. history.

Chapter Twenty-seven

Life in Nauvoo

Any political aspirations the Prophet's Washington trip may have inspired were, of necessity, pushed into the background temporarily by other pressing matters that faced him upon his return to Nauvoo. Chief among these was the settlement of the thousands of Latter-day Saints who poured into the area in a constant, never-ending stream. What occurred in Nauvoo was essentially a repetition of what had happened before in Ohio and Missouri. The church organization had moved intact to the new location, and the bishops and other ecclesiastical officers responsible for the welfare of the Saints had automatically gone about their work, applying the techniques they had learned from the Prophet in Kirtland and in Missouri.

Since most of the Saints at this time were of British stock, Nauvoo took on the appearance of the English-inspired towns and villages of the kind found throughout New England. The solid, two-story brick or wooden colonial homes, the quiet, tree-lined streets, and the air of purposeful activity branded the community as nothing else could have done.

By July 1841 about 1200 new homes and other buildings had been completed and hundreds of others were in progress. A temple, to occupy a prominent site on the crest of a slight incline above the riverside lands, was authorized by a general conference on October 6, 1840. By the following general conference in April 1841, the basement had been dug and walled and was ready for the laying of the cornerstone.

The over-all impression the bustling community conveyed to outsiders is typified by the lyrics of a favorite Latter-day Saint hymn whose refrain breathes the spirit that pervaded the building of Nauvoo and other Mormon communities: "Then wake up, and do something more / Than dream of your mansion above; / Doing good is a pleasure, a joy beyond measure, / A blessing of duty and love." The same hymn contains this significant phrase, which conveys the essence of the Mormon character: "Only he who does something is worthy to live, / The world has no use for the drone." ("Have I Done Any Good in the World," *Hymns,* No. 58.) The lazy or shiftless never felt quite at ease in Nauvoo or in any other Latter-day Saint community. The glorification of work and the condemnatory attitude toward loafers and idlers tended to cause guilt feelings over engaging in purely recreational activities unless they produced some objective or tangible good.

But this should not be interpreted to mean that life among the Saints was ascetic or dull, for it was not. In fact, judged by the standards of the day, they were the most forward-looking and daring of all the religious sects in the nature of their entertainments. Unlike many contemporary churches, the Latter-day Saints did not prohibit or frown upon dancing. On the contrary; they approved and promoted it as a means of raising the spirits of the people and improving their social graces. Concerts, lectures, debates, scientific societies, and athletic competitions thrived and were encouraged and participated in by Church leaders. At the same time, the city was entirely devoid of brothels and saloons and other marks of a dissolute society. Crime was practically nonexistent, except for infrequent cases of theft or violation of an ordinance against damage to crops by untended animals.

Underlying the novel and refreshing life-style of the Saints were, of course, the religious concepts inculcated in them by the Prophet Joseph Smith. He had taught them that the glory of God is intelligence, and that the chief purpose of the Creator is to bring about the immortality and eternal life of man. He also taught that earth life is the time allotted to men to prepare to return to God, and that their status in the hereafter depends on the extent to which they, in this life, learn and apply eternal principles of truth. Further, they were taught that any degree of intelligence attained or any quality of character developed in earth life would rise with them in the resurrection. Thus, the Saints were alert to avoid any conduct that tended to debauch the mind and the spirit or to weaken the body. At the same time, they avidly embraced those activities that were wholesome and elevating in nature.

Assured that the industry and skill of the people and the high motivations that impelled them would lead inexorably to the creation of a model city, Joseph, in the early stages of Nauvoo's development, set about to structure a political organization that would afford the people the civil protections they had sorely lacked in Ohio and Missouri. In this, he pursued the vague, indistinct impressions that had come to him along the way and that had come more sharply into focus as his knowledge of civil government increased through study and bitter experience and as he was enlightened by further revelation. All this culminated in the drafting of the Nauvoo City charter, which is without parallel in the history of the United States. The city's courts were empowered to issue writs of habeas corpus, and the city was empowered to raise and maintain an army and to organize a university. So broad were its powers that political scientists have likened it to the ancient Greek city-states, which had almost complete autonomy. Joseph was determined that he would not again be exposed to the kind of governmental banditry that had brought about his arrest and imprisonment in Missouri.

The enactment of the unusual legislation permitting the city to put its charter into effect was made possible by the way in which it was handled by the Prophet and his associates and by the desire of the Illinois legislature to attract more taxpayers to its borders. In a journal entry dated December 16, 1840, he recorded with satisfaction: "This day the act chartering the 'City of Navuoo,' the 'Nauvoo Legion,' and the 'University of the City of Nauvoo,' was signed by the Governor, having previously passed the House and Senate." (HC 4:239.)

Later he noted: "The City Charter of Nauvoo is of my own plan and device. I concocted it for the salvation of the Church, and on principles so broad, that every honest man might dwell secure under its protective influence without distinction of sect or party." (HC 4:249.)

The Prophet's chief aide in obtaining passage of the charter was an ambitious new convert named John C. Bennett. A physician and former university professor, Bennett also had a flair for military matters; at the time the Prophet was working to get passage of the Nauvoo Charter, he was quartermaster general of the state. His acquaintance with leading personalities in the state government and his intimate knowledge of government procedures were vital in getting the charter passed.

Later events were to prove that the Prophet never quite trusted John C. Bennett, although he elevated him to positions of principal importance in the Church and supported him in his ambitious reach for power in the civil government. In Bennett, Joseph recognized a man of ability and influence who was in a position to advance the cause of the Church. This always seemed to be the criterion that the Prophet applied in extending or withholding calls to service. The age, the relationship, or the seniority in service of a person being considered for a position seemed to carry little weight with the Prophet if it was apparent that someone else could do a better job. The hard question he seemed always to put to himself as he juggled administrative assignments was: Can this person do the work more effectively than anyone else? If the answer to that inquiry was yes, the person ordinarily was selected, unless, through spiritual direction or Joseph's intuitive sense, some other candidate was indicated.

It was this sound principle of management, as much as almost anything else, that accounted for the unusually high degree of enthusiasm and initiative among Joseph's co-workers. They came to realize that recognition, in terms of appointment to office, was based largely upon the merit of their past work or upon special qualifications to perform a certain task. Yet underlying all this was a conviction that because of Joseph's unusual, prophetic role, the special qualities of an individual, as yet unrevealed by objective performance, would be taken into account.

There is little doubt that Joseph's tendency to ignore personal relationships and length of service in making administrative appointments alienated some of his followers. We have already seen how the Whitmers, Oliver Cowdery, Martin Harris, and others were alienated when the Prophet failed to accord them recognition to which they felt entitled by their years of service. However, the advantages that accrued from this wise policy far outweighed the disadvantages, particularly by avoiding the dulling effect of nepotism, by emphasizing performance over personal influence, and by fueling the energies of members who came to realize that superior performance would not go unrewarded or unrecognized. Furthermore, most of those who were alienated from the Prophet through false feelings of neglect or of having been passed over later became reconciled as they gained maturity and experience.

Special mention has been made of the emergence of John C. Bennett at this time because of the key role he played in obtaining the Nauvoo Charter. But he was only one of a number of comparative newcomers—including Wilson and William Law and Chauncey Higbee—to the inner circle of leadership who were to play important roles in the unfolding drama of Nauvoo, and especially in the final tragic act that was to see the brutal assassination of the Prophet and his loyal brother Hyrum. These men were to play key roles in the building up of Nauvoo; and although the Prophet had serious reservations about them from time to time, he continued to use them as long as their affirmative contributions continued to outweigh the negative.

Preeminent among the Prophet's followers was his father, who never wavered in supporting his famous and controversial son. Others might abandon or turn on the Prophet, but never his constant, dependable father. Thus, the unexpected death of Joseph Smith, Sr., on September 14, 1840, brought special sorrow to the Prophet. The short journal entry that appears under that date fails to convey the deep sense of loss Joseph felt at the time. It read: "My father, Joseph Smith, Sen., Patriarch of the whole Church of Jesus Christ of Latter-day Saints, died at Nauvoo." (HC 4:192.) His feelings can best be gauged by an excerpt from the funeral sermon Joseph included in his record and by an obituary he prepared himself. Of the deceased, the speaker, Robert B. Thompson, declared: "If ever there was a man who had claims on the affections of the community, it was our beloved but now deceased Patriarch. If ever there was an event calculated to raise the feelings of sorrow in the human breast, . . . it certainly is the present; for truly we can say with the king of Israel, 'A prince and a great man has fallen in Israel.' . . . A man faithful to his God and to the Church in every situation and under all circumstances through which he was called to pass." (HC 4:192.) Excerpts from the obituary provide a special insight into the character of this unusual man: "He was the first person who received my testimony after I had seen the angel," Joseph wrote, "and exhorted me to be faithful and diligent to the message I had received. . . . He was one of the most benevolent of men; opening his house to all who were destitute. While at Quincy, Illinois, he fed hundreds of the poor Saints who were flying from the Missouri persecutions, although he had arrived there penniless himself." (HC 4:190-91.)

During a funeral sermon he preached for Colonel Seymour Brunson just a few weeks before the death of his father, the Prophet laid before his followers a new and far-reaching doctrinal concept. Reading 1 Corinthians 15:29—"Else what shall they do which are baptized for the dead, if the dead rise not at all? why are they then baptized for the dead?"—Joseph declared that the Savior's disciples understood and practiced the ordinance of baptism for the dead, which had been lost through the apostasy. Since Joseph's followers understood that the spirit in man survives bodily death and has intelligence and reasoning powers, it was clear that a disembodied spirit could understand and assent to the principles of the gospel during the interval between death and resurrection. And since baptism, an earthly ordinance, requires bodily immersion in water, the doctrine of vicarious baptism provides the means whereby one acting as a proxy upon the earth can be baptized in behalf of another who is dead, thus complying with a requirement that is essential to salvation. Joseph emphasized that to be effective, a vicarious baptism would, of necessity, have to be accompanied by the exercise of faith in the Savior by the disembodied spirit for whom the vicarious baptism is performed.

It was not difficult for the members of the Church, and others of like mind, to accept this principle. The idea of vicarious work—doing for another something which he is incapable of doing himself—lies at the very root of Christian doctrine. Jesus, the central figure of Christianity, was the great exemplar of the principle of vicarious work, since he did something for all which they could not do for themselves by reconciling man to God through the atonement. The clear reference to vicarious baptism in 1 Corinthians had until now been a great source of speculation and puzzlement to the Saints. In elaborating upon the principle, the Prophet explained that in his first letter to the Corinthian Saints, the apostle Paul was making an argument for the universality of the resurrection, to convince those in Corinth who did not believe in a life after death. To support the argument, Paul alluded to the practice of baptism for the dead, which apparently was commonplace at the time, and asked why, if there were no resurrection, the people were performing the otherwise meaningless ordinance of baptism for the dead.

Joseph's introduction of this principle added a vital element of reasonableness to the doctrines of Christianity that before this had seemed to some to be unduly restrictive and narrow, limiting the blessings of salvation, or even the chance of salvation, to a favored and lucky few who, because of chance, happened to be in the right place at the right time. Furthermore, many were repulsed by the doctrine of infant baptism, which followed from the mistaken belief that all who are not baptized during earth life are damned eternally. In addition, the unreasonable doctrines of predestination and original sin have their roots sunk deep in the misconception that unless one is baptized during his mortal existence, all is lost.

This new doctrine of baptism for the dead touched off a wave of unbridled enthusiasm among Joseph's followers. It was as if the weight of the world had been lifted from the shoulders of some, who had become resigned to the belief that departed loved ones who had died without baptism were consigned either to oblivion or to eternal punishment. Elated by the prospect that they might be reunited with these loved ones, some members acted precipitously to perform proxy baptisms for them. There followed thousands of these baptisms, with little thought being given to preparing an accurate, official record. Nor were there precise rules to govern the conditions under which a proxy baptism could be performed, or any delineation about the identity and the qualifications of those standing as proxy, Thus, for a time men and women indiscriminately stood as proxy for deceased persons of the opposite sex.

This uncontrolled situation did not continue for long. On September 6, 1842, Joseph received a revelation which, among other things, required that a "book containing the records of our dead [be kept], which shall be worthy of all acceptation." (D&C 128:24.) Since that time, an elaborate, almost overwhelming, system of record gathering and record keeping has developed, entailing the microfilming and systematic storage of millions of genealogical records from around the world. From these voluminous records, avid researchers glean the data which, according to strict rules of procedure, will entitle a person to have a vicarious baptism performed in behalf of a departed ancestor.

Some detail about the origin and the development of the doctrine of vicarious baptism for the dead among the Latter-day Saints has been included in order to provide further insight into the methodology of Joseph Smith as an ecclesiastical leader. Of particular significance is the offhand, almost casual way in which the doctrine was first introduced to the Church. It was not ushered in with any special fanfare, nor was it based upon an exhaustive study and analysis of the subject, nor was the announcement of it accompanied by detailed instructions or explanations. One who was in attendance at that meeting reported that the Prophet singled out Jane Neyman in the course of his remarks, saying that he "saw a widow in that congregation that had a son who had died without being baptized." (Barrett, p. 489.) This was all it took for Jane Neyman to ask Harvey Olmstead to baptize her in behalf of her deceased son Cyrus. It was reported that the Prophet later inquired about the words Olmstead used in performing the ordinance and, upon hearing them, put his stamp of approval upon them. It was from this inauspicious beginning that the doctrine and practice of baptism for the dead grew in modern times. Today it includes among its parts vast genealogical libraries and research facilities, temples, and thousands of temple workers who labor diligently to perform this and other vicarious ordinances.

The Prophet made it clear to his followers that while they were in straitened circumstances, it was permissible to perform vicarious baptisms in the streams and lakes and in ordinary baptismal fonts; but the most acceptable place to perform them was in a holy, specially dedicated temple. This led to work on the Nauvoo Temple being pushed forward with all due haste. By April 1841, the work had progressed to the point that it was possible for the cornerstones of the temple to be laid. As a means of dramatizing this historic event and of demonstrating to the Church and to the outside world how the Saints had survived violence and persecution and had risen stronger than ever, an elaborate commemorative ceremony was prepared. "At an early hour," the Prophet recorded, "the several companies comprising the 'Nauvoo Legion,' with two volunteer companies from Iowa Territory, making sixteen companies in all, assembled at their several places of rendezvous, and were conducted in due order to the ground assigned for general review. The appearance, order and movements of the Legion, were chaste, grand and imposing. . . . At half-past seven o'clock a.m., the fire of artillery announced the arrival of Brigadier-Generals Law and Don Carlos Smith, . . . and at 8 o'clock Major-General Bennett was conducted to his post, under the discharge of cannon. . . . At half-past nine o'clock a.m., Lieutenant-General Smith, with his guard, staff and field officers arrived at the ground, and were presented with a beautiful silk national flag by the ladies of Nauvoo." (HC 4:326-27.)

Following this colorful pageantry, Sidney Rigdon delivered a major address in which he traced the trials and persecutions of the Saints, lauded them for their faithfulness, reaffirmed the role of the

Church as the earthly instrument by which the doctrines of the Savior would be taught and his goals achieved, and outlined the purpose and use of the temple. There then followed the laying of the four cornerstones, commencing with the southeast corner, where the stone was laid at the direction of the First Presidency. In doing so, the Prophet declared: "This principal corner stone in representation of the First Presidency, is now duly laid in honor of the Great God; and may it there remain until the whole fabric is completed; and may the same be accomplished speedily; that the Saints may have a place to worship God, and the Son of Man have where to lay His head." (HC 4:329.) The other cornerstones were then laid in turn by the stake presidency, the high council, and the bishops, with comments being made by William Marks, Elias Higbee, and Newell Whitney.

The obvious purpose Joseph had in organizing the Nauvoo Legion was to provide the protection the Saints had sorely lacked in Ohio and Missouri. And the apparent reason why he, as commander in chief of the legion, chose to demonstrate its strength and discipline on the occasion of the cornerstone laying was to serve notice on all that the legion was a fit instrument to protect his people in their worship. But, as usual, his enemies and detractors attributed an entirely different motive to his conduct. Instead of viewing the legion as a means of self-defense, they saw in it a bold design of conquest. They remembered well the vicious rumors that had circulated in Missouri after Thomas B. Marsh had published his insidious Mohammed affidavit. Did not Joseph have designs of empire? they asked. And was not a loyal, disciplined army the most essential tool of one bent on conquest?

The fact that Joseph had raised and trained such a formidable military force in two short years while burdened with the multiple tasks of relocating an entire people, building a new city from the foundation up, and directing a far-flung proselyting effort inspired feelings of awe and fear in his enemies. And the prospect that his power and influence would become even more formidable as the ranks of the Church were swelled by conversions caused them to renew their efforts to destroy him. Thus in June 1841, the Missouri enemies sought to extradite the Prophet under a requisition from Governor Boggs of Missouri that had been issued several months earlier. The requisition was based on the charge that Joseph was a fugitive from justice under the old indictments handed down in

Missouri. He was arrested on June 5 while staying at Heberlin's Hotel, Bear Creek, about twenty-eight miles south of Nauvoo. The arrest was unexpected because only a few hours before, Joseph had visited with Illinois' Governor Carlin at his home in Quincy, and he had said nothing about the requisition from Governor Boggs. Showing the legal acumen he had gained through long experience with various courts, Joseph obtained a writ of habeas corpus from a master of chancery in Quincy, which blocked his immediate removal to Missouri. Judge Stephen A. Douglas, who happened to be in Quincy that evening, set the hearing on the writ for the following Tuesday in Monmouth.

News of Joseph's arrest aroused great excitement and concern among his followers in Nauvoo. Upon learning of it, Hosea Stout, one of the Prophet's bodyguards, and several other brethren obtained a skiff and commenced rowing toward Quincy. Strong headwinds greatly impeded them, and by the time they arrived at their destination, Joseph and his party had left for Monmouth, traveling overland via Nauvoo. En route, the sheriff who had custody of the prisoner had a recurrence of a prior illness and Joseph nursed him as solicitously as if he were one of his own.

In Monmouth, Joseph found the feelings against him there ran very high. By this time the falsehoods and distortions about him and his people, which had been so assiduously broadcast by his enemies in Missouri and Ohio, had commenced to take root and to ferment in Illinois. Like a virulent disease, these false ideas infected many who were exposed to them and produced the customary symptoms of bigotry and irrationality. As the Prophet sought counsel to represent him at the hearing, he found that veiled or overt threats had been made to the legal fraternity that any lawyer who accepted employment as his attorney would be boycotted by the community. Fortunately for Joseph, the Monmouth bar included men of independence and courage to whom such threats were a spur instead of a rein. Goaded by them, O. H. Browning, one of the most eminent of the local lawyers, agreed to handle the case. As if to demonstrate they could not be intimidated, five other lawyers joined with Mr. Browning as defense counsel.

The basic issue Judge Douglas had to decide was whether the writ issued on the extradition order from Missouri should be honored and enforced. Joseph's lawyers attacked the writ on two grounds, one procedural and one on the merits. As to the latter, they argued that the Missouri indictments upon which the extradition order was based were fraudulent and therefore invalid. Judge Douglas rejected this argument but held for the Prophet on the procedural ground that the writ issued in Illinois on the Missouri extradition order was unenforceable since it had been served once before and returned and was, therefore, dead.

While he failed to convince the judge to decide the case on the merits, Mr. Browning succeeded in showing that the Prophet's conduct in Missouri had been a reasonable and necessary response to Governor Boggs' extermination order and to the lawless mobbings to which Joseph and the Saints had been subjected. So eloquent was the argument that "Judge Douglas . . . and most of the officers . . . wept." Mr. Browning's words carried conviction because he had witnessed the suffering and anguish produced by the brutal expulsion of the Saints from Missouri. He recited some of the tragic happenings he had seen at Quincy "where he tracked the persecuted women and children by their bloody footmarks in the snow." (HC 4:369.)

Although this highly emotional argument failed to dispose of the question whether the state of Missouri still had a legal hold on the embattled Mormon leader, it produced a helpful residual effect. It influenced the thinking of many important people in attendance at the trial; this in turn had a moderating effect upon the public and helped to postpone temporarily the avalanche of hatred and ill will that ultimately was to come crashing down on Joseph's head.

Chapter Twenty-eight

The Twelve Return: New Directions and Problems

The great drama of the Twelve in England, which the Prophet had watched with such avid interest, drew to a close in the late summer of 1841. By August all of them had returned to Nauvoo except Willard Richards and Wilford Woodruff. Anxious to learn the details of their ministry abroad that correspondence had failed to provide, Joseph spent long hours with the Twelve. Of particular interest to him were reports of the manifestations of God's power and of the spirit of enthusiasm and commitment these produced among the converts. Of interest also was the mechanism that had been set up to transport them to the new places of gathering in Illinois and across the river in Iowa.

As he listened, probed, and evaluated, Joseph was frankly amazed at the awesome results achieved by this small corps of dedicated men. Of their accomplishments he wrote with pride and appreciation: "Perhaps no men ever undertook such an important mission under such peculiarly distressing and unpropitious circumstances." After describing the adverse conditions under which they had departed for their mission and the travails through which they had passed in performing it, he offered his explanation for their phenomenal success: "But knowing that they had been called by the God of Heaven to preach the Gospel to other nations, they conferred not with flesh and blood, but obedient to the heavenly mandate, without purse or scrip, they commenced a journey of five thousand miles entirely dependent on the providence of that God who had called them to such a holy calling." In conclusion, the Prophet noted: "They, truly, 'went forth weeping, bearing precious seed,' but have 'returned with rejoicing, bearing their sheaves with them.' " (HC 4:390-91.)

These comments typified the special relationship between Joseph and his disciples. He gloried in their successes as if they were his own, never attempting to take credit for their accomplishments nor in any way to upstage them. As if to reciprocate for his selfless attitude toward them, his disciples ordinarily ascribed to the

Prophet much of the credit for any success they achieved.

Aside from his joy in hearing their reports and in again having the pleasure of their daily companionship, there was another special reason why Joseph was happy for the return of the Twelve. He had commenced to feel some uneasiness about the loyalty and designs of some of those in the top echelons of Church leadership. Especially was this true of John C. Bennett, whose egotistical and corrupt qualities had commenced to emerge. Some lingering doubts about the character and motivation of Sidney Rigdon had also begun to crystallize in the Prophet's mind. The conduct of the Law brothers, the Higbees, William Marks, and other influential leaders had given him the feeling of being hemmed in by false or unreliable brethren. Thus, to have about him a corps of men who had proved the depth of their convictions by going abroad to labor under the most stressful conditions inspired Joseph with new zeal and assurance. With men of this calibre at his side, he could carry forward his heavy duties confident that they would not betray or undercut him.

It was with these thoughts in mind that the Prophet scheduled a special conference to be held in Nauvoo on August 16, 1841. He was late in arriving at the conference because of the death on the day before of his infant son Don Carlos, and he sent word that Brigham Young was to conduct the meetings. Because until that time the Twelve had been restricted in their ministry to proselyting in the mission fields and had not been authorized to direct the affairs of the Church in the organized stakes, Elder Young approached this assignment with feelings of ambivalence. He was anxious, of course, to follow the instructions of his leader, but, at the same time, he did not wish to antagonize the local brethren who had not been accustomed to the Twelve intervening in local affairs. Some sense of the awkwardness he felt as he arose to conduct is found in this excerpt from the minutes of the meeting: "The speaker hoped that no one would view him and his brethren as aspiring, because they had come forward to take part in the proceedings before the conference; he could assure the brethren that nothing could be further from his wishes, and those of his quorum, than to interfere with Church affairs in Zion and her stakes. He had been in the vineyard so long, he had become attached to foreign missions, and nothing could induce him to retire therefrom and attend to the affairs of the Church at home but a sense of duty, the requirements of heaven, or the revelations of God; to which he would always submit, be the consequence what it might." Echoing the sentiments of their leader "the brethren of his (Brigham Young's) quorum responded, Amen."

The unusual procedure of having the Twelve take charge of a conference at the headquarters of the Church created no small stir among local members and leaders. There was busy speculation between the morning and afternoon sessions as to what this portended. All uncertainty was removed at the afternoon session when Joseph made an important announcement: "President Joseph Smith now arriving," the minutes of the meeting read, "proceeded to state to the conference at considerable length, the object of their present meeting, and, in addition to what President Young had stated in the morning, said that the time had come when the Twelve should be called upon to stand in their place next to the First Presidency, and attend to the settling of emigrants and the business of the Church at the stakes, and assist to bear off the kingdom victoriously to the nations. . . .' " (HC 4:402-3.)

It is doubtful that many in attendance at this meeting grasped the far-reaching significance of what took place. They could not foresee that within less than three years, Joseph would be dead and the Twelve, who until that time had hardly been visible on the local scene, would be in full control of the Church to the exclusion of other men whom they had come to regard as being higher than the Twelve in the scale of leadership. However, careful students of the revelations were not surprised by this change. They knew that in the formal hierarchy of the Church, the Twelve comprised a quorum equal in authority and responsibility to the First Presidency so that inherently this body had the power to act in any capacity to which it might be assigned by the Prophet, who held the ultimate authority or key. Now the key had been turned further to give the Twelve access to the broader powers of administration that until then they had possessed but had not been permitted to exercise.

Aside from the need for moral support and for assistance in handling the complex, fast-growing administrative affairs of the Church, there was another important reason why Joseph was anxious for the return of the Twelve. Only a few months before, after years of reluctance and trepidation, he had taken a step that he knew full well would further poison the public mind against him and the Church and would lead to scenes of violent persecution that would overshadow anything the Saints had previously endured. In April 1841 the Prophet had married his first plural wife! This step was not taken precipitously nor was it taken in ignorance of the consequences. He was intelligent enough and wise enough in the ways of the world to know that while a large segment of the public might tolerate adultery and fornication, which had been part of human conduct for so long, they would be incensed at the thought of a man having more than one wife, merely because the practice was novel and strange. He knew also that regardless of how pure and circumspect a man might be in entering into this relationship, he would be denounced by enemies who would ascribe to his actions the same base motives such a relationship might suggest to a carnal mind. It was for these reasons, and others equally compelling, that he had suppressed a revelation he received as early as 1831. (HC 5:xxix.) Like many other revelations he received, the one on the eternity of the marriage covenant and the plurality of wives came because of an earnest question he put to the Lord in prayer. While he and Sidney Rigdon were engaged in revising the Bible at Kirtland, Ohio, in the early 1830s, Joseph had begun to wonder about the propriety of the ancient patriarchs having more than one wife. Logic convinced him that if an unchangeable God justified Abraham, Isaac, and Jacob and other ancients in this practice, there would seem no apparent reason why the Lord would condemn modern prophets and Saints for adopting it. Never content with surface reasoning and explanations, however, Joseph sought an answer to this question by the only sure means he knew about.

The revelation he received was not reduced to writing until July 12, 1843, almost twelve years later. The circumstances under which it was recorded on that date are described by William Clayton, who took it in shorthand as the Prophet dictated: "On the morning of the 12th of July, 1843; Joseph and Hyrum Smith came into the office in the upper story of the brick store, on the bank of the Mississippi river. They were talking on the subject of plural marriage." In the discussion that followed, Hyrum persuaded Joseph to reduce the revelation to writing. Continuing with his narrative, William Clayton said: "He then requested me to get paper and prepare to write. Hyrum very urgently requested Joseph to write the revelation by means of the Urim and Thummim, but Joseph in reply, said he did not need to, for he knew the revelation perfectly from beginning to end. Joseph and Hyrum then sat down and Joseph commenced to dictate the revelation on celestial marriage, and I wrote it, sentence by sentence, as he dictated. After the whole was written, Joseph asked me to read it through, slowly and carefully, which I did, and he pronounced it correct. He then remarked that there was much more that he could write on the same subject, but what was written was sufficient for the present." (HC 4:xxxii-xxxiii.)

During the long years Joseph kept this revelation locked in his mind, he reflected upon it often. He shrank from publishing it or from putting it into practice because it ran against the grain of his own strict, Christian upbringing. It also threatened to load upon the new, struggling church an extra burden of criticism and abuse that might stunt, if not destroy, its growth and that, because of prejudice and misunderstanding, might permanently close the minds of many honest people who otherwise would be receptive to its message. So, with few exceptions, he kept this explosive revelation to himself through these many years. Occasionally he would divulge portions of it to some of his confidants, emphasizing that the time was not ripe, either to publish the revelation or to put into practice the principles it enjoined.

To his dismay, the Prophet found that either through laxity or through a desire to show the closer relationship they bore to the head of the Church, some of these confidants had leaked word about the revelation to persons outside Joseph's inner circle. Once this volatile information was loose, it spread rapidly by word of mouth. So widespread were the rumors by 1835 that at a special conference held in August, which Joseph did not attend, the following statement was presented by W. W. Phelps and accepted by the conference: "Inasmuch as this Church of Christ has been reproached with the crime of fornication and polygamy, we declare that we believe that one man should have one wife, and one woman but one husband, except in case of death, when either is at liberty to marry again." (HC 2:247.)

While this statement accurately reflected the official policy of the Church at the time, Joseph knew that it would have to be changed when the time was ripe. However, it placed him in a vulnerable position, requiring him to support a policy adopted by the conference that was at variance with revelation he had received .

It was this tangled condition that produced the apparent inconsistencies that developed when Joseph commenced to follow the mandate of the revelation. Since many in the Church, some in positions of high leadership, were ignorant of it, there were occasional, vehement, and wholly honest denials by influential members that the Church was involved in this doctrine in any way. Thus some members, when they first learned of Joseph's advocacy and practice of the doctrine, denounced him as a "fallen" prophet without knowing the source and background of it.

So it was that by 1841, after ten years of anguished reflection and delay, Joseph finally took the fateful step that he knew, deep within, would lead inevitably to his death. Having, in effect, opened the last fateful chapter of his life, he wanted around him the men whom he trusted most, both for moral support and administrative assistance, as well as to enable him to instruct them in the principles of the revelation.

The Prophet occasionally employed unusual means to test the faith and conviction of his followers. This was done deliberately to enable him to learn who had genuine faith in God and could be trusted implicitly. It is reported that he once directed a Nauvoo storekeeper, Edwin D. Woolley, to box up all the goods on his shelves prior to moving to an undisclosed location. The storekeeper obediently complied; and when he later asked what to do with some goods he had on consignment, Joseph surprised and thrilled him by saying, "Brother Woolley, you can return all these boxed goods to their shelves. You have demonstrated that, like Abraham of old, you are prepared to do all that is required of you without question."

Those whom Joseph tried in this way were said to have passed the "Abrahamic test." Little did the Twelve know, as they returned triumphantly from their mission to England, that soon they would be subjected to an Abrahamic test, which would make Bishop Woolley's experience look insignificant by comparison.

Heber C. Kimball was among the first of the Twelve whom Joseph taught the principles of the eternity of the marriage covenant and the plurality of wives. Preliminary to teaching the first of these principles, Joseph shocked Elder Kimball by directing him to give his wife Vilate to Joseph in marriage. Having been raised strictly in the Christian tradition of monogamy, Elder Kimball's first impression was that the Prophet was not serious. Seeing that he was, the apostle was thrown into a state of turmoil. Was he to reject what he had believed all his life, or was he to turn his back on the man whom he knew to be a prophet of God? He fasted and prayed for three days over this dilemma, following which he led his beloved Vilate to Joseph's home and presented her to the Prophet. "Joseph wept at this proof of devotion, and embracing Heber, told him that was all that the Lord required. He had proved him, as a child of Abraham, that he would 'do the works of Abraham,' holding back nothing, but laying all upon the altar for God's glory." (Whitney, p. 324.) The Prophet then sealed Elder Kimball to Vilate "for time and eternity" by the authority of the priesthood.

Later Elder Kimball and his wife were to undergo further, severe testing when the Prophet directed him to take another wife. Three times Elder Kimball declined to follow this direction, but finally he complied when Joseph commanded him to do so in the name of the Lord.

In turn, other members of the Twelve were taught this principle and with like results. They ultimately accepted it as a matter of faith, relying solely on their knowledge that the man who required it of them was a prophet.

Further insight into the traumatic effect the introduction of the principle of plural marriage had upon the Twelve is gained from this account left by Elder John Taylor: "I had always entertained strict ideas of virtue, and I felt as a married man that this was to me, outside of this principle, an appalling thing to do. The idea of going and asking a young lady to be married to me when I had already a wife! It was a thing calculated to stir up feelings from the innermost depths of the human soul. I had always entertained the strictest regard of chastity. . . . Hence, with the feelings I had entertained, nothing but a knowledge of God, and the revelations of God, and the truth of them, could have induced me to embrace such a principle as this." (Roberts, *The Life of John Taylor,* p. 100.)

It is apparent that the doctrine of plural marriage as practiced by the Latter-day Saints had its origin in their unquestioning faith in Joseph Smith as a prophet of God. It was not based upon any theory of social need or reform, nor upon any desire to satisfy a prurient interest. And, significantly, the discontinuance of the practice of the doctrine in 1890 was based upon the same ground that supported it at first.

Then, as now, those who deride Joseph Smith for teaching plural marriage do so at the level of their own moral elevation. It has been said that one cannot believe in honor until he achieves it. Similarly, one cannot believe in virtue unless he himself is virtuous. Consequently, those who revel in gossip, who are shallow in mind, who enjoy tales of lascivious conduct, and who belittle the idea that prophets of God exist, see Joseph Smith as an unprincipled man who invented the doctrine of plural marriage to mask his lust or to cloak his dissolute habits with some respectability. These critics savor any information that casts Joseph in a bad light. They delight in speculating about the number of plural wives he had, the conditions surrounding the marriages, and any nebulous circumstances that attended them.

In this, such critics have in part fallen prey to the distortions of the next to the last major apostate with whom the Prophet had to contend. This man, John C. Bennett, was the one who set in motion the chain of events that led ultimately to the martyrdom of Joseph and Hyrum Smith in the Carthage jail.

The secrecy Joseph used to institute plural marriage created the precise conditions in which John C. Bennett's immoral conduct flourished. When this glib man first became affiliated with the Church, little was known about him other than his involvement in Illinois politics and that he was adroit and knowledgeable in business and political matters. He soon gravitated to positions of honor and responsibility both in the Church, where he served as a counselor to the Prophet, and in civil government, where, among other things, he served as mayor of Nauvoo and as major general of the Nauvoo Legion. While from the beginning he was bombastic and arrogant, Joseph overlooked these defects in the hope that they and the harm they might produce would be more than counterbalanced by the good Bennett might render to the community.

However, not long after General Bennett cast his lot with the Saints, Joseph received a disquieting report that he was an adulterer and a married man with children, although he had presented himself as a bachelor. Joseph discounted these reports as representing the kind of unfounded criticism to which he himself had always been subjected. However, as similar reports continued to filter in and as the Prophet noted facets of Bennett's character that coincided with them, grave doubts arose about this new and as yet untried associate. At last, rumblings were heard about his seduction of several women in Nauvoo who, it was reported, had been enticed by false representations that the Church condoned promiscuous sex relations. It was also rumored that he had performed abortions, misusing the medical and surgical skills he had learned as a young man. While there was no hard evidence as yet to substantiate these rumors, they were so persistent, and the corroborating signs in Bennett's attitudes and conduct were so glaring, that Joseph became convinced he was an evil and dangerous man. Thereafter, he was highly suspicious and wary of anything his counselor said or did. This changed attitude was detected with alarm by Bennett, who ultimately concluded that the only way out of his difficulty was to do away with Joseph. It was then that he devised a scheme of having the Prophet killed during mock maneuvers of the Nauvoo Legion so that it would be made to appear as an accident or, this failing, so that detection of the murderer would be all but impossible.

This attempt at assassination failed because Joseph, who by then was alert to any false moves on the part of his counselor, refused to take the places in the sham battle that General Bennett assigned to him. In recording these events, the Prophet noted: "General Bennett next requested me to take my station in the rear of the cavalry, without my staff, during the engagement; but this was counteracted by Captain A. P. Rockwood, commander of my life guards, who kept close to my side, and I chose my own position. And if General Bennett's true feelings toward me are not made manifest to the world in a very short time, then it may be possible that the gentle breathings of that Spirit, which whispered me on parade, that there was mischief concealed in that sham battle, were false; a short time will determine the point. Let John C. Bennett answer at the day of judgment, 'Why did you request me to command one of the cohorts, and also to take my position without my staff, during the sham battle, on the 7th of May, 1842, where my life might have been the forfeit, and no man have known who did the deed?' " (HC 5:4.)

Within a week, General Bennett resigned as the mayor of Nauvoo at a tense meeting of the city council. The Prophet was elected to succeed him, and Hyrum Smith was elected vice-mayor. Because of the wild rumors flying about the city that he had condoned promiscuous sex relations, Joseph called upon the ex-mayor before the meeting ended to inquire "if he had aught against me." Responding, Bennett said in part: "I publicly avow that any one who has said that I have stated that General Joseph Smith has given me authority to hold illicit intercourse with women is a liar in the face of God. . . . I intend to continue with you, and hope the time may come when I may be restored to full confidence (and) fellowship . . . and should the time ever come that I may have the opportunity to test my faith, it will then be known whether I am a traitor or true man." (HC 5:13.)

A week after this confrontation, Bennett met with about a hundred of the leading brethren in Nauvoo, where he "acknowledged his wicked and licentious conduct toward certain females in Nauvoo" and admitted "that he was worthy of the severest chastisements." At the conclusion of this emotion-packed meeting he "cried like a child, and begged that he might be spared, in any possible way." Whether through a genuine show of contrition at the moment or through an artful deception, Joseph was moved to compassion and to "plead for mercy for him." (HC 5:18-19.)

Events that followed revealed that these expressions of the ex-mayor were merely a facade intended to mislead the Prophet until he was free to execute his plan of attack. Within weeks, he left Nauvoo and launched a blistering campaign whose object was to discredit the Church and to humiliate and to destroy its leader, the Prophet Joseph Smith.

Chapter Twenty-nine

Apostasy and Conspiracy

One of the unusual aspects of The Church of Jesus Christ of Latter-day Saints is the powerful, life-long effect it exerts upon both members and former members. To the member, it is a way of life that occupies the center stage of his thoughts and actions. Its doctrines provide the mainspring of his motivations and filter into every aspect of daily living. While to the former member, the apostate, or the excommunicant, the Church has a different focus, it ordinarily is no less influential in his life. In fact, if anything, most apostates are more obsessive in their attitudes toward the Church than are members. These have an impelling urge to demean and, if possible, to destroy that which once was the focal point of their lives.

John C. Bennett stands as one of the most notorious apostates from the Church. No sooner had he severed relations with his former associates in Nauvoo than he launched a furious campaign to smear and to destroy them, especially the Prophet.

At the threshhold of his apostate career, Dr. Bennett, as he liked to be called, was faced with two embarrassing questions. First, if the Mormons and their leaders were as depraved as he made them out to be, why did he join with them at all? And second, how did he explain the incriminating confession he made upon resigning as mayor of Nauvoo? To one so skilled in the arts of deception, these presented no real obstacle. In his usual self-confident way, he answered the first question by ascribing a patriotic motive to his joining the Church. It was common knowledge, he explained, that Joseph Smith aspired to conquer and to dominate the western United States. To prevent this, he had selflessly decided to join the Church in order to spy from within. He asserted that the answer to the second question was even more obvious: his confession had been obtained under duress, including threats upon his life, despite the lack of corroboration from any of the more than one hundred persons who heard his confession.

These questions having been disposed of to his satisfaction, Dr.

Bennett proceeded to execute the plan he had devised for Joseph's destruction. Using the important connections he had made while serving as quartermaster general in the Illinois capital, he arranged with the *Sangamo Journal* in Springfield to publish a series of scandalous letters in which he repeated most of the sensational stories that had been circulated about the Prophet and his followers.

The first letter in the series, on July 8, 1842, set the tone for what was to follow: "I write you now from the Mormon Zion, the city of the Saints," the letter began, "where I am threatened with death by the Holy Joe, and his Danite band of murderers." These scurrilous letters were printed intermittently over a period of about three months, following which they were revised and published in a book entitled *The History of the Saints: or, An Exposé of Joe Smith and Mormonism.* When completed, this volume took its place on the shelf alongside *Mormonism Unvailed,* issued under the editorship of Eber D. Howe; and over the years, these two books were quoted as authoritative by most anti-Mormon critics and biographers. Almost any evil one can conceive concerning Joseph Smith will be found in these two books. Even today, many uninformed readers will accept at face value the characterizations of the Prophet found in them.

To their credit, some of the contemporary newspapers, while willing to print Dr. Bennett's libelous letters as a means of increasing circulation, recognized the basic falsity of his writings. Shortly after their first appearance, the New York Herald characterized them as "obscene and licentious in the highest degree." About the same time, the Quincy *Whig,* which would have been inclined to excuse defects in the letters because of Dr. Bennett's affiliation with the Whig party, wrote accusingly: "We can hardly put reliance upon the statements of Bennett." And the *Illinois State Register,* a Democratic party newspaper, scored the Whig gubernatorial candidate for printing and distributing excerpts from the letters, characterizing him and those of like mind as "panderers of licentiousness and moral depravity." But these feeble voices of dissent hardly reached the public ear, which was being bombarded by Dr. Bennett's invective. And those who did not subscribe to the *Sangamo Journal* or who did not purchase his book heard the stories third or fourth hand, embellished with juicy details his own imagination had failed to provide.

To the Prophet it seemed for a while that he and the Saints

would be engulfed by the tide of public enmity Dr. Bennett's attack produced. Displaying his usual endurance and pugnacity, however, he refused to take this assault lying down. But in planning his counterattack, he felt much like the fighter who enters the ring with one arm strapped to his side. Though the practice of plural marriage was not yet known publicly, he could not, and did not, deny that he had taught and practiced the principle; and if he were to admit he had done so, it would have given some credence to the stories being circulated by Dr. Bennett. Furthermore, to disclose the principle at this time would have created grave misunderstandings among the Saints and opened the door to possible excesses and misapplications. For these and other reasons, Joseph decided to attack the ex-mayor at his most vulnerable point, his sordid past. Adopting the approach that had been used so effectively in countering the lies and misrepresentations leveled against the Saints in Missouri, the Prophet obtained and had published numerous affidavits about Dr. Bennett's spotted past and about the voluntary confessions he had made of his adulteries and other misconduct. Joseph also denied categorically that he or the Church had ever condoned or sanctioned promiscuous sexual conduct. While this was effective to a large degree within the limited circulation area of the Nauvoo newspapers, it did little good elsewhere. The poison had been so widely disseminated and the Prophet's enemies and detractors were so anxious to believe any falsehoods about him that it was almost useless to try to change their views.

During May 1842, while the Bennett affair was moving to a conclusion, a sensational occurrence took place in Missouri that was to bring a new and unforeseen burden to the already harassed Prophet. On the sixth of that month, former governor Lilburn W. Boggs was shot in the head by an unknown assailant as he sat in his Independence home. Since Governor Boggs was the chief instrument in the expulsion of the Saints from Missouri and the attendant persecution to which they were subjected, suspicion was instantly fixed upon them and their leader. This was heightened by idle rumors that Joseph had prophesied Governor Boggs would suffer a violent death. To most of the Prophet's enemies, the mere suspicion of his guilt was sufficient to convict him in their minds, and so, following the attempted assassination, the rumor mills commenced to grind out incriminating statements connecting him with the crime. These were fueled by false and provocative news articles. One such article in the May 21 issue of the Quincy *Whig* was especially offensive to the Prophet and evoked a prompt response from him the following day: "Boggs was a candidate for the state senate," he wrote, "and, I presume, fell by the hand of a political opponent, with 'his hands and face yet dripping with the blood of murder;' but he died not through my instrumentality." In conclusion, the Prophet expressed understandable annoyance with these unfounded charges: "I am tired of the misrepresentations, calumny and detraction, heaped upon me by wicked men," he wrote, "and desire and claim, only those principles guaranteed to all men by the Constitution and laws of the United States and of Illinois." (HC 5:15.)

John C. Bennett seized upon the Boggs incident as a means of retaliating against the Prophet. He industriously fed misinformation to the ex-governor to the effect that the assailant who had gunned him down was Orrin Porter Rockwell, who, he said, had acted under orders from the Prophet. In a false affidavit, Mr. Boggs was able to persuade Governor Reynolds of Missouri to seek to extradite the Mormon leader on the ground that he was "an accessory to an assault with intent to kill." (HC 5:87.) Governor Carlin of Illinois, who by this time was an avowed enemy of the Saints, honored this requisition and issued a warrant for the Prophet's arrest, despite the fact that any alleged misconduct on his part would have occurred in Illinois, not Missouri.

Joseph was arrested on August 8 and promptly obtained his release on a writ of habeas corpus. Looking forward to a hearing on the writ, and remembering how in past similar legal skirmishes the Prophet had been unable to obtain a judgment on the merits, those responsible for his defense induced the Nauvoo city council to adopt a special ordinance that contained these key provisions: ". . . the court shall in every such case have power and authority, and [is] hereby required to examine into the origin, validity and legality of the writ of process, under which such arrest was made, and . . . shall then proceed and fully hear the merits of the case, . . . and . . . if upon investigation it shall be proven . . . that the writ or process has been issued, either through private pique, malicious intent, or religious or other persecution, falsehood or misrepresentation, . . . the said writ or process shall be quashed." (HC 5:88.)

This legal maneuver, while it effectively prevented Joseph from being taken into custody at this time, aroused bitter criticism among Illinois officials, who saw in it a bold attempt to thwart the normal legal processes of the state courts and to set the Nauvoo city court above them. Thus, explosive fuel was added to the ever-mounting demands that the Nauvoo Charter be revoked, thereby stripping Joseph of the legal safeguards he had so carefully devised.

So it was that the Prophet went into retirement for four long, difficult months. For one as gregarious and active as he, this period of enforced seclusion was difficult to bear; in some ways, it was even more onerous than imprisonment. In order to avoid detection, he moved frequently from one place to another, either on the outskirts of Nauvoo or across the river near Montrose, Iowa. Periodically members of his family or associates in the ministry would rendezvous with him at prearranged points to give him reports and impart necessary instructions. On one occasion, such a rendezvous was held on skiffs in the Mississippi River.

Although he was frequently on the move and under great pressure during this period, there was no significant change in his work habits. He dictated endlessly whenever he could find a scribe, and the range of the subjects he covered was as broad as his multifarious interests and responsibilities. One letter might contain detailed instructions about the conduct of the Nauvoo Legion, while the next might be a letter to Emma, informing her of his planned movements and giving her instructions and advice about family matters.

More significant, however, were letters addressed to the Saints in general. One of these elaborated in great detail the doctrine of vicarious work for the dead and was considered to be of such importance that it was later included as section 128 of the Doctrine and Covenants. In it, the Prophet surveyed the whole scope of the work that had been established through his instrumentality. Alluding to the appearances of Moroni, Peter, James, and John and other "divers angels, from Michael or Adam down to the present time," he exulted in the fact that these personages had given "line upon line, precept upon precept; here a little, and there a little; giving us consolation by holding forth that which is to come." (D&C 128:21.) Reaching deep into his seemingly inexhaustible store of optimism, he uttered words that were calculated to focus the minds of his followers on what lay ahead, rather than on their present difficulties. Wrote he: "Brethren, shall we not go on in so great a cause? Go forward and not backward. Courage, brethren; and on, on to the victory." Toward the end of this remarkable letter, he revealed again the poetic quality in his character that gave a special illumination to his work: "Let your hearts rejoice, and be exceedingly glad. Let the earth break forth into singing. Let the dead speak forth anthems of eternal praise to the King Immanuel, who hath ordained, before the world was, that which would enable us to redeem them out of their prison; for the prisoners shall go free. Let the mountains shout for joy, and all ye valleys cry aloud; and all ye seas and dry lands tell the wonders of your Eternal King! And ye rivers, and brooks, and rills, flow down with gladness. . . . And again I say, how glorious is the voice we hear from heaven, proclaiming in our ears, glory, and salvation, and honor, and immortality, and eternal life; kingdoms, principalities, and powers!" (D&C 128:22-23.)

If this letter was calculated to elevate the minds and the spirits of the Prophet's followers, as it surely did, one written a few days before was designed to stiffen their backbone and resolve in anticipation of the more difficult and tragic events that were to follow. In it is mirrored the implacable quality of his will and determination: "And as for the perils which I am called to pass through," he wrote, "they seem but a small thing to me, as the envy and wrath of man have been my common lot all the days of my life; and for what cause it seems mysterious, unless I was ordained from before the foundation of the world for some good end, or bad, as you may choose to call it. Judge ye for yourselves. God knoweth all these things, whether it be good or bad. But nevertheless, deep water is what I am wont to swim in. It all has become a second nature to me; and I feel, like Paul, to glory in tribulation; for to this day has the God of my fathers delivered me out of them all, and will deliver me from henceforth; for behold, and lo, I shall triumph over all my enemies, for the Lord God hath spoken it." (D&C 127:2.)

It was also during this period of enforced seclusion that Joseph seemed to reach the zenith of his sense of love and appreciation for his family and associates. Every act of kindness toward him was duly noted and appreciated. Of those who had given him special succor he wrote: "How good and glorious it has seemed unto me, to find pure and holy friends, who are faithful, just, and true, and whose hearts fail not; and whose knees are confirmed and do not falter, while they wait upon the Lord, in administering to my necessities, in the day when the wrath of mine enemies was poured out upon me." Reflecting upon the love and faithfulness of his beloved wife Emma, he wrote: "Oh what a commingling of thought filled my mind for the moment, again she is here, even in the seventh trouble—undaunted, firm, and unwavering—unchangeable, affectionate Emma!" Of his loyal brother Hyrum he noted: "What a faithful heart you have got! Oh may the Eternal Jehovah crown eternal blessings upon your head, as a reward for the care you have had for my soul." He commented specially about his long-time friend, Newel K. Whitney: "Thou art a faithful friend in whom the afflicted sons of men can confide, with the most perfect safety." Then listing a number of other men who had cared for him in time of need, he recorded: "My heart feels to reciprocate the unwearied kindnesses that have been bestowed upon me by these men. They are men of noble stature, of noble hands, and of noble deeds; possessing noble, and daring, and giant hearts and souls." (HC 5:107-9.)

In retrospect, one cannot but wonder whether this unusual outpouring was inspired by vague feelings stirring within the Prophet that his time had about come and that the dramatic winding-up scenes were near at hand.

Everyone who objectively studied the facts and the law behind ex-governor Boggs' effort to return Joseph to Missouri to stand trial as an accessory in the attempted assassination agreed there was no valid basis for extradition. But the Prophet was uncertain whether the Illinois officials would decide the matter on the basis of law and fact or on the basis of personal prejudice.

As if by providential intervention, Governor Carlin was replaced by Governor Thomas Ford in December 1842. Despite the fact that Governor Ford had called for the revocation of the Nauvoo Charter in his inaugural address, enough confidence was felt in his basic fairness that a few days later, Joseph asked him to rescind the warrant of arrest. The governor responded that he had consulted the supreme court judges, and they were of the unanimous opinion that there was no valid basis for extradition, but that it would be improper for him to rescind Governor Carlin's warrant. Having received a similar opinion from reputable legal counsel, and feeling that the climate toward him and the Church in Springfield had improved with the departure of Governor

Carlin, Joseph decided that the time was ripe to test the attempted extradition in the courts. So he came out of retirement and, the day after Christmas, with a large entourage to accompany him, started for Springfield, where his trial was to take place.

Because of the extent to which the news media had been saturated with reports about him and the Saints, Joseph was by now a genuine celebrity. Wherever he went, people looked at him with interest and curiosity. Both the believer and the scoffer attempted to engage him in conversation. And because of his fine appearance, his knowledge of men and affairs, and his highly developed ability to express his thoughts, he was a welcome guest among the most cultured and educated society of the day. In Springfield, the governor and other high officials received him or waited on him. Arrangements were made for Mormon services to be held, and large, interested crowds came to see this unusual man.

The recent charges of John C. Bennett about the so-called spiritual-wife doctrine had titillated the interest of many curiosity seekers. At one of the court hearings, an unheard-of precedent was set in the court of Judge Pope when a section was reserved for some women, mostly the wives and friends of court officials and prominent local leaders, who wanted to enjoy the spectacle. Invariably during recesses of the court or at other times when he was in public, the Prophet would be surrounded by groups of spectators who plied him with questions, some of which were insolent and annoying, but most of which were sincere questions posed by persons who were genuinely interested in hearing his views.

Many legal maneuverings were necessary in order to bring the matter to the point of final decision. When these were cleared away, the court was left with the basic issue of whether Missouri could extradite the Prophet on a writ based upon alleged misconduct in Illinois. As expected, the court answered this question in the negative.

The fact that a favorable decision had been issued lifted a load of care from the shoulders of the Prophet and his followers and reinforced their confidence, which admittedly had wavered at times, in the judicial system. Evidence of the lighthearted feeling the decision produced is found in the fact that on the return trip to Nauvoo, two of the brethren composed a "Jubilee Song," which was dedicated "to all lovers of Illinois' liberties." (HC 5:246.) Later, when an axletree of one of their carriages was broken in an accident, the company jokingly agreed that "Lilburn W. Boggs should pay the damage."

At Nauvoo the Prophet and his party were met by a large assembly of Saints who, alternately laughing and crying, demonstrated in a touching way the love and affection they had for him. The carefree spirit ended with a special dinner hosted by the Prophet and Emma to which were invited most of the principal leaders of Nauvoo and their wives. And after the celebrating and jubilation had subsided, a sense of gratitude and thanksgiving settled upon the members of the Church, heightened by a proclamation issued by the Twelve and signed by Brigham Young. In it, President Young invited the Saints to dedicate the 17th of January "as a day of humiliation, fasting, praise, prayer, and thanksgiving before the great Eloheim" as a means of expressing gratitude for "the deliverance of our beloved President, Joseph Smith." (HC 5:248.)

Chapter Thirty

An Interval of Peace

With the voices of his enemies stilled for the moment, and surrounded by a few trustworthy associates, the Prophet enjoyed a brief interval of peace during the first part of 1843. But it was not a period of idleness. There was much in bustling Nauvoo to claim his attention. Everywhere the sound of the saw and hammer and the brick mason's trowel could be heard, as homes and other buildings sprang up all over the city.

Work on the temple was being pushed forward aggressively, and Joseph spent many hours at the site, making certain that the feisty non-Mormon architect faithfully executed the design of the building the Prophet had envisioned. The architect had tried to dissuade him from including a series of circular windows, but all arguments advanced were rejected—not for an aesthetic reason, but merely because Joseph had seen the temple in vision long before work on it was commenced, and he was adamant that the form he had seen be faithfully reproduced. The architect was annoyed at being overruled by a layman in a matter he felt lay exlusively within his professional competence, but it soon became evident that the issue of the temple's design was one upon which his continued employment might hinge. And seeing that Joseph was immoveable, he drew the plans as directed, although he did it grudgingly and remained convinced that he was right and Joseph wrong.

Joseph never stepped out of his role of leadership. Whether speaking in public meetings or engaged in private conversation, he constantly instructed his people as the exigencies of the moment required. His views covered the whole gamut of human experience. No period of his life better illustrates this facet of his character than during this interval of peace. In a series of discourses delivered between January and May, he added a rich store to the doctrines of the Church. He elaborated upon the kingdom of God, asserting that where an authorized minister of God can be found, there is His kingdom. He provided a key to the interpretation of the scriptures, emphasizing the need to understand the background against which they were given. He also gave instructions for distinguishing between good and bad spirits or angels. He expounded on the resurrection, the characteristics of God, the eternal nature of human intelligence, salvation through knowledge, and the indestructability of matter. Sandwiched in between, he found time to offer his views on the powers of constitutional government and the vagaries of the currency system. Indeed, over the years there seem to be few subjects, whether pertaining to ecclesiastical or secular matters, that did not claim his attention.

In the meantime, he was laying plans for a revamped newspaper, to be called the *Nauvoo Neighbor,* which he hoped would help counteract the false rumors that were circulating.

In the midst of these activities, the Prophet did not neglect his administrative duties as the head of the Church. He inaugurated a program for the youth that was the forerunner of the elaborate activity programs that were to emerge in the years ahead. He also launched a new and aggressive proselyting campaign.

To one unacquainted with the undercurrents buffeting him, Joseph would have appeared at this juncture to be merely a vigorous and highly successful, albeit controversial, man, intent only on fulfilling his duties as leader of a thriving new church. The evidence of his talent and industry was to be seen on every hand. Nauvoo itself was an impressive monument to his genius. He exuded an air of confidence, which inspired his followers in the belief that the present difficulties would vanish as had others in the past and that he would emerge from them stronger than ever. But deep within, nagging concerns were troubling Joseph as summer approached. Foremost among these was Emma's refusal to accept the principle of the plurality of wives. It was not that she really doubted her husband's prophetic calling. She, above all others, had been in a position to observe his emergence as a man of God whose spiritual qualities had opened the heavens to him. She had been a witness of his strugglings as he had translated the Book of Mormon. She had been present on many occasions when the influence of God had rested upon him as he had uttered prophecies, rebuked evil, or healed the sick. Often she had seen his handsome face pale and his eyes partially close as, through powerful exertion, he served as a conduit through whom God's power was manifested. The cumulative effect of these experiences as well as her knowledge of Joseph's forthright character convinced her that the mandate was true. Nevertheless, she rejected it and fought bitterly against it. In her moments of anguish, she was greatly influenced by prominent but weak men who had rejected the doctrine. Torn between her knowledge and better instincts and the basic jealousy of her nature, Emma oscillated between joy and despair, outgoing love and suspicion, depending on whose company she was in. Thus was manifested in her character a gross inconstancy that was both reminiscent of her agnostic father and prophetic of the wavering course she would follow once the steadying influence of her husband was gone.

In addition to his concerns over Emma's conduct, Joseph was troubled by the mounting demands of his enemies that the Nauvoo Charter be revoked. The legal safeguards this document provided were both a practical and a psychological shelter for him. Time and again he had relied upon it as a shield from unwarranted legal attacks. The Nauvoo period was really the first time the scales of justice had been tipped in favor of the Saints, and Joseph was anxious to retain this advantage. But the chances of doing so were waning. Enemies and apostates outside the Church and traitors within it sought to crush Joseph by removing this protection. Some neutrals favored its abolition on legal grounds, arguing that the anomalous powers of the charter created a dangerous precedent for the future. Only the faithful favored its retention, and their limited political influence rendered them impotent for the task. Seeing his support dissolve, Joseph knew this legal umbrella could be preserved only by divine intervention or by adroit maneuvers on his part. He sought to avail himself of both remedies, but he was to discover it was not in God's economy to preserve the charter. His rear-guard efforts to do so, while heroic in their proportions, fell short.

The third leg on his tripod of woe was the impression that death was near. It was not that he feared the end. On the contrary, he looked forward to it. His understanding of eternity led him to expect both a continuation and a burgeoning of life beyond the grave. The anxiety he felt proceeded from an uncertainty whether the Church was fit enough to withstand the storms he foresaw, and whether his disciples had been sufficiently taught to steer a true course. It was this concern that would take the center stage of his thoughts during his remaining year of life. Of course, polygamy and politics were to play major roles too, but these were side issues. Joseph's chief focus was on perpetuating the system of religion created through his agency. He was not unmindful of the lesson history taught: that the growth of a religion or a philosophy is due as much to the fervor of its disciples as to the work of its founder. He had discerned this principle at work in the lives of Jesus and Socrates. He also knew, despite the reality of his own experience, that the work established through him would falter unless energetic disciples succeeded him, unless men imbued with the dedication of a Paul or a Plato were to pick up the torch he had lighted. So, during the last year of his life, he never missed an opportunity to train his disciples in the operation of the Church. Like a master mechanic, he took pains and delight in explaining the intricacies of church government.

The Twelve were the chief recipients of the Prophet's frequent briefings. He saw in them the qualities necessary to propagate the faith and build securely on the foundation he had laid. The revelations clearly stated that the Twelve stood next to the President in authority and responsibility. These, then, were the heirs apparent, the men upon whom the burden of leadership would fall once Joseph was gone, and he spared no effort in making certain that they learned their lessons well.

Chapter Thirty-one

A Family Vacation Interrupted

The early June sun flooded Main Street in Nauvoo as Joseph carefully fitted the last valise into the new carriage, heavily loaded now with clothing and foodstuffs and his four lively children. As he turned to go back for Emma, he paused momentarily, attracted by the beauty of his new home with its green trim framed sharply against the pure white walls glistening in the morning sun. Across Water Street looking toward the river, Joseph could see the uncompleted Nauvoo House, which faced his original Nauvoo residence, the Homestead. Only recently Joseph and his family had moved into the spacious luxury of their new two-story federal-style home. The name selected for it, the Mansion House, eloquently expressed the pride they felt toward it.

Compared with the Homestead, which was a jumbled melange of additions and renovations to what was once a rough-hewn log cabin, the new residence was a mansion indeed. With more and larger bedrooms, the Smith children were less likely to be relegated to sleeping on the floor, or outside in the summer, because of crowding created by the constant stream of visitors that flowed in and out of the Smith household. On almost any Sunday during the year when the Prophet was in town and the weather was good, his yard and the adjacent streets would be crowded with the wagons and buggies of visitors who had come to dine or to visit. This state of affairs, which had begun early in Joseph and Emma's married life and had grown steadily worse as his fame spread, had, in effect, converted the Smith household from a private residence into a public hostelry, with Emma shouldering the chief burden of caring for the hordes of visitors. Realizing the need to give her some relief and, at the same time, to provide a source of personal income, Joseph had begun construction of the Nauvoo House. However, public apathy toward the project and Joseph's own financial condition, which had thrown him into bankruptcy, caused a suspension of work on the building.

Faced with uncertain delays in completion of the Nauvoo

House, the Prophet had begun to rent spare rooms in the Mansion House to out-of-town visitors. As the number of guests increased, the facilities had to be enlarged. Thus, almost before the family could get settled into their new home, workmen were busily adding a wing to the rear of the structure. This inconvenience, added to worries about her husband's safety, pressures from the new doctrine of polygamy, the constant demands of a growing family, and the steady stream of visitors, had made Emma irritable and languid. After months of pressure from administering the affairs of the Church and the city and defending against attacks from within and outside the Church, Joseph also felt the need for a change of scene. Thus he and Emma carefully planned the only family vacation they were ever to take together with their children.

They decided to visit Emma's sister, Elizabeth Wassen, and her family near Dixon, Lee County, Illinois, about two hundred miles northeast of Nauvoo. In the vicinity of Dixon were another sister, Tryal, the wife of Michael Morse; and two brothers, Alva and David Hale, who had recently moved to Illinois from Pennsylvania. Years had passed since Emma had seen her family, and the prospect of seeing four of them and their growing families filled her with joy.

For several days before the departure Emma had been busily packing and putting everything at home in order. Julia, the adopted Murdock twin, now twelve years old, was a great help. She took her big sister role seriously, assisting Emma with the household chores and with her three energetic brothers, Joseph, eighteen months her junior; Frederick, who was to celebrate his seventh birthday during the trip; and Alexander, five.

Parting instructions having been given to the construction workers and the domestic help who would remain at the Mansion House in their absence, Joseph and Emma joined the children, who were noisily discussing seating arrangements in the carriage. They were accompanied by Loren Walker, a long-time handyman in the Smith household. Hitched to the carriage were two of the Prophet's favorite horses, Black Charlie and a big sorrel whimsically named Tom Carlin after the former governor of Illinois. Once Joseph and Emma had taken their places in the front seat, Brother Walker clucked at the horses and the Smiths were off for their holiday.

Reining the horses right on to Water Street off Main, the

driver angled northeasterly, following the contours of the river road, toward the main highway leading to Galesburg. To the right could be seen the silhouette of the half-finished temple. At intervals along the route, the vacationers were greeted by friendly neighbors whose attention usually focused upon the affable, handsome man in the front seat who was fondly addressed as "Brother Joseph" by young and old alike.

As the carriage rumbled past the last of the homes on Water Street, Brother Walker lightly flapped the reins against the backs of the team, which responded by accelerating into the comfortable pace it was to maintain most of the day. Even as the last of the farms on the outskirts of Nauvoo was left in the dust of the carriage, the ever-hungry children were anticipating the delicious picnic lunch their mother had prepared.

This was a close-knit family. The parents had bestowed the ultimate security upon their children through the deep love they had always had for each other. This emotion had ripened with the years into a constant feeling of mutual admiration and affection.

Emma was the Prophet's strongest supporter, save only on the sensitive issue of the plurality of wives. Warmly affectionate, she was a woman of intelligence and spirit. When Joseph was in trouble, she defended him tenaciously. When he was ill, she nursed and comforted him. When he did something worthy of note, she was in the front rank of his admirers. When he was disheartened, she was the first to give him encouragement.

These qualities were not lost on Joseph. He loved Emma as no one else. To him, she was the "elect lady." She had endured every privation with stoic calm. She had shown a remarkable resiliency in the face of misfortune. Their marital trail was marked by the graves of four infants. She had experienced the terror of seeing her husband beaten, tarred and feathered, and threatened with death. She had endured the trauma of seeing him jailed in filthy prisons, surrounded by vicious men. These and other difficulties she faced without complaint as being the common lot of the wife of an uncommon man.

But the thought of sharing her husband with another woman was an extremity Emma was not prepared to face. After her first violent reaction to the idea, she moderated even to the extent of participating in the selection of other mates for her husband, but her basic insecurity then dominated, and she returned to her original stance of unyielding opposition. It was in this rigid mold that her attitudes were finally cast, and so inflexible did they become that after the Prophet's death, she refused even to admit that he had ever taken another wife. So industriously did she inculcate this false idea in the minds of her children that young Joseph, in writing his memoirs as an old man, prefaced them by declaring that his mother, Emma, was the only wife the Prophet Joseph Smith ever had.

All this, however, was shrouded in the cloak of an uncertain future as the Smith children gloried in the luxury of having their parents all to themselves. They regarded their father with mixed feelings of awe and affection. At this time, all of them were old enough to take note of the deferential respect most people paid to their famous parent. And while they were shielded, to a large extent, from the ugly hatred of their father's enemies, they were aware of the controversy that surrounded him. This aspect of their father, however, was of relatively minor importance to the Smith children. What counted most with them was the unfailing kindness and love he showed toward them, as well as his exuberance, his athletic interests, and his friendly nature. Most important, however, they were touched by his profoundly spiritual nature. They had heard him pray in their family circle with a fervor and humility that thrilled them. They had been blessed under his hands and had felt the spiritual power which emanated from him as he had rebuked disease or had given comfort or made promises. Young Joseph was never to forget a special blessing conferred upon him while the Prophet was imprisoned in the Liberty jail. In later years, he could not recall the specifics of it, but he was never to forget the incident itself nor the solemn, majestic manner in which his father had spoken.

As for the Prophet, his world was centered in his family. All he had done or was to do, as an ecclesiastic, was aimed toward establishing the patriarchal order, under which every worthy man would stand at the head of his family, inseparably linked by heavenly authority to them as well as to his lineal ancestors and descendants. Like Abraham of old, he confidently expected that he would eventually stand at the head of a progeny as numerous as the sands on the seashore. And, looking beyond the veil of time, he envisioned that, conditioned upon his worthiness and obedience, he ultimately would acquire the capacity to procreate spiritual offspring, thus being elevated to the status of godhood, where he would experience a continuation of the seeds forever. This was Joseph's lofty goal and the one toward which all his teaching had pointed. And while to many it would have been difficult to envision, Joseph could see in the little family then gathered about him the genesis of a vast progeny who in the centuries and the eternity ahead would emulate his example, would call him prophet and patriarch.

Joseph's sense of well-being heightened as the distance from Nauvoo increased. After a day on the road, away from the pressing cares of his offices and surrounded by those who loved him most, he settled into the pleasurable holiday routine he was to enjoy for over a week. The long distances between villages afforded a rare opportunity for uninterrupted conversation. Ever the teacher, he instructed the children about the new things they saw and heard and shared intimate experiences of the past and plans for the future.

So intent was Joseph on enjoying Emma and the children that he did not allow his mind to dwell on the difficulties at home. Had he done so, his highly developed prophetic sense, which had illuminated his path through many dark days, would have revealed that serious trouble lay ahead. While he basked in the companionship of his family, the wheels of a giant conspiracy, set in motion by John C. Bennett, ground toward him. The peripatetic doctor had succeeded in reviving the stale charge of treason in Missouri, had obtained a new indictment there against the Prophet, had persuaded Missouri Governor Thomas Reynolds to seek extradition, and, through adroit maneuvers, had induced Illinois Governor Thomas Ford to honor the writ and issue a warrant of arrest. This was placed in the hands of a Carthage, Illinois, lawman, Harmon T. Wilson, who, accompanied by a special agent from Missouri, Joseph H. Reynolds, went immediately to Nauvoo to serve the warrant, only to find his quarry had gone north to Dixon. Armed with guns and the warrant, they drove confidently out of Nauvoo along the Galesburg highway in search of the Mormon prophet.

Ahead of this pair on the road by several hours were two horsemen, William Clayton and Stephen Markham, who had been sent to Dixon by Hyrum Smith to warn his brother of the conspiracy that was afoot. Word of it had been leaked to Nauvoo by Judge Adams, a solid friend of the Mormons, who had been given advance notice by Governor Ford of his intention to issue the warrant of arrest.

In the meantime, the Smith family arrived at its destination. The Wassens, converts to the Church, received the visitors warmly. Arrangements had been made for the Morses and the two Hale families to join in a family gathering; and in order for those outside the family circle to meet the man who was the talk of Illinois, Benjamin Wassen had arranged for him to speak at a meeting.

Joseph felt no rancor toward Emma's family because of the ill treatment he had received at the hands of their father, Isaac Hale. Having been separated for so long, the Hales and the Smiths could scarcely find enough hours in the day for visiting and reminiscing. Joseph and Emma were plied with endless questions about their harrowing experiences in Missouri and about the exciting growth of Nauvoo. Only one subject was taboo, and that was the one uppermost in the minds of Emma's brothers and sisters—polygamy. The Prophet was unwilling to broach it because as yet he had divulged the principle to only a few of his most trusted associates. And Emma had already settled into that obstinate delusion that was to obsess her throughout life and that barred her from facing the reality of what had happened.

The favorite topic of conversation among the adults, however, was their children who, after overcoming the awkward shyness that always marks the first contact between children who are strangers, had become fast friends. Young Joseph was to recall the gathering with nostalgic pleasure in the reminiscences he wrote in the sunset of a long life: ". . . the visiting there with my hitherto unknown cousins—and there was quite a number of them—the fishing in the brook which ran through the farm, the freedom of the whole place, and the hilarity natural to such a jolly mingling of healthy youngsters made quite an impression upon me." (Mary Audentia Smith Anderson, ed., *Joseph Smith III and the Restoration* [Independence, Mo.: Herald Publishing House, 1952], p. 73.)

The first pair of horsemen to arrive at the Wassen farm scarcely drew the attention of the children, who were too preoccupied with their play. Young Joseph recognized them as Elders Clayton and Markham, close associates of his father, and merely assumed they were there to transact Church business. The horsemen immediately sought out the Prophet and informed him of Judge Adams's warning. After questioning the messengers carefully, Joseph responded with his accustomed self-assurance and deliberateness: "I have no fear," he said. "I shall find friends, and Missourians cannot hurt me, I tell you in the name of the Lord." (Joseph Fielding Smith, *Essentials in Church History* [Deseret Book, 1950], p. 284.)

Joseph sent William Clayton back along the road to watch for the intruders, who had already arrived in Dixon and had introduced themselves as Mormon elders who were looking for the head of the Church. Directed to the Wassen farm by accommodating neighbors, the two lawmen passed Elder Clayton, who failed to recognize them behind their disguises. At the farm, they were led to the honored guest by a well-intentioned relative.

Once in the presence of their victim, Wilson and Reynolds acted with speed. They quickly drew concealed weapons and threatened to kill him instantly if he resisted, punctuating their threats by coarse profanities and repeated jabbings with their weapons. (This physical abuse was so violent that the prisoner's whole rib cage later turned black and blue.) Anxious to be on the road, away from potential hindrance by Joseph's family and friends, the lawmen insisted that he go with them immediately. Attracted by the commotion, Elder Markham came on the scene in time to grab the reins of the horses and to insist that the prisoner at least be permitted to get his coat and hat. The intruders then made a grave error that was to tie them in a frustrating legal snarl. They leveled their guns at Elder Markham and threatened to shoot him.

Emma barely had time to hand Joseph his coat and hat and to bid him a hurried goodbye before the carriage was rumbling toward Dixon. Through the dust and commotion, Joseph shouted a final instruction. "Go get a writ of habeas," he directed Elder Markham.

This faithful disciple was to do much more than his leader had enjoined. He hurried to Dixon, where he swore out a warrant for the arrest of Reynolds and Wilson for threatening his life. Adding a second string to his legal bow, he later obtained a warrant against the lawmen for threatening Joseph's life. The hapless pair was then arrested by the local sheriff. In the meantime, Joseph succeeded in obtaining a writ of habeas corpus through lawyers in Dixon. Finally, the legal circus was made complete when Reynolds and Wilson were released from the custody of the local sheriff on a writ of habeas corpus.

In the course of those intricate legal maneuverings, Joseph obtained the services of a noted lawyer, Cyrus Walker, who was in the neighborhood campaigning for the U.S. House of Representatives. Sensing that he might make political capital out of the affair, he conditioned his service upon Joseph's promise of support in the coming election. Under the circumstances, Joseph agreed and later fulfilled the condition, although, as will be seen, he did it in a way that robbed the candidate of his high expectations—the entire Mormon vote.

When word of the legal entanglements reached Nauvoo, a large group of brethren was organized and sent along to protect their leader. When these joined the entourage that had formed at Dixon and that had been augmented along the way, the combined company looked like a large posse.

What happened in Nauvoo was anti-climactic and wholly expected. The writ of habeas corpus Joseph had obtained was heard by the municipal court and he was discharged from the custody of Reynolds and Wilson. The decision not only declared the warrant of arrest to be defective, but also held that the indictments issued by the state of Missouri were invalid.

Chapter Thirty-two

Into the Political Cauldron

Stung by the humiliation of becoming captives of the man whom they had been sent to arrest, Reynolds and Wilson and their principals made a futile attempt to persuade Governor Ford to call out the militia to arrest Joseph. This ploy, which had proven so successful in Missouri, failed because the governor, ever sensitive to the political winds, was unwilling to risk any further alienation of the Mormon vote on the eve of the upcoming congressional election. Cyrus Walker, the Whig candidate, had made no secret of Joseph's promise to vote for him. Alarmed that this might evolve into a general endorsement, the governor and his party had adopted a conciliatory attitude toward the Prophet—for the time being, at least. It was this softening that stalled the effort, originally set in motion by Governor Ford, to revoke the Nauvoo charters.

In the meantime, a political tug-of-war was developing within the Prophet's inner circle. Shortly before the election, Hyrum Smith announced his support for the Democratic candidate, Joseph Hoge. William Law favored the Whig candidate, Cyrus Walker. Their differences on this issue were magnified by the fact that in the hierarchy of the Church, these two men stood closer to Joseph than any others. On January 24, 1841, Hyrum had been elevated from second counselor in the First Presidency to assistant president, a move apparently designed to short-circuit the authority of the first counselor, Sidney Rigdon, who by then had lost Joseph's confidence. On the same day, William Law, an ambitious, untried convert from Canada, was called to replace Hyrum as second counselor. Catapulted into the front rank of Mormon leadership at age thirty-one after having been a member for only a short time, Law had missed the early seasoning and discipline other, more mature leaders had gained. He was arrogant, aspiring, and cocksure. Having brought some modest capital with him from Canada, he had invested successfully in a variety of businesses in Nauvoo. More entrepreneur than spiritual leader, his energies were directed almost exclusively toward material objectives. While he ostensibly rested it on a high moral ground, his real opposition to polygamy arose from a conviction that it was bad for business.

Hyrum soon learned that his antagonist was both untiring and vicious. In campaigning for Walker, Law hinted that Hyrum's real purpose in supporting Hoge was to gain political favors, which were to be cashed in later when Hyrum sought political office. Whatever his motives, the Prophet's brother played the role as he did all others in life—earnestly and with typical Smith vigor and determination. As election day neared, the heat generated by the campaign brought the cauldron to its boiling point. At this crucial moment, the Nauvoo *Neighbor* threw its support to Hoge. Shortly afterward, Joseph announced in a public speech that his personal vote would go to Walker as promised, but in conclusion, he mentioned significantly that Hyrum had told him he had a "testimony" it would be better for the people to vote for Hoge and that he had never known Hyrum to have a revelation that failed.

This casual statement, taken with the item in the *Neighbor,* was sufficient to give the election to Hoge. It also produced a violent reaction against Joseph on the part of the Whigs, who had assumed that his promise to vote for Walker also meant he would urge his followers to do likewise. This election, more than any other incident, demonstrated the political muscle the Latter-day Saints had developed in Illinois in four short years, for Hoge, who won the election by the thin margin of 700 votes, had polled about 2,000 votes in Nauvoo.

The outcome of this election was an eye-opener to the Mormon prophet. While he instinctively knew he wielded significant political power as the head of a monolithic church, the extent and potentialities of it had never been brought home to him before with such force, for it was now evident that the Mormons held the balance of political power in the state of Illinois. But Joseph was perceptive enough also to recognize that in victory lay the seeds of future dissensions and turmoil, for the supporters of the defeated candidate laid the blame at his door, and the victors had no real interest in the Latter-day Saints except as they might help to further their ambitions. Furthermore, he knew that any superiority in voting power could be quickly nullified by the ascendancy of a spirit of mob rule, as had happened in Missouri. Aside from all this, however, Joseph knew that becoming embroiled in the intrigues of local politics would divert him from his responsibilities as the head of a rapidly growing international church. For these reasons, he never seriously entertained the idea of becoming a working politician. Yet a few months later, he would declare his candidacy for the presidency of the United States and divert the energies of many of his leading men from their ecclesiastical duties to hit the campaign trail.

The anomaly of a man who eschewed politics seeking the highest political office in the land deserves an explanation. It rested solely upon the Mormon leader's desire to protect his people, enforce their rights, and broadcast the gospel message. And the circumstances prompting the move had their roots in the Missouri persecutions and in the political intrigues in Illinois.

Bitterness and suspicion toward the Latter-day Saints followed in the wake of the Walker-Hoge contest and the court hearing in Nauvoo that freed Joseph from the custody of Wilson and Reynolds. The Whigs especially were incensed at what they interpreted as a sell-out on the part of the Prophet, and influential men from both parties expressed alarm at the frequent use of the broad powers in the Nauvoo charters to protect the city's most prominent citizen. These irritations were constantly inflamed by threats and harassing legal actions of old enemies in Missouri, strengthened now by the support of John C. Bennett and other apostates from Illinois.

Foreseeing that these trends would sound the death knell of his people in Illinois if not checked, Joseph undertook several extraordinary initiatives in late 1843 and early 1844 designed to relieve the tremendous pressures being exerted on him and the Saints. In the autumn of 1843 he wrote to several of the presidential candidates, asking their views about federal help in obtaining redress for the Missouri depredations. Only two of them—Henry Clay and John C. Calhoun—answered. Clay implied he was not a candidate, but said if he were, he would want to take office uncommitted to anyone. Calhoun merely repeated the stock answers Joseph had previously heard from Martin Van Buren, and with like result. These men adhered to the prevailing view that because the federal government was a creature of the Constitution, which did not expressly give it jurisdiction in these matters, it was powerless to act. Years later, the interpretation Joseph advanced became the prevailing view with the expansion of the concept of implied powers and the adoption of the Fourteenth Amendment.

To say that Joseph was displeased with these answers hardly tells the story. In fact, he was enraged—so much so that he fired off answers which, for bluntness, are without peer among his correspondence. One excerpt from the letter to Calhoun conveys the bitterness of his feelings: "If the General Government has no power to reinstate expelled citizens to their rights, there is a monstrous hypocrite fed and fostered from the hard earnings of the people! A real 'bull beggar' upheld by sycophants." (G. Homer Durham, *Joseph Smith: Prophet-Statesman* [Bookcraft, 1944], p. 135.)

It was the sense of helpless exasperation reflected in this letter that led ultimately to the Prophet's decision to run for president. But before that step was to be taken, there were two other initiatives he undertook for self-protection.

On December 21, 1843, Joseph petitioned Congress, proposing that Nauvoo be constituted as a federal military district, while retaining its self-governing status under the charter. This contemplated that the citizens of Nauvoo would be vested with all "rights, privileges and immunities" belonging to federal territories and that the mayor be empowered to commandeer federal troops to augment the Nauvoo Legion when circumstances required it. Constitutional authority for this proposal was seen in the provision that empowers the national government to exercise exclusive jurisdiction over territory ceded or sold to it by the states.

The apathy of the federal government toward the Latter-day Saints and the ripening hostility in Illinois doomed this request to oblivion from the outset. Its only effect was to provide an interesting historical footnote attesting to the imaginative resourcefulness of the Prophet.

The second initiative involved the enactment of two ordinances by the Nauvoo City Council, intended to strengthen the legal safeguards protecting the Prophet and other leading men. The first provided for the arrest and imprisonment of anyone who attempted to enforce a warrant against the Prophet based upon the old Missouri charges. The second made it a criminal offense for any officer to issue a warrant in Nauvoo without the countersignature of the mayor, who was Joseph Smith.

The enemies of the Church instantly seized upon these ordinances as fresh evidence of the intent of the Mormons to subvert the normal legal processes of the state and federal governments and to place the leaders at Nauvoo beyond the reach of either. This added fuel to the movement to revoke the charter and produced a violent reaction among the more extreme antagonists. So intense was this reaction that the city council repealed the offending ordinances within weeks after they were adopted.

It was against this background that the Council of the Twelve Apostles held a special meeting in Joseph's office in Nauvoo on January 29, 1844, to consider the political and legal dilemmas that faced them. Present also were Hyrum Smith and John P. Greene. After analyzing the various candidates and deciding that none of them held views consistent with the best interests of the Saints, it was decided that Joseph Smith run for the presidency as an independent candidate and that those present "use all honorable means" to secure his election.

This action was the signal for another dramatic demonstration of the Prophet's genius for organization and discipline. Thirty-seven special conferences would be held throughout the country before election in the fall, with the final ones in the nation's capital in the forepart of September. Missionaries were sent into all of the twenty-six existing states with instructions both to expound the gospel and to advance the Prophet's candidacy. These included many of the leading men in the Church and ranged in number from two in some states to a high forty-nine in the state of New York. Commenting on the forensic skills of these supporters, Joseph wryly observed: "There is oratory enough in the Church to carry me into the presidential chair the first slide." (HC 6:187.)

Into the hands of these missionary-campaigners was placed an unusual document that embodied the candidate's platform—unusual not only because of the audacity of its author, but also because of the perceptive and unorthodox remedies it prescribed for the ills of the day. It proposed a substantial decrease in the size of Congress and the compensation of its members; sweeping prison reforms, with emphasis on rehabilitative instead of punitive treatment of inmates; abolition of slavery by the purchase of slaves from their owners; development of a national banking system; annexation of Texas, Mexico, Oregon, and Canada; and power in the president to suppress mobs and to intervene in state affairs to protect the civil liberties of United States citizens. In these planks were reflected many of the difficulties the Saints had faced in Ohio, Missouri, and Illinois.

Even the most ardent of Joseph's supporters held out little hope that he could be elected, but they were convinced that the collateral benefits to the Church from the campaign would repay fully any efforts they might exert. Bearing this in mind, they campaigned with vigor and enthusiasm. Every argument for Joseph's candidacy was, in effect, an argument for the equitable treatment of the Latter-day Saints, and anyone who turned a listening ear to their oratory inevitably received a liberal serving of the theology that had distinguished them.

While the publicity gained for the candidate by these itinerant campaigners was substantial, it was modest compared to the wide coverage he received in the press. Some of the large eastern papers published Joseph's platform with editorial comment about his views and character. The more cynical of these poked fun at him, treating his candidacy as a ludicrous joke. But more important to Joseph's purpose was the wide publicity given to the doctrines and policies of the Church through the campaign and the dramatization of the sad plight of the Saints. He was determined that at the very least, the campaign would establish a public record of the wrongs suffered by the Saints by which the nation, and succeeding generations, could weigh their motives and conduct against those of their enemies.

The innovative talents of the Mormon prophet were not exhausted with the announcement of his presidential candidacy. Pushed into a corner at this critical time, he showed the resourceful qualities of his grandfather, Solomon Mack, moving from alternative to alternative in search of an answer to the perplexing problems at hand. It was at this point that he turned his face westward in earnest. Often he had given thought to the possibility of moving the Saints into the remote western wilderness where they could live in isolated peace. As early as August 1842 he had prophesied that they would be driven to the West, where they would "become a mighty people in the midst of the Rocky Mountains." (HC 5:85, footnote.) He later discussed this event privately with some of the brethren, but no positive steps were taken to bring the prophecy to fruition until February 1844, when he instructed the Twelve to send out a delegation to investigate potential sites. He made it clear that any projected move would be delayed until the Nauvoo Temple had been completed.

Joseph Smith possessed all the instincts of a good field general.

When confronted with a problem, he assayed the alternatives, computed the risks, and embarked on the path best calculated to lead to his objectives. This trait surfaced again at this time. He accompanied the thrust westward in search of places of settlement with a thrust eastward in search of financing and security. On March 26, 1844, he again petitioned Congress, proposing that he be empowered to raise a military force of one hundred thousand volunteers "to extend the arm of deliverance to Texas; to protect the inhabitants of Oregon from foreign aggressions and . . . to prevent the crowned nations from encircling us as a nation on our western and southern borders." This suggestion had appeal for the national leaders, who were wrestling with the thorny problems of annexing Texas and of resolving disputes with Mexico and Great Britain over California and Oregon. The reasonableness of it was not far-fetched, since Joseph was the commander of a disciplined military force, holding the rank of lieutenant general, and had proven his ability as an organizer and administrator.

Joseph assigned two of the most articulate members of the Twelve, Orson Pratt and Orson Hyde, to lobby for the measure in Washington. Later they were joined by Heber C. Kimball and Lyman Wight. These brethren were able to get bills embodying the substance of Joseph's memorial introduced in both houses of Congress. A supporting money bill was also proposed, which authorized the payment of two million dollars to the Nauvoo City council to be paid to those who suffered losses in Missouri. The novice lobbyists worked industriously with the Illinois delegation, which included the recently elected Joseph Hoge and Stephen A. Douglas. Mr. Douglas was especially helpful, providing the brethren with maps of the West along with copies of the recently published report of John C. Fremont, who had explored extensively in the Rockies. They were also granted an audience with President John Tyler.

These efforts failed of their main objective, but they provided excellent training in the complexities of politics and government for the leaders of the Church and furnished a workable pattern that would be followed with success a few years later, after the martyrdom of Joseph Smith, when the United States commissioned the Mormon Battalion.

Chapter Thirty-three

Prelude to Death

While Joseph struggled to contend with the external forces that threatened his destruction, a fatal contagion festered within the heart of the Church's leadership. At the core of this malignancy was the Prophet's counselor, William Law. It seemed almost inconceivable that within the span of less than five years, the Prophet would witness the rise and fall of two counselors and then see them link hands to bring about his destruction.

It was a lust for women that first propelled John C. Bennett toward apostasy, while William Law was blinded by the allurements of wealth and power, although he, too, was an admitted adulterer. (HC 6:435.)

The first crevice in the Prophet's relationship with William Law appeared when Joseph commenced to instruct his inner circle in the doctrine of plural wives. This occurred in 1841, a few months after Law was called as a counselor in the First Presidency. From then until the final rupture of their relationship, Law knew, either directly or indirectly, of the doctrine.

While he resisted it from the beginning, he did so from a selfish motive and not from any moral or idealistic qualms. For him, it was simply a matter of dollars and cents. His shrewd business judgment convinced him that once the doctrine of plural wives surfaced, Nauvoo was doomed, and with it, his wealth. So he argued and cajoled with Joseph behind the scenes to persuade him to abandon the doctrine, to no avail. Knowing of Emma's repugnance toward it, he played upon her sympathies, thinking to influence her husband toward his views, again to no avail. It was then that he opened negotiations with the Prophet's Missouri enemies to betray him into their hands. This failing, Law conspired unsuccessfully with a group of men and women in Nauvoo to kill him. The later efforts of these conspirators to destroy the reputation of the Prophet through the pages of the Nauvoo *Expositor* opened the curtain on the act of his martyrdom.

The links in the chain of events that transformed William Law

from a counselor to a conspirator present an interesting meta-
morphic study. He emigrated from Canada to Nauvoo as a new
convert with high hopes and some capital, which mostly was invested in real estate. In this, he became associated with Robert D.
Foster, a real estate promoter and financier. The business skill he
showed soon brought him to the attention of Joseph Smith and
other leaders, who saw in him qualities essential in building a new
city. He soon gravitated to positions of importance, serving as an
officer in the Nauvoo Legion, as a trustee of the Agricultural and
Manufacturing Association, and as registrar of the Nauvoo
University. In addition to real estate, his diverse business interests
included ownership of steam, grain, and saw mills. So immersed
did he become in the complexities of his business ventures that he
commenced to lose sight of the high motives that had led him to
join the Church and emigrate to Nauvoo. This change in focus
was accompanied by a reappraisal of the man whom he originally
had accepted as a prophet of God but who, after personal association, he decided was his inferior in business judgment. From this
premise, it was an easy step for him to begin to question and criticize Joseph's policies, which seemed to him to lie within the scope
of his own business expertise. Thus, he was negative about the
construction of the Nauvoo House, largely because of his opinion
that the area on the hill near the temple should be built up com-
mercially, instead of the bottom lands. He also doubted the
wisdom of speeding the construction of the temple, believing that
other construction in the city should be given priority, including
the many buildings he and his partner Robert Foster were building. These attitudes brought him into direct conflict with the
Prophet, who was aggressively pushing for prompt completion of
both the temple and the Nauvoo House and who sorely needed
the materials and labor that were being diverted to the Law-Foster
enterprises.

As his relationship with Joseph deteriorated, the pressures
upon William Law became increasingly intense. To alienate the
Prophet meant to alienate most of his followers, who were Law's
potential customers and employees. Alongside these agonies stood
the spectre of insolvency, threatened because his wealth was frozen
in assets that he could not readily liquidate. Caught in this vise, he
began to search frantically for alternatives to protect his invest-
ments. He despaired of remaining with Joseph, whose policies, he

felt, were too unpredictable, particularly the plural wife doctrine and the possibility of migrating to the West. Under these circumstances, it seemed to him there were only three directions in which he could go: he could coerce Joseph into accepting his views, dispose of him, or try to isolate and downgrade him by attacks upon his character and morals.

When Law realized that his leader could not be deterred from teaching and practicing the doctrine of plural wives, he decided to join forces with Joseph's enemies in Missouri, who had been thirsting for his blood. Although he took elaborate precautions to mask his identity and the extent of his involvement, he learned belatedly, as all conspirators do, that no plot to kill another is leakproof, and that the word always gets out, one way or another.

Not long after Law opened negotiations with his co-conspirators in Missouri, the efficient grapevine picked up and broadcast the news that one of Joseph Smith's most intimate associates had betrayed him and was plotting his death. This was intercepted and passed on by Joseph's bodyguard, Porter Rockwell, whose frequent exposure to Missourian wrath had made him especially alert to these subterranean messages.

Learning of this new danger, and being concerned about the mounting threats from enemies in nearby Warsaw and Carthage, Joseph and the Nauvoo city council beefed up the city police force in late December 1843 and established a system of night patrols. During a speech delivered to the enlarged police force on December 29, the Prophet made a statement that frightened William Law and others who were in league with him. Said Joseph: "My life is more in danger from some little dough-head of a fool in this city than from all my numerous and inveterate enemies abroad. I am exposed to far greater danger from traitors among ourselves, than from enemies without. . . ." Later he observed that he could live as Caesar might have lived "were it not for a right-hand Brutus." (HC 5:152.)

No sooner were these words out of Joseph's mouth than all Nauvoo buzzed with speculation about his meaning. The gossipers focused their attention on William Law and William Marks as the most likely objects of his obscure allusion. The rumors and insinuations floating around the city so intensified the pressure on these men that they became spooked, discerning imaginary dangers in the most innocent occurrences. William Marks, for example, read some dark meaning into the fact that several policemen built a fire across the street from his house one cold winter night in order to keep themselves warm. So agitated was he by the incident that he insisted a session of inquiry be called by the city council at which the policemen were sworn and interrogated. At about the same time, William Law demanded a hearing before the council to voice complaint about the buildup of the police force. After observing these proceedings, Joseph mused in his journal: "What can be the matter with these men? Is it that the wicked flee when no man pursueth, that hit pigeons always flutter, that drowning men catch at straws, or that Presidents Law and Marks are absolutely traitors to the Church, that my remarks should produce such an excitement in their minds? Can it be possible that the traitor whom Porter Rockwell reports to me as being in correspondence with my Missouri enemies, is one of my quorum?" (HC 6:170.)

Although these investigations revealed nothing that William Law did not already know, they somehow multiplied the anxieties his betrayal of the Prophet had set in motion. Consequently, he moved further underground and commenced to plot against the Prophet with some of the local people while maintaining his ties with his co-conspirators in Missouri. The ring in Nauvoo with which he became allied included his brother, Wilson Law, Chauncey L. Higbee, Joseph II. Jackson, his own wife, Jane Law, and Robert D. Foster and his wife.

The attack that the Nauvoo conspirators made upon Joseph began when he was accused of trying to seduce the wives of William Law and Robert D. Foster. The impact of this accusation was defused when Joseph published the affidavits of two men, A. B. Williams and M. G. Eaton, who had heard Foster speak of the supposed attempt at the seduction of his wife. Foster's wife later denied that the alleged incident ever occurred. One of these informants also revealed that the conspirators were actually plotting Joseph's death. Mounting the stand near the temple on Sunday, March 24, 1844, Joseph laid the whole affair before the public, specifically naming the Laws and Foster as being among those who were conspiring to kill him. (HC 6:272.) Nauvoo was electrified by this announcement. No longer was there a need to speculate about the identity of the Brutus to whom the Prophet had made veiled reference earlier. It was none other than his counselor.

With these facts out in the open, the final rupture in the official relationship between William Law and the Prophet occurred on April 18, 1844. On that date, Law, his wife, his brother Wilson, and Robert D. Foster were excommunicated from the Church for "unchristianlike conduct." (HC 6:341.) Foster's wife escaped this fate because she ultimately denied the false rumors that Joseph had tried to seduce her.

Once the mask had been ripped away, Law had to abandon any plans for a surreptitious killing. He and his co-conspirators then turned to the last weapon available to them in the death struggle with their former leader—character assassination by libel, slander, and gossip. To make certain that their strident voice of calumny and dissent would be clearly heard, they invested some of their dwindling funds in a press and announced plans to commence the publication of a newspaper in Nauvoo under the provocative name *Expositor.*

While waiting for the press to arrive, the apostates intensified their campaign of vilification by invoking the power of the courts. William Law persuaded a grand jury in Carthage to indict Joseph for polygamy and adultery; Jackson and Foster were able to get an indictment for false swearing; and Francis Higbee pressed an earlier suit against him for alleged slander. The anti-Mormon press trumpeted the news of these suits abroad as if the allegations upon which they were based were true, further inflaming the public mind against the Mormon leader.

In an effort to hide his vicious intentions under a cloak of respectability, William Law organized a church at this time, patterned after the church from which he had just been excommunicated. Declaring himself to be its president, he held it out as a "reformed" church, adopting the basic tenets of Mormonism while rejecting the doctrine of plural wives and Joseph's prophetic status. The selective acceptance of some of Joseph's teachings was explained on the premise that he had "fallen."

The dissidents in Nauvoo flocked to this standard, bringing with them the pent-up hatreds and enmities they had nurtured over the years. Feeding on each others' venom, these dissenters generated the lethal toxin that was to bring death to the Prophet. And the corrupt foundation upon which William Law's church was built caused it to crumble and fall soon after it was formed, leaving hardly a trace that it had ever existed.

Except for the case of the Nauvoo *Expositor,* the annals of history are devoid of an instance where the enduring fame of a newspaper was guaranteed by the publication of only one number. The single issue of this journalistic bomb exploded on Nauvoo on June 7, 1844. Twenty days later, the shock waves from it produced the martyrdom of Joseph and his brother Hyrum in Carthage jail.

Viewing the unfolding drama of the *Expositor* through the pages of Joseph's diary imparts the sense of one observing the approach of a devastating storm. Under date of May 7, the Prophet noted cryptically: "An opposition printing press arrives at Doctor Foster's." Three days later, he recorded: "A prospectus of the Nauvoo Expositor was distributed among the people by the apostates." And on the day the paper hit the streets, he wrote with prophetic finality, "The first and only number of the Nauvoo Expositor was published, edited by Sylvester Emmons." (HC 6:357, 363, 430.)

The content and tone of the *Expositor* were more offensive than Joseph had been led to expect they would be. He was portrayed as a fallen prophet, ambitious and power hungry. A fictional story implied that the missionary effort abroad was merely a lure to trap unsuspecting women into polygamy. Joseph was condemned for his political activity, accused of being venal and dictatorial, and labeled as a blasphemer.

The language in which these charges were couched was both vulgar and intemperate. Joseph, for example, was characterized as "one of the blackest and basest scoundrels that has appeared upon the stage of human existence since the days of Nero, and Caligula." The remedy proposed foreshadowed the bloody killings which were to take place in less than three weeks. "Let us arise in the majesty of our strength," the writer intoned, "and sweep the influence of tyrants and miscreants from the face of the land, as with the breath of heaven." (Nauvoo *Expositor,* June 7, 1844, p. 3.)

Unfortunately for Joseph, a germ of truth lay buried beneath the monstrous lies and calumnies that glutted the *Expositor.* The truth was that he had commenced to practice polygamy and had taught the principle to many of his associates. William Law knew this and also knew, under the circumstances, that Joseph would not admit the fact, for to do so would carry the false implication that the other charges made against him were likewise true. But if Joseph would not admit this fact, it was equally clear that he would not deny it, for to do so would violate his moral integrity and hold him up to disdain and ridicule in the eyes of those who meant the most to him. Thus precluded from either admitting or denying this underlying charge, Joseph diverted attention from it by focusing on the *Expositor*'s palpable falsehoods and strident tone. These, he contended at a meeting of the Nauvoo council the next day, would inevitably produce a seething mob spirit in the city if they were permitted to continue. He argued, therefore, that the *Expositor* should be declared a nuisance and, as such, should be abated.

So vast were the consequences that hinged on this decision that the city council debated this issue all that day, Saturday, and, unable to reach a decision, adjourned until the following Monday, when the debate continued. The feeling was strong from the beginning that the paper should be declared a nuisance. Respectable common law authority existed to support this conclusion. Consequently, the issue in dispute was the remedy to be applied to redress the damage inflicted or to be inflicted by the paper.

The moderate view, urged by Councilman Warrington, a non-Mormon, was that in lieu of abatement, a $3,000 fine be imposed for each libel. Joseph insisted that this would be a remedy without substance, since to enforce it would require repeated trips to the county seat at Carthage, thereby endangering the lives of the Church leaders. In the meantime, the publishers would be free to spew their poisonous falsehoods into the public mind. The Prophet genuinely feared that this would produce the kind of polarization that had occurred in Ohio and Missouri, with his enemies enraged and goaded to violence and his loyal followers militantly prepared to stand in self-defense.

Glossing over the legal niceties in favor of a decision that, they felt, was in the best interests of the city, the council accepted Joseph's views and adopted an ordinance that declared the *Expositor* a nuisance and ordered the mayor to have it abated. Acting without delay, the Prophet, in his role as mayor, ordered the city marshal to destroy the press with the assistance of members of the Nauvoo Legion.

This order was executed immediately, and by Monday evening, June 10, only an hour and a half after the council meeting ended, the *Expositor* press had been destroyed and the type scattered.

The fury that this bold act unleashed must have made Joseph feel as if he had stilled one obscene voice while unstopping a thousand others. Newspapers in nearby Quincy, LaHarpe, and Warsaw fulminated with self-righteous indignation at what they considered to be the ultimate affront by the hated Mormons. Thomas C. Sharp, the dissipated and worldly-wise editor of the neighboring Warsaw *Signal,* was the most explicit and deadly of all in his violent rhetoric and in the remedy he proposed. Wrote he, "We hold ourselves at all times in readiness to cooperate with our fellow citizens . . . to exterminate, utterly exterminate the wicked and abominable Mormon leaders." (Dallin H. Oaks, "The Suppression of the Nauvoo Expositor," *Utah Law Review,* 9.)

In retrospect, it seemed ironic to the Latter-day Saints that the event which triggered the fatal storm in Illinois had an almost exact parallel in Missouri, except the destruction of the Mormon press in Jackson County had no semblance of legality about it, and the event went almost unnoticed in the public media. But in Nauvoo, an action taken under color of law, following two days of debate by a proper government body having jurisdiction, was made to appear as a hideous thing.

While the hostile press whipped up the anger of Joseph's enemies with a steady stream of invective and abuse, the apostates, led by William Law, were busy agitating for legal action against him. Two days after the *Expositor* press was destroyed, a spurious charge of inciting to riot was issued by the court in Carthage. The constable sent to make the arrest refused to permit the matter to be heard before a Nauvoo court as the procedure allowed, and later was frustrated by Joseph's favorite legal device, a writ of habeas corpus. At a trial held on the writ, Joseph was acquitted by a non-Mormon judge.

When the constable returned home empty-handed, Carthage erupted with excitement and rage. Recalling the recent fiasco involving Reynolds and Wilson, who were made a laughingstock when they failed in their attempt to arrest Joseph, and who were themselves arrested, the conspirators were determined that the Mormon prophet be arrested and tried again, this time in their own forum. Urgent calls for arms and money to capture Joseph circulated among anti-Mormon cliques within a wide radius of Carthage. A delegation waited on Governor Ford, who was urged to direct the state militia to take the Mormon leader into custody.

And the Prophet's most inveterate enemies, sensing a golden opportunity to crush him once and for all, whipped up support among the Mormon-haters in Missouri and across the river in Iowa.

Alarmed at the menacing tone of his enemies and at reports of the size and deployment of the mobs being raised and enlarged daily, the Prophet declared martial law in Nauvoo and called out the legion to defend it against what he thought was imminent attack. Governor Ford, who feared that a full-scale civil war would be precipitated, and responding to pleas from both sides, intervened to try to mediate the dispute. Traveling to Carthage, he established his headquarters in the Hamilton Hotel. His natural hostility toward the Latter-day Saints was confirmed as he heard damning accusations against Joseph Smith, which were made chiefly by the knot of apostates, headed by William Law. So intense was hatred of the Prophet in Carthage, and so voluble and uncompromising were his enemies, that any voice raised in his defense was either not heard or was promptly shouted down. In this electric atmosphere, and given his anti-Mormon bias, it came as no surprise that the governor yielded completely to the demands of Joseph's mortal enemies. Their object was to pry him loose from the security of the Nauvoo Legion and the Nauvoo courts and to get him under their control on their own ground.

Preserving a show of neutrality, Governor Ford invited the Prophet to send emissaries to Carthage to explain his actions, rejecting the suggestion that the governor go to Nauvoo to investigate the conditions and to gauge in person the temper and the intent of the Mormon leader. The delegation sent from Nauvoo was chagrined to find that their side of the story had to be presented to the governor in the presence of Joseph's bitter enemies, who repeatedly interrupted their presentation with heckling and profane denials.

The decision reached by Governor Ford revealed a glaring inconsistency. He ordered Joseph to submit to arrest and to be tried in Carthage under the inciting to riot charge as a means of vindicating the authority of the courts. In doing so, however, he ignored the judgment of the Nauvoo court rendered on the writ of habeas corpus on the apparent assumption that it was void. Thus, the chief executive officer of the state usurped judicial authority as a means of affirming the independence and power of the court at

Carthage. This incongruous result moved the Prophet to note bitingly that Governor Ford had "turned supreme court."

When Joseph became aware of the elaborate plans laid by his enemies either to trap him into going to Carthage to answer to false indictment or to overwhelm him by force in Nauvoo, he prepared to defend against either in his customary thorough and determined way. In his legal arsenal to defend against the attempt to force him to Carthage was the court in Nauvoo and the ever-ready writ of habeas corpus; the legion was his main shield against an armed attack upon Nauvoo.

Joseph's earlier declaration of martial law was designed to afford internal protection against any conspirators who may have remained behind. As a further security measure, all roads connecting Nauvoo with the outside world were placed under guard to control movements in and out of the city. In order to provide leadership and personal moral strength, the Prophet ordered the Twelve, who were away campaigning in support of his presidential candidacy, to return to Nauvoo immediately. In the meantime, he was occupied gathering evidence through affidavits to support pleas to both Governor Ford and President John Tyler for help in quelling the mobs being raised against him.

It was against this background that Joseph received a disheartening letter from Governor Ford dated June 22. In it, the governor acceded to the demands of the mob in every detail. Joseph was ordered to submit to arrest by the Carthage constable and to stand trial in the midst of enemies who had sworn to kill him. He was also ordered to forgo the exercise of any legal remedies in Nauvoo and was forbade specifically from invoking the writ of habeas corpus. What was more alarming to Joseph was the stipulation that if he and the others involved submitted peacefully to arrest, they were not to be accompanied to Carthage by anyone else, not even their witnesses.

The ostensible reason given to support these extraordinary demands was that the authority and jurisdiction of the courts must be vindicated. The only alternative offered to Joseph was the blunt threat to call out the state militia to enforce the order of the court.

Faced with the prospect of entering the lair of his mortal enemies without a bodyguard, Joseph took no comfort in the governor's assurance that he would guarantee Joseph's safety. It seemed clear to him that the governor lacked both the inclination and the authority to deliver on this hollow promise. And so, as Joseph pondered the chilling facts and calculated his next move, he realized that once again he was near checkmate in the deadly game with his unrelenting persecutors.

Only three feasible courses of action remained open to him. He could stand and fight, backed by the arms and discipline of the Nauvoo Legion and supported by the loyalty of his followers. Reason convinced him, however, that this was the least acceptable of the three because of the real prospect it held of injury or death to many of his followers. Behind the furious mobs that then ringed Nauvoo, Joseph could see the ranks of the Illinois militia, which Governor Ford had threatened to order into the fray; and beyond them loomed the spectre of federal troops, backed by the unlimited resources of the American government. The possibility of intervention by federal troops was not a mere parade of horrors. Were Governor Ford to commit the state militia and were a stalemate to ensue, the federal government could ill afford to remain aloof, and the general apathy or enmity toward the Saints that existed in all branches of the government left little doubt as to the side it would champion.

Joseph shrank from the second alternative of submitting to arrest and trial in Carthage. He knew this would mean the end for him. Several times he declared that if he were to go to Carthage, he would be killed. On one occasion, he used the word "butchered." On another, he emphatically predicted his death in Carthage, saying that if it did not occur, he was not a prophet of God.

Faced with imminent death if he were to remain or if he were to submit to arrest, it was inevitable that this charismatic young leader, not yet thirty-nine, would select the third alternative, which would take him and his people into the vast wilderness beyond the Mississippi. His plans for an orderly mass exodus had not yet matured, but he had so often been forced to improvise and to adjust to radical changes without adequate preparation that the thought of plunging into the unchartered plains and mountains to the West did not give him a moment's hesitation.

The decision to go west was made late Saturday night, June 22. Plans were immediately laid to take the first step when Joseph and Hyrum arranged to cross the river.

Chapter Thirty-four

Martyrdom

Night had fallen on Nauvoo as Joseph stepped from the Mansion House and headed for the river. He was unabashed by the tears streaking his face, poignant evidence of the emotion-packed goodbyes that had just been spoken to his family.

It was no ordinary impetus that had caused him to leave the comfort of his home on a Saturday night—the last one of his turbulent life—and to ford the Mississippi River in a leaky boat. It was the threat of death that impelled him.

He had been threatened before. In fact, so often had he been faced with death or the threat of it that it almost had become commonplace. But this time was different. This time he had the overpowering feeling that the end was near. And this feeling, which he could not suppress, found expression in the frequent references to death that were to mark the last five days of his life. Intermittently, flashes of his old self-confidence and optimism would appear; then his buoyancy would subside into the gnawing uncertainty that characterized most of his few remaining days of mortal life.

Once outside the house and away from the tears and anguish of Emma and the children, the Prophet immediately composed himself and was driven in a carriage to a predetermined rendezvous on the east bank of the river. There he counseled in a deliberate, unhurried way with his staunchly faithful brother Hyrum and one of his most dependable clerks, Willard Richards. Out of this discussion came the decision to send their families to Cincinnati for safety. Joseph believed that he and Hyrum were the only prey the mob truly sought, and that once they and their families, who were potential hostages, had left Nauvoo, the furor would die down. William W. Phelps was sent for and given instructions about the evacuation of their families.

This important matter having been disposed of, Joseph sent for Porter Rockwell. When he joined the party after midnight, they all went upstream to a waiting boat owned by Aaron Johnson. It was after 2:00 A.M. when Porter Rockwell pushed off from shore and maneuvered the boat out into the river's powerful current.

Joseph knew from experience that the river was schizophrenic, oscillating from a benign to a malignant aspect. Today, it might wear a friendly face, serving docilely as a channel of commerce or pleasure, while tomorrow, it might don a fearsome mask, wreaking havoc and destruction. This night the river added a subtle touch to its ugly nature. About the time the boat reached the point of no return in the river, the passengers discovered with alarm that water was seeping through the small boat's sieve-like bottom. As Porter Rockwell bent his powerful back to the oars in a race for the opposite shore, the other three passengers bailed out the water with their shoes and boots.

Exhausted and wet, they reached the Montrose side of the river at dawn. Porter Rockwell barely had time to catch his breath before he was sent back across the river to get horses, supplies, and equipment for the trip into the wilderness. It was intended that he return the following night. In the meantime, the Prophet and his companions established their headquarters at the home of William Jordan.

Sunday morning, June 23, Emma heard disquieting reports that the Illinois militia would lay siege to Nauvoo until Joseph and Hyrum were surrendered, even "if it took three years to do it." (HC 6:549.) These reports carried ominous overtones to Joseph's family, who, it was hinted, would be held hostage until he returned. Foreseeing an indefinite period of fear and turmoil for her and the children, and being blind to the dire consequences that would flow from Joseph's surrender to his enemies, Emma impetuously called for Porter Rockwell, who she knew had recrossed the river, and pleaded with him to persuade Joseph to return and submit to Governor Ford's demands. She was encouraged in this by three men of poor judgment and questionable motives, Reynolds Cahoon, Hiram Kimball, and her nephew Lorenzo D. Wassen, none of whom professed to see any danger in Joseph entering the trap his enemies had set for him in Carthage. Emma ws either ignorant of, had lost sight of, or chose to ignore incriminating revelations her husband had received about Brothers Cahoon and Kimball, else she might not have relied upon their counsel. In November 1835, a revelation given to the Prophet reproved Cahoon for "his iniquities, his covetous and dishonest principles, in himself and family." (HC 2:299.) And in May 1842, the Prophet was warned by "the voice of [the] Spirit" that Hiram Kimball, with others, had been "insinuating evil, and forming evil opinions" against him. (HC 5:12.) Also, perhaps because of her blood relationship, Emma failed to recognize in her nephew some of the censurable qualities that existed in her father, Isaac Hale.

Porter Rockwell was unwilling to try to persuade him to return, but he did agree to permit Emma's three advisers to accompany him on the return trip to the Iowa side of the river. Reynolds Cahoon carried with him a letter of entreaty from Emma to her husband. On arriving at William Jordan's, they found Joseph and his companions sorting out flour and other provisions they would take with them in their planned move west.

Even after Joseph had read Emma's letter and had heard Reynolds Cahoon explain about additional guarantees of safety Governor Ford had offered, including the promise of an escort, he remained convinced that going to Carthage would mean his death. Had the matter rested there, he and his companions likely would have gone forward with their plans to go west. Sensing this, Emma's advisers put forward the argument that instantly changed Joseph's mind: They accused him of cowardice and likened him to a shepherd who deserts his flock at the appearance of wolves. Such a charge coming from anyone would have been sufficient to arouse Joseph's combative instincts. Considering the source, however, and the insinuating manner in which the accusations were made, he found it almost unbearably repugnant. The insult was aggravated by the fact that from the beginning, valorous conduct under the most adverse circumstances had been one of Joseph's most noted characteristics, and now, in the twilight of life, to have his name and reputation branded with a false charge of cowardice was more than he was prepared to endure. Suppressing any inclination to retaliate or to try to justify or explain his actions, the Prophet responded in a calm, almost indifferent, manner: "If my life is of no value to my friends it is of none to myself." (HC 6:549.)

This dramatic moment marked the point at which Joseph became resigned to his fate. From then until the final curtain descended with the fatal shots in the Carthage jail, he knew that he was destined for martyrdom. There were, of course, intervening moments during the next four days when hope of escape flickered momentarily, but it was quickly extinguished. And there were other moments when he yearned that the bitter cup would pass from him or when he wondered whether even God had forsaken him.

Before recrossing the river, Joseph and Hyrum dictated a letter to Governor Ford, advising him of their intention to surrender. In it, they referred to the governor's promises of protection, made the assumption they would be given an impartial trial, and acknowledged the governor's agreement to provide an escort. Joseph then sent letters to attorneys H. T. Huggins and D. J. Wakefield, asking them to represent him at the hearings in Carthage.

Upon reaching Nauvoo late Sunday afternoon, the Prophet dispatched Jedediah M. Grant and Theodore Turley to Carthage with the letter to Governor Ford. Arriving at their destination at 9:00 P.M., the messengers were given a cold reception by the governor, who rescinded his earlier promise to provide an escort for the Prophet and who ordered that the Smiths surrender themselves in Carthage at 10:00 A.M. the following morning.

It was obvious that Governor Ford had closed his mind to the Prophet and Hyrum and was determined that they yield completely to the demands of their enemies. This, along with the violent atmosphere that pervaded Carthage, made Elders Grant and Turley fearful for the Prophet's safety. Pushing their mounts to the limit of their endurance, they arrived back in Nauvoo at 4:00 A.M. Monday. Routing Joseph out of bed, they reported on what they had learned and expressed concern for his safety were he to go forward with his intention to surrender. Joseph listened to the report and to the entreaties of the messengers, and of other followers who had joined them, that he not go to Carthage. While he knew that safety lay in the direction toward which his friends pointed and that death awaited him in Carthage, he commenced his preparations to leave. In his mind burned the accusations of cowardice made by Reynolds Cahoon and the others. If for no other reason than to demonstrate the error of these inferior men, Joseph was determined to submit to Governor Ford's demands.

It took the Prophet two hours to make ready for the trip to Carthage and to exchange another round of tearful farewells to Emma and the children. He held no malice toward his wife for the key role she played in sending him to his death trap, for he knew that she desired to protect herself and the children from threatened harm and failed to realize the fatal consequences to her husband.

Joseph departed for Carthage with a coterie of over twenty-five horsemen, who had gathered in front of the Mansion House. The company included all of the eighteen defendants who had been charged in the false inciting-to-riot indictment obtained by the owners of the *Expositor*. The group left the Mansion House at 6:30 A.M., riding into the glare of an early morning sun. Except for the clatter of horses' hooves echoing through Nauvoo's sleepy streets and the occasional snort of one of the animals, the party rode in silence until it reached the temple site. Pausing there, Joseph carefully surveyed the beautiful building, which was beginning to take its final form; then, permitting his eyes to sweep over the residential neighborhoods that stretched below him toward the river, he said, almost in a reverie: "This is the loveliest place and the best people under the heavens; little do they know the trials that await them." (HC 6:554.)

On the outskirts of the city the party stopped again, this time at the home of a non-Mormon, Daniel H. Wells, who had been ailing. After visiting with the man, who always had been a staunch friend of the Saints and who was later to join the Church and to play a key role in the development of the empire in the Rocky Mountains, the Prophet said, in parting: "Squire Wells, I wish you to cherish my memory, and not to think me the worst man in the world either." (HC 6:554.)

About four miles west of Carthage shortly before ten A.M., as the group approached the farm of Albert G. Fellows, they were startled to see a large company of mounted militia riding toward them. Uncertain about the motives of these armed riders and sensing an undercurrent of anxiety among his companions, Joseph commented: "Do not be alarmed, brethren, for they cannot do more to you than the enemies of truth did to the ancient Saints— they can only kill the body." (HC 6:554-55.)

To their relief, Joseph and the brethren found no belligerency in this company of Illinois militia, which was led by a courteous, mild-mannered man, Captain Dunn, who presented an order from Governor Ford to surrender all the state arms in the possession of the Nauvoo Legion. While he may have had some mental reservations in doing so, Joseph promptly countersigned this order as commander-in-chief of the legion. He also agreed to accompany Captain Dunn to Nauvoo to help supervise the surrender of the arms.

Before retracing his steps, Joseph dictated and dispatched two letters, one to Governor Ford, explaining his delay in reaching Carthage, and the other to an officer of the legion in Nauvoo, giving directions about collecting the arms.

As he relaxed at the Fellows farm before commencing the trip back to Nauvoo, the Prophet drifted into one of his contemplative moods. Reflecting upon his perilous condition and the ordeal that lay ahead, he uttered a statement, simple, yet majestic, that ever since has been associated with his name and that gave voice to his deepest feelings: "I am going like a lamb to the slaughter," he predicted, "but I am calm as a summer's morning. I have a conscience void of offense toward God and toward all men. If they take my life I shall die an innocent man, and my blood shall cry from the ground for vengeance, and it shall be said of me, 'He was murdered in cold blood.' " (HC 5:555.)

It took from late morning until nine o'clock Monday night for the group to make the round trip to Nauvoo and back to the Fellows farm and to effect the transfer of the arms to Captain Dunn. While he was in Nauvoo during the afternoon, Joseph made two trips to the Mansion House to give further comfort to his family. As he bade them farewell, Emma and the children saw him alive for the last time.

Although it was near midnight when the travelers arrived, Carthage was as awake and boisterous as if it were midday. The militia and the mobs, whose attitudes toward the Mormon leader and his brother were hardly distinguishable, had been waiting expectantly since late morning. As the day wore on, the excitement and anticipation heightened in the quiet little country town, which bulged with hundreds of strangers who had come to witness the spectacle. The militia and several of the local volunteer units were quartered in tents pitched on or near the public square, as were some of the mobocrats who had been drawn to Carthage by the lure of an assassination that had been openly discussed for weeks. The Hamilton Hotel was filled to capacity with those who could afford more luxurious accommodations. Its guest list included Governor Ford and his party from the state capital and all of the principal apostates from Nauvoo, including William and Wilson Law, the Higbees and Fosters, and Augustine Spencer.

Through the day these apostates worked over a scheme to detain Joseph and Hyrum in Carthage as long as would be necessary to accomplish their purpose. What they had in mind was evident from a statement attributed to them that "the law could not reach" Joseph and Hyrum, "but powder and ball would." Aware of the flimsy nature of the contrived charge of riot and the likelihood that the defendants would win that contest quickly or would be freed on bail, they invented eighteen other false charges against Joseph so that "as one failed, they would try another to detain him there." They freely acknowledged "that they had had so much trouble and hazard, and worked so hard in getting him [Joseph] to Carthage, that they would not let him get out of it alive." (HC 6:566, 569.)

As night fell on Carthage, the exhilaration was intensified by the free flow of cheap liquor, and by midnight, when Joseph and his party arrived, many of the militia and mobocrats were wildly intoxicated. As Joseph and his party passed through the public square on their way to the hotel, they were insulted and threatened by the drunken militiamen who ostensibly were there for their protection. Especially vile and abusive were the Carthage Greys. "Where is the damned prophet?" they shouted. "Stand away, you McDonough boys, and let us shoot the damned Mormons." "G— D— you, old Joe, we've got you now." "Clear the way and let us have a view of Joe Smith, the prophet of God. He has seen the last of Nauvoo. We'll use him up now, and kill all the damned Mormons." (HC 6:559.)

These threats were accompanied by a wierd ritual performed by the rear platoon of the Carthage Greys, who threw their guns backward over their heads in a sweeping arc to land bayonet down, breech up. While whooping, yelling, and cursing, they would run to retrieve their guns, only to repeat the macabre procedure.

By the time the weary travelers reined up in front of the Hamilton Hotel, hundreds of curious spectators had assembled, alerted by the news that the Mormons had reached town. The shouting and cursing, mingled with the general commotion of the large crowd, brought Governor Ford to the window of his room. Instead of censuring the drunken troops, he merely placated them by saying that a parade would be arranged the next day to enable them to see the prisoners clearly. With this, and to the accompaniment of scattered "hurrahs" for the governor, the crowd began to disperse, and Joseph and his companions disappeared into the hotel.

Joseph arose early Tuesday morning. After conferring with H. T. Reid and James W. Woods, who had been retained as legal counsel, he and the other defendants voluntarily surrendered to Constable Bettisworth on the writ issued under the charge of riot. Later, the apostates sprang the first of the legal surprises they had concocted. Shortly after eight A.M., the Prophet was interrupted in a conversation and arrested again by Constable Bettisworth under a writ for treason, based upon an affidavit sworn to by the apostate Augustine Spencer. The alleged treasonable act was the Prophet's declaration of martial law at Nauvoo. With this extra hold on him, Joseph's enemies felt confident of their ability to retain custody, despite the outcome of the hearing that afternoon on the riot charge.

It was midmorning when Joseph and Hyrum joined the governor to review the militia and volunteers who had been assembled in formation on the town square. Several times in the course of the review, Governor Ford stopped before troop units to introduce the Smiths as "General Joseph Smith and General Hyrum Smith." With the soberness a night's sleep had brought, most of the troops maintained silence. The glaring exception was the Carthage Greys. When the Prophet and Hyrum were introduced to them, some of the officers threw their hats in the air and drew swords, declaring that they would introduce themselves to the "damned Mormons" in their own way. (HC 6:564.) It was with some difficulty that the governor was able to restore order, and there are indications that he later censured them, if he did not have them arrested. Under the circumstances, it is a paradox that he would have assigned these same Carthage Greys, the most violent and insubordinate of all, to guard the prisoners when they were later confined to jail—a paradox unless the governor harbored a secret, deadly intent toward Joseph and Hyrum.

Even the imminence of death did not alter the Prophet's work habits. Between the morning review of the troops and his arraignment in late afternoon, he counseled with the governor about a report that the apostates intended to go to Nauvoo to plunder; dictated several letters, including one to Emma and one to Porter Rockwell; and received a large group of militia officers who came out of curiosity to converse with him in his room. These men left with a healthy respect for his composure under extreme pressure and not a little shaken by the chilling prediction he made about them, delivered with his accustomed aplomb and detachment. Answering a facetious statement by one of the officers that Joseph's mild appearance was no index to his thoughts or intentions, he startled them by saying that while his intentions were masked from them, he could read theirs with clarity. "I can see that you thirst for blood," he told them, and then he prophesied "in the name of the Lord" that they would "witness scenes of blood and sorrow to [their] entire satisfaction" and that their souls would be "perfectly satiated with blood." (HC 6:566.)

No one who heard Joseph Smith prophesy in this manner ever forgot the occasion nor failed to be impressed by the solemnity of his manner or the substance of what he said. This instance was no exception. As the officers filed from Joseph's room, they were more subdued and thoughtful than when they entered. Had they been willing to share their deepest impressions with each other, they likely would have acknowledged that this man who then stood on the threshhold of death was one of the most truly remarkable persons they had ever encountered.

Joseph and his fellow defendants thought it strange at the late afternoon hearing in the riot case that they were arraigned before Justice Robert F. Smith. Governor Ford had "turned supreme court," as Joseph put it, and had rejected the decision of Justice Daniel H. Wells in Nauvoo precisely because the writ had not been returned to the justice who issued it, Thomas Morrison. What was even more disconcerting, however, was the fact that this same Robert Smith, who now had legal jurisdiction over them, was also a commander of a company of Carthage Greys. And they took no comfort from the fact that one of the prosecutors was the apostate Chauncey L. Higbee.

Following the arraignment, the prisoners were bound over for trial to be held at the next term of the circuit court, and bail was set at $500 for each defendant, an amount that was considered high under the circumstances. To the surprise of the court and the apostates, the full amount of the bail was posted immediately. According to prearrangement, however, the justice adjourned the court without calling up the treason case, which had the effect of leaving Joseph and Hyrum in the custody of the constable while setting free the other defendants who were not charged with treason.

So far, the strategy of the conspirators had worked. The first legal hurdle had been passed safely and Joseph and Hyrum were still in custody in Carthage. It was a matter of indifference to the conspirators that the other defendants were at liberty on bail, since they were interested only in the Smiths. Still, there were some loose ends that troubled them. They were uncertain, for example, of the effect of the day's events on Governor Ford. While they knew of his sympathy toward their position and of his animus toward the Smith brothers, they recognized also that he was an elected politician, inclined to follow the drift of public opinion, and vain enough to be concerned about the record he would leave behind. In view of this, they conjectured whether he might commence to shift position because the Mormon leaders had not been taken before Justice Morrison as the governor had originally decreed or because Joseph and Hyrum were now being held in custody on a charge that did not exist when the governor had invoked the power of the state militia. They also knew that the Prophet had been trying unsuccessfully to obtain an interview with Governor Ford since Monday night, and they were uncertain about the effect on the governor of the Prophet's persuasive eloquence, especially since his side of the controversy had not as yet been presented. Finally, it was not clear to them whether Joseph and Hyrum, in appraising the new developments, might decide they had complied with the spirit if not the letter of Governor Ford's demands, might elude Constable Bettisworth at the hotel, and might flee to Nauvoo, where a friendly court and an ever-ready writ of habeas corpus awaited them.

Weighing all these factors, the conspirators decided upon a course of action that was patently illegal and high-handed but that was calculated to put Joseph and Hyrum behind bars where they could be securely held until the assassination plans had matured. By some means never made clear, they induced Justice Smith to issue an order committing Joseph and Hyrum to jail under the treason suit, even though a preliminary hearing to determine the probability of guilt had never been held. Constable Bettisworth served this on them in their hotel rooms after dinner Tuesday evening. Actually, the constable did not produce it until Joseph and Hyrum demanded to know the authority by which he proposed to lock them up. Once they had seen the order, which falsely stated that a hearing had been postponed for lack of a material witness, they immediately sent for their legal counsel.

Pleas were made to Governor Ford to intervene, in view of the pledges of protection and impartial treatment he had made to induce the Mormon leaders to come to Carthage. Although he had felt no compunction about intervening earlier to demands that Joseph and Hyrum ignore the judgment of the Nauvoo court on the writ of habeas corpus, he now balked at any interference with an order that he knew to be false, the effect of which was to violate the promises he had made to the prisoners.

After more than an hour of fruitless arguing and remonstrance, the brothers realized that without force of arms or the power of an impartial judiciary, neither of which was available to them, there was no way to avoid being imprisoned. Consequently, they submitted to the constable, who prepared to escort them across the square to the jail.

During the debate over the commitment order, word leaked out that the Smith brothers were about to be moved, and a large, unruly crowd assembled to witness the dramatic happening. Elder John Taylor, who had argued valiantly but unsuccessfully with Governor Ford, was fearful for the safety of the Church leaders if they were taken unescorted through the ever-enlarging crowd, so he arranged for Captain Dunn and about twenty other members of the militia to escort the prisoners to jail. A number of friends also gathered close around them to form an additional protective shield.

As Joseph emerged from the hotel, he was flanked by Stephen Markham and Dan Jones, who carried heavy canes, which they were prepared to use to ward off any would-be attackers. Ahead and further out on the flanks were Constable Bettisworth and members of Captain Dunn's escort. These formed a literal phalanx that plunged quickly into and through the milling, angry crowd.

The jailer, George W. Stigall, checked in the prisoners and, at first, lodged them in the criminal's cell, a small, rectangular, iron-barred room upstairs at the rear of the building. Since they requested it, he permitted the prisoners' friends to be locked up with them. Later in the evening he moved the entire party to the larger debtors' quarters in the front of the upstairs floor, at the head of a steep stairway. The door to this room was a conventional wooden door, and the glassed windows in the room had no bars. Here the Prophet, Hyrum, and their friends spent the night, sleeping either on the double bed in the southeast corner or on the floor.

From the moment he entered the Carthage jail, Joseph seemed to be under the influence of an oppressive, foreboding spirit. On Wednesday, following an unproductive meeting with Governor Ford, he revealed the depth of these feelings: "I have had a good deal of anxiety about my safety since I left Nauvoo," he said, "which I never had before when I was under arrest. I could not help those feelings, and they have depressed me." (HC 6:572.)

This day of confinement seemed interminably long for the Prophet. Never idle, he managed to keep occupied in dictating, reading, counseling with the brethren, and sending and receiving messages through the visitors who came and went. But nothing he did seemed to matter much nor to be directed toward any meaningful end. There was movement and activity, but no progress. Unlike the days in Missouri jails when he was confidently projecting plans for the future and actively giving directions to the Church from his cell, he now seemed to be in a state of suspension. He continued to manifest in his actions and speech the sense of calmness and self-confidence that had characterized most of his life, but the essential ingredient of forward-looking action was missing.

One need not search long for an explanation for this radical change in the Prophet's demeanor. He knew the end was near. He knew that his work was finished. He knew that whatever time was left for him would be spent playing a defensive, waiting game. The effect of this was to increase the intensity of his concentration upon any subject that claimed his attention for the moment. Since his work had been completed and he foresaw no earthly future, all that remained to be done was to live out the moment, the hour, the day—however long God would permit him to remain in mortality in a manner consistent with his prophetic calling.

In late afternoon, the prisoners were aroused from their make-work activities by loud, argumentative voices from the jailers' quarters downstairs. The issue being debated so hotly was whether the conscientious jailer, Stigall, would relinquish custody of the prisoners to Constable Bettisworth, who carried another order from Justice Robert Smith for Joseph and Hyrum to appear before him for a hearing on the charge of treason. The order stated that the prisoners were committed to jail without the benefit of a hearing "for safe keeping until trial could be had." (HC 6:596.)

The jailer refused to relinquish custody because he held the prisoners under a direct order from the court, while the present order was addressed only to Constable Bettisworth. Also, an angry crowd had assembled in front of the jail and, in view of the loose talk about assassination that had circulated around town for days, he feared that to give them up would be to consign them to their graves. However, his loud insistence on legal formality was unavailing, for when the constable saw that he could not win his way by argument, he did so by force and intimidation. Enlisting the help of several willing Carthage Greys in the crowd, he brushed the jailer aside and, taking his keys to the debtors' room, gained entrance and ordered the prisoners to accompany him.

Noting the ugly mood of the crowd outside, and being aware of the many threats that had been made against their lives, Joseph and Hyrum were not at all sure but that their hour had arrived. Perhaps this was merely a ruse to get them out in the open, where their enemies could deliver on their threats. The vigorous protest of the jailer was a signal to them that the constable's action was of dubious legality, but with Bettisworth standing at the door and some of the Carthage Greys there to back him up, there was little else to do but to go along. Sizing up the situation in a glance, Joseph decided that the best thing to do was to act positively and with assurance. Putting on his hat, he walked briskly outside, with Hyrum close behind. With no sense of hesitation or fear, he plunged into the crowd, politely linking arms with the most vicious mobocrat in sight, and, linking the other arm with Hyrum's, strode quickly to the court.

The so-called court hearing before Justice Robert Smith was a charade. Since the prisoners had no witnesses with which to contest the treason charge, the court ordered that witnesses be subpoenaed and a hearing be set for the next day at noon. He then entered another order of commitment and the prisoners were returned to jail, again being required to run the gauntlet of a boisterous, profane crowd.

Safely back in jail, the prisoners and their friends had a light supper and then retired to the debtors' room where they were to spend the night—the last one for the Prophet and his brother. Sensing that his life had about run its course, Joseph spent several hours affirming to his brethren the truthfulness of the things he had taught during his ministry. With the guards listening in, he bore powerful testimony of the divine authenticity of the Book of Mormon. He testified of the reality of the spirit world and of the communications through the veil by resurrected beings. He also affirmed that the kingdom of God had been established upon the earth, and that it was for this cause and not because of any violation of law that he was in prison.

It was late when Joseph and Hyrum retired to the only bed in the room. The others lay on the floor to rest, except Willard Richards, who stayed up to finish some of the many letters Joseph had dictated to him during the day. He remained at this task until the last dim candle flickered out; then he joined the others on the floor.

A loud gunshot nearby awakened the sleepers during the night. Joseph arose to look about and, instead of returning to the bed, stretched out on the floor between John Fullmer and Dan Jones. Not being able to go back to sleep, he visited in quiet tones with these loyal followers. Believing Brother Fullmer was uncomfortable on the hard floor, he whispered, "Lay your head on my arm for a pillow, Brother John." He then confided in these brethren the presentiments he had that death for him was near. This reminded him of the two things that were most dear, prompting him to express the wish that he could see his family and preach to the Saints once again. After a long pause, he made his last nocturnal comments. To Dan Jones he whispered, "Are you afraid to die?" When his friend, in answering, asked whether the questioner thought that time had come for him, Joseph responded with the final prophetic utterance that was to escape his mortal lips. Pausing for emphasis, he said, "You will yet see Wales, and fulfill the mission appointed you before you die." (HC 6:601.)

The brethren were awakened from an uneasy sleep at five A.M. by John P. Greene and William W. Phelps, who were on their way to Nauvoo. After giving them messages for the family and the leaders there, Joseph asked Dan Jones to inquire about the reason for the shot during the night. When he put this question to Frank Worrell, an officer of the Carthage Greys who was on guard duty, he got more than he bargained for. Instead of responding to the question, Worrell warned that unless Jones left town, he would be killed along with the Smiths, and anyone else who was with them. He said they had waited too long to get "old Joe" in their power to let him slip away.

When the report of this conversation was conveyed to the Prophet, he sent Brother Jones to advise Governor Ford of what he had heard. The governor, who was preparing to go to Nauvoo with the militia, brushed off the report with the observation that Joseph and his friends were unduly alarmed and that "the people [were] not that cruel." (HC 6:603.) As if to dramatize his rejection of any idea that the prisoners were in danger, he took all the militia with him, including Captain Dunn and his company, assigned the Carthage Greys to guard the jail, and dismissed all the other volunteer troops.

Despite several unsuccessful attempts to do so, Dan Jones was never able to get back into the jail to be with the Prophet and Hyrum. On every side, he heard reports of plans for an assassination discussed freely. The apostate Chauncey Higbee frankly told him that "Joe and Hyrum" were to be killed and that he had better leave town.

In the meantime, inside the jail, Joseph pursued with dogged persistence the limited tasks available to him. He continued to dictate to Willard Richards, including a last letter to Emma. Devoid of any self-pity or reproach, the letter was designed to calm his wife's fears. He took pains to assure her that there was "no danger of any extermination order." Then, in a touching postscript, he said, "I am very much resigned to my lot, knowing I am justified, and have done the best that could be done." (HC 6:605.)

There were others outside the jail besides Dan Jones who were concerned by the widespread reports of plans for assassination. Among these was Cyrus H. Wheelock. He too went to Governor Ford for help and he too was brushed off. Feeling impotent to halt the deadly forces that had been set in motion, he decided to do what he could to provide at least a meager defense for the prisoners.

Obtaining a pass from the governor to visit the jail, Wheelock carried a six-shooter with him, concealed in the overcoat he wore as protection against a light rain that fell in the morning. While visiting with the Prophet, he passed this gun to him, which, added to a small pistol John Fullmer had left the brethren, gave them two guns.

Shortly after lunch Willard Richards took ill and Stephen Markham was sent to get some medication for his relief. As he was returning to the jail, he was surrounded by several members of the Carthage Greys and forced to leave town without conveying any message to the brethren. With his departure, the number of occupants in the debtors' room of the jail was reduced to four: the Prophet, Hyrum, John Taylor, and Willard Richards.

Late in the afternoon, John Taylor, who had a fine baritone voice, sang all fourteen verses of the mournful song "A Poor Wayfaring Man of Grief." This seemed to touch a melancholy chord in the Prophet's feelings, and he asked Elder Taylor to sing it again, which he did. Hyrum read aloud several excerpts from Josephus.

About five P.M., the jailer became concerned about the safety of his prisoners when he learned that Elder Markham had been forced out of town. He suggested, therefore, that they transfer back to the criminal cells where they would enjoy better protection. It was decided that this transfer would take place following supper.

Soon after, as one of the guards was leaving after having brought some refreshments to the prisoners, a loud commotion was heard outside the jail, followed by several shots. Glancing out the window, Elder Richards saw a group of about a hundred armed men. Some circled the building while others forced their way through the door and ran upstairs, firing as they came. Instantly and instinctively the four occupants of the room seized the weapons at hand, Joseph the six-shooter, Hyrum the single-barrelled gun, John Taylor a cane Elder Markham had left behind, and Elder Richards, Elder Taylor's cane.

The Prophet and Elders Taylor and Richards sprang to the left of the door, where the two cane bearers commenced to flail away at the guns of the attackers that were thrust through the door. Hyrum, who had been unable to maneuver out of the way, was standing in the line of fire when the first fusillade of shots was discharged through the door. He was hit first by a ball on the left side of his nose, which snapped his head back violently and sent him crashing to the floor. As he fell, he cried out in anguish, "I am a dead man." In quick succession, he was hit by three other balls, one entering his left side, the second his head, via his throat, as he lay prone on the floor, and the other lodging in his left leg.

When Joseph saw his brother fall and the blood gush from his ugly wounds, he cried out, "Oh dear, brother Hyrum!" At that, he thrust his six-shooter out through a small crack in the door and fired it blindly.

In the meantime, John Taylor, seeing that Elder Markham's cane was no match for the determined killers and their guns, ran for a window and attempted to jump out. As he did so, a ball from inside crashed into his left thigh, causing him to fall on the windowsill, where he teetered momentarily until a ball from the outside hit him in the vest pocket, throwing him back into the room. Fortunately, his watch stopped this second ball, sparing his life.

Joseph realized the futility of trying to parry the guns of the killers about the same time as did Elder Taylor, and, dropping his pistol to the floor, he tried to jump out another window. As he did so, he was hit almost simultaneously by three balls, two from inside the room and one from the outside. He then fell headlong out the window, landing on the ground near a well near the southeast corner of the jail.

Almost miraculously, Willard Richards, a large, corpulent man, survived a literal rain of gunfire, both from within and outside the jail, and was unscathed except for one bullet grazing his left ear lobe. This unusual circumstance brought to fulfillment a striking prophecy Joseph Smith made a year before when he told Elder Richards that "the time would come that the balls would fly around him like hail, and he should see his friends fall on the right and on the left, but that there should not be a hole in his garment." (HC 6:619.)

Once their bloody work had been finished, the assassins disappeared, leaving behind the corpses of two noble men. But without realizing it and without ever having intended to do it, they left much more. They left two martyrs crowns that they had helped to forge with their senseless brutality. In their temporary bloody victory lay their greatest defeat, for the men whom they had murdered, having sealed their testimonies with their blood, became in death even more powerful instruments for advancing the principles they had taught in life.

Epilogue

Joseph Smith's enemies seemed to have a penchant for miscalculation. From the beginning to the end of his career, they misjudged his intentions and objectives and, perhaps more significant, they misjudged the effect of their opposition upon him and his work. Preserved Harris, when she stole the Book of Mormon manuscript; Isaac Hale, when he wrote his libelous affidavit against Joseph; Philastus Hurlburt, when he collected or invented the series of false affidavits that formed the basis of E. D. Howe's anti-Mormon book; the mobbers in Ohio, Missouri, and Illinois, when they persecuted and drove Joseph and his people; and John C. Bennett, when he apostatized and wrote his scurrilous book—all these seemed to believe at the time that they had dealt a death blow to Joseph Smith or the church he founded. Time and the maturing of events have shown them to be in the wrong and have demonstrated that far from impeding Joseph Smith's work, some of them actually helped to accelerate and strengthen it.

In no instance is this phenomenon more evident than in the case of Joseph Smith's martyrdom. It is hard to conceive of a circumstance that would have been better calculated to insure the rapid growth and development of the Church. His death, under the circumstances that brought it about, added a ring of authenticity to his work it otherwise would have lacked, and provided an impetus that is still felt.

Yet, at the time, William Law and the other conspirators thought they had achieved a great victory, erroneously believed they had in some way demonstrated a superiority over him and had destroyed his work. But time, the great healer and leveler, has proven them wrong. Today, Joseph Smith's life and work find vindication in the stature and achievements of the organization he founded and in the high regard in which he is held by over three million disciples. On the other hand, there are no voices raised to commend those who conspired to kill him; their words and deeds have long since fallen into oblivion.

Some Contemporary Appraisals of the Prophet

What kind of man was the Prophet Joseph Smith? What did he look like? What kinds of impressions did he leave on those who met him, both the Latter-day Saints and nonmembers? What can we learn about him from his own words?

The life and works of the Prophet have been chronicled from beginning to end as have those of few other persons. We can see him through the eyes of sympathetic and unsympathetic family members; friends, disciples, and associates; enemies and apostates; the curious outsider whose interest was piqued by the enormous achievements of this remarkable man; and finally, through his own eyes. Chronicled here are some contemporary appraisals of the man who saw and spoke with the Father and the Son, who was visited and instructed by other heavenly beings, who founded a church that has become one of the major religions in the world today.

A comprehension of the mainsprings that moved Joseph Smith and molded his attitudes and activities must begin with the man himself and his self-image and his understanding of his relationship to God. Two sermons delivered near the end of his life disclose the Prophet's concept of his status and mission. The first, delivered in the Nauvoo Temple a little over a year before his death, included this revealing self-analysis:

> I am like a huge, rough stone rolling down from a high mountain; and the only polishing I get is when some corner gets rubbed off by coming in contact with something else, striking with accelerated force against religious bigotry, priestcraft, lawyer-craft, doctor-craft, lying editors, suborned judges and jurors, and the authority of perjured executives, backed by mobs, blasphemers, licentious and corrupt men and women—all hell knocking off a corner here and a corner there. Thus I will become a smooth and polished shaft in the quiver of the Almighty, who will give me dominion over all and every one of them, when their refuge of lies shall fail, and their hiding place shall be destroyed, while these smooth-polished stones with which I come in contact become marred. (HC 5:401.)

Thus is laid bare an interesting dichotomy in the character of Joseph Smith. On the one hand there exists a recognition of his frailties, suggested by the analogy of the rough stone; on the other stands his highly developed sense of superiority, shown by the declaration of ultimate triumph over all his enemies. The statement reveals the basic toughness in the Prophet's character, which enabled him to survive and achieve despite bitter and sometimes violent opposition. The perceptive reader also detects here the fine blending of the qualities of self-reliance, intelligence, and articulateness.

The second sermon, delivered barely three months before the Prophet's martyrdom, contains this enigmatic and oft-quoted statement:

You don't know me; you never knew my heart. No man knows my history. I cannot tell it; I shall never undertake it. I don't blame any one for not believing my history. If I had not experienced what I have, I would not have believed it myself. (HC 6:317.)

At least one of the Prophet's detractors reads into this statement a fraudulent intent to deceive and mislead. According to this view, his reported visions and other spiritual manifestations were manufactured either to feed a hungry ego or to satisfy his ambition for wealth and power. The answer to this charge lies in the following statement made by the Prophet immediately following the one just quoted, but which the critic chooses to ignore: "When I am called by the trump of the archangel and weighed in the balance, you will all know me then." Here, then, is an open invitation to weigh and consider the extensive evidence about the character and work of the Prophet in deciding what kind of a man he was.

From a time early in his career, the Prophet knew that his mission would evoke widespread comment and criticism. At the time of the first appearance to him of the Angel Moroni, he was informed "that God had a work for [him] to do; and that [his] name should be had for good and evil among all nations, kindreds, and tongues, or that it should be both good and evil spoken of among all people." (HC 1:11-12.)

This sense of destiny accounted in large part for his enormous self-confidence and his fatalistic attitude and was certainly fed by the striking prophecy concerning him and his father found in the ancient record that he translated. There he learned:

A seer shall the Lord my God raise up, who shall be a choice seer unto the fruit of my loins. . . .

And his name shall be called after me; and it shall be after the name of his father. And he shall be like unto me; for the thing, which the Lord shall bring forth by his hand, by the power of the Lord shall bring my people unto salvation. (Book of Mormon, 2 Nephi 3:6, 15.)

Thus was planted in the Prophet's mind the knowledge that centuries before he was born he had been designated as "a choice seer," like unto Joseph of old, and that he would bring the people to salvation by the power of the Lord. Not only that, but it was also divulged to him that the dispensation he headed was the most significant and important of all the dispensations. In comparing his status and role with the greats of the past, the Prophet came to the conclusion that he was unusual and distinct from all others, a fact that weighed heavily in determining his attitudes and conduct throughout a productive and turbulent life. It was precisely this kind of self-image that evoked from him a statement to his cousin George A. Smith to the effect that though the Prophet were buried in the deepest pit of Nova Scotia with all the world piled on top of him, still he would "hang on and exercise faith" and that ultimately he would "come out on top."

Not only was the Prophet convinced that the role he had been called on to play in life was important and significant, but also that he was one of the chief actors in a preexistent life. A record he translated from ancient papyrus scrolls contained this striking reference to the pre-existence:

> Now the Lord had shown unto me, Abraham, the intelligences that were organized before the world was; and among all these there were many of the noble and great ones;
>
> And God saw these souls that they were good, and he stood in the midst of them, and he said: These I will make my rulers; for he stood among those that were spirits, and he saw that they were good; and he said unto me: Abraham, thou art one of them; thou wast chosen before thou wast born. (Pearl of Great Price, Abraham 3:22-23.)

The Prophet's self-image was further enhanced by his concept of the character of God and His relationship to man, which was elaborated in a sermon delivered shortly before his death:

> God himself was once as we are now, and is an exalted man, and sits enthroned in yonder heavens! That is the great secret. If the veil were rent today, and the great God who holds this world in its orbit, and who upholds all worlds and all things by His power, was to make himself visible—I say, if you were to see him today, you would see him like a man in form—like yourselves in all the person, image, and very form as a man; for Adam was created in the very fashion, image and likeness of God, and received instruction from, and walked, talked and conversed with Him, as one man talks and communes with another.
>
> . . . Here, then, is eternal life—to know the only wise and true God; and you have got to learn how to be gods yourselves, and to be kings and priests to God, the same as all gods have done before you, namely, by going from one small degree to another, and from a small capacity to a great one; from grace to grace, from exaltation to exaltation, until you attain to the resurrection of the dead, and are able to dwell in everlasting burnings, and to sit in glory, as do those who sit enthroned in everlasting power. (HC 6:305-6.)

In this same sermon, the Prophet enunciated the doctrine that the intelligence of man is co-eternal with that of God and was not created nor could be. Expanding upon this concept he added,

> The first principles of man are self-existent with God. God himself, finding he was in the midst of spirits and glory, because he was more intelligent, saw proper to institute laws whereby the rest could have a privilege to advance like himself. The relationship we have with God places us in a situation to advance in knowledge. He has power to institute laws to instruct the weaker intelligences, that they may be exalted with Himself, so that they might have one glory upon another, and all that knowledge, power, glory, and intelligence, which is requisite in order to save them in the world of spirits. (HC 6:312.)

It is apparent that the Prophet not only considered himself to be a leading spirit in the preexistence whose birth and mission had been heralded centuries before he was born, but he also viewed himself as a god in embryo who had been visited personally by the Creator and into whose hands had been placed the responsibility of establishing the kingdom of God upon the earth.

One who hopes to understand the Prophet Joseph Smith must first understand the powerful, motivating effect of these concepts upon his life and works. They explain his refusal to be balked by adverse circumstances, his resilient, self-confident attitude in all situations, and his imaginative solution of perplexing problems. They explain his innate sense of superiority, his basic assumption that all must or should defer to him, and the ease with which he commanded the respect and obedience of persons of all ages and backgrounds. They explain his innovative approach to ancient religious, social, and political problems, his assertion that God is a real person in whose image we have been created, and his confident expectation that the problems of the individual, the family, and the state would yield to the doctrines he expounded.

It is not often that a man's self-image coincides with the image he projects to others. In the case of the Prophet, however, the image we get of him through the eyes of his close associates and family is even more striking than the one he entertained of himself.

Of all his disciples, none was more prolific or more exact in his writing than was Wilford Woodruff, who became the fourth president of the Church. Throughout his life he was an accurate diarist and speaker, and he left many incisive comments about men and events, including many about the Prophet. In reporting a conference held in April 1837, he said:

> The Prophet Joseph then arose and addressed the congregation for the space of three hours, clothed with the power, spirit and image of God. He presented many things of vast importance to the Elders of Israel. O! that the record could be written as with an iron pen of the light, principles and virtue that came forth out of the mouth and heart of the Prophet Joseph whose soul like Enoch's seems wide as eternity. That day showed strikingly that he is in very deed a Prophet of God raised up for the deliverance of Israel. (Andrus, pp. 62-63.)

President Woodruff's report of the same conference also noted:

> Joseph then arose and like the lion of the Tribe of Judah poured out his soul in the midst of the congregation of Saints. While listening I thought "Who can find language to write his words and teachings as with an iron pen in a rock, that they might stand for future generations to look upon!" He seemed a fountain of knowledge from whose mouth streams of eternal wisdom flowed; and as he stood before the people he showed that the authority of God was upon him. (Andrus, p. 63.)

In the same vein, President Woodruff later commented on the scope and impact of the Prophet's teachings:

> His mind was opened by the visions of the Almighty, and the Lord taught him many things by vision and revelation that were never taught publicly in his days; for the people could not bear the flood of intelligence which God poured into his mind. (JD 5:83-84.)

President Woodruff left us this revealing summary of the impression the Prophet made upon him:

There is not so great a man as Joseph standing in this generation. The gentiles look upon him and he is like a bed of gold concealed from human view. They know not his principles, his spirit, his wisdom, his virtues, his philanthropy, nor his calling. His mind, like Enoch's expands as eternity, and only God can comprehend his soul. (Andrus, p. 140.)

Parley P. Pratt, an early convert to the Church and an original member of the Quorum of Twelve in this dispensation, painted this interesting word picture of the Prophet:

President Joseph Smith was in person tall and well built, strong and active; of light complexion, light hair, blue eyes, very little beard, and of an expression peculiar to himself, on which the eye naturally rested with interest, and was never weary of beholding. His countenance was ever mild, affable, beaming with intelligence and benevolence; mingled with a look of interest and an unconscious smile, or cheerfulness, and entirely free from all restraint or affectation of gravity; and there was something connected with the serene and steady penetrating glance of his eye, as if he would penetrate the deepest abyss of the human heart, gaze into eternity, penetrate the heaven and comprehend all worlds.

He possessed a noble boldness and independence of character; his manner was easy and familiar; his rebuke terrible as the lion; his benevolence unbounded as the ocean; his intelligence universal, and his language abounding in original eloquence peculiar to himself—not polished—not studied—not smoothed and softened by education and refined by art; but flowing forth in its own native simplicity, and profusely abounding in variety of subject and manner. He interested and edified, while, at the same time, he amused and entertained his audience; and none listened to him who were ever weary with his discourse. I have even known him to retain a congregation of willing and anxious listeners for many hours together, in the midst of cold or sunshine, rain or wind, while they were laughing at one moment and weeping the next. Even his most bitter enemies were generally overcome, if he could once get their ears. . . .

In short, in him the character of a Daniel and a Cyrus were wonderfully blended. The gifts, wisdom and devotion of a Daniel were united with the boldness, courage, temperance, perseverance and generosity of a Cyrus. And had he been spared a martyr's fate till mature manhood and age, he was certainly endowed with powers and ability to have revolutionized the world in many respects, and to have transmitted to posterity a name associated with more brilliant and glorious acts than has yet fallen to the lot of mortal. (Andrus, pp. 13-14.)

Of the many trials Joseph endured, none was more difficult and exasperating than the Zions Camp episode. We see him under these stressful conditions through the eyes of a cousin, George A. Smith, who later became a member of the First Presidency of the Church:

The Prophet Joseph took a full share of the fatigues of the entire journey. In addition to the care of providing for the Camp and presiding over it, he walked most of the time and had a full proportion of blistered, bloody and sore feet, which was the natural result of walking from 25 to 40 miles a day in a hot season of the year. But during the entire trip he never uttered a murmur or complaint, while most of the men in the Camp complained to him of sore toes, blistered feet, long drives, scanty supply of provisions, poor quality of bread, bad corn dodger, frouzey butter, strong honey, maggotty bacon and cheese, etc., even a dog could not bark at some men without their murmuring at Joseph. If they had to camp with bad water it would nearly cause rebellion, yet we were the Camp of Zion, and many of us were prayerless, thoughtless, careless, heedless, foolish or devilish and yet we did not know it. Joseph had to bear with us and tutor us, like children. There were many, however, in the Camp who never murmured and who were always ready and willing to do as our leaders desired. (Andrus, pp. 23-24.)

An early convert to the Church, Orson Spencer, a teacher by profession, left us this character analysis of the Prophet:

. . . he is kind and obliging; pitiful and courteous; as far from dissimulation as any man; frank and loquacious to all men, friends or foes. He seems to employ no studied effort to guard himself against misrepresentation, but often leaves himself exposed to misconstructions by those who watch for faults. He is remarkably cheerful for one who had seen well-tried friends martyred around him, and felt the inflictions of calumny—the vexations of lawsuits—the treachery of intimates—and multiplied violent attempts upon his person and life, together with the cares of much business. His influence, after which you inquire, is very great. His friends are as ardently attached to him as his enemies are violently opposed. . . . That lurking fear and suspicion that he may become a dictator or despot, gradually gives place to confidence and fondness, as believers become acquainted with him. (Orson Spencer, *Letters Exhibiting the Most Prominent Doctrines of The Church of Jesus Christ of Latter-day Saints* [Salt Lake City: George Q. Cannon & Sons Co., 1891], p. 26.)

The powerful impact the Prophet had upon his followers, hinted at in these words of Orson Spencer, is clearly revealed in character sketches written by two practical men of affairs, Angus M. Cannon and Amasa M. Lyman, who held positions of high leadership in the Church during their lives. Cannon, later a stake president, observed:

He was one of the grandest samples of manhood that I ever saw walk or ride at the head of a legion of men. In listening to him as he has addressed the Saints his words have so affected me that I would rise upon my feet in the agitation that would take hold of my mind. (Andrus, p. 4.)

Lyman, who was elevated to the apostleship about two years before the Prophet's death, recorded this impression:

When he grasped my hand in that cordial way (known to those who have met him in the honest simplicity of truth), I felt as one of old in the presence of the Lord, my strength seemed to be gone, so that it required an effort on my part to stand on my feet; but in all this there was no fear, but the serenity and peace of heaven pervaded my soul, and the still small voice of the spirit whispered its living testimony in the depths of my soul, where it has ever remained, that he was a Man of God. (Andrus, p. 4.)

During the tense period following the Nauvoo *Expositor* affair, Dr. John M. Bernhisel, a prominent physician-convert from New York, wrote to Governor Thomas Ford, explaining the circumstances under which the newspaper had been destroyed. His letter contained this interesting analysis of the Prophet:

General Joseph Smith is naturally a man of strong mental powers, and is possessed of much energy and decision of character, great penetration, and a profound knowledge of human nature. He is a man of calm judgment, enlarged views, and is eminently distinguished by his love of justice. He is kind and obliging, generous and benevolent, sociable and cheerful, and is possessed of a mind and a contemplative and reflective character. He is honest, frank, fearless and independent, and as free from dissimulation as any man to be found.

But it is in the gentle charities of domestic life, as the tender and affectionate husband and parent, the warm and sympathizing friend, that the prominent traits of his character are revealed, and his heart is felt to be keenly alive to the kindest and softest emotions of which human nature is susceptible; and I feel assured that his family and friends formed one of the greatest consolations to him while the vials of wrath were poured upon his head, while his footsteps were pursued by malice and envy, and reproach and slander were strewn in his path, as well as during numerous and cruel persecutions, and severe and protracted sufferings in chains and loathsome prisons, for worshiping God according to the dictates of his own conscience.

He is a true lover of his country, and a bright and shining example of integrity and moral excellence in all the relations of life. As a religious teacher, as well as a man, he is greatly beloved by this people. It is almost superfluous to add that the numerous ridiculous and scandalous reports in circulation respecting him have not the least foundation in truth. (HC 6:468.)

One cannot review the vast achievements of Joseph Smith during the short thirty-eight-year period of his life without being struck by the implacable quality of his self-confidence and will to excel that made them possible. Three close associates observed and recorded this aspect of his many-sided personality. Benjamin F. Johnson left us this insight:

And yet, although so social and even convivial at times, he would allow no arrogance or undue liberties, and criticisms, even by his associates, were rarely acceptable, and contradictions would rouse in him the lion at once, for by no one of his fellows would he be superseded. (Andrus, p. 36.)

George Q. Cannon, one of the Prophet's biographers, observed:

But whether engaging in manly sport, during hours of relaxation, or proclaiming words of wisdom in pulpit or grove, he was ever the leader. His magnetism was masterful, and his heroic qualities won universal admiration. Where he moved all classes were forced to recognize in him the man of power. Strangers journeying to see him from a distance, knew him the moment their eyes beheld his person. (George Q. Cannon, *Life of Joseph Smith the Prophet* [Salt Lake City: Deseret Book Co., 1958], p. 20.)

Newel Knight, the man upon whom the Prophet performed the first miracle of his ministry, wrote:

His noble deportment, his faithfulness, and his kind address, could not fail to win the esteem of those who had the pleasure of his acquaintance. One thing I will mention, which seemed to be a peculiar characteristic with him in all his boyish sports and amusements. I never knew anyone to gain advantage over him and yet he was always kind and kept the good will of his playmates. (Andrus, p. 37.)

These and other similar appraisals of the Prophet's character reveal a highly competitive if not combative nature. Ordinarily, the Prophet kept this temperament under tight rein. Occasionally, however, it erupted into physical violence. One such occasion involved a tax collecter named Bagby in Nauvoo. The Prophet left his own account of the incident.

. . . I . . . complained to the clerks that Mr. Hamilton had got a tax title from the sheriff on one of my city lots. Mr. Bagby, the collector, came up in the midst of our conversation, and when asked about it denied all knowledge of it. I told him that I had always been ready to pay all my taxes when I was called upon; and I did not think it gentlemanly treatment to sell any of my lots for taxes; and I told him that he was continually abusing the citizens here. Bagby called me a liar, and picked up a stone to throw at me, which so enraged me that I followed him a few steps, and struck him two or three times. Esquire Daniel H. Wells stepped between us and succeeded in separating us. I told the Esquire to assess the fine for the assault, and I was willing to pay it. He not doing it, I rode down to Alderman Whitney, stated the circumstances, and he imposed a fine which I paid, and then returned to the political meeting. Bagby stayed awhile, muttering threats against me. I went home, commenced to work awhile, but soon was very sick. (HC 5:523-24.)

On another occasion, the Prophet became embroiled in a fight with his brother William Smith, which erupted at a debating society held at William's home. While William was clearly the aggressor and inflicted serious injury upon the Prophet, Joseph, when he saw the attack coming, quickly removed his coat in order to defend himself and to be free to counterattack. (HC 2:341.) There are also reports of a fight that the Prophet had with his brother-in-law Calvin Stoddard over some water rights. It is said that Stoddard called Joseph a "damned false prophet" whereupon Joseph knocked him down. A suit for assault against the Prophet ended in an acquittal after Stoddard publicly forgave him. (Brodie, p. 164.)

Before rendering a harsh judgment against the Prophet for these manifestations of physical violence, one must remember that he lived in a violent day when combat, including dueling, was commonplace and in frontier communities where the qualities of physical force and aggressiveness were much admired. Physically the Prophet was a powerful man over six feet in height. He enjoyed the popular athletic events of the day and frequently participated in them. His fine physique and competitive spirit made him a formidable opponent. A spectator at a wrestling match where the Prophet was attempting to raise money for the release of his friend Orrin Porter Rockwell from prison painted this scene:

When Joseph came to the crowd he told them what he wanted, passed around the hat, raised what money he could and then went into the ring to take part with the young men and boys in their games. So he was invited to wrestle with this bully. The man was eager to have a tussle with the Prophet, so Joseph stepped forward and took hold of the man. The first pass he made Joseph whirled him around and took him by the collar and seat of his trousers and walked out to a ditch and threw him in it. Then, taking him by the arm, he helped him up and patted him on the back and said "You must not mind this. When I am with the boys I make all the fun I can for them." (Andrus, p. 35.)

The Prophet was exceedingly proud of his physical strength and on one occasion alluded to it in a speech in these somewhat boastful words:

I am well—I am hearty. . . . I feel as strong as a giant. I pulled sticks with the men coming along, and I pulled up with one hand the strongest man that could be found. Then two men tried, but they could not pull me up. . . . (HC 5:466.)

Participation in sports became a useful diversion for the Prophet, providing needed relaxation from the heavy burden of leadership that he carried. One observer reported his development of this theme:

He said it tried some of the pious folks to see him play ball with the boys. He then related a story of a certain prophet who was sitting under the shade of a tree amusing himself in some way, when a hunter came along with his bow and arrow, and reproved him. The prophet asked him if he kept his bow strung up all the time. The hunter answered that he did not. The prophet asked why, and he said it would lose its elasticity if he did. The prophet said it was just so with his mind, he did not want it strung up all the time. (Andrus, p. 16.)

But the Prophet's tendency toward combativeness and vigorous physical activity was far overshadowed by a strain of great gentleness and kindness, which was especially evident in his relationship to children. L. O. Littlefield recalled:

He was naturally fond of the young—especially the little children. He did not like to pass a child, however small, without speaking to it. He has been known to actually cross a street if he saw a child alone on the opposite side, to speak to it or to inquire if it had lost its way. (Andrus, pp. 38-39.)

The same writer told of an incident while he was a young boy when the Prophet went out of his way to acknowledge him and give him comfort:

He stepped to where I sat alone. It might have been my isolated position that attracted him. I knew not the motive; but that man, who to me appeared so good and so godlike, really halted in his hurry to notice me—only a little boy. Placing one of his hands upon my head, he said, "Well, bub, is there no place for you?" (Ibid.)

In the same vein, we have been left this picture of the Prophet's kindly demeanor toward children:

In Kirtland when wagon loads of grown people and children came in from the country to meeting, Joseph would make his way to as many of the wagons as he could and cordially shake the hand of each person. Every child and young babe in the company were especially noted by him and tenderly taken by the hand, with his kind words and blessings. He loved innocence and purity, and he seemed to find it in the greatest perfection with the prattling child. (Andrus, pp. 39-40.)

His tenderness toward children appeared to be but another facet of the love he had for all. In his view, it was this quality that gave him such influence with the people. He once declared:

Sectarian priests cry out concerning me, and ask "Why is it this babbler gains so many followers, and retains them?" I answer, It is because I possess the principle of love. All I can offer the world is a good heart and a good hand. The Saints can testify whether I am willing to lay down my life for my brethren. (HC 5:498.)

This feeling of love he had for the Saints was reciprocated by them. Illustrative of this are these words from the pen of a convert:

The love the Saints had for him was inexpressible. They would willingly have laid down their lives for him. If he was to talk, every task would be laid aside that they might listen to his words. He was not an ordinary man. Saints and sinners alike felt and recognized a power and influence which he carried with him. It was impossible to meet him and not be impressed by the strength of his personality and influence.

In May, 1844, he went to the stone shops where the men were working on the Nauvoo Temple and blessed them, each man by the power of his Priesthood. Brother Lambert . . . he gathered right into his arms and blessed, and it was ever his testimony that he was thrilled from head to foot by that blessing.

In the same vein an acquaintance, William Taylor, said of him, "Much has been said of his geniality and personal magnetism. I was a witness of this—people, old and young, loved him and trusted him instinctively." (Andrus, p. 42.)

The magnetism of the Prophet and the thrilling impact he had upon his associates constituted one of his most striking qualities. It seemed to be produced by a combination of his penetrating glance, which was said to be steady and searching; his facial expression, which ordinarily was pleasant with a light smile playing around the lips, and which often paled when the spiritual power was manifested through him; his voice, which had an urgent, penetrating quality about it; and his solemn, almost majestic demeanor. Several episodes in the Prophet's life dramatically demonstrated this magnetic, almost electrifying, impact of his personality.

After finishing the translation of the Book of Mormon at the Peter Whitmer farm in Pennsylvania, the Prophet sent word to his parents, who were in Palmyra, New York, to come to him immediately. They notified Martin Harris, who went with them. The evening after their arrival was spent reading the manuscript together. The next morning the group gathered together for what Lucy Smith, the Prophet's mother, referred to as "the usual services," consisting of "reading, singing and praying." Following these services, there occurred one of those shocking, unexpected episodes in the life of the Prophet, which Lucy recorded in these words:

Joseph arose from his knees, and approaching Martin Harris with a solemnity that thrills through my veins to this day, when it occurs to my recollection, said, 'Martin Harris, you have got to humble yourself before God this day, that you may obtain a forgiveness of your sins. If you do, it is the will of God that you should look upon the plates, in company with Oliver Cowdery and David Whitmer." (Lucy Mack Smith, pp. 151-52.)

The prophetic nature of that utterance and the stimulating effect it had upon Martin, Oliver, and David are recorded in their testimony, which appears in the front page of each Book of Mormon. Among other things, that testimony states:

And we declare with words of soberness, that an angel of God came down from heaven, and he brought and laid before our eyes, that we beheld and saw the plates, and the engravings thereon; and we know that it is by the grace of God the Father, and our Lord Jesus Christ, that we beheld and bear record that these things are true.

The *History of the Church,* which was dictated for the most part by the Prophet, contains this off-hand reference to an apostate: "About this

time [September, 1831] Ezra Booth came out as an apostate. He came
into the Church upon seeing a person healed of an infirmity of many
years standing." (HC 1:215.) It was left to a historian of a Protestant sect
to furnish the details of this healing, which provide another insight into
the sometimes electrifying effect of the Prophet's words and demeanor.
The scene was set in Kirtland in 1831 in the living room of the Prophet.
Present were a number of people, including Booth, a Methodist preacher
of some note, and a Mrs. Johnson, who had a lame arm that she could
not lift to her head. During the course of the conversation the subject
turned to supernatural gifts and someone, alluding to Mrs. Johnson's
lame arm, inquired whether God had given anyone the power to heal it.
Later when the conversation had turned to another subject, the Prophet
arose from his chair, walked across the room, and, taking Mrs. Johnson
by the hand, said, "in the most solemn and impressive manner: 'Woman,
in the name of the Lord Jesus Christ I command thee to be whole,' and
immediately left the room." The effect of this dramatic episode upon
those present was recorded by the Protestant historian:

> The company were awe-stricken at the infinite presumption of the man, and the
> calm assurance with which he spoke. The sudden mental and moral shock—I know not
> how better to explain the well-attested fact—electrified the rheumatic arm—Mrs.
> Johnson at once lifted it up with ease, and on her return home the next day she was able
> to do her washing without difficulty or pain. (HC 1:215-16.)

Kirtland, Ohio, was the first community where the Latter-day Saints
were established in force, and it later became the site of the first temple
constructed in this dispensation. The first act performed by the Prophet
upon his arrival in Kirtland illustrates again the magnetic, startling effect
of his personality. It took place at the store of Gilbert and Whitney in
Kirtland, where Newel K. Whitney, one of the proprietors, was on duty.
The incident stands as a highlight in the folklore of the Whitney family:

> About the first of February, 1831, a sleigh containing four persons drove through
> the streets of Kirtland and drew up in front of the store of Gilbert and Whitney. One of
> the men, a young and stalwart personage alighted, and springing up the steps walked
> into the store and to where the junior partner was standing. "Newel K. Whitney! Thou
> art the man!" he exclaimed, extending his hand cordially, as if to an old and familiar ac-
> quaintance. "You have the advantage of me," replied the merchant, as he mechanically
> took the proffered hand. "I could not call you by name as you have me." "I am Joseph
> the Prophet," said the stranger smiling. "You've prayed me here, now what do you want
> of me?" (HC 1:146.)

We may gain some idea about the effect of this unconventional
greeting from the fact that the Whitneys hospitably entertained the
Prophet and his family for many months and thereafter remained his devoted followers throughout their lives.

It is comparatively easy for a man of perception and ability to
influence and impress his associates while he occupies a dominant position. This was the situation that existed in the three episodes just related.

However, another incident that shows the charismatic effect of the Prophet's personality and demeanor occurred while he was imprisoned in a Missouri jail. It was graphically related by one of his cellmates, Parley P. Pratt.

In one of those tedious nights we had lain as if in sleep till the hour of midnight had passed, and our ears and hearts had been pained, while we had listened for hours to the obscene jests, the horrid oaths, the dreadful blasphemies and filthy language of our guards . . . as they accounted to each other their deeds of rapine, murder, robbery, etc., which they had committed among the *"Mormons"* while at Far West and vicinity. They even boasted of defiling by force wives, daughters and virgins, and of shooting or dashing out the brains of men, women and children.

I had listened till I became so disgusted, shocked, horrified, and so filled with the spirit of indignant justice that I could scarcely refrain from rising upon my feet and rebuking the guards; but had said nothing to Joseph, or any one else, although I lay next to him and knew he was awake. On a sudden he arose to his feet, and spoke in a voice of thunder, or as the roaring lion, uttering, as near as I can recollect, the following words.

"SILENCE, ye fiends of the infernal pit. In the name of Jesus Christ I rebuke you, and command you to be still; I will not live another minute and hear such language. Cease such talk, or you or I die THIS INSTANT!"

He ceased to speak. He stood erect in terrible majesty. Chained, and without a weapon; calm, unruffled and dignified as an angel, he looked upon the quailing guards, whose weapons were lowered or dropped to the ground; whose knees smote together, and who, shrinking into a corner, or crouching at his feet, begged his pardon, and remained quiet till a change of guards. (Pratt, pp. 210-11.)

It is interesting that this event, which had such a profound effect upon Elder Pratt, received only scant attention in the Prophet's record. Of it he merely observed that the officers in charge permitted "all manner of abuses to be heaped upon us" and that "during this time my afflictions were great and our situation truly painful."

The foregoing appraisals of the Prophet's character and accounts of his unusual deeds came for the most part from his disciples or family. One might expect, therefore, that they would be tinged with some bias and would not be wholly objective. This is doubtless true to some degree. Even after discounting these stories, however, one is left with the clear impression that here was an uncommonly able and gifted man who by reason of his personality, his intellect, and his deeply spiritual nature set a standard of achievement unexcelled by any of his contemporaries. One of his sympathetic biographers has left us this somewhat poetic summary of these achievements:

Here is a man who was born in the stark hills of Vermont; who was reared in the backwoods of New York; who never looked inside a college or high school; who lived in six States, no one of which would own him during his lifetime; who spent months in the vile prisons of the period; who, even when he had his freedom, was hounded like a fugitive; who was covered once with a coat of tar and feathers, and left for dead; who, with his following, was driven by irate neighbors from New York to Ohio, from Ohio to Missouri, and from Missouri to Illinois; and who, at the unripe age of thirty-eight, was shot to death by a mob with painted faces.

Yet this man became mayor of the biggest town in Illinois and the state's most prominent citizen, the commander of the largest body of trained soldiers in the nation outside the Federal army, the founder of cities and of a university, and aspired to become President of the United States.

He wrote a book which has baffled the literary critics for a hundred years and which is today more widely read than any other volume save the Bible. On the threshold of an organizing age he established the most nearly perfect social mechanism in the modern world, and developed a religious philosophy that challenges anything of the kind in history, for completeness and cohesion. And he set up the machinery for an economic system that would take the brood of Fears out of the heart of man—the fear of want through sickness, old age, unemployment, and poverty.

In thirty nations are men and women who look upon him as a greater leader than Moses and a greater prophet than Isaiah. (Evans, frontispiece.)

The appraisals of the Prophet by many outsiders are hardly less generous than those by his disciples. One of the most frequently quoted analyses of the Prophet made by a non-Mormon, and perhaps one of the most reliable, was the one made by Josiah Quincy, a Harvard graduate, lawyer, president of the Massachusetts Senate, and mayor of Boston, who, in his *Figures of the Past,* gave these impressions of Joseph Smith:

It is by no means improbable that some future textbook, for the use of generations yet unborn, will contain a question something like this: What historical American of the nineteenth century has exerted the most powerful influence upon the destinies of his countrymen? And it is by no means impossible that the answer to that interrogatory may be thus written: Joseph Smith, the Mormon Prophet. And the reply, absurd as it doubtless seems to most men now living, may be an obvious commonplace to their descendants. History deals in surprises and paradoxes quite as startling as this. The man who established a religion in this age of free debate, who was and is today accepted by hundreds of thousands as a direct emissary from the Most High—such a rare human being is not to be disposed of by pelting his memory with unsavory epithets. (B.H. Roberts, *Joseph Smith the Prophet-Teacher* [Princeton, N.J.: Deseret Club of Princeton University, 1967], pp. 8-9.)

Quincy also left us this interesting glimpse of the lasting impression the personality of the Prophet made upon him:

When I made the acquaintance of the Mormon prophet I was haunted with a provoking sense of having known him before; or, at least, of having known some one whom he greatly resembled. And then followed a painful groping and peering 'in the dark backward and abysm of time,' in search of the figure that was provokingly undiscoverable. At last the Washington of 1826 came up before me, and the form of Elisha R. Potter thrust itself through the gorges of memory. Yes, that was the man I was seeking; yet the resemblance, after all, could scarcely be called physical, and I am loath to borrow the word 'impressional' from the vocabulary of spirit mediums. Both were of commanding appearance, men whom it seemed natural to obey. Wide as were the differences between the lives and character of these Americans, there emanated from each of them a certain peculiar moral stress and compulsion which I have never felt in the presence of others of their countrymen. (Andrus, p. 27.)

Another professional non-Mormon writer, a reporter for the St. Louis *Weekly Gazette,* interviewed the Prophet just a few days before his martyrdom and wrote this interesting description, which indicates that the author may have had some phrenological training.

General Smith is in stature and proportion a very large man; and his figure would probably be called a fine one, although by no means distinguished for symmetry or grace.

His chest and shoulders are broad and muscular, although his arms and hands seem never to have been developed by physical toil, and the latter are quite small for his proportions. His foot, however, is massive enough, and extensive enough, in all conscience, to make up for any deficiency in his hand.

The shape of his head is a very oblong oval—the coronal region high, denoting a resolved will—the basilar and occipital full, indicating powerful impulses, and the frontal retreating, although the region devoted by phrenologists to the organization of the perceptive powers is unusually prominent.

His forehead is white, without a furrow, and, notwithstanding the small facial angle, somewhat symmetrical. His hair is quite light and fine—complexion pale—cheeks full—temperament evidently sanguine—lips thin rather than thick, and by no means indicative of boldness or decision of character.

But the Prophet's most remarkable feature is his eye; not that it is very large, or very bright—very thoughtful or very restless—even very deep in its expression or location; for it is usually neither of these. The hue is light hazel, and is shaded, and, at times, almost veiled, by the longest, thickest light lashes you ever saw belonging to a man, whatever the facts respecting the 'dear ladies.'

The brows are, also, light and thick—indeed, precisely of that description called beetle-brow. The expression of the Prophet's eyes when half closed and shaded by their long lashes was quite as crafty as I ever beheld.

His voice is low and soft, and his smile, which is frequent, is agreeable. (Evans, pp. 178-79.)

A historian prepared this summary of the Prophet's character and conduct during the last trying days of his life:

The bearing of the Prophet throughout the closing months with which this volume deals is admirable. There is no faltering or evidence of weakness at any point of his conduct. If criticised at all it would be for over-daring, for over self-confidence, that approached sublimity. Strong men through wickedness fell away from their discipleship, and conspired against him; the Prophet reproved them in the gate, and proclaimed their iniquities in public when hope of reforming them was gone. He saw mobs forming for the destruction of himself and Nauvoo and his people; he calmly prepared to meet force with force, and drilled and prepared his legion for the conflict, entrenched some of the approaches to the city, and picketed them with guards; as mayor of the city he placed the city under martial law; and as lieutenant-general he took personal command of the Nauvoo Legion and stood ready to defend the rights of himself and his people, for which his revolutionary ancestry had fought in the war for American independence. He believed gloriously in the right of self-defense, and resistance to oppression by physical force if necessary. To his uncle John Smith at Ramus who had asked for counsel in the disturbed state of things, he wrote ten days before his death:

"I write these few lines to inform you that we feel determined in this place not to be dismayed if hell boils over all at once. We feel to hope for the best, and determined to prepare for the worst, and we want this to be your motto in common with us: *We will never ground our arms until we give them up by death.*"

And from Carthage prison, on the morning of the day of his martyrdom, he wrote to his wife for transmission to his people:

"There is one principle which is eternal: It is the duty of all men to protect their lives and the lives of their household, whenever necessity requires, and no power has a right to forbid it, should the last extreme arrive; but I anticipate no such extreme; *but caution is the parent of safety.*"

When the jail in Carthage was assailed, and the mob was pouring murderous volleys into the room occupied by himself and friends, the Prophet turned from the prostrate form of his murdered brother to face death-dealing guns and bravely returned the fire of his assailants, "bringing his man down every time," and compelling even John Hay, who but reluctantly accords the Prophet any quality of virtue, to confess that he "made a handsome fight" in the jail. (HC 6:xl-xli.)

The word that there existed a man who claimed to have seen and conversed with God caused many to want to see or hear the Prophet out of mere curiosity. One such was a congressman, M.L. Davis, who heard the Prophet speak in Washington, D.C., during February 1840. He later wrote a lengthy letter to his wife describing the Prophet and summarizing his remarks. The letter has special significance since the author was a man of ability and independence who had no connection with the Church and whose observations, therefore, have a special objectivity:

I went last evening to hear "Joe Smith," the celebrated Mormon, expound his doctrine. I, with several others, had a desire to understand his tenets as explained by himself. He is not an educated man; but he is a plain, sensible, strong minded man. Everything he says, is said in a manner to leave an impression that he is sincere. There is no levity, no fanaticism, no want of dignity in his deportment. He is apparently from forty to forty-five years of age, rather above the middle stature, and what you ladies would call a very good looking man. In his garb there are no peculiarities; his dress being that of a plain, unpretending citizen. He is by profession a farmer, but is evidently well read.

. . . During the whole of his address, and it occupied more than two hours, there was no opinion or belief that he expressed, that was calculated, in the slightest degree, to impair the morals of society, or in any manner to degrade and brutalize the human species. There was much in his precepts, if they were followed, that would soften the asperities of man towards man, and that would tend to make him a more rational being than he is generally found to be. There was no violence, no fury, no denunciation. His religion appears to be the religion of meekness, lowliness, and mild persuasion.

Towards the close of his address, he remarked that he had been represented as pretending to be a Savior, a worker of miracles, etc. All this was false. He made no such pretensions. He was but a man, he said; a plain, untutored man; seeking what he should do to be saved. He performed no miracles. He did not pretend to possess any such power. He closed by referring to the Mormon Bible, which he said, contained nothing inconsistent or conflicting with the Christian Bible, and he again repeated that all who would follow the precepts of the Bible, whether Mormon or not, would assuredly be saved.

Throughout his whole address, he displayed strongly a spirit of charity and forbearance. The Mormon Bible, he said, was communicated to him, *direct from heaven.* If there was such a thing on earth, as the author of it, then he (Smith) was the author; but the idea that he wished to impress was, that he had penned it as dictated by God.

I have taken some pains to explain the man's beliefs, as he himself explained it. I have done so because it might satisfy your curiosity, and might be interesting to you, and some of your friends. *I have changed my opinion of the Mormons.* They are an injured and much-abused people. (HC 4:78-79.)

Viewed in retrospect, the impact the Prophet's two-hour talk had upon Congressman Davis is quite remarkable. His allusions to "Joe Smith" and to the fact that the Prophet's followers were an "injured and much-abused people" clearly imply that the reports he had heard about the Mormons and their leader were derogatory and uncomplimentary. As a result, he went to the meeting with his mind set against the Prophet. Yet in the short space of two hours, the eloquence and demeanor of Joseph caused him to declare *"I have changed my opinion of the Mormons."*

The reasons that brought about this radical change in attitude toward the Prophet are either stated or clearly implied in Mr. Davis's letter. He was impressed by the Prophet's sincerity, by his obvious intelligence, and by his calmness and reasonableness. He saw nothing of the charlatan or imposter in him. At the same time, he was unaffected by the doctrine the Prophet expounded, for near the end of his letter, he said, "Of matters of *faith,* you know I express no opinion." This was not an uncommon reaction, for the overwhelming majority of those who heard the new doctrine rejected it. But most of those who took the time to listen to the Prophet were almost invariably convinced of his personal ability and stature, and it was precisely this circumstance that caused many to assert that the success of Mormonism was dependent entirely upon the magnetism of Joseph Smith and to predict that the organization he established would wither and disappear after his death. Subsequent events have proven this assumption to be false, a fact that clearly implies that the motivating force of the doctrines Joseph advanced accounts in part for the unusual impact he had upon experienced observers and men of affairs like Congressman Davis and Josiah Quincy.

An essential test of a man's greatness is his capacity for growth. Judged by this standard, the Prophet stands high in the scale of achievement. A historian, viewing an eighteen-month period near the end of the Prophet's career, comments upon the growth in his capacity for love and compassion, qualities which, in the final analysis, measure the true stature of one who speaks and acts for God:

During the trying events of the fifteen months of which this volume is a history, the nature of the Prophet underwent a remarkable development. There never was, of course, any doubt as to the physical courage of the Prophet. From boyhood he had been noted for his fearlessness under trying circumstances, but during the period here considered he was the constant object of assault, both by legal processes, under the leadership of cunning, malicious men, and the physical brutality of officials charged with the execution of the law; and both when facing the maliciously skillful in their proceedings under the color of law, and the threats of physical force from brutal captors, the conduct of the Prophet was most admirable. Also in seclusion, when others were easily excited and manifested symptoms of panic under the circumstances of conflicting rumors of impending dangers, it is refreshing to see how calmly the Prophet keeps his balance and rightly judges the true status of many trying situations. But what is most pleasing to record of this period of enforced seclusion while avoiding his enemies, is the development of the tenderness of soul manifested in his reflections upon the friends who had stood by him from the commencement of his public career: for his father and mother, for his brother Alvin, for Emma, his wife, for his brother Hyrum, the Knights, who were his friends even before the Book of Mormon was translated, and especially for the friends who received him and ministered unto him during his retirement from public ministry. No act of kindness seems to go unmentioned. No risk run for him that is not appreciated. Indeed he gathers much benefit from those trials, since their effect upon his nature seems to be a softening rather than a hardening influence; and the trials of life are always beneficial where they do not harden and brutalize men's souls; and every day under his trials the Prophet seems to have grown more tender-hearted, more universal in his sympathies; his moments of spiritual exaltation are superb. No one can read them and doubt that the inspiration of God was giving this man's spirit understanding. (HC 5:xxviii.)

Sources Cited

BOOKS

Anderson, Mary Audentia Smith, ed. *Joseph Smith III and the Restoration.* Independence, Mo.: Herald Publishing House, 1952.

Anderson, Richard Lloyd. *Joseph Smith's New England Heritage.* Salt Lake City: Deseret Book, 1971.

Andrus, Hyrum. *Joseph Smith, the Man and the Seer.* Salt Lake City: Deseret Book, 1960.

Backman, Milton V., Jr. *Joseph Smith's First Vision.* Salt Lake City: Bookcraft, 1971.

Barrett, Ivan J. *Joseph Smith and the Restoration: A History of the Church to 1846.* 2nd ed. Provo, Utah: Brigham Young University Press, Young House, 1973.

Berrett, William E., and Alma P. Burton. *Readings in L.D.S. Church History, from Original Manuscripts.* 3 vols. Salt Lake City: Deseret Book, 1953-58.

Book of Mormon.

Brodie, Fawn M. *No Man Knows My History: The Life of Joseph Smith, the Mormon Prophet.* New York: Alfred A. Knopf, 1945.

Cannon, George Q. *Life of Joseph Smith the Prophet.* Salt Lake City: Deseret Book, 1964.

Cowley, Matthias F. *Wilford Woodruff.* Salt Lake City: Bookcraft, 1964.

Doctrine and Covenants (D&C).

Durham, G. Homer. *Joseph Smith: Prophet-Statesman.* Salt Lake City: Bookcraft, 1944.

Evans, John Henry. *Joseph Smith, An American Prophet.* Salt Lake City: Deseret Book, 1946.

Lundwall, N. B. *The Fate of the Persecutors of the Prophet Joseph Smith.* Salt Lake City: n.p., 1952.

Nibley, Preston. *The Witnesses of the Book of Mormon.* Salt Lake City: Deseret Book, 1953.

Pearl of Great Price.

Pratt, Parley P. *Autobiography of Parley Parker Pratt.* First published in 1874; reprinted Salt Lake City: Deseret Book Co., 1961.

Roberts, B. H. *A Comprehensive History of The Church of Jesus Christ of Latter-day Saints, Century I* (cited as CHC). 6 vols. Salt Lake City: The Church of Jesus Christ of Latter-day Saints, 1930.

_____ . *Joseph Smith, the Prophet-Teacher.* Princeton, New Jersey: Deseret Club of Princeton University, 1967.

_____ . *The Life of John Taylor.* Salt Lake City: Bookcraft, 1965.

_____ . *The Missouri Persecutions.* Salt Lake City: George Q. Cannon and Sons Co., 1900.

Smith, Joseph. *History of the Church of Jesus Christ of Latter-day Saints. Period I: History of Joseph Smith, the Prophet,* and *Period II: From the Manuscript History of Brigham Young and Other Original Documents* (cited as HC). Edited by B. H. Roberts. 7 vols. Salt Lake City: The Church of Jesus Christ of Latter-day Saints, 1902-1932. Sometimes referred to as the "Documentary History," it is more properly cited by the title *History of the Church.*

Smith, Joseph Fielding, comp. *Teachings of the Prophet Joseph Smith.* Salt Lake City: Deseret Book, 1976.

Smith, Lucy Mack. *History of Joseph Smith by His Mother.* Salt Lake City: Bookcraft, 1958.

Spencer, Orson. *Letters.* Salt Lake City: George Q. Cannon and Sons Co., 1891.

Whitmer, David. *An Address to All Believers in Christ.* Richmond, Mo., 1887.

Whitney, Orson F. *Life of Heber C. Kimball.* Salt Lake City: Bookcraft, 1967.

ARTICLES, PERIODICALS, MISCELLANEOUS

Bennett, Archibald F. "Solomon Mack and His Family." *Improvement Era* 59 (February 1956): 90, 110.

Jessee, Dean C., and William G. Hartley. "Joseph Smith's Missionary Journal." *New Era* 4 (February 1974): 34-36.

Journal of Discourses. 26 vols. London: Latter-day Saints' Book Depot, 1854-1886. A serial publication issued by British Mission officials of talks given by early Church leaders from transcriptions provided by George D. Watt and many other reporters.

Nauvoo Expositor. June 7, 1844. Nauvoo, Illinois.
Nauvoo Neighbor 51. Nauvoo, Illinois.
Oaks, Dallin H. "The Suppression of the Nauvoo Expositor."
　　Utah Law Review 9 (1965): 869-903.
Times and Seasons. July 1, 1843. Nauvoo, Illinois.

Index

Hitchcock, Seth, 162
Hoge, Joseph, 313-14
Holmes, Erastus, 188
Holy Ghost, 207

Howe, E. D., 51, 92, 138
Huntley, Hannah, 4
Hurlburt, "Doctor" Philastus: attempts
  to slander Joseph, 43-44, 136-38; excommunication of, 136, 152-53
Hyde, Heman T., baptism of, 154
Hyde, Orson: sent to Missouri, 144;
  reproved as member of Twelve, 186-
  87; apostasy of, 230-31
Hymns, Emma Smith to make collection
  of, 90; publication of, 117

Illinois, Joseph looks for permanent set-
  tlement in, 252-53
Immortality, revelation concerning, 88
Imposter, Joseph charged with being,
  45-46
Independence, Missouri: site for temple
  in, 105-6; revelation concerning co-
  operative living in, 116-17; prisoners
  arrive in, 238-39
Indians to be preached to, 94
Intelligence, 351
Internal eruption in the Church:
  between Sidney Rigdon and Edward
  Partridge, 116-17; with Oliver
  Cowdery and David Whitmer, 135-
  36; in Kirtland, 152, 214; in Far
  West, 214-15

Jackson County, Missouri, expulsion of
  Saints from, 146. *See also* Missouri;
  Zion
John, the apostle, 62
John the Baptist confers Aaronic Priest-
  hood on Joseph and Oliver, 64
Johnson, Benjamin F., 355
Jones, Dan, 344
Joseph of Egypt, account of, found, 180
"Joshua, the Jewish Minister," 187-88
Judging, Joseph's teachings on, 262

Kimball, Heber C.: conversion of, 121;
  describes Zion's Camp stricken by
  cholera, 162; chosen as member of
  Quorum of Twelve, 173; has gift of
  prophecy, 201-2; called on mission to
  England, 206; departs for England,

258-59; taught principle of plural
  marriage, 287-88
Kimball, Hiram, 332-33
Kirtland: Saints gather in, 96-97; temple
  to be constructed in, 132-33, 144-45;
  threats from enemies in, 147-48; need
  for temple in, 191; preparation of
  brethren for temple in, 192; dedication of temple in, 195-200; internal
  eruption in, 214
Kirtland Safety Society Bank, organization of, 203
Kirtland Safety Society Anti-Banking
  Company, 204-5
Kirtland Temple, 132-33, 144-45, 191,
  192, 195-200
Knight, Joseph, 47
Knight, Newel, 82-83, 355
Knight, Vinson, 225

Lamanite, skeleton of, 161
Lane, Reverend, inspires Joseph's interest
  in Methodism, 28; rejects Joseph's vision, 31
Latter-day Saints Messenger and Advocate,
  145; publication of, 167; letters to
  elders in, 181-82
Law, William, 313-14; rejects plural marriage, 320; business attitudes of, 321;
  joins Joseph's enemies, 322; com-
  plains about buildup of police force,
  323; conspiracy of, revealed, 323; excommunication of, 324; organizes a
  church, 324
Lawyer: who defended Joseph in
  Colesville, 86-87; defends Joseph
  against Missouri enemies, 280-81
Lawyers defend Joseph in Richmond,
  248-49
"Lectures on Faith," 168
"Lectures on Theology," 168
Letter: to Chicago *Democrat,* 38; to
  Emma, 122-23, 247; concerning
  Church in Missouri, 124-25; repri-
  manding W. W. Phelps and Sidney
  Gilbert, 127-28; concerning persecu-
  tion, 147-48, 148-49; from Sylvester
  Smith to *Latter-day Saints Messenger
  and Advocate,* 157-58; to Saints in
  Kirtland, 215-16; from Sashiel
  Woods, 231; included in Doctrine
  and Covenants, 244; from Con-

receives plates, 47-48; not to replace lost translation, 56; called conjurer by critic, 71; organizes Church, 78-80; arrested in Colesville, 85-87; poisoned, 119; exercises gift of tongues, 129-30; plans City of Zion, 131-32; goes on mission to Canada, 145-46; recruits for Zion's Camp, 154-55; disagreement between William and, 183-84; reproves brethren when necessary, 185-86, 211-12; expectations of people who visited, 187-88; visited by Savior, Moses, Elias, and Elijah, 199-200; near death due to illness, 205-6; writes history of the Church, 218; taken prisoner at Far West, 233-34; sentenced to be shot, 235; commands guards to be silent, 240; tried at Richmond, 240-41; character of, 245, 301-2, 362-63, 364-65; escape of, 248; heals Saints in Nauvoo, 260-61; speaks in Washington, D.C. 268-69; Missouri enemies seek to extradite, 279-81; enters into plural marriage, 285; accused of shooting Governor Boggs, 294-95; goes into retirement, 296; knew death was near, 303; family life of, 307-8; arrest of, while on vacation, 311-12; runs for presidency, 317-18; goes to Carthage, 332-33; receives group of officers, 338-39; martyrdom of, 346-47; self analysis of, 349-52; physical appearance of, 356-57, 361-62

Smith, Joseph, Sr.: illness of, 2, 184-85; marriage of, 11; business enterprise of, 11-12; moves to Palmyra, 12, 23-26; religious attitude of, 12-13; series of dreams of, 16-18; teaches school, 20; confidence of, in Joseph, Jr., 35; writes notice concerning Alvin's body, 42; revelation concerning, 57; death of, 275

Smith, Joseph, III, 123, 310

Smith, Lucy Mack: marriage of, 11; religious attitude of, 12-13; death of sister of, 13; spiritual conversion of, 14-15; dream of, concerning conversion of husband, 15-16; takes family to Palmyra, 23-25; describes family listening to account of vision, 37-38;

journey of, to Kirtland, 96-97
Smith, Mary Duty, 9-10
Smith, Samuel, 3, 12, 66, 185
Smith, Sophronia, 20-21
Smith, Sylvester, 156-58
Smith, William, 12, 183-84, 356
Snow, Eliza R., 130
Social life of Saints, 272
Spaulding manuscript, 137-38
Spaulding, Solomon, 137
Spencer, Orson, 354
Spiritual manifestations, to Solomon Mack, 5-6; to Lucy Mack Smith, 14-15; to Joseph Smith, Sr., 16-18; to three witnesses, 69-70
Squirrel, Joseph shoots, 159-60
Stewardship, principle of, 101, 124
Stigall, George W., 341, 342-43
Stoddard, Calvin, 356
Stowel (Stoal), Josiah, 44, 47
Sword of Laban to be shown to three witnesses, 68

Tar and feathering: of Joseph, 114; of Bishop Partridge, 143
Tax collector, 355-56
Taylor, John, states prophets who appeared to Joseph, 38; conversion of, 202; taught plural marriage, 288; accompanies Joseph to jail, 341; sings in jail, 346; shooting of, 346-47
Teamster of Smith family, 24-25
Temple: Independence as site of, 105-6; to be constructed in Kirtland, 132-33; cornerstone laid in Kirtland, 144-45; need for, 191; preparation of brethren for, 192; dedication of Kirtland, 195-200; in Nauvoo, 39, 271; cornerstone of Nauvoo, laid, 278-79; design of Nauvoo, 301
Three witnesses: revelation concerning, 58; statement in translation concerning, 67; revelation identifying, 67-68; viewing of the plates by, 68-70, 358; testimony of, criticized as a conspiracy, 71-72
Tithing: Joseph and Oliver promise to pay, 170; revelation concerning, 221
Tongues, speaking in, 167
Translation, taken to Charles Anthon, 51; Martin Harris loses pages of, 53-55; Joseph not to replace lost, 56;